The YC-130, 53-3397, in flight over California. Apart from the addition of an extended nose radome, the Hercules has undergone little obvious external alteration during the past 30 years (Lockheed Aircraft Corporation, Neg No C6331).

LOCKHEED HERCULES

LOCKHEED HERCULES

Francis K Mason

Patrick Stephens, Wellingborough

First published in 1984

British Library Cataloguing in Publication Data

Mason, Francis K.
    Lockheed Hercules.
    1. Hercules (Turboprop transports)
    I. Title
    623.74'65   UG1242.T7

ISBN 0-85059-698-X

Patrick Stephens Limited is part of the Thorsons Publishing Group.

Photoset in 10 pt Plantin by MJL Typesetting, Hitchin, Herts. Printed in Great Britain on 115 gsm Fineblade coated cartridge, and bound, by The Garden City Press, Letchworth, Herts, for the publishers, Patrick Stephens Limited, Denington Estate, Wellingborough, Northants, NN8 2QD, England.

Title page *The withdrawal from Vietnam. Troops of the US 3rd Marine Division boarding a KC-130F transport/tanker of VMGR-152 at MCAS Futema, Okinawa, on their way home in 1974* (Staff Sergeant Mennillo, USMC, Neg No A291417).

Page 6 *Second pilot Captain T. J. Doyle, USMC, starts his pre-flight cockpit checks in a VMGR-252 KC-130F tanker at MCAS Cherry Point, North Carolina, April 12 1973* (Master Sergeant B.V. Davidson, USMC, Neg No A142556).

Contents

Introduction

Some 30 years ago, at a time when the world was still struggling to find its feet after the most devastating war in history, there was born in California an aeroplane which, despite its military *raison d'être*, was to become one of the most remarkable tools of world reconstruction and development, an aircraft so powerful and robust, and capable of moving great loads, that it could bear but one name—Hercules.

There are always those of us who deprecate the assumed waste of resources in the manufacture of weapons of war, yet it was unquestionably the very stringent military demands made in the original requirement for which the C-130 was conceived that brought forth an aeroplane that could undertake tasks for the benefit of mankind hitherto thought to be impossible. Of course, the Hercules is first and foremost a military transport; it is, however, only the extent of military usage that has enabled its cost and reliability to suit the needs of the world's developing nations.

The United States of America had led the world in military transportation during the Second World War, particularly with the C-47 Skytrain/Dakota, and when that splendid aircraft appeared to be reaching the evening of its illustrious life the world cried out for a successor and this role was assumed by the Hercules.

Even prior to its vigorous involvement in the trauma of Vietnam—a conflict which, by its irregular military definition, taxed the ingenuity and steadfastness of the American nation as never before—the Hercules had astonished military authorities with its 'do anything, go anywhere' capabilities. Those capabilities have been manifest in an unparalleled catalogue of achievement, compiled by a score of agencies worldwide, including spectacular operations, such as support of geophysical research in Antarctica, the creation of an air bridge to the remote Falkland Islands, the construction of the Trans-Gabon Railway, the exploitation of mineral resources in Canada and Alaska, famine relief in Africa, Asia and South America, not to mention countless instances of individual rescue and relief operations.

Among aviation literature one frequently encounters statements that this or that aircraft possesses claims to greatness: Camel, Spitfire, Mustang, Fortress, all have their advocates, yet all were shortlived sparks of genius which flashed in time of war, for on them and their airmen rested the destiny of nations briefly at great moments of peril. To shine in peace is another matter, yet the forces of nature are no less destructive nor forbidding than the man-made weapons of war, and less selective of their victims. Who will gainsay the effects of famine, fire, flood, earthquake and storm? This has been the scenario of Hercules for more than a quarter-century among mankind, whose tantrums are no less predictable than those of the elements.

The politics of Hercules have mercifully been uncomplicated, seldom the target or victim of financial controversy and intrigue—as are so many military aeroplanes of today. Perhaps therein lies the secret of its longevity. Hopefully when, in the years to come, history records the technological, social and humanitarian strides achieved by mankind in the latter half of the 20th century, a word may be spared for Hercules; truly a fitting name in the legend of endeavour.

In conclusion I should state that views expressed in this book are perhaps mine alone and may not be shared by others. I do, however, take responsibility for them. The book is an attempt to record history and therefore opinions may be considered academic at best, superfluous at worst. I have made a number of observations on and about the outcome of past policies (or perhaps the absence of such policies) within the British Ministry of Defence and the Air Staff. The observations are perhaps speculative on my part; the outcome was fact. Farsightedness is the blessing of the planner; hindsight the weapon of the historian.

Acknowledgements

One of the gratifying aspects of researching the history of an aeroplane such as the Lockheed Hercules is that, not being primarily an active combat aircraft, people associated with it feel less constrained by possibly sensitive considerations and are more forthcoming about its achievements, employment and physical attributes. On the other hand, one does not have to have been intimately involved with the Hercules to realise that its achievements have gone far past those of a transport aeroplane in the accepted sense, and it was not long before I realised that almost every one of the 1,700-odd aircraft produced over the past 30 years seems to have been purchased individually to perform a specific job! And I should therefore single out Mr Joe Dabney at the Lockheed-Georgia Company at Marietta for particular gratitude in regard to his painstaking efforts to keep me informed of the growing family of C-130 variants, supplying information releases and numerous Company photographs over a long period. Colonel Lars Olausson, whose professional task it is to keep *Flygvapnet's* fleet of Hercules in the air, has also kept me abreast of recent Hercules' histories and permitted me to use material from his own Lockheed Hercules Production List, and for this I owe him a considerable debt of gratitude.

Others to whom I should acknowledge my thanks include Mr Christopher Buisseret, Aircraft Division, Marshall of Cambridge (Engineering) Ltd, and the Board of Directors of that Company; Mr Danny J. Crawford, Head of Reference Section, History and Museums Division, US Marine Corps; Commander Rance D. Dunmire, USN, Commanding VQ-3, US Navy; Lieutenant-Colonel W.S. Evans, USAF, formerly of the 50th TAS, 314th TAW, and presently of the 16th SOS, 1st SOW, USAF; Technical Sergeant Jesse L. Frey AFRES, 193d ECG, Pennsylvania Air National Guard; Captain P.A.M. Griber USN, Commanding VR-3, US Navy; Mr Roy A. Grossnick, Naval Aviation History and Archives, US Navy,

Washington; Captain Glen Hatch USN, Commanding VR-24, US Navy; Captain Sarah Hayes, USAF, of the 513th TAW, Mildenhall; Mr G.E. Holland, Aircraft Readiness and Analysis Branch, US Navy; Sergeant Marvin Kasumoco USAF, 513th TAW, Mildenhall; Captain Edwin L. Keim USN, Commanding VR-1, US Navy; Captain William H. Munson USN, Commanding VX-3, US Navy; Master-Sergeant James Renshaw USAF, of the 301st ARRS, USAF; Colonel Charles F. Scrull AFRES, Commanding the 305th ARRS, AFRES; Lieutenant-Colonel John C. Stafford USAF, Commanding the 144th TAS, 176th TAG, Alaska Air National Guard; Staff-Sergeant A.L. Wagner USAF, of the 50th TAS, 314th TAW; Staff-Sergeant Lynn A. Yocum AFRES, Public Affairs, 911th TAG, AFRES.

In the matters of picture research I am indebted to Mr Keith Wilson of Starliner Aviation Press, to Mr Brian Pickering of Military Aircraft Photographs, to Mr D.K. McCarthy and Mr W.F. Wilson at Marshall of Cambridge (Engineering) Ltd, and to Mr Bob Dorr at the US Embassy in London. Others whose help I must acknowledge are Mr B.D. Wilkinson, previously of Cairo, Mr John Melrose, GPU Ltd, Mrs Ruth Dvornik of Khyber Studios, and the late Mr Geoffrey Bates-Smythe, previously of Thailand.

Finally, a special word of appreciation to Mr Bill Granley of Echo Bay Mines Ltd, one of long association with the Hercules and who loaned me numerous photos and videos, and who obviously gave so much of his time to assist me with this book.

Dedicated to the memory of
Bob Beaton
A very good man, a true son of Canada
and a Herculean pilot in every sense

Chapter 1

To the sound of the guns

The past 50 years have brought about total change to the means of delivering fighting men to the battlefield. Prior to the period between the World Wars the soldier either marched or was carried by ship, horse or wheeled vehicle to the sound of the guns. Air transport changed all that.

During the period of police mandate between the World Wars Britain engaged in the air movement of troops about the Middle East, a relatively efficient undertaking in regard to the distances involved and the limited number of transport aircraft at her disposal. The first major air transport operation involving quasi-military aircraft was performed by the German air detachment sent to Spain in 1936, whose small fleet of Junkers Ju 52/3m bomber transports airlifted some 10,000 troops from Morocco to the Civil War battlefields on behalf of the Nationalist armies. There is no doubt that the swift delivery of such a force of fighting men did much to sustain the Nationalists' early vital operations, pending the arrival of other powerful assistance from their Fascist allies.

Indeed, while Britain and America were content to pursue the development of air transport for commercial purposes and with imperial motivation, the great dictatorships of Germany, Italy and Russia were hard at work establishing powerful military air transport fleets. Central to the theme of *Blitzkrieg* was the surprise delivery by air of highly-trained shock troops with limited support weapons. Countless key points throughout Europe were to fall in 1939–41 to assault by paratroops, glider-borne forces and other units flown into battle by the fast-growing numbers of Ju 52/3ms of the *Luftwaffe*. It can probably be said that the German General Kurt Student, although later accused of misappropriation of military manpower in the *Wehrmacht*, was the true architect of air transport for combat purposes.

On the other hand the Royal Air Force, to whom fell the responsibility of transporting British fighting forces by air, was utterly unable to match this mobility throughout the first three years of the Second World War, having been not only painfully unaware of the extent of the enemy's activity in the training and development of military air transport, but for years starved of funds so that it could do no more than produce air combat aircraft and aircrews. Not surprisingly the RAF's transport squadrons throughout those three years had to make do with a hotchpotch of impressed commercial airliners and flying boats, or hurried adaptations of obsolete bombers. The so-called 'bomber-transport' was the hall-mark of planning ineptitude and a parsimonious Treasury. With scarcely an exception there was no artillery larger than a soldier's mortar capable of being loaded into an aircraft—and even then it was probably being evacuated.

In America however, chance, and certainly not pre-meditation, had played its hand. Since the mid-1930s the Douglas Aircraft Corporation had been building large numbers (for those days) of the DC-2 and DC-3 airliners for commercial companies; aircraft which in their category of 20-seat medium-range carriers led the world in technology and reliability. First flown in 1935 the DC-3 was not ordered into production for the United States Army Air Corps until 1940 but thereafter, as the C-47 Skytrain and Dakota, provided the backbone of the American air transport fleet, and from 1943 equipped Royal Air Force Transport Command as well. Though never itself employed as an assault transport, as the Ju 53/3m had been, the C-47 (*Old Bucket Seats* or the *Gooney Bird*, as it became to countless Allied soldiers and airmen) nevertheless provided the essential air bridge between war theatres and to the fighting fronts in the years of British and American advance and re-conquest. No finer testimony was ever bestowed upon its place in history than by General Eisenhower who declared that the C-47 was one of the four decisive weapons in the Allied victory (joining the jeep, bazooka and the atom bomb).

If the C-47 was itself not used as an assault weapon that is not to say that it did not deliver soldiers and their weapons into battle; for while the C-47 would have required a fairly long and level landing strip (and much greater power from its engines than it possessed to fly out of very short strips) the troop-carrying assault gliders which it towed during the War did not. And it was upon these gliders—the British Horsa and Hamilcar, and the American Hadrian—that the RAF and USAAF came largely to depend upon in the classic air operations over Sicily, Normandy and the Rhine. In each of these and many other campaigns the glider-towing C-47 dominated the operations. For example, during the first 50 hours of the Allied assault on Normandy in June 1944 C-47s alone delivered more than 60,000 troops together with their equipment into battle.

More than 9,500 DC-3s and C-47 variants were built in the United States between 1935 and 1945, plus an unknown number in the Soviet Union. Not un-naturally many of these remained in service with post-war air forces or were disposed of throughout the world to assist in the enormous tasks of returning the fighting men to their homelands and resettling vast numbers of people displaced by war, not to mention the re-creation of international communications and commercial air transportation. In short, the Dakota had become the epitome of air communication the world over; it was the willing workhorse, born in peace, and a robust and reliable beast of burden in war. Soon, as these aged workhorses began to fall by the wayside, there would sound the universal call: 'Find a Dakota replacement.'

*   *   *

At the end of the Second World War the C-47 was by no means the only transport aeroplane in service with the USAAF, the Curtiss C-46 Commando twin-engine transport and the four-engine Douglas C-54 Skymaster were both serving in relatively large numbers; the latter in particular being widely used both for freight and passenger-carrying over long distances. The Skymaster gave excellent service with the USAAF's Air Transport Command and in the course of nearly 80,000 ocean crossings only three aircraft were lost; a hitherto unmatched safety record rendered possible by the use of four reliable Pratt & Whitney radial engines.

Before the United States even entered the Second World War American military observers and planners had taken note of the part being played by German air transport in the deployment and support of armies on the widely dispersed fronts of Europe and North Africa. It followed therefore that in the event that the USA became involved in the war, either in Europe or the Far East, or both, the demand for air transport would be enormous, and the implications of these demands brought about far-reaching re-assessment of the basic requirements of the transport aeroplane.

In the first place the use of large gliders (only then just beginning to appear in prototype form) was recognised in the longer view as being no more than a transient and relatively wasteful expedient, for obvious reasons, yet served to highlight the fundamental deficiencies of transport aircraft extant. Indeed the only fighting vehicles, and relatively small ones at that,

delivered to the battlefield itself by Allied aircraft during the War were those carried in gliders, owing simply to their use of folding or disposable sections of the fuselage for ease of loading and unloading, and of horizontal cabin floors. The obvious deficiencies of the existing wartime transports lay in the supposed weakening of the fuselage structure by large side-loading doors (soon to be dispelled in later versions of the C-46, C-47 and C-54) and by the traditional use of tailwheel undercarriages which resulted in a steeply inclined cabin floor (not, however, present in the C-54).

Indeed, it was in 1941 that the Fairchild Airplane and Engine Corporation of Hagerstown, Maryland, produced its radical Model F-78 design to a US Army requirement, in which the dominant factors were to provide an uninterrupted, low-set cabin floor with fore-and-aft loading and unloading access through rear clam-shell doors. To achieve this Fairchild adopted a shoulder-wing, twin-engine configuration with twin booms carrying the tailplane high, so as to provide clearance above loads being moved to and from the rear loading doors. By placing the cockpit and main wing spars above the cabin an almost uninterrupted cabin cross-section was maintained over much of its length, and therefore was able to accommodate a light tank, an Army truck, half-track or howitzers—all items of ordnance previously impossible to carry in an aero-plane. Alternatively up to 42 paratroops could be accommodated, their parachute exit being through doors set in each side of the rear fuselage. A mock-up of the Fairchild F-78 was approved in 1942, designated the C-82 and orders placed for a prototype XC-82, then subsequently for 100 production C-82A Packets. First flown on September 10 1944, the Packet was produced too late to see service during the Second World War, deliveries to the USAF not being made until the end of 1945.

There is no doubt that the Packet was an exceptional aircraft and certainly created entirely new parameters for military transport design and operations, for which Fairchild and the US Army can share the accolades. Indeed, as will become evident in the course of this book, the C-82 and it's derivative, the C-119, were to provide the means by which countless operational techniques were to be evolved, continued and extended by the Lockheed C-130 Hercules over the next quarter-century.

Before the end of the War North American Aviation had been asked to join the production programme and a new C-82 production line had been established at Dallas, Texas. Contracts for an improved version, the C-82N, totalling 792 aircraft, were placed but were cancelled immediately after VJ-Day. Fairchild how-ever, completed 220 C-82As.

Deliveries of C-82As to Troop Carrier Squadrons

Top *Scarcely a nation in the world has not flown the Douglas DC-3/C-47 either militarily or commercially. The example shown here is a C-47 of the Chilean Navy* (MAP, Neg No 98/126).

Above *Representing a makeshift generation of post-War RAF transports, the Handley Page Hastings owed something to the Halifax, but as a freighter was always handicapped by a tailwheel undercarriage and side loading* (MAP, Neg No 98/500).

Below *The Douglas DC-4/C-54 represented a yet further significant advance on the DC-3, but was largely developed as a military transport owing to the demands of the Second World War. The aircraft shown here served with the Royal Danish Air Force; note the tricycle landing gear and large side-loading freight doors* (Air and General Photos).

(Medium) of Tactical Air Command began in 1946 and in due course five aircraft were also assigned for duty with the Berlin Air Lift, their clam-shell loading doors being employed to allow transport of vehicles to the city. By the end of 1948 production of the Packet had run out and a new version, the C-119 Flying Boxcar, began deliveries the following year. An entirely new, extended and widened fuselage was introduced in which the crew cabin level was lowered and moved forward to give a smooth nose profile, and a strengthened, extended wing with two 3,500-hp Pratt & Whitney R-4360-20 piston engines allowed an all-up weight of 74,000 lb (compared with 54,000 lb in the C-82). Troop accommodation was increased to 62.

Undoubtedly the outbreak of the Korean War spurred production of the C-119, 55 C-119Bs and being produced by Fairchild, 347 C-119Cs (with water-injection in 120WB engines) by Fairchild and the Kaiser Manufacturing Company, 210 C-119Fs (with -85 engines and all-up weight increased to 85,000 lb) by the same two companies, and 480 C-119Gs (with Aeroproducts propellers) by Fairchild alone.

Flying Boxcars equipped the 314th Troop Carrier Group in the Far East during the Korean War and went on to serve with the Air Force Reserve's Troop Carrier Wings, as well as the Air National Guard's 14th and 183d Aeromedical Transport Squadrons. In 1960 nine specially-equipped C-119Js flew with the 6593d Test Squadron as satellite recovery aircraft in the Discoverer satellite programme, using trapeze gear to snatch the capsules as they returned to earth from orbit. Other C-119s were employed to carry personnel and equipment to Alaska and northern Canada during the construction of the Distant Early Warning radar line. Much more will be said about these activities in the context of the C-130.

Above *The French Nord Noratlas, similar in concept to the Fairchild C-82 Packet, was an efficient transport and has given considerable service during the post-War period. The aeroplane shown here carries the markings of the German* Luftwaffe *(Air and General Photos).*

Below *The British transport that nearly got it right; representing a sort of transient stage between the C-119 Flying Boxcar and the C-130 Hercules, the Armstrong Whitworth Argosy was, in truth, not adequately robust to meet the punishing tactical transport demands (MAP, Neg No 99/105).*

The most widely-used American military transport of the immediate post-War period was the excellent Fairchild C-119 Flying Boxcar, an example of which (a C-119J) is shown here in the markings of 46 Abg, Aeronautica Militare Italiana (MAP, Neg No 99/38).

By the beginning of the armed involvement of American forces in Vietnam the C-119's use as a military transport had declined considerably and the aircraft was not based as such in South Vietnam, although some Reserve Units flew occasional supply missions from overseas. However, with increasing numbers of surplus Flying Boxcars becoming available it was natural that with the evolution of the gunship the C-119 should constitute the interim aircraft so modified. Two such versions were produced, the AC-119G Shadow with four 7.62-mm Miniguns and the AC-119K with two additional 20-mm cannon (and two auxiliary turbojets under the wings). These AC-119s joined the 14th Special Operations Wing at Nha Trang Air Base in 1968, one Squadron operating the AC-119G and another AC-119K. All were eventually transferred to the South Vietnamese Air Force and struck off USAF charge.

*   *   *

The fortunes of the C-82/C-119 aircraft have been described at some length for these aircraft formed the backbone of the USAF's modern medium-weight airlift element at the time of the Korean War. The aircraft, good though they were by the standards of the time, were still not truly tactical aircraft in the sense that they still required fully-paved and hardened surfaces, which were to be found only at expensively-established transport bases. Moreover, limited by the use of only two piston engines, their load-carrying was still somewhat meagre (hence the progressively increased engine power in the successive versions), while the long main landing gear components imposed limitations on landing weight and ground surface operating conditions.

In truth, the demise of the heavy transport glider of the Second World War had deprived the Air Force of its ability to bring airborne troops with their equipment right in to the battlefield, save by parachute. When next America found herself at war, in Vietnam, the US Army itself overcame this deficiency by acquiring such huge numbers of helicopters that, in numerical terms, that Service became the world's third largest Air Force!

Thus it was in 1951, that following a policy decision by the USAF to seek introduction of a turboprop-powered family of transport aircraft to replace all remaining piston-engine aircraft in service by the end of the decade, work started at Lockheed's Burbank offices on a new design, the Model 82—a four turboprop-powered transport. It should perhaps be remarked in passing, that the company possessed no recent design experience in transport aircraft, other than the Constellation airliner which was an aeroplane of very different concept.

In common with a growing number of operational requirements—initiated with the integrated aircraft/missile/ground-control Weapons System concept then or about to be pursued in the Century-series fighters with the WS-105 (F-101), WS-303 (F-104) and WS-306 (F-105)—the same system concept was extended to the transport requirement, SS-400L, and under a single System Authority, the Model 82 was tailored to match the Service requirement.

Even if Lockheed would be loath to admit any reference to the C-82/C-119 design concept, there must surely be no doubt that these aircraft provided the Service's parameters for the drafting of the requirement, parameters which, from the outset, seemed capable of embracing the potential of the Model 82. Attracted by the four-engine layout and rough-field operating capability promised by the new design, the USAF gained authority to place a contract for two prototypes of the Model 82 in September 1952.

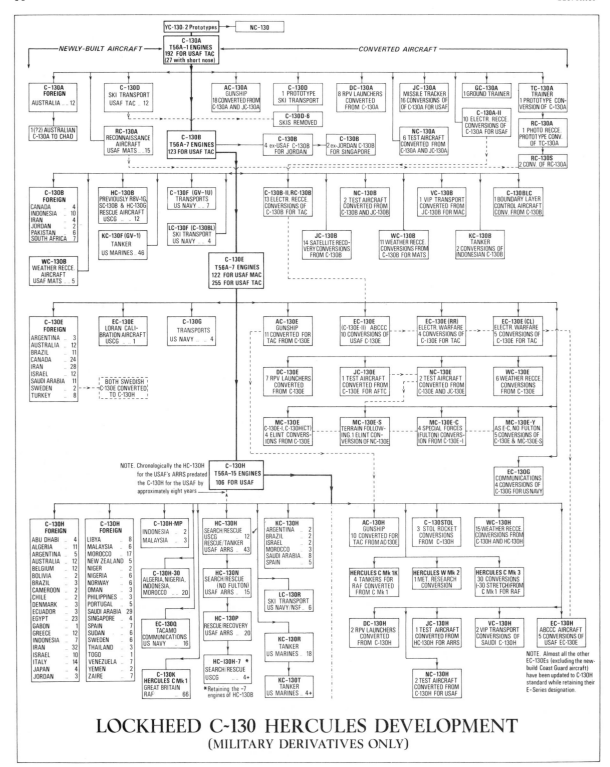

LOCKHEED C-130 HERCULES DEVELOPMENT
(MILITARY DERIVATIVES ONLY)

Chapter 2

The birth of Hercules

It is not unnatural that, having conceived the Requirement that brought about the Hercules, the United States Air Force has remained the biggest user of the aircraft. Moreover, the Hercules in its various forms has remained in service with and in production for the USAF for 30 years; an achievement not matched by any other large aeroplane in history.

Broadly speaking the life of the C-130 may be divided into two parts for convenience, the first embracing the A-, B- and E-Series (and their immediate derivatives), and the second comprising the H-Series and its variations*. Like most convenient segregations however, there is some blurring of the division (particularly among those versions for the US Navy and US Marine Corps), but the division is adequately defined for the purposes of the USAF's aeroplanes to be described here in two separate chapters.

Hercules is born

After issue of contracts for two YC-130 prototypes in September 1952 detail design went ahead at Burbank, California, and late the following year construction of

* Up to the end of the 1950s USAF and US Navy aircraft were designated according to different nomenclature series, the former perpetuating an age-old system comprising function letter (F for fighters, B for bombers, C for transports, etc), followed by a number whose sequence had, in some cases, reached the hundreds by the 1950s. Thus the Hercules had been conceived as the C-130, of which the first Service version was the C-130A. Fundamental changes in the design, such as new powerplant, different loading access or a new fuel system, might identify the C-130B or C-130E. A change of operational role that did not affect the aircraft's basic structure, systems or powerplant would be identified by a prefix letter, for example the AC-130A (attack) gunship, the DC-130A drone launcher and the RC-130A reconnaissance aircraft. As the adaptability of the Hercules was exploited, so these fairly simple rules became 'bent', sometimes on the pretext of security, and some new conventions were adopted (with such aircraft as the MC-130E-S and EC-130E (RR) whose significance, if not their logicality, will become apparent). So much for the 'rules of designation'. In the 1960s, incidentally, the USAF decided to abandon the traditional numerical sequence and return to No 1, but aircraft in being at the time of change retained their old number, so the Hercules remained the C-130; however, the change involved standardising the US Navy's designation system with that of the USAF, so that Hercules versions such as the GV-1 and R8V-1G (the latter of the Coast Guard) were included henceforth in the C-130 designation in one form or another.

these aircraft started. With the announcement that production would be centred at Lockheed-Marietta, Georgia, at that time the world's largest aircraft manufacturing plant, orders for six development aircraft, a test specimen and 20 production aircraft were placed.

Powered by 3,750-eshp Allison T56A-1A turboprops driving three-blade Aeroproducts propellers, the YC-130s featured a short, blunt nose without radome, it being intended in due course to introduce a weather-mapping radar with nose radome. In an excellent exercise in ergonomics, every facet of the tactical requirement was allowed free rein and, in a fashion that has come to characterise so many post-War Lockheed projects (be they F-104 Starfighter, U-2, C-5 Galaxy or SR-71 Blackbird), conventional design and structural limitations and parameters underwent fundamental redefinition.

To provide low-loading facility a very short undercarriage was adopted, the main units of the tricycle gear incorporating twin tandem wheels to impose the largest surface footprint, being retracted into large fairings on the sides of the fuselage so as to avoid heavy retracting oleos, the landing loads being carried vertically up to the main wing spar. The shoulder mounted high aspect ratio wing, of considerable weight lifting characteristics, achieved much of its strength and stiffness by use of huge (48-ft) integrally-machined planks which, attached to front and rear spars, provided accommodation for integral fuel tanks. The parallel-width fuselage of near-circular cross-section with strengthened floor was a huge cargo hold with loading ramp at the rear, and, to maintain full-height aperture for loading, the rear section of the under-fuselage hinged upwards into the hull, so that any load which extended to the full height of the cabin would still clear the underside of the rear fuselage during loading. The cabin floor height was chosen to match that of the standard American low-bed truck.

The two YC-130s, *53-3396* and *53-3397* (C/Ns 1001 and 1002) were completed in reverse numerical sequence, '96 being delayed by installation of instrumentation, and on August 23 1954 '97 was first flown by Stanley Beltz at Burbank, where it remained

Above left *First flight by the YC-130, 53-3397, at Burbank, California, on August 23 1954, with Stanley Beltz at the controls* (Lockheed Aircraft Corporation, Neg No RL 2394).

Above *The first development C-130A, 53-3129, during a test flight over Stone Mountain, near Atlanta, Georgia* (Lockheed Aircraft Corporation, Neg No C9682).

Left *Take-off for first flight by the first development C-130A, 53-3129, at Marietta, Georgia, on April 7 1954. When landing from its third flight it was badly damaged by fire in the port wing, but was repaired and was still flying some 30 years later* (Lockheed Aircraft Corporation, Neg No C9627).

until December when it was flown to Marietta for completion of prototype flight trials; after brief visits to Edwards AFB and elsewhere during the next four years, it was delivered to General Motors' Allison Division at Indianapolis in July 1959. The second YC-130 was delivered from Burbank to Edwards AFB in August 1955 for performance trials, and then joined the first aircraft at Marietta in March 1956. Both aircraft were redesignated NC-130s for Air Force test programmes starting in 1959, but by that time their standard of preparation had become so outdated by new production versions as to render them superfluous, and both had been dismantled by 1962.

The six development aircraft were undoubtedly of greater value in the C-130 trials programme and, being built on the Marietta production line, were more closely representative of the production aircraft following behind. The first aircraft, *53-3129* (C/N 3001) was flown on April 7 1955 but, after landing from its third

flight, a fuel leak in the port wing led to a fire which destroyed the wing before it could be extinguished. The aircraft was repaired and rejoined the test programme at Marietta. In 1957 it was modified as a JC-130A missile tracker (see below), but remained with the manufacturers until October 1959, when it was delivered to the Cambridge Air Research Center Hanscom Field, Massachusettes. The following April it went to the Air Force Missile Center, and to Majors Field, Texas, in 1961. In August 1962 it joined the 6550th Support Wing (Range) at Patrick AFB, Florida. Later it was converted to an AC-130A gunship and served in Vietnam; it was still flying in 1981 with the 711th Special Operations Squadron. The second development aircraft, *53-3130*, was the contracted structural test airframe and, after being modified as a JC-130A test aircraft in September 1957, was tested to destruction in the rig at Marietta the following February.

Top *Pre-delivery line-up of very early unpainted C-130As on the ramp at Marietta; note the short nose, three-blade propellers and rounded vertical tail* (Lockheed-Georgia, Neg No RE 0119-3).

Above *Eighteenth full-production C-130A, 54-1638, identified by the short nose and outboard fuel tanks as a very early production Hercules. The low visibility national markings and four-blade propellers indicate a recent picture of this veteran aircraft, still serving with the AFRES some 25 years after manufacture* (MAP, Neg No 98/324).

The remaining five development aircraft were all completed before the end of 1956 and all were subjects of wide-ranging test programmes during the next four years, all being redesignated JC-130As and serving variously at the Edwards and El Centro Air Force Test Centers, the Armament Development and Test Center, Eglin AFB (for gunship development), and the 4900th, 6401st, 6515th and 6549th Test Squadrons before taking their place in regular service with Tactical Air Command.

The first 20 production C-130As (*54-1621* to *54-1640*) were withheld for various development and evaluation programmes, and although most eventually also served in regular line Squadrons of the USAF, their immediate presence at Marietta often resulted in their selection for trial installations which in turn led to conversion to such derivatives as the AC-130A, JC-130A, NC-130A and RC-130A.

Into service with TAC

The C-130A entered regular operational service with the USAF's Tactical Air Command in November 1956 with the delivery of about 38 aircraft to the 772d, 773d and 774th Troop Carrier Squadrons (TCS) of the 463d

Top *Last of the first batch of 20 true production C-130As, 54-1640, with the short nose; this aircraft was still serving in 1981, named* Nashville, *with the 105th TAS, 118th TAW, Tennessee Air National Guard (Starliner Aviation Press, Neg No CS 855).*

Above *Another famous example of the early C-130A, 55-0023, this time with the characteristic nose radome, was originally named* City of Ardmore *with the 463d TCW; it still carried the name with the 64th TAS, 928th TAG, of the AFRES in 1982 (Starliner Aviation Press, Neg No CS 856).* **Right** *Close-up of* City of Ardmore *(Starliner Aviation Press, Neg No CS 857).*

Troop Carrier Wing (TCW) at Ardmore in southern Oklahoma, much of the early Service working-up being performed by these Squadrons during the course of the next eight months. The 314th TCW followed in the summer of 1957, its 50th, 61st and 62d Squadrons being allotted 48 C-130As at Sewart Air Force Base, Tennessee. The first Hercules to be deployed overseas were C-130As assigned in September that year to the 314th TCW's 40th TCS at Evreux-Fauville Air Base (AB) in northern France—then a full military component of NATO; before the end of the year the Wing's 39th and 41st Squadrons had also received their full establishment of C-130As.

1958 was a year of considerable re-organisation of the USAF, not least of TAC itself. In January C-130As were delivered to the 21st TCS, 483d TCW, at Ashiya AB, Japan, and the Wing's 815th and 817th Squadrons followed suit the next month. However, in September as part of the 315th Air Division. The 815th and 817th remained at Ashiya until mid-1960 when the former moved to Tachikawa AB, Japan, also in the 315th Air Division, and the latter to Naha AB, but as a component of the 374th TCW. These three Squadrons retained their C-130As right up to the end of the 1960s when they were inactivated after five strenuous years' operations in Vietnam.

In France the 39th, 40th and 41st Squadrons at Evreux transferred to the 322d Air Division (Troop Carrier) in September, remaining in this command until mid-1963 when the 317th Wing command was re-instated. In the States, the pioneer Hercules squadrons of the 463d TCW at Ardmore moved to Sewart AFB, Tennessee, this base becoming the principal centre of C-130 operations in the USA for about three years.

With some 180 C-130As delivered to TAC, no further Squadrons were equipped with Hercules in 1959, but before the end of that year the 61st TCS at Sewart had exchanged its early C-130As for a new version, the ski-equipped C-130D, and as this version has continued in service ever since it is convenient to recount here its history in full.

The C-130D ski-Hercules

Anticipating a requirement to conduct transport operations in the harsh Arctic conditions of Alaska, the Air Force had in late 1956 set aside a C-130A (*55-0021*, C/N 3048) for modification to include a wheel-ski undercarriage and after its first flight as the prototype C-130D on January 29 1957 successful trials leds to an order for 12 production examples in the 1957 Appropriations (*57-0484* to *57-0495*, C/Ns 3191 to 3202). At this time however, proposals were in hand to extend the USAF's Distant Early Warning (DEW) Line, a radar 'fence', the construction of whose radar stations between Cape Lisburne in Alaska and Cape Dyer on

Canada's Atlantic Coast had been completed in 1957. Extensions to this radar fence were proposed, including six auxiliary sites along the Aleutian chain in the Pacific, and five to the north-east of Canada, of which four (DYE I, II, III and IV) were in Greenland and one in Iceland. Being located on the remote ice-cap, the construction of DYE II and III would demand a considerable airlift effort. It was the realisation that the existing ski-equipped Fairchild C-123J Providers, then serving the Arctic stations, would be unequal to the task of supporting construction work on the Greenland bases that hastened development and delivery of the C-130Ds.

The C-130Ds, together with ski-equipped Hercules of the US Navy, (see Chapter 4) are the largest ski-equipped aeroplanes ever built, featuring two main skis of 20 ft long by 5 ft 6 in wide, and a nose ski 10 ft long by 5 ft 6 in wide; all three being coated with Teflon on their undersurfaces to resist ice and snow accretion and to reduce friction. All are retractable on to external fairings and the normal wheel undercarriage is retained; on selecting the undercarriage down the wheels extend normally and the skis may be raised or lowered around the wheels (which extend through apertures in the skis), thereby providing an ability to operate both from snow and paved/hardened surfaces. Total weight of the ski installation is around 4,200 lb.

Two further standard C-130As (*57-0473* and *57-0474*, C/Ns 3180 and 3181) were modified to C-130D standard, but these served only for test purposes and were returned to C-130As when delivery of the production aircraft started.

As already mentioned, the C-130Ds were delivered to the 61st TCS in 1959, the Squadron being tasked with airlifting the components and materials needed to build DYE II, 100 miles east of Sondrestrom, 90 miles south of the Arctic Circle and at an altitude of 7,600 ft above sea level. The first aircraft arrived on deployment at Sondrestrom AB early in 1959, the first delivery mission of Phase 1 in the building of DYE II being flown to its site on March 23. By December the following year construction of the stations had been completed with the 12 C-130Ds having lifted no less than 243,000 tons of cargo to the sites and on August 1 1961, after delivery of operational equipment, DYE II and III were handed over to Air Defense Command. Support of DYE II and III now passed to the 17th TCS, 64th TCW, at Dyess AFB, Texas, this Squadron taking over the 12 C-130Ds as the 61st TCS converted to C-130Bs. Gradually the support task eased and late in 1962 the Sondrestrom detachment was reduced to six aircraft, the other six having their ski landing gear removed (and their designation becoming C-130D-6) so as to resume normal airlift duties.

In December 1963 it was decided to move the 17th TCS to Alaska (under Alaska Air Command) where the

Above *Ski-equipped C-130D, 57-0493 (C/N 3200) of the 139th TAS, New York ANG, taxying near one of the DYE Line radar stations in Greenland in the late 1970s* (Lockheed-Georgia, Neg No 9825-2). **Below** *Amidst the wastes of Greenland a C-130D discharges fuel oil into the buried fuel tanks near a DYE Line station* (Lockheed-Georgia, Neg No RMO 389-2).

Left *One of the six C-130Ds, 57-0486 (C/N 3193), which were modified to C-130D-6 by removal of the ski components of the landing gear. The outboard fuel tanks and three-blade propellers disclose the C-130D's relationship with the C-130A (MAP, Neg No U08911 dated October 1980).* **Below left** *A C-130D-6, 57-0488 (C/N 3195), without skis, seldom pictured while serving with the 17th TAS, 21st Composite Wing, in August 1974 (MAP, Neg No U08295).*

Bottom left *A C-130D with wheel-ski landing gear, 57-0493 (C/N 3200), of the 139th TAS, 109th TAG, New York ANG. This aircraft appeared at the 1979 Greenham Common Air Tattoo in immaculate paint having only just completed repairs following a minor accident (Starliner Aviation Press, Neg No CS 859).* **Right** *Close-up of the C-130D showing details of the nose ski; note also the four RATOG bottles attached aft (Starliner Aviation Press, Neg No CS 860).*

Below *In conditions of near white-out, a C-130D discharges fuel oil at a DYE Line station in Greenland (Lockheed-Georgia, Neg No RMO 389-5).*

Fairchild C-123s were proving unequal to the task of servicing the DEW Line stations. The distance moreover, between Elmendorf, whither the 17th TCS went, and Sondrestrom in Greenland was less than that between Sondrestrom and Dyess. Thereafter the ski-equipped C-130Ds continued to service the Greenland sites, while the wheel-only D-6s serviced the Alaska sites, most of which possessed gravel strips. For ten years this pattern of gruelling operations continued, two aircraft being stationed on rotation at Sondrestrom. One aircraft was lost in an accident on June 5 1972 when *57-0495* stalled while overshooting at DYE III; the crew escaped with minor injuries but the aircraft was written off.

In 1974, with the Service operation of early warning satellites introduced, the DEW Line was relegated to back-up status, its day-to-day support being contracted commercially, although a single ski-equipped C-130D of the 17th Tactical Airlift Squadron (so renamed on July 1 1967) was kept at Sondrestrom to provide a heavy-lift element.

On July 1 1975, the heavy-lift responsibility was passed to the Air National Guard, the 139th TAS, 109th TAG, New York ANG, based at Schenectady Airport, NY, being selected for the task. At the same time the 11 surviving C-130Ds and D-6s were taken over from the 17th TAS. In June 1976 two of the D-6s were withdrawn to storage at Davis Montham AFB, but ever since then the remaining nine aircraft have continued to perform the support task with scarcely a hitch.

Finally, to illustrate the scale of operation undertaken to build and support the DYE II and III stations, it is worth describing briefly these huge structures which were built by the US Army Corps of Engineers. Between them the stations weigh 300,000 tons, each being supported on eight columns sunk into the ice cap. Each of these columns incorporates a pair of hydraulic jacks which raise and lower the entire station according to the seasonal accumulation of snow, so as to maintain a consistent aerial height above the surrounding surface. The station itself is a two-storey communications centre, surmounted by the AN/FPS-30 search radar. Electrical power is provided by six huge diesel generators whose Arctic diesel fuel is stored in four 100,000-US gal under-ice tanks. Each site uses 300,000-US gal of fuel annually, all of which has to be airlifted in from Sondrestrom by the C-130Ds, where it has been cold-soaked to prevent it from melting the ice when it arrives at the DYE sites.

★   ★   ★

Returning to the deployment of Hercules in the USAF during the late 1950s, 1958 had seen the end of C-130A production with 192 aircraft completed, with an extra dozen similar aircraft for the Royal Australian Air Force (see Chapter 8), and the 12 C-130D ski transports. In 1959 production of 15 RC-130As was completed for Military Airlift Command, these Hercules (*57-0510* to *57-0524*, C/Ns 3217 to 3231) being developed for aerial survey and charting duties, equipped with radar dielectric panels and windows for cameras in the underside of the fuselage and a small TV viewfinder under the nose search radar. The interior layout made accommodation for a photo-navigator, air photographer, and airborne profile recorder operator and two HIRAN operators, up to four vertical cameras, cartographic equipment, a dark room and a galley. After trials has been completed using a converted C-130A (an early aircraft, *54-1632*, C/N 3019) that had served as prototype of a proposed Hercules trainer, the TC-130A, deliveries of all 16 aircraft were completed in 1959 to the 1375th Mapping and Charting Squadron (MCS), 1370th Photo Mapping Wing (PMW), Air Photographic and Charting Service (APCS) of MATS. They remained with this Wing for about ten years, some aircraft being passed to the 1st Aerospace Cartographic and Geodetic Squadron (ACGS) between May 1968 and 1972, and four aircraft to the 1866th Facility Checking Squadron (FCS) at Scott AFB, Illinois, in 1971–72. Two years later 15 of the RC-130As were converted to standard C-130As and one to a DC-130A drone launcher.

Two other reconnaissance Hercules were produced later, designated RC-130S (*56-0493* and *56-0497*, C/Ns 3101 and 3105) after conversion from JC-130A test aircraft; these were intended for low-level night reconnaissance and carried searchlights; both were returned to standard C-130As in the late 1960s.

The designation JC-130A, just referred to, covered 16 C-130As converted for a multitude of trial installations beginning in 1956, when all seven development ('pre-production') C-130As underwent test instrumentation on behalf of the Cambridge Air Research Center, Hanscom Field, Massachusetts, and the Air Force Flight Test Center at Edwards AFB, California. Apart from *53-3130*, which underwent structural test to destruction in 1958, these and nine other conversions were later employed for missile tracking on the Atlantic range, serving with a number

An RC-130A of the 1375th Mapping and Charting Squadron, 1370th Photo Mapping Wing, Military Airlift Command, in the late 1960s (MAP, Neg No U03009).

Flying view of an RC-130A of the 1375th MCS, 1370th PMW. Note the large camera ports and dielectric panels under the fuselage; the aircraft was painted with high-visibility panels on nose, wings and tail (Lockheed-Georgia, Neg No RF 8759).

of test establishments as well as the 6515th Test Squadron, the instrumentation being installed as palletised containers in the cabins.

Finally, conversions of the C-130A included eight DC-130As (originally referred to as GC-130As, but changed to avoid confusion with a single GC-130A ground trainer used for ground instruction at the Sheppard Technical Training Center, Texas). The first two conversion (*57-0496* and *57-0497*, C/Ns 3203 and 3204) were carried out on the last two C-130As to leave Marietta to a requirement prepared for Air Research and Development Command. Equipped with a nose radome lengthened by 30 in and an additional 'chin' radome with ground control

antenna, the DC-130A could carry up to four drones on underwing pylons, capable of release at altitudes up to 35,000 ft, the seven/eight crew members operating the release, control and monitoring equipment installed in palletised and portable consoles mounted in the cargo cabin. Systems developed for the DC-130A were compatible with the whole range of Ryan and Northrop drones ordered for the USAF and US Navy. Enlarged fuselage windows facilitated camera recording.

The aircraft served in turn and variously with the 3225th Drone Squadron, the 4453d Combat Crew Training Wing, the 6514th Test Squadron, the 11th Target Drone Squadron and the 350th Strategic

Above left *One of the JC-130As, 55-0022 (C/N 3049), being employed for trials with the Aeronautical Systems Division, Air Force Systems Command, Wright Paterson AFB, seen here in the markings of the 4950th Test Wing in 1976. Note the modified wing tips and the various sensors and radome on the fuselage (MAP, Neg No U01318).* **Left** *Another JC-130A, 56-0490 (C/N 3098), with much larger dorsal radome, probably in about 1970. The aircraft was subsequently modified as an AC-130A gunship and lost in Vietnam in 1972 (MAP, Neg No U03052).*

Below left *One of eight converted DC-130As, 57-0461 (C/N 3168), this aircraft served with the 350th Strategic Reconnaissance Squadron and probably flew with Ryan AQM-34 reconnaissance drones over Vietnam. Note the additional chin radome and lengthened nose (Starliner Aviation Press, Neg No CS 858).* **Above** *One of the two original GC-130As which became the DC-130A, 57-0496 (C/N 3203), seen here in the markings of the 11th Target Drone Squadron, 355th Tactical Fighter Wing, probably in about 1975 (MAP, Neg No U01365).*

Below *One of ten C-130A-IIs, 56-0525 (C/N 3133), of the 7406th Combat Support Squadron, 7407th Combat Support Wing, seen here in August 1966 in Germany. Considerable secrecy surrounded the work done by these aircraft (MAP, Neg No U03033).*

Reconnaissance Squadron, and two of them (*55-0021* and *56-0491*) underwent updating for transfer to the US Navy in 1969.

The C-130B and -7 engines

Development by the Allison division of the T56A-7 turboprop, in which the inlet guide vanes were removed from the compressor intake to increase mass flow, thereby increasing the power output from 3,750 to 4,050 eshp, resulted in the introduction of the Lockheed Model 282 C-130B Hercules. The first example of this, *57-0525* (C/N 3501), was flown on November 20 1958 and the first production delivery made to TAC on June 12 the following year. Among other modifications incorporated were the adoption of four-blade propellers, strengthened undercarriage and the additional capacity of 1,710 US gal of fuel in the wings inboard of the inner engine nacelles. A forward side-loading cargo door was included and the provision for 450-gal external tanks outboard of the outer engines was retained. A total of 123 C-130Bs was built for TAC in the USAF Appropriations of 1957–61; the first deliveries being to the 463d TCW at Sewart AFB in the latter half of 1959, followed by the 314th TCW at the same base in 1960–61. By the end of 1962 C-130As were serving with the 322d Air Division in France, the 815th TAS, 315th Air Division, at Tachikawa AB, the 345th and 817th TAS, 374th TAW at Naha AB, and the 18th TAS, 64th TAW, at Dyess AFB, Texas. C-130Bs served with the 50th, 61st and 62d TAS, 314th TAW, and the 772d, 773d and 774th TAS, 463d TAW, all at Sewart AFB. In addition, C-130As and Bs had been delivered as initial equipment of the 4442d Combat Crew Training Squadron (CCTS), also at Sewart.

Apart from 40 C-130Bs built for export (see Chapter 8), 46 tankers were produced for the US Marine Corps as the KC-130F (see Chapter 5), four LC-130F transports for the US Navy (see Chapter 4) and 12 HC-130B rescue aircraft for the US Coast Guard (see Chapter 7). As already recounted, five weather reconnaissance WC-130Bs were built for MATS.

The largest C-130B conversion programme was undertaken on 14 aircraft, JC-130Bs, for recovery of Discoverer satellites over the Pacific to replace Fairchild C-119s of the 6593d Test Squadron (TS) at Hickam AFB, Hawaii. Equipped with a retractable trapeze gear, which extended from the rear loading ramp of the Hercules, these aircraft underwent progressive modification, at least one aircraft later being fitted with a large dorsal radome. At the end of the Discoverer programme, most of the JC-130Bs were returned to standard C-130B configuration, although some remained with the 6593d TS; one however, (*57-0715*, C/N 3510) was modified as a VIP transport,

Standard C-130B, 59-1525 (C/N 3561), serving with the 164th TAS, Ohio Air National Guard, in the late 1970s and wearing 'lizard' camouflage. This aircraft had previously served with the 556th Reconnaissance Squadron, 347th Tactical Fighter Wing, as a C-130B-II electronic reconnaissance aircraft in Japan (MAP, Neg No 98/320).

Above *A JC-130B test aircraft, 57-0527 (C/N 3503), serving with the 6593d Test Squadron in the late 1970s (MAP, Neg No 100/415).*

Below *The single VC-130B VIP transport, 58-0715 (C/N 3510), converted from a JC-130B and serving with the 1174th Support Squadron at Norton Air Force Base in December 1969 (MAP, Neg No U00687).*

A C-130B, 58-0756 (C/N 3557), serving with the California ANG, demonstrating the Modular Airborne Fire Fighting System (MAFFS), probably about 1975. The aircraft was later sold to Singapore (Starliner Aviation Press, Neg No CS 861).

the VC-130B, and this flew with the 1174th SS, Norton AFB, California, during the early 1970s.

The field of radar reconnaissance embraced the whole gamut of radar search, identification and frequency compilation, and involved the mounting of multiple radar sensors in aircraft flown both tactically and strategically by the USAF to gain intelligence on potentially hostile radar defences. A total of 13 Hercules was converted to C-130B-II, a designation intended to avoid any allusion to the covert operations flown. Most aircraft were delivered to the 6091st Reconnaissance Squadron (RS) in 1964–65, during the early stages of the Vietnam War, then to the 556th RS in about 1967, a component of the 347th Tactical Fighter Wing at Yokota AB, Japan; some remained with the 556th after inactivation of the 347th TFW, becoming part of the 475th Base Wing in 1973, while others went on to serve with the 7406th Combat Support Squadron.

The C-130E

The C-130E was the most extensively used USAF Hercules, a total of 377 being produced for that Service at Marietta between 1961 and 1974. It was in effect, a much modified version, largely tailored to meet the specific requirements of Military Airlift Command, although the C-130B's T56A-7 turboprops were retain-

ed. The side-loading freight door continued to be used in the first eight aircraft, but thereafter was omitted. Externally the distinguishing feature of the C-130E was it's ability to carry two large 1,360-US gal underwing fuel tanks between the engine nacelles, whereas aircraft delivered to MAC featured station keeping equipment (SKE) from the outset; these were identified by a small dorsal cylindrical radome above the crew cabin. Ironically perhaps all MAC units were transferred to TAC during 1964–66, only to return to MAC late in 1974, by which time almost all C-130s with the USAF had acquired SKE.

The first flight by a MAC-destined C-130E (*61-2358*, C/N 3609) was made on August 15 1961 and was followed by 121 others, which were delivered to the 29th and 30th Air Transport Squadrons (ATS), 1611th Air Transport Wing (ATW), at McGuire AFB, New Jersey, the 41st and 76th ATS, 1608th ATW, at Charleston AFB, South Carolina, and the 86th ATS, 1501st ATW, at Travis AFB, California.★

The first TAC unit to fly the C-130B was the 345th TCS, which re-activated with the 516th TCW at Dyess

---

★*On July 1 1965 the 1611th, 1608th and 1501st ATW became the 438th, 437th and 60th Military Airlift Wings respectively; their component Squadrons retained their numbers unchanged but became Military Airlift Squadrons.*

Above *This C-130E, 64-18240 (C/N 4105), was a 'one-off' order in the 1964 Appropriations for TAC to replace 64-0546 which had been diverted to the Swedish Air Force in September 1965; it is seen here serving with the 40th TAS, 317th TAW, in October 1971* (MAP, Neg No U03043).

Below *C-130E, 63-7823 (C/N 3891), said to be serving with the 435th TAW, displaying sand camouflage and low visibility markings* (Starliner Aviation Press, Neg No CS 870).

Left *C-130E, 64-0504 (C/N 3988), of the 317th TAW wearing an experimental two-tone grey camouflage in the late 1970s, seen here at Mildenhall, England* (MAP, Neg No U06576).

Below left *Three C-130Es of the 435th TAW at the conclusion of an air display at RAF Mildenhall, England* (Starliner Aviation Press, Neg No CS 900).

Above right *DC-130E, 61-2362 (C/N 3663), serving with the 22nd Target Drone Squadron, 432d Target Drone Group, in 1978. This aircraft had previously served with the 350th Strategic Reconnaissance Squadron, carrying reconnaissance drones in South-east Asia* (Starliner Aviation Press, Neg No CS 865). **Right** *Close-up of the AQM-34 carried under the wing of a DC-130E* (Starliner Aviation Press, Neg No CS 866).

on January 1 1963, followed by the Wing's 346th TCS two months later, and the 347th TCS in June. The next Wing to equip with Es was the 464th TCW at Pope AFB, North Carolina, the 777th TCS also activating in June, the 778th on January 1 1964 and the 779th about two months later. By the end of 1966 C-130Es equipped the 4446th and 4447th CCTS of the 4442d CCTW, and the 61st and 62d TCS of the 64th TCW, all at Sewart AFB; the 346th and 347th TCS of the 516th TCW at Dyess AFB, and the 777th, 778th and 779th TCS of the 464th TCW at Pope AFB; another component of the 464th TCW, the 776th TCS, was based in South East Asia at Ching Chuan Kang ROCAB, Taiwan, home also of the 314th TCW's 50th and 345th TCS, all with C-130Es.

On July 1 1967 all Troop Carrier Squadrons and Wings were redesignated Tactical Airlift Squadrons and Wings, and subsequently C-130Es also equipped the 47th and 38th TAS, 313th TAW (the latter becoming the 48th TAS), at Forbes AFB, Kansas, the 61st and 62d TAS, 314th TAW, Little Rock AFB, Arkansas, the 774th TAS, 463d TAW, at Dyess AFB and the 776th TAS, 464th TAW at Clark AB.

Considerable redeployment of the large numbers of C-130Es produced for the USAF has taken place during the past 17 years and the current distribution and location of all C-130 units is given in Chapter 3. Conversions of C-130Es have also been numerous. Eleven gunships (AC-130Es, see below) were converted during the early Vietnam War period, as were seven DC-130Es, similar to the DC-130B, some of these serving at the Missile Development Center, Holloman AFB, New Mexico, and with the 11th and 22d Target Drone Squadrons, before being returned to C-130E standard.

The electronic warfare and intelligence gathering installations initiated in the C-130B-II conversions were followed by a whole range of installations, in some respects related but all made possible by the adaptability of the Hercules, its long range, heavy load-carrying and rough field operating concept. To begin with, ten aircraft started conversion in 1966 as EC-130Es for the Airborne Battlefield Command Control Centre (ABCCC) role, for the communication with and surveillance of special ground forces' missions. Developed in parallel was the 20,000-lb. ABCCC/USC-15 airborne command capsule that could be installed in the cargo hold of the C-130, and which in turn accommo-

Right *Original development C-130A, 53-3129 (C/N 3001), as converted to an AC-130A gunship and serving with the 711th Special Operations Squadron, 919th Special Operations Group, AFRES, at Duke Field, Florida* (Starliner Aviation Press, Neg No BW 1254).

Below right *The AC-130A gunship, 53-3129, while in service with the 415th SOTS, 834th TCW; at this time it was armed with four 7.62 mm Miniguns and two 40 mm Bofors guns; it carried the usual array of infra-red sensor 'bulbs' fore and aft* (MAP, Neg No U02895).

Bottom right *Standard C-130E, 64-0499 (C/N 3983), serving with the 317th TAW, seen at Mildenhall. Note the 'sitting bird' and 'diving bird' incorporated into the pale camouflage scheme on tail and forward fuselage—something of a trademark of the 317th* (MAP, Neg No 99/174).

dated up to 16 personnel together with four UF, eight UHF, four VHF and four FM radio transceivers, secure teletype, automatic radio relay and voice communication equipment. Externally these aircraft were distinguishable by a pair of large air conditioning system intakes on the upper sides of the fuselage forward of the wings, as well as numerous additional antenna wires between fuselage and tail. The majority of these aircraft served with the 7th Airborne Command and Control Squadron (ACCS), 552d Airborne Warning and Control Wing (AWCW). (See also Chapter 3).

Much later a number of EC-130Es, as well as 20 MC-130E electronic reconnaissance aircraft, were converted for air support of special forces, their development being carried out alongside the C-130H. It is, therefore, convenient to describe them in the following chapter.

The Hercules gunships

As American involvement in Vietnam escallated during the early 1960s it became all too clear that the nature of the country's terrain—and hence the infiltration tactics of the enemy guerillas—could well serve to eliminate any numerical strength and firepower advantage built up by the forces of South Vietnam. Even prior to the start of open warfare by American forces in Vietnam attempts had been made to effect local defoliation of jungle areas by spraying chemicals from Fairchild C-123K Providers (the controversial 'Ranch Hand' missions); while this served to deprive enemy forces of ground concealment in specific localities, it could never come near to creating the conditions for general warfare over open ground for which Western armies were conventionally trained. Indeed, so adept were the guerillas at operating in the jungle that only by bringing to bear a deluge of gunfire over an area suspected of being occupied by enemy forces could effective action be taken against them.

It was a proposal by Captain Ronald Terry of the USAF's Aeronautical Systems Division that led to the installation of guns firing laterally from the cabin of a Convair C-131 Samaritan for trials by the Armament Development and Test Center at Eglin AFB, Florida. The first operational gunship to arrive in the war theatre was a converted AC-47 Skytrain (dubbed *Puff*

the Magic Dragon), which landed at Tan Son Nhut in November 1965. Flown by the 1st Special Operations Wing, these slow-flying aeroplanes could pour a withering torrent of small-calibre gunfire from their three 7.62-mm rotary-barrelled Miniguns into a small area of ground as they circled above. In due course the AC-47s were joined by AC-119K Shadow and Stinger gunships, but none was to prove so effective as the Hercules in this role.

As early operations by AC-47s and AC-119s quickly confirmed the value of Captain Terry's proposals, a C-130A, *54-1626*, in 1967 serving with the 4950th Test Wing, was modified to feature three, and later four 7.62-mm Miniguns, firing laterally from the port side of the fuselage (the port side was chosen so that in a left-hand turn the pilot, seated in the left-hand cockpit position, would have a clear view of the ground). This aircraft, in turn, was later armed with an additional pair of 40-mm Bofors guns, and delivered to the 16th Special Operations Squadron (SOS), 14th Special Operations Wing (SOW), at Nha Trang AB, Vietnam, in 1969. In due course a total of 18 AC-130As was converted, including the very first production Hercules (*53-3129, C/N 3001*), and these served with the 16th SOS, remaining with it after transfer to the 8th Tactical Fighter Wing (the 'Wolf Pack') at Ubon RTAFB, Thailand.

The AC-130As quickly acquired all manner of sensing devices (including large infra-red sensing 'bulbs', 'Igloo White' receivers and laser designators), and were joined in service by 11 AC-130Es, ten of which were converted to AC-130Hs in 1973. The other AC-130E (*69-6571*) had been shot down near An Loc on March 30 1972.

The AC-130H configuration took the gunship's armoury one stage further by the substitution of one of the Bofors guns by a 105-mm howitzer, one of the largest weapons mounted by any aircraft.

Today 11 of the surviving AC-130As serve on the 711th SOS, 919th Special Operations Group (SOG), of the Air Force Reserve at Duke Field, Florida, and the AC-130Hs on the 16th SOS, 1st SOW, at Hurlburt Field, Florida. None of their crews will admit to their showing their age, but the record shows that they have certainly been cost-effective over a very long service period.

Chapter 3

The last twenty years with the USAF

During the past 20 years the C-130 has served with almost every command component of the United States Air Force, not simply as a support aircraft but as principal equipment, be it transport, rescue aircraft, weather reconnaissance aircraft, gunship, electronic reconnaissance and intelligence aircraft or airborne command/communications relay aircraft.

The previous chapter indicated the extent to which the USAF became committed to the C-130E, with production of the version for MAC and TAC extending right up to and including the 1972 Appropriations. The FY 1973 Appropriations however, covered the production of 20 C-130Hs for Tactical Air Command, it being intended initially to re-equip the 32d TAS, 314th TAW, at Little Rock AFB, Arkansas completely; however, five of these aircraft were diverted for delivery to the Canadian Armed Forces—these aircraft being made good by the following year's Appropriations. The first USAF C-130Hs were completed in mid-1974 and the first half-dozen or so aircraft were delivered to the 32d TAS during the second half of the year. Powered by the more forceful 4,510-eshp Allison

T56A-15 turboprops these 1973 aircraft featured provision for RATOG attachment and were externally indistinguishable from the earlier C-130Es, but it soon became apparent that rocket assisted take-off was superfluous in normal airlift circumstances, so from *74-1658* onwards this provision was omitted.

Moreover, by the time the 1974 aircraft were being delivered (starting in March 1975) all airlift squadrons of Tactical Air Command had been transferred once more to Military Airlift Command; the Special Operations Squadrons, however, remained with TAC.

Rescue and recovery

Although the airlift C-130H did not arrive in USAF service until 1974, another T56A-15-powered version had been in production for the USAF for ten years; this was the HC-130H rescue and recovery aircraft, of which the first example, *64-14852* (C/N 4036), had been flown on November 30 1964.

This version incorporated the Fulton recovery system, increased fuel capacity in additional fuselage tanks, a Cook Electric Company aerial tracker and a DF

Below left *Standard USAF airlift C-130H, 74-2066, of the 463d TAW, based at Little Rock AFB, Arkansas, seen late in 1982* (Starliner Aviation Press, Neg No CS 897).

This page *The second HC-130H delivered to the USAF ARRS, in February 1965, 64-14853 (C/N 4037), serving with the 305th ARRS throughout the 1970s. Note the removal of the nose Fulton yoke* (Starliner Aviation Press, Neg Nos CS 878 and 879).

Left *Uncamouflaged HC-130H, 65-0970 (C/N 4112), serving with the 303d ARRS, AFRES, at Richards-Gebaur AFB during the 1970s* (Starliner Aviation Press, Neg No CS 884).

Below left *Camouflaged HC-130H, 65-0974 (C/N 4123), with the 102d ARRS, New York Air National Guard, seen at Greenham Common* (Starliner Aviation Press, Neg No CS 885).

Bottom left *HC-130H, 65-0982 (C/N 4135), serving with the 305th ARRS, AFRES. Note the camouflaged dorsal fairing and low visibility markings* (MAP, Neg No 99/334).

Right *Uncamouflaged HC-130N, 69-5826 (C/N 4375), rescue tanker, of the 67th ARRS, based at RAF Woodbridge in the United Kingdom* (Starliner Aviation Press, Neg No CS 890).

system in a large dorsal fairing, and an overhead delivery system (ODS) for loading, unloading and aerial delivery of rescue kits. Originally developed under contract from the US Navy's Office of Naval Research, the rescue system (named after its inventor Robert Fulton), comprised a large two-piece yoke installation in the nose which was folded back along the sides of the nose when not in use. To recover a man from the sea (or land), the Hercules or an attendant helicopter first dropped a special recovery kit which included a harness attached to a 24 ft × 6 ft helium balloon by a 500 ft nylon line. As the man to be rescued donned the harness and released the balloon, the Hercules would return up-wind flying at about 150 mph, snagging the balloon line in the nose yoke. The nylon line would be severed, releasing the balloon and mechanically securing and knotting the line attached to the rescued man's harness. Imposing forces no greater than those encountered during parachuting, the man would then be lifted away and winched into the Hercules, being recovered on the rear loading ramp. To prevent the nylon line from fouling the aircraft's propellers, guard wires extended from the nose to the wing tips. Some HC-130Hs, intended for retrieving objects descending by parachute, such as satellite capsules, carried the All American Engineering air-to-air retrieval system; this version was sometimes referred to as the JHC-130H.

Originally envisaged as being employed solely for air-sea rescue (being a naval concept), the onset of the Vietnam War quickly caused the system to be extended to land recovery, both of downed airmen and of Special Forces personnel, as it was also able to recover two men simultaneously; this having the advantage of being applicable in instances when a medical attendant might

have to be parachuted to assist an injured man to don the rescue harness. For occasions when aerial recovery was not immediately feasible, the HC-130H carried as standard equipment four six-man rafts and ten flare launchers, as well as two casualty litters, recovery winches and additional rest bunks. The rescue kits and rafts were normally precision-dropped from longitudinal overhead rails by means of an intervalometer.

A typical long range rescue mission was the 'Contingency Visual Search and Recovery' sortie. Using two additional fuselage tanks and with a crew of 13, the HC-130H would take off at a weight of 173,320 lb (including 86,320 lb of fuel), cruise out 2,476 statute miles, search at sea level for almost three hours, complete three Fulton recoveries and return to base with full statutory reserves. Mission time would be 18.4 hours. Alternatively a standby emergency rescue mission, known as the 'Orbit Duck Butt', would be possible using a single additional fuselage tank. The HC-130H could fly out 1,150 statute miles, search for ten hours, make two Fulton recoveries and return to base; such a mission would occupy 17.6 hours.

Some HC-130Hs, particularly those deployed to Vietnam, were equipped as tankers and a new version, the HC-130P, started delivery in 1966 specially equipped to air refuel helicopters, it being capable of delivering 48,500 lb of fuel to large helicopters 575 miles from the tanker's base.

A total of 43 HC-130Hs was completed by the end of 1967 for the USAF's Air Rescue Service, serving in turn with the 31st, 33d, 35th, 36th, 41st, 48th, 57th, 67th, 76th an 79th Aerospace Rescue and Recovery Squadrons (ARRS); one or two aircraft also served with the 71st ARRS in the mid-1970s, being painted with prominent high-visibility markings for work in polar

Above *HC-130N, 69-5827, (C/N 4376) before receiving camouflage; overall finish was pale grey with yellow fuselage band and wing tips (Starliner Aviation Press, Neg No CS 891).*

Left *Camouflaged HC-130N, 69-5827, also with the 67th ARRS, seen at Greenham Common in 1979 (Starliner Aviation Press, Neg No CS 892).*

Right *Originally built as an HC-130H, this aircraft, 65-0979 (C/N 4131), was modified as one of two DC-130Hs in the mid-1970s, and carried a record external load of 40,000 lb as part of trials with five-ton RPVs with the 6514th Test Squadron, Hill AFB, Utah (Lockheed-Georgia, Neg No RL 9612).*

regions. Another version, of which 15 were built, the HC-130N, was equipped with advanced direction-finding electronics and started delivery to the 67th ARRS, being specially intended for retrieval of space capsules and was not equipped with Fulton gear. Later a number of HC-130Hs was converted for use as weather reconnaissance WC-130Hs with their Fulton yokes removed.

At the time of writing Military Airlift Command deploys four regular squadrons in the Aerospace Rescue and Recovery Service; there are three such squadrons (the 301st, 303d and 305th) in the AFRES and two with the Air National Guard (the 102d and 129th). A measure of the manner in which the AFRES HC-130 squadrons are integrated into routine Air Force duties may be gained by the fact that the 305th ARRS, which currently possesses five HC-130N/Ps at Selfridge ANGB, Michigan, flew two HC-130Ns in direct support of the 1981–82 Space Shuttle launch and recovery programme.

The Special Operations MC-130Es

For obvious reasons little has been published about the sinister-looking MC-130Es of the United States Air Force, and even the designation prefix is probably deliberately misleading, it being variously stated (with equal authority) that the M-prefix refers to Missile, Module (Command), or countermeasures.

Early in the American passive involvement in Vietnam the employment of Special Forces for covert intelligence gathering (and possibly even sabotage and semi-overt acts of war)—generically referred to as Combat Talon missions—there emerged a requirement for a specialist version of the Hercules to support these forces in a wide range of tasks, demanding special flying techniques. These included the day and night pinpoint infiltration (air dropping) of small groups of operators and their supply and retrieval; which in turn demanded such equipment as terrain-following radar, an inertial navigation system, Fulton STAR yoke, automatic computed air-release system, high-speed

low-level aerial delivery and container release systems, and equipment for psychological warfare. Communications equipment would include ground acquisition receiver-interrogator, secure voice UHF/VHF/FM radio, angle of attack probe, FLIR pod and ALQ-8 ECM pod. In certain cases provision would be made to mount decoy flares for operations in the vicinity of SAM-defended areas, as well as Shrike (and later Standard) anti-radiation missiles. Such was the daunting catalogue of equipment and systems deemed necessary for the proposed 'Special Forces Hercules'. Following in the tradition of the electronic intelligence gathering (euphemistically referred to as electronic reconnaissance) C-130A-II and C-130B-II versions of the early 1960s, four C-130Es, *64-0508, 64-0547, 64-0558* and *64-0563*, were withdrawn from service and underwent extensive conversion, including installation of T56A-15 turboprops, although they never officially adopted the H-series designation. The aircraft were in turn designated HC-130E (to conceal the

purpose of the Fulton STAR gear), C-130E-I Skyhook and, unofficially, C-130H(CT). With a crew of between nine and 11, depending on the nature of the mission, at least three of these aircraft, eventually termed officially the MC-130E, served in Vietnam with the 1st, 15th and 318th Special Operations Squadrons. All were to be lost, *'08* shot down in April 1972, *'47* shot down in December 1967, *'58* lost in an air collision over the States in April 1972 and *'63* destroyed in a mortar attack on Nha Trang in November 1967. Several other C-130E-Is also served in Vietnam.

There followed 16 further conversions during the 1970s, enigmatically referred to as MC-130E-S (for Swap), MC-130E-C (Clamp) and MC-130E-Y (Yank). The E-S aircraft, of which only one example, *64-0671* was produced, featured terrain-following radar and in-flight refuelling provision, and was serving with the 8th SOS at Hurlburt Field in 1982. It was scheduled to be converted to an E-Y in 1983 for issue to the 1st SOS at Clark AB, Philippines.

Top *An MC-130E-I Skyhook (sometimes referred to as an HC-130E or C-130H(CT)) electronic reconnaissance aircraft with Fulton recovery gear and ATO bottles, serving with the 1st SOS. This aircraft was destroyed in a collision with a Convair F-102A over South Carolina in December 1972 (Lockheed Aircraft, Neg No RL 2166-10).*

Above *64-0523 (C/N 4007), a C-130E-I (later MC-130E) complete with Fulton yoke and guard to wing tips; note the fin-tip pitot, hallmark of the countermeasures/MC family. This aircraft served with the 7th and 8th SOS. Note the absence of the twin blisters below the windscreens (MAP, Neg No U06407).*

Below *64-0523 (C/N 4007) as an MC-130E with the 7th SOS in all-black finish and with no visible national markings; almost invisible are the flares carried under the drop tanks. Note the addition of the blisters below the windscreens (MAP, Neg No 40561 dated May 1983).*

Top *Seldom photographed version of the C-130, this MC-130E-C(Clamp) 64-0561 (C/N 4065), with Fulton gear and chin radome, was one of four such aircraft modified from C-130E-Is, and served with the 7th SOS, 7575th SOG, Rhein-Main AB, Germany* (Starliner Aviation Press, Neg No CS 875).

Above *MC-130E-C, 64-0561 (C/N 4065), with under-tank flare installation* (MAP, Neg No U10525, dated May 1983).

Below *Sinister-looking MC-130E-C, 64-0523, complete with under-tank flares and ventral fins whose purpose is not known* (MAP, Neg No U09552).

Ten E-Cs, *64-0523, 64-0551, 64-0555, 64-0559, 64-0562, 64-0566, 64-0567, 64-0568* and *64-0572*, were produced in 1978 by conversion from C-130E-Is, retaining the Fulton STAR gear and are currently serving with the 8th SOS. The last-mentioned aircraft took part in Operation Eagle Claw, the attempted rescue of the hostages being held in Iran on April 25 1980 (see page 50).

Four E-Ys were originally produced in 1978, *62-1843, 63-7785, 64-0564* and *64-0565*, all being converted from C-130E-Is; *'65*, also an Eagle Claw aircraft, carried the command staff module for the rescue operation.

Development and employment of the M-Series has taken place in parallel with the AC-130E and AC-130H gunships as well as the surveillance, communication and command EC-130Es and EC-130Hs, all being integrated within the operational scope of the Special Forces and Special Operations Squadrons based at Clark AB, Philippines, Hurlburt Field, Florida, and Rhein-Main AB, Germany, as well as the 7th Airborne Command and Control Squadron at Keesler AFB, Mississippi, and the 41st Electronic Countermeasures Squadron at Davis Monthan AFB, Arizona. Systems development and testing of the specialist equipment is undertaken by the 4950th Test Wing at Wright-Patterson AFB, Ohio.

Weather reconnaissance

Weather reconnaissance has been undertaken by USAF Hercules since 1964, originally under the command structure of the Military Air Transport Service and latterly as part of the Rescue and Weather Reconnaissance Wings (RWRW) of the Aerospace Rescue and Recovery Service (ARRS). It is undertaken on an *ad hoc* world-wide basis to provide weather forecast data in preparation for specific operations by the US air forces and as a routine task in respect of seasonal weather phenomena, such as hurricane tracking over the seas adjacent to the United States. In addition to this Service responsibility, weather research has been performed by the civilian US National Oceanic and Atmospheric Administration (NOAA) using a single Hercules.

For all its importance and wide ranging responsibilities, weather reconnaissance has never involved the use of more than 20 Hercules simultaneously by the USAF.

The first weather reconnaissance C-130s were five new-built WC-130Bs (allocated from the USAF's 1962 Appropriations, *62-3492* to *62-3496*, C/Ns 3702, 3707, 3708, 3721 and 3722), originally ordered for Military Airlift Command. These entered service in 1964 with the 54th Weather Reconnaissance Squadron (WRS), but were almost immediately transferred to Tactical

First of five new-built WC-130B weather reconnaissance aircraft, 62-3492 (C/N 3702), serving with MAC's 53d WRS at Keesler AFB. Note the blister hatch on the side of the nose. All five WC-130Bs were modified to standard C-130Bs in 1979 (MAP, Neg No 530/98).

Above *Take-off photograph of a Model 282 WC-130B, 62-3496 (C/N 3722), of a MATS Weather Reconnaissance Squadron (Lockheed-Georgia, Neg No RG 1088).*

Below *One of six WC-130E weather reconnaissance aircraft, 64-0554 (C/N 4049), converted from standard C-130Es, serving with the 53d Weather Reconnaissance Squadron, 41st RWRW, at Keesler AFB (Starliner Aviation Press, Neg No CS 874).*

Above *WC-130H, 65-0963 (C/N 4103), of the 53d WRS, 41st RWRW, MAC; this differed from the AFRES weather aircraft in retaining the large dorsal radome (Starliner Aviation Press, Neg No CS 883).*

Above right *Previously one of 15 HC-130Hs that had been converted from standard C-130Hs, this WC-130H, 65-0964 (C/N 4104), served with the 815th WRS, 920th WRG, 403d RWRW. Note the tally of 25 hurricane sorties flown, painted forward of the door.*

Right *Another 815th WRS WC-130H, 65-0972 (C/N 4120); note the large observation hatch in the side of the nose.*

Bottom right *815th WRS WC-130H, 65-0977 (C/N 4127), seen at Keesler AFB; like the Squadron's other aircraft, this had been converted from an HC-130H (courtesy of the 920th WRG, AFRES).*

Air Command, along with almost all MAC's Hercules in 1964–66. Simultaneously, three fairly new C-130Es were also converted in 1965 to increase the 54th WRS' establishment to eight aircraft. A second Weather Reconnaissance Squadron, the 53d, was equipped with Hercules in 1968–69 after the conversion of 11 further WC-130Bs.

While the bulk of the weather reporting task was performed during the late 1960s by the WC-130Bs, advances in data link technology suggested that much greater utilisation and reporting scope would be possible using the greater range potential of the C-130E (and the new C-130H) carrying a more sophisticated equipment fit and it was accordingly decided to introduce the C-130H as basic WR aircraft and update the WC-130E.

Three further ex-TAS C-130Es were converted to WC-130Es in about 1969, these aircraft serving with the 53d WRS between 1970 and 1972 when they were transferred to a third Squadron, the 55th WRS. In 1973–74 15 HC-130Hs of the ARRS were converted to WC-130Hs (their Fulton recovery yokes being removed from the nose) and these joined the 53d and 54th WRS in 1974, replacing 15 of the 16 WC-130Bs; the remaining aircraft (ex-*58-0731*, C/N 3256), after manufacturers' update, corrosion inspection and control, and life extension modifications, had been re-registered *N8037* to the US Department of Commerce and was to be used by the NOAA operating from Miami, Florida, on hurricane tracking research. Very

soon after entering service in 1974 one of the WC-130Hs (*65-0965*) was lost when it disappeared on a flight over the South China Sea, 650 miles NNW of Clark Air Base in the Philippines on October 13 that year. Its fate was never established.

The 14 remaining WC-130Hs and six WC-130Es continue in service today, equipping the ARRS's 53d WRS at Keesler AFB, Mississippi, and the 54th WRS at Anderson AFB, Guam, while the 815th WRS, 920th Weather Reconnaissance Group of the 403d Rescue and Weather Reporting Wing, USAF Reserve, flies WC-130Hs, also at Keesler AFB. The WC-130Es and Hs currently in service are extensively modified (by Mod 1C-130(W)-507) to undertake weather patrols, both versions accommodating three extra crew members, the Aerial Reconnaissance Weather Officer's (ARWO) station being located immediately aft of the pilots, a Weather Observer's station amidships and a radiosonde dispenser's station just forward of the rear loading ramp. A pair of U-1 sensing foils carried in fairings on the sides of the nose, together with an I-2 foil in the WC-130E have been omitted in the H version which includes a 1,800-US gal auxiliary fuel tank in the cabin together with a pressure relief system which vents under the aircraft's tail. The radio dropsonde dispenser is located in the cabin floor immediately forward of the rear loading ramp.

The Omega Dropwindsonde (ODWS) System, AN/AMQ-29A, comprises a number of expendable sondes, AN/AMT-13A, which are dispensed from the aircraft

and record vertical profile measurements of pressure, temperature, humidity, wind speed and direction in real time; on release from the aircraft the sonde's parachute actuates it's transmitter aerial. Signals from the sonde are received by the aircraft on-board computer via key-board entry and two teleprinters record real-time data. The ODWS may be used to edit the data prior to transmission to base by satellite communication. Normally up to about a dozen sondes are carried, being discharged at about 200–300 mile intervals; they are effective at any height below 40,000 ft (normally being released by the Hercules at around 25,000 ft), and may be tracked at ranges up to 200 miles.

The work of the 815th Weather Reconnaissance Squadron, AFRES, is typical of the WRS based in the USA. In peacetime the Squadron undertakes four routine tasks: *Volant Eye,* the surveillance of hurricanes (wind speeds in excess of 64 kt) in the Atlantic, Caribbean, Gulf of Mexico and Eastern Pacific; *Volant Coast,* weather reconnaissance during the winter months along the Atlantic Coast and in the Gulf of Mexico; *Volant Met,* weather reconnaissance in areas of sparse data (eg, the Gulf of Alaska) for the Air Force Global Weather Center; and *Volant Cross,* specific weather data gathering missions required for flight planning of overseas deployment of TAC fighter units.

Tropical storm and hurricane reconnaissance involves flying through severe frontal weather into the eye of the storm, collecting force and movement data, determining the storm area and then tracking it to provide warning of possible landfall. In 1976, the first year the 815th WRS was fully equipped with WC-130Hs, nine named hurricanes were penetrated, in 1977 seven storms, in 1978 11 storms in the Atlantic and two in the Pacific, in 1979 eight in the Atlantic and one in the Pacific, in 1980 eight in the Atlantic, and in 1981 11 storms (seven of hurricane force) were penetrated. 1982 proved to be the century's most tranquil, there being only five named storms, of which two were hurricanes. Those seven years involved more than 4,200 storm flying hours, with tasking assessed at over 99 per cent effective, and flown entirely accident free.

Carrying the registration *N6541C* NOAA's WC-130B was returned to Marietta in the mid-1970s to be given a more powerful radar and was recommissioned in service in August 1977. During its ten years' research it has flown scientific sorties in 11 countries as well as the United States, plotted hurricanes off the US coasts and performed a hail suppression programme over Colorado.

The US Air Force Reserve

Generally regarded as an air force within an air force, the US Air Force Reserve (AFRES) came into being shortly after the end of the Second World War to employ the manpower and skills rendered operationally redundant by the end of hostilities. The value of this force was well demonstrated during the Korean War when no fewer than 36 Reserve Wings were called to active duty in almost every aspect of combat and support operations. During the later 1950s however, a gradual reduction in strength followed and by the end of the decade the number of Wings had fallen to 15, of which 14 flew the C-119 and the other C-123, the total nominal strength being 50 Troop Carrier and Air Sea Rescue Squadrons. Strength of the AFRES fluctuated considerably during the early 1960s, with manpower recalls during the Berlin crises, the Cuban missile crisis and with the American decision in 1965 to intervene in the Dominican problem, the year in which USRES squadrons also started to fly airlift missions into South East Asia soon after the start of operations by combat elements of the USAF and US Navy in Vietnam.

For a long time having to be satisfied with using aircraft previously discarded by regular units of the USAF—often with the difficulties associated with long-term fatigue and corrosion problems, such as when operating the AC-119G gunship in Vietnam—the AFRES continued during the 1970s to engage in most operational tasks, of which the airlift role remained paramount. Gradually, the C-119, C-123 and C-124 were phased out of service, and as regular units began to re-equip wholly with C-130Es and Hs, the older C-130As and Bs joined the Reserve, having in almost all cases been subject of fatigue and corrosion inspection and re-engineering to extend their operational lives. By the end of the decade the Hercules had become the most widely-used aircraft in the AFRES inventory, one of the primary routine tasks being to airlift American reservists to their monthly Unit Training Assembly (UTA) areas within the USA, as well as to their annual active-duty training (AcDuTra) units, often overseas. A measure of this task may be judged by the achievements during 1982 when the AFRES C-130 squadrons carried nearly 90,000 personnel, airdropped about 40,000 combat troops and airlifted more than 5,500 tons of freight. At the same time, working with ANG C-130 squadrons, the AFRES has since 1979 contributed to the 'Volant Oak' airlift of personnel between the USA and Howard AFB, Panama Canal Zone, for their annual 15-day AcDuTra commitment.

With a current 'recallable' strength of around 100,000 personnel in the 'Ready' and 'Standby' categories, the Air Force Reserve deploys a total of 20 C-130 squadrons, all in the USA, of which 15 perform the tactical airlift role, with C-130As, Bs and Es, three are rescue and recovery squadrons with HC-130Hs and Ns, one is a Weather Reconnaissance Squadron (the 815th WRS with WC-130Hs) and one a Special

A Hercules with an eventful history. Originally delivered to the USAF in August 1963 as a standard C-130E, 62-1857 (C/N 3821), it was damaged in a wheels-up landing at Eglin AFB in 1965. Repaired and modified to EC-130E in 1967, it joined the 7th Airborne Command and Control Squadron in 1971. Equipped with underwing refuelling probe, air conditioning intakes on the fuselage sides forward of the wings and additional aerial wires on the tail, the aircraft became an EC-130E-II in 1977 and an EC-130H in 1978, and was among the C-130s that participated in the hostage rescue attempt in Iran on April 25 1980 (MAP, Neg No 529/98).

Operations Squadron (the 711th SOS with C-130As and AC-130As).

Like the Air National Guard, the Air Force Reserve is today moving beyond the implied austere stigma of second-line status with no more than 'cast-off' aircraft, and regularly mans some of the latest types of aircraft in the USAF's inventory such as the C-141B and KC-10A. It is moreover currently receiving factory-fresh C-130Hs, the FY 1981 Appropriations covering seven brand-new C-130Hs delivered to the 700th TAS at Dobbins AFB, Georgia, in 1982, replacing C-7s.

It seems likely that the C-130A and B (both now over a quarter-century old) will gradually disappear from AFRES service during the next half-decade and the Command fairly quickly standardise on the E and H in the airlift role.

Operation 'Eagle Claw'

A major operation undertaken by the US Air Force, as well as the US Army, US Navy and US Marine Corps, involving the use of C-130s, was the attempted rescue of United States nationals being held hostage by the revolutionary regime which had seized power in Iran in 1979. News of the hostages' confinement in the American Embassy in Teheran was flashed to Fort Bragg, North Carolina, on Sunday November 4 that year, headquarters of Delta Force (1st Special Forces Operational Detachment—Delta), the special American force trained and organised in counter-terrorist operations

on the lines of the British Special Air Service. At once plans were put in hand to investigate the mounting of an attempt to stage an airborne rescue, and Operation 'Rice Bowl'—a series of dress rehearsals—got underway.

The two main problems with any such rescue attempt were the long distance of Teheran from any external staging base and the fact that Teheran itself was a city teaming with four million fanatically hostile revolutionaries. Iran, moreover, was possessed of a modern air force and defence system.

In due course a plan was evolved in great secrecy. Three bases would be established outside Iran, one at Wadi Kena, Egypt (previously constructed by the Soviet Union), one at Masirah Island in the Gulf of Oman and one aboard the USS *Nimitz* (CVN-69), the nuclear-powered carrier that would be steaming in the Indian Ocean. Three operating bases or sites would be secured within Iran, at Manzariyeh (35 miles southwest of Teheran), at Garmsar (60 miles south-east of Teheran) and at a desert site at Poshti-i-Badam, known as 'Desert One' (200 miles south-east of Teheran).

Three alternative operational plans were studied, including one involving a flight by specially modified STOL C-130s equipped with downward-firing rockets direct to a stadium in Teheran where the aircraft would land and, following an assault by Delta forces covered by AC-130H gunships, take on board the hostages who would then be flown to Manzariyeh for airlifting out of Iran by a pair of Lockheed C-141 Starlifters. This plan was discarded owing to the obvious vulnerability of the C-130s from SAMs whose crews would have been fully alerted. (Three Hercules, C-130Hs *74-1683*, *74-1686* and *74-2065*, were eventually fitted with the STOL rockets, but '*83* crashed later in 1980 during a landing demonstration when the computer accidentally fired the rockets too soon.)

The second plan involved flying helicopters from USS *Nimitz* to Desert One where they would refuel from large fuel blivets air-dropped by Hercules; they would then fly to Teheran where, with covert assistance from pre-positioned CIA and other personnel, assault parties of Delta and a Joint Task Force would secure the hostages' release for airlifting out as in the previous plan. This idea survived for some time, but during the first night rehearsal in the States, all but two of the huge blivets burst when their parachutes failed. When they were eventually dropped successfully they were found to be unmanageable on the ground, and to have to hand-pump fuel to the helicopters too time-consuming.

The final operational plan—Operation 'Eagle Claw'—involved staging three MC-130 command and communication transport aircraft (including an MC-130E-Y, *64-0565*, and an MC-130E-C, *64-0572*, of the 8th Special Operations Squadron) together with three EC-130Hs equipped as tankers with wing probes (*62-1809*, *62-1818* and *62-1857* of the 7th Airborne Command and Control Squadron) to Masirah Island; all these aircraft were upgraded to include T56A-15 engines. Meanwhile USS *Nimitz* would sail into the

Gulf of Oman with eight RH-53D Sea Stallion helicopters of Navy Helicopter Mine Countermeasures Squadron HM-16 embarked from USS *Kitty Hawk* (CVA-63), as the C-141 Starlifters and a C-9 Nightingale transport carrying a hospital and burns unit deployed to Egypt.

The six Hercules, carrying some 120 Joint Task Force and Delta Force specialist assault personnel, under the command of Colonel Charlie Beckwith aboard the MC-130Es, and with large fuel containers in the EC-130Hs, would fly to Desert One, jamming Iranian radar en route if necessary and arriving there in darkness. The helicopters would fly the 900 miles from the *Nimitz* to Desert One, (timed to arrive 30 min after the Hercules) position themselves near the tankers, refuel and then fly the assault force to the Hide Site at Garmsar, where they would lie-up during daylight under camouflage netting. On the second night Delta Force would then be taken into Teheran in Mercedes coaches, already assembled and concealed in Iran for the purpose, for the final rescue attempt. The helicopters would then lift the 53 hostages and the assault force out of the Embassy grounds, or the neighbouring stadium, to the airfield at Manzariyeh, which would by then have been secured by a force of US Rangers. The final act of preparation would be to discover whether the desert floor at Desert One would be adequate to support the weight of heavily-laden Hercules without their sinking too deep and being unable to take-off for the return to Masirah.

Towards the end of March 1980 a twin-engine STOL aircraft with three crew members aboard was

Another of the hostage rescue aircraft, 62-1818 (C/N 3780), also equipped with refuelling probe; it was flown by the 7th ACCS (MAP, Neg No U09718).

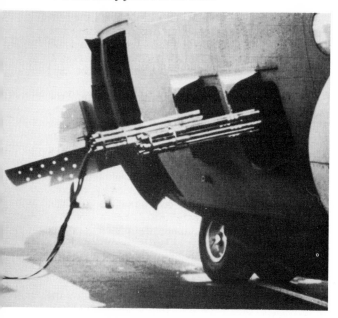

Left *The two forward MXU-470/A gun modules housing 7.62 mm 'Gatling' miniguns in the AC-130H Spectre.* **Right** *The Army 105 mm howitzer and the M2A1 40 mm Bofors gun in a 1st Special Operations Wing AC-130H Spectre. These aircraft currently equip the 16th Special Operations Squadron at Hurlburt Field, Florida, and were to have been used to cover Teheran during the hostage rescue attempt in 1980 (USAF, via R. Dorr).*

secretly flown to the proposed Desert One site where soil and rock samples were gathered and runway lights (which could be switched on by the approaching Hercules pilots) laid. This group confirmed that the site was adequate for use by the C-130s. One extra provision was added to the plan: two AC-130Hs (plus two back-up aicraft) were to be deployed to Iran, to keep station over the final rescue assault and prevent any interference by Iranian Soviet-made ZSU-23-4 AFVs which mounted four 23-mm guns with target-acquisition and tracking radar. They were to protect the Embassy compound and stadium while the helicopters were awaited, and then, using their 105-mm howitzers and 40-mm Bofors guns, utterly destroy the Embassy to prevent any subsequent intelligence gathering by the Iranians.

It was not discovered until a late stage that the Navy helicopter pilots of HM-16 were unable to cope with the difficult flying conditions likely to be encountered over Iran in the darkness, so Marine Corps assault pilots, under Colonel Edward Seiffert USMC, were introduced into the training programme and then transferred to the Indian Ocean.

On April 21 the C-141s landed at Wadi Kena with the men of Delta Force and two days later carried on to Masirah Island, where the C-130s had arrived from Hurlburt Field, Florida, (flown by the 8th SOS), having staged through Europe and picked up a special assault party in Germany. At 18:00 hrs on the 24th the

first MC-130 took off from Masirah for Desert One, carrying the Delta Command element and part of the assault force, together with a jeep, motor cycles and a satellite communications module. Four hours later the Hercules touched down safely at its destination, soon followed by the other five aircraft. Almost immediately, as the troops were disembarking to await the arrival of the helicopters, an Iranian bus with 45 civilians stumbled into the site; it was quickly stopped and its passengers assembled under guard nearby. It was now that matters started to go seriously wrong.

The planned time of the helicopters' arrival came and went, and all the time the engines of the Hercules had to be kept running. With dawn at Teheran at 05:30 and the time necessary to refuel the Sea Stallions, it soon became all too obvious that the helicopters could not reach the Hide Site until after daylight. Eventually the first two Sea Stallions arrived—90 min late and from different directions, followed by four more. It soon transpired that they encountered severe sand storms; one had had to land in the desert with a rotor blade malfunction (its crew being picked up by another helicopter), and another had turned back with instrument failure. Contingency planning had, however, allowed for the operation to go ahead with a minimum of six RH-53Ds, so the Marine pilots quickly positioned themselves near the Hercules tankers and began the long job of refuelling in the darkness. Then one of the Marine pilots reported his aircraft to be unserviceable with a major hydraulic fault. Faced with an agonising decision whether to recommend going ahead with only five helicopters, and being forced to leave behind 20 vital members of the assault force, Colonel Beckwith also had to consider the likelihood of the loss of a further helicopter later on, which would have left insufficient capacity to recover the hostages and the assault force. Just as the order was being given to disembark from the Sea Stallions and return to C-130s, one of the helicopters, flown by Major James Schaefer USMC, which was moving away from its tanker amidst a great swirling cloud of dust and sand, seemed to sink backwards and struck the port side of the EC-130H, *62-1809*, of Major Richard Bakke. At once there was a colossal explosion as the fuel erupted in a great fireball and Redeye missiles started discharging in the intense heat. The operation was finally ruined.

Now faced with immediate withdrawal, Delta Force was rapidly embarked, together with the Marine helicopter pilots, in the C-130s. It was intended to lay on an air strike to destroy the remaining helicopters, but in fact this was never carried out. The Iranian bus passengers were left standing huddled in the desert. Miraculously Major Schaefer had escaped with his life, although suffering from severe burns; he, as well as the bodies of five airmen and three Marines, were brought back to Masirah. The MC-130E-Y in which Colonel Beckwith was flying almost crashed on take-off from Desert One; it struck a high sand ridge just as it was becoming airborne and reared up steeply, only being saved by the pilot easing the nose down and slamming open the throttles; the 5g load however, severely overstressed the C-130's structure.

As news of the mission abort was flashed to those waiting at the Hide Site, the C-141 medevac aircraft and the C-9 with its burns unit now flew to Masirah to meet the returning assault force. The mission had failed, defeated not in combat or by any lack of determination, but by a chapter of accidents. If any weakness existed in the plan it probably lay in the deployment of a force of helicopters whose use overstretched a reasonable expectation of success, and fate had played on that weakness. Their pilots, some of the best in the Marine Corps, had been taxed to their limit even by the time they arrived at Desert One. Once more the availability of the C-130 in its various guises—transport, command vehicle, tanker, gunship, radar suppressor—all with its unique rough strip operating ability, had rendered the whole operation conceivable. In every respect it had carried out the tasks demanded of it.

Current USAF Hercules deployment

Recent years have seen little change in the heavy-lift equipment of the USAF, both the C-5 and C-141 being progressively modernised and retained, although some 70 C-5Bs are due to be delivered in the next decade. By far the greatest dependence still rests on the Hercules in the transport role, not to mention all the other operational tasks it undertakes.

Thirty years after the C-130 first flew 30 squadrons of the USAF, 18 squadrons of the Air Force Reserve and 22 of the Air National Guard still fly the Hercules, some 630 aircraft being listed at ramp strength.

Military Airlift Command the 317th Tactical Airlift Wing, based at Pope AFB, North Carolina, flies

One of the most distinctive of all Hercules versions, the EC-130E (RR) electronic warfare aircraft, 63-7783 (C/N 3850), of the 193d SOS (later ECS), Pennsylvania ANG. It carried five large blade antennae or reflectors, under the outer wings, on the sides of the rear fuselage and as a massive dorsal fin. Electronic equipment was housed in outboard wing pods and a fairing in the exteme tail (courtesy of the 193d ECS, Pa ANG).

C-130Es, with the 39th, 40th and 41st Tactical Airlift Squadrons, as well as the 37th TAS, 435th TAW, 322d Air Division, and the 7405th Support Squadron, 435th TAW, at Rhein-Main Air Base, Germany. In the 22d Air Force, the 36th TAS, 62d Military Airlift Wing, flies C-130Es at McChord AFB, Washington, while at Little Rock AFB, Arkansas, the 48th, 61st and 62d TAS and 16th Tactical Airlift Training Squadron, all of the 314th TAW, fly both C-130Es and Hs. The 463d TAW's 772d, 773d and 774th TAS operate C-130Hs out of Dyess AFB, Texas. In Alaska the 17th TAS of the 616th Military Airlift Group fly C-130Es at Elmendorf AFB, while overseas the 21st TAS, 374th TAW of the 834th Air Division is based at Clark Air Base in the Philippines with C-130Hs, and the 34th TAS, 316th TAG, at Yokota Air Base in Japan with C-130Es and Hs.

In Tactical Air Command the 1st Special Operations Wing at Hurlburt Field, Florida, comprises the 8th Special Operations Squadron with MC-130Es and the 16th SOS with AC-130Hs. At Davis Monthan AFB the 41st Electronic Countermeasures Squadron flies the EC-130H, as does the 7th Airborne Command and Control Squadron, 52d Airborne Warning and Control Wing at Keesler AFB, Mississippi.

Military Airlift Command's Aerospace Rescue and Recovery Service is deployed world-wide; the 39th ARRW deploys the 55th ARRS at Eglin, Florida, with HC-130Ns and Ps, and the 67th ARRS at RAF Woodbridge in England with HC-130Hs, Ns and Ps; the 1551st Flying Training Squadron of the 1550th Aircrew Training and Test Wing at Kirtland AFB, New Mexico, flies HC-130Hs and Ps. The 41st Rescue and Weather Reconnaissance Wing comprises the 33d ARRS at Kadena Air Base, Okinawa (HC-130H, N and P), the 41st ARRS at McClellan AFB, California (HC-130H, N and P), the 53d Weather Reconnaissance Squadron at Keesler AFB, Mississippi (WC-130E and H), and the 54th WRS at Anderson AFB, Guam (WC-130E and H).

Directly under the command of the United States Air Forces in Europe (USAFE) the 7th SOS, 1505th Special Operations Group of the 17th Air Force is based at Rhein-Main Air Base in Germany with MC-130Es.

Special Operations in the Pacific theatre (Pacific Air Force) are the responsibility of the 1st SOS, responsible to the 3rd Tactical Fighter Wing at Clark Air Base in the Philippines, also with MC-130Es.

Test Establishments under the Air Force Systems Command include the Air Systems Division's 4950th Test Wing at Wright-Patterson AFB, Ohio, which includes NC-130As and an MC-130E in its inventory, and the Space Divisions 6593d Test Squadron, 6594th Test Wing, at Los Angeles Air Force Station, California, which flies an NC-130B and an NC-130H.

The Air Force Flight Test Center at Hill AFB, Utah, includes the 6514th Drone and Remotely Piloted Vehicle Test Squadron with C-130Es and the two DC-130Hs.

Complementing the first line USAF deployment are the squadrons of the Air Force Reserve which are tasked with transportation, weather reporting and rescue work, and one Squadron, the 711th SOS of the 919th SOG at Duke Field, Florida, flies AC-130A gunships. The transport squadrons still flying C-130As are the 63d TAS, 927th TAG, at Selfridge Air National Guard Base, Michigan, the 95th TAS, 440th TAW, at Mitchell Field, Wisconsin, the 328th TAS, 914th TAG, at Niagara Falls International Airport, New York, the 356th TAS, 302d TAW, at Rickenbacker AFB, Ohio, and the 758th TAS, 302d TAW, at Pittsburgh Airport, Pennsylvania. All the aircraft flown by these squadrons are at least a quarter-century old!

About 50 C-130Bs serve with the 64th TAS, 440th TAW, at O'Hare International Airport, Illinois, the 68th TAS, 433d TAW, at Kelly AFB, Texas, the 731st TAS, 439th TAW, at Peterson AFB, Colorado, and the 757th TAS, 434th TAW, Youngstown Municipal Airport, Ohio.

As C-130Hs gradually replace the Es with USAF squadrons the redundant aircraft in turn replace C-130As and Bs with the AFRES units. E-equipped transport squadrons are the 303d TAS, 442d TAW, at Richards-Gebaur AFB, Missouri, the 327th TAS, 459th TAW, at Willow Grove Naval Air Station, Pennsylvania, the 337th TAS, 439th TAW, at Westover AFB, Maine, and the 756th TAS, 459th TAW, Andrews AFB, Maryland.

Rescue work is undertaken by HC-130Hs and Ns on the 301st ARRS at Homestead AFB, Florida, the 303d ARRS at March AFB, California, the 305th ARRS at Selfridge, all these Squadrons forming the 403d Rescue and Weather Reconnaissance Wing, which also embraces the 815th Weather Reconnaissance Squadron with WC-130Hs at Keesler AFB, Mississippi.

The Air National Guard Undertakes a very wide range of operational duties, of which air transportation is the principal task of the Guard's C-130s. Five Squadrons still fly C-130As, the 105th TAS, 118th TAW, of the Tennessee ANG at Nashville Airport, the 142d TAS, 166th TAG, of the Delaware ANG at Greater Wilmington Airport, the 143d TAS, 143d TAG, of the Rhode Island ANG at Quonset State Airport, the 155th TAS, 164th TAG, of the Tennessee ANG at Memphis International Airport, and the 180th TAS, 139th TAG, Missouri ANG at St Joseph Airport. The six Squadrons with C-130Bs are the 135th TAS, 135th TAG, Maryland ANG at Glenn L. Martin State Airport, Baltimore, the 156th TAS, 145th TAG, of the North Carolina ANG at Charlotte

Top *Newly applied paint scheme on the 193d ECS's EC-130E (RR), 63-9817 (C/N 3978), in which all stores and blade antennae have been camouflaged; scarcely visible is the large air intake on the fuselage side under the wing root, presumably for air conditioning* (MAP, Neg No 347/98).

Above *Wearing lizard camouflage is an EC-130H, 73-1587 (C/N 4549), with large side fairings on the rear fuselage, extensive aerial array around the tail and air intakes over the wheel fairings. The aircraft was serving with the 41st Electronic Countermeasures Squadron, 552d AWACW* (MAP, Neg No U09708).

Airport, the 164th TAS, 179th TAG, of the Ohio ANG at Mansfield Lahm Airport, the 167th TAS, 167thTAG, of the West Virginia ANG at Martinsburg Airport, the 181st TAS, 136th TAW, of the Texas ANG at Hensley Field, Dallas, and the 187th TAS, 153d TAG, of the Wyoming ANG at Cheyenne Airport.

Four Guard Squadrons fly the C-130E, the 109th TAS, 133d TAW, of the Minnesota ANG at Minneapolis St Paul International Airport, the 115th TAS, 146th TAW, of the California ANG at Van Nuys Airport, the 130th TAS, 130th TAG, of the West Virginia ANG at Charleston Airport, and the 144th TAS, 176th TAG, of the Alaska ANG at Kulis Air National Guard Base. Three squadrons have received C-130Hs, the 158th TAS, 165th TAG, of the Georgia ANG at Savannah Airport, the 183d TAS, 172d TAG, of the Mississippi ANG at Jackson Airport, and the 185th

TAS, 137th TAW, of the Oklahoma ANG at Oklahoma City Airport.

In the Aerospace Rescue and Recovery Service there are two Guard Squadrons, both with HC-130Hs and Ps, the 102d ARRS, 106th ARRG, of the New York ANG at Suffolk County Airport, and the 129th ARRS, 129th ARRG, of the California ANG at Moffett Field Naval Air Station.

One other Squadron, the 139th TAS, 109th TAG, of the New York ANG at Schenectady Airport, flies the C-130D and D-6 with and without ski landing gear on support work for the DYE line in Greenland.

Gaining command of all the above Guard Squadrons is Military Airlift Command, but a single unit, the 193d Electronic Countermeasures Squadron, 193d ECG, of the Pennsylvania ANG at Harrisburg International Airport, with EC-130Es (and some C-130Es) is subordinate to Tactical Airlift Command.

Chapter 4

Hercules with the Navy

The United States Navy is tasked with three principal world-wide responsibilities: maintaining the freedom and security of the world's shipping routes, the safe movement by sea of American fighting personnel to theatres of war overseas and the operation of a nuclear deterrent in submarines. In only the latter task has the Hercules been closely involved. However, to a rather lesser extent the aircraft has been associated with some of the Navy's 'fringe' responsibilities—performing highly specialised duties for all that.

At the time of the Korean War, when the US Air Force was evolving its own future transport requirements, which brought forth the C-130A, no parallel requirement for a heavy-lift or tactical assault transport existed in the US Navy and such limited transport needs that arose (for routine movement overseas of Navy personnel) were undertaken by the USAF's Military Air Transport Service or by existing aircraft in service with the US Marine Corps. Indeed, it was to be the Marine Corps, whose aircraft are in any case funded through Navy Appropriations, that was to be the first to put forward an operational requirement involving the maritime use of the Hercules, following air refuelling trials with two C-130As on loan from the USAF in 1957 (see Chapter 5).

The appearance of Soviet naval forces in European waters in the late 1950s resulted in increased deployment of American naval forces, particularly in the Mediterranean, and it soon became apparent that a naval heavy-lift element (at least partly independent of the USAF's MATS) would be required. Accordingly in 1959, the US Navy submitted a limited requirement for a small number of Hercules to be similar to the USAF's C-130B which was then in current production at Marietta. This requirement followed closely behind a call for a specialised, ski-equipped version of the C-130 to support the Navy's Antarctic Detachment. The resulting aircraft were the GV-1U (later termed the C-130F) and the C-130BL (later to become the LC-130F), of which seven and four examples respectively were produced. From the work of these 11 Hercules stemmed two huge tasks, of totally differing natures, that have occupied the US Navy for 25 years.

Operation 'Deep Freeze'

With almost 30 years behind it, the American Antarctic Research Programme has involved some of the most hazardous and spectacular operations ever undertaken by aircraft, with huge areas of desolate, freezing wastes, primitive operating bases and few sophisticated navigation, maintenance and weather forecasting facilities available.

In 1955 the first formal use of a US Navy air echelon was inaugurated in the exploration of the Antarctic land mass with the deployment of Navy Air Development Squadron VX-6 to the South Polar region for the first Operation 'Deep Freeze', becoming part of the US Naval Support Force. Initially the squadron was equipped with Douglas R4Ds (a Navy version of the C-47 Sytrain, in this instance fitted with ski landing gear), one of which made the first ever aeroplane landing at the geographic South Pole in 1956; shortly afterwards VX-6 received the Lockheed P2V Neptune, to take part in further annual Deep Freezes.

By 1960 VX-6 was scheduled to receive a new, ski-equipped version of the Hercules. Four aircraft, originally termed the C-130BL and funded from 1959 USAF Appropriations to speed delivery, were produced in 1960. The Bureau of Aeronautics raised a special requirement, SAR 398, to provide support for the new aircraft by the manufacturers, including training of crews in their flying and maintenance, both at Marietta and VX-6's home base at NAS Point Mugu, California, until such time that the US Navy could itself take over this responsibility. SAR 398 remained in being until September 1961 when the Navy's own SAR 400 support system took over.

Having regard to the climatic enviroment of Antarctica, with the fact that no other in-service aircraft was powered by the Allison T56 turboprops or fitted with AN/APN-59 radar or the AN/APA-52 Doppler drift system and that the Hercules was the largest-ever ski-equipped aircraft with the US Navy, these training and support programmes were vital for the Hercules' successful employment.

On August 4 1960 the first two C-130BLs (*148318*

and *148319*) landed at NAS Quonset Point, Rhode Island, for handing over to VX-6. By the end of Deep Freeze 61 these and a third aircraft, *148320*, had lifted over 1,800 tons of supplies between Pole and Byrd stations; they also flew the longest-ever trans-Antarctic flight, the 2,800-mile journey from McMurdo Sound to set up a scientific field station at Eight's Coast on Bellingshausen Sea. In 1962 the aircraft, together with a fourth (*148321*, which had been retained in the States for development testing), were redesignated LC-130Fs. In April that year VX-6, comprising 70 officers and 400 other ranks, and commanded by Commander Martin D Creenwell USN, was awarded the US Navy Unit Commendation for 'exceptionally meritorious conduct' during the first six Deep Freeze Operations. In most respects the combined wheel/ski landing gear on the LC-130F was similar to that fitted on the USAF's C-130D, arranged so that all components were semi-retractable, the skis capable of being lifted to expose the wheels for use on normal paved runways. The total ski installation weight was about 5,500 lb, this reducing the range by about five per cent from that of a standard C-130B. The bearing surfaces of each ski

were coated with Teflon to reduce friction and to combat ice adhesion.

The pattern of air operations in Antarctica had already become established before the arrival of the Hercules, the principal limiting factor being the onset of the Polar winter between about April and September which prohibits such operations under normal circumstances; during this 'closed season' VX-6 flew north to the USA, normally staging at Christchurch, Fiji and Hawaii, returning to McMurdo Sound at the beginning of October each year. The Squadron's achievements were impressive indeed; on February 22 1963 an LC-130F made the longest flight in the histroy of Antarctica when, piloted by Commander William H. Everett and with Rear Admiral James R. Reedy USN aboard, it flew 3,470 miles from McMurdo south beyond the Pole to the Shackleton Mountains, southeast to the pole of inaccessibility before returning to McMurdo; much of the territory over which the aircraft flew had never before been seen by mankind.

During the South Polar winter of 1964 VX-6 was asked to participate in flying supplies from Thule AFB in Greenland to an ice island, known as T-3, close to the

All that was visible of 148321 (see front cover) in deep snow (note the propeller tips) after it had crashed in Antarctica when a RATOG bottle tore loose during take-off. Despite the remote crash site, the Hercules was repaired and rejoined VX-6 (US Navy, via Robert F. Dorr).

Another ski-equipped LC-130F, 148319 (C/N 3564), of VX-6, US Navy, that crashed in Antarctica after a RATOG bottle broke loose and smashed into the starboard wing, this time at Dome Charlie on January 15 during Deep Freeze 75. In this instance an entire new wing and engines were airlifted to the crash site where repairs were completed and the aircraft flown back to base 11 months later (M.W. Moore, US Navy, Neg No 700008 dated 26-10-76, via Robert F. Dorr).

Above *The LC-130R, 159129, of US Navy Squadron VXE-6* (Lockheed-Georgia, Neg No RJ-9350-IC).

Right *One of six US Navy LC-130Rs flying with VXE-6, 159129 (C/N 4508), but carrying the tail codes of VX-6. This aircraft was damaged on January 15 1975 when its nose ski failed on take-off while bringing out the crew of the damaged LC-130F, 148321, which had also just crashed (via US Navy).*

North Pole. Two of the LC-130Fs accordingly flew north from Quonset Point to Thule and each flew seven trips to T-3 between May 8 and 12 1964.

Occasionally emergencies demanded mid-winter flying by VX-6 in Antarctica as witnessed in a LC-130F flight from Christchurch to McMurdo on June 26 1964 when Lieutenant Robert V. Meyer brought out a critically injured seaman, after having first flown a medical team all the way from the States. A similar emergency flight in mid-winter was made by Commander Marion Morris on June 7 1966. Another milestone was reached at the beginning of the 1966–67 summer season when an LC-130F made the earliest deep penetration of the Antarctic continent; flown by the Squadron Commander, Commander Don Balish, the aircraft opened up Plateau Station on October 13, 1,250 miles from McMurdo, landing at the 12,000 ft high ice strip were the temperature was recorded at minus 67° F. In 1967 VX-6 received a second Navy Unit Commendation. Also in that year VX-6 started limited routine winter flying (as distinct from emergency flights) to and from Antarctica, an LC-130F being flown from Christchurch to Williams Field, near McMurdo, by Commander Fred Schneider USN, the Squadron's Commanding Officer on June 18. The purpose of these flights was to deliver mail, fresh fruits and vegetables to

the 'wintering-over' ground personnel. A record-breaking flight by *148318*, by then christened 'City of Christchurch', piloted by Lieutenant-Commander Robert D. McLin USN, covered the 2,300-mile distance from Christchurch to McMurdo early in September 1967 in six hours two minutes, landing on the ice strip in total darkness.

One of the most spectacular rescue flights was performed by LC-130Fs of VX-6, starting on December 4 1967 when a British medical officer at the Halley Bay Station, Dr John Brotherhood, suffered spinal injuries and a fractured jaw. Two LC-130Fs flew out of McMurdo, the second 400 miles behind the first to act as radio relay and, in event of mishap, to conduct search and rescue. Because of rough, hard-packed ice, the strip at Halley Bay had not been used for ten years, so the British scientists marked out the best available ski-way, using up all their cocoa stores to do so! The pilot of the leading Hercules (flown by VX-6's previous Commanding Officer, Commander Schneider) landed safely and returned with the injured doctor to McMurdo, 1,600 miles away. For this feat Commander Schneider was awarded the Distinguished Flying Cross and Sir Vivian Fuchs, Director of the British Antarctic Survey, presented a commemmorative plaque to VX-6.

By the start of Deep Freeze 16 of 1970-71 VX-6 had been renamed 'Antarctic Development Squadron VXE-6', with its semi-permanent base established at Christchurch, New Zealand, largely as the result of the elimination of the winter flying limitations. It had also taken delivery in the previous year of the first of a new version of the Hercules, the LC-130R (*155917*), which in effect was a ski-equipped C-130H and therefore more powerful than the LC-130F. It also opened up longer flights, due to its ability to lift a greater load of fuel, a capability further enhanced by the increased use of JATO (jet-assisted take-off, or more accurately rocket-assisted take-off), particularly with the earlier aircraft.

The Squadron's fine accident-free record with the Hercules suffered a setback on February 15 1971, when the veteran *City of Christchurch* struck a snow wall at McMurdo, caught fire and was destroyed. Halfway through Deep Freeze 17, on December 4 1971, a second LC-130F *(148321)* was badly damaged during take-off from Care Four station, 750 miles from McMurdo, when a JATO bottle tore loose and struck the wing; with spares flown out from Christchurch to the remote site the aircraft was repaired and flown back to McMurdo towards the end of the Antarctic summer. The decision to repair *148321*, despite the considerable logistic and technical problems involved, was to some extent determined by the 25 per cent decrease in aircraft strength its loss would have entailed. Worse was to follow on January 28 1973 when, during the next Deep Freeze, the only LC-130R so far delivered crashed while landing at the Amundsen-Scott South Pole station and was written off. By then *148321* was flying again and VXE-6 was back up to three Hercules. There is no doubt that this spate of accidents was due to the much higher limits to which the Hercules were being flown; greater distances covered, lower weather criteria and heavier loads all reduced the safety margins, against which could be set the considerable store of experience amassed in the Antarctic flying conditions.

Towards the end of 1973 a second LC-130R was completed for the National Science Foundation's (NSF) contribution to Deep Freeze, the aircraft, *159129*, being crewed by VXE-6 personnel on behalf of the NSF. However, on January 15 1975 one of the original LC-130Fs, *149319*, also suffered a JATO

bottle breakaway on take-off, this time at Dome Charlie station. The next mishap occured when the LC-130R *159129* arrived at Dome Charlie the same day to bring out the downed crew, its nose ski breaking off during take-off, so that VX-6 now had two badly damaged aircraft stranded and out of operation. Both were to remain at Dome Charlie for much of 1975, *149319* requiring an entire new wing and powerplant to be airlifted out to the crash site. Moreover the one remaining LC-130F, *148320*, to have thus far remained unscathed also crashed at Dome Charlie on November 4 1975, although in this case the repairs were effected within six weeks.

Between December 1973 and May 1977 the four remaining LC-130Rs were completed for the NSF and were flown without further mishap and by 1981 VXE-6 was still flying the three veteran LC-130Fs and five LC-130Rs. The astonishing achievements of this Squadron over nearly 20 years would fill a book on their own; vast tracts of barren wastelands surveyed and photographed, countless support and supply flights made, rescue and evacuation of injured American, British and Soviet personnel, to mention but a few of the tasks successfully accomplished.

VXE-6 is tasked during the current 1983–84 Deep Freeze operation, on behalf of the NSF, to fly through the plume of steam and smoke that emits from the active volcano Mount Erebus that rises to 13,000 ft on

Ross Island near McMurdo. An LC-130 has been specially equipped with a correlation spectrometer to analyse the sulphur dioxide content of the emissions; it also carries a quartz crystal micro-balancing device to accumulate solid particles through the aircraft's sextant port for laboratory analysis. By comparison with ice core samples gathered throughout Antarctica it will then be possible to chart the volcano's plume dispersal pattern, to evolve a history of the volcano itself and to discover whether any other volcano has been active on that continent.

KC-130Fs with the US Navy

Although the KC-130F tanker was strictly a Marine Corps Hercules, ordered through and funded by the US Navy, about eight of these aircraft were at some time flown on Navy assignments.

The most famous of these aeroplanes was *149798*, the 23rd KC-130F completed, which was delivered to the Naval Air Test Center, Patuxent River, on October 8 1963 to begin trials to test the feasibility of operating an aircraft of the Hercules' size and weight from the deck of an aircraft carrier at sea, a study that had been ordered by the US Chief of Naval Operations. It was, in effect, an exercise to discover whether, if necessary, the Hercules could perform 'carrier onboard delivery' to a fleet at sea.

To begin with a simulated *Forrestal*-class carrier

The largest aircraft ever to fly from the deck of a carrier, KC-130F 149798 took off from the USS Forrestal *(CVA-59) on October 30 1963 (Lockheed-Georgia, Neg No RG 4124-C).*

deck was marked out at Patuxent River, with the Hercules making 95 take-offs and 141 landings at aircraft weights between 80,000 and 100,000 lb. For the purpose of the trials the KC-130F was modified by the removal of the in-flight refuelling pods, reduction of the nose-wheel retraction aperture and inclusion of a Hytrol Antiskid Braking System MK 2 as used in the Boeing 727 airliner. The principal objects of the 'dry land' flying were to find the best means of controlling and reducing the sink rate on landing to no more than 9 ft/sec (in fact the average achieved was 5.6 ft/sec), and to reduce the likely touchdown dispersion—bearing in mind that no arrester equipment could be used.

Trials involving USS *Forrestal* (CVA-59) herself, with Lieutenant James H. Flatley III, USN, at the controls of the Hercules, started on October 30 with 44 approaches, of which 16 resulted in touch-and-go landings, all down the centre-line of the axial deck. A week later the second stage of the trials involved three-touch-and-go landings and four full-stop landings at weights up to 92,000 lb. During the four deck take-offs lift-off speeds varied between 60 and 80 kts, with roll distances around 330 ft. The final stage, conducted on November 21 and 22, comprised 24 approaches, seven touch-and-go landings and 17 full-stop landings on both wet and dry decks at weights up to 121,000 lb.

Seventeen take-offs were performed, including several at 90,000 lb on the angled deck. Perhaps the most interesting achievements of the trials was that, despite some pitching of the *Forrestal*, Lieutenant Flatley managed to *average* a sink rate on landing of only 5.2 ft/sec.

There is no doubt that these trials were highly successful in proving the feasibility of operating a Hercules from a carrier of the *Forrestal*'s size and, incidentally, constituted an all-time record for size and weight of an aircraft operating from a carrier. The study was, however, of academic interest only and no plan ever existed to extend the use of such large aircraft to routine operations of this nature to the fleet. For his skill in completing the trials successfully, Lieutenant Flatley was awarded the Distinguished Flying Cross and in 1982 was serving as a Rear Admiral in the US Navy.

Fleet Tactical Support Squadrons and TACAMO

Before going on to recount the manner in which the Hercules contributes to one of the principal US Navy fleet tasks it is necessary to describe briefly its service with the Fleet Tactical Support Squadrons, for it was

First flown as a C-130A for the USAF in 1956 as 55-0021 (C/N 3048), this Hercules was converted as the prototype C-130D in 1957 and later flown with the AFSC. It was converted to a GC-130A (later DC-130A) but without 'chin' radome and was purchased by the US Navy as 158228, serving with VC-3, as shown here with four underwing target drones. The upper surfaces were white, the fin red and the wings yellow (MAP, Neg No U-00516).

from this service that the use of the Hercules in the long-range communications role sprang.

Fleet Tactical Support Squadron VR-1 had originally been formed on March 9 1942, just three months after Pearl Harbor, to provide transport and communications services between units of the US Navy which would be on station in war theatres throughout the world. After the War, to avoid costly duplication of services, it was decided that a single Command, the USAF's Military Air Transport Service (MATS), would assume all world-wide transport responsibilities of the American armed forces combining those of Air Transport Command (ATC) and the Naval Air Transport Service (NATS). However, VR-1 remained in being as something of a utility unit, flying all manner of aircraft until in March

1962 when the first GV-1U Hercules arrived at VR-1's Patuxent River station. As already stated above, the GV-1U was a standard transport version of the Marine Corps' GV-1 tanker (KC-130F), which was soon to be retermed the C-130F. VR-1 remained at Patuxent River until 1968 when it moved to its original base at NAS Norfolk, Virginia. Officially this was the occasion that the Squadron divided into two parts, one section becoming Fleet Air Reconnaissance Squadron VQ-4 which remained at Patuxent River; the other part had already split away, about which more is said below.

Meanwhile other Hercules of MATS were being flown by US Navy Fleet Tactical Support Squadrons, VR-3 taking over USAF C-130Es in January 1964 at McGuire Air Force Base, New Jersey—a full complement of 16 aircraft being delivered that year. The

Above left *Seen here in more stylised markings with US Navy Squadron VC-3 is the second converted DC-130A, 158229 (ex-56-0491, C/N 3099)* (MAP, Neg No U-01411).

Left *Although bearing USAF marks and 'old'-prefixed BuAer No 56-0514, this DC-130A was serving with US Navy Squadron VC-3 in 1979 and, with 'chin' radome, is seen here with a single Ryan AQM-34 reconnaissance drone under the starboard wing. The aircraft was later given the familiar red, white and yellow paint scheme and normal Navy marks* (MAP, Neg No 99/316).

Above *One of the seven C-130Fs (GV-1U), 149797 (C/N 3666), of VR-24, normally based at Naples, Italy, for Navy transport duties* (Starliner Aviation Press, Neg No CS 902).

Right *Close-up of C-130F, 149797* (Starliner Aviation Press, Neg No CS 903).

Squadron was to specialise in world-wide supply operations, both landing and air dropping supplies (using 'computed air release point, or CARP, procedures) to American units from the Arctic to the Middle East, first taking part in Operation 'Delaware' in the Middle East in April 1964, and in Operation 'Desert Strike' in the United States the following month. While VR-3's responsibilities lay largely to the east of the United States, VR-7, also with C-130Es, covered fleet support in the Pacific, but with an associated maintenance Squadron, VR-8, based at Moffett Field, California. Other Squadrons to fly the C-130E were VR-21, VR-22 and VR-24, as well as a related but autonomous Fleet Logistic Support Squadron VRC-50, serving the US Seventh Fleet in the Far East. VRC-50 received its C-130Fs from VR-21, which was

decommissioned on March 31 1977. For a short time in the mid-1960s a Hercules of VR-24 was assigned the task of field support of the US Navy's formation aerobatic team, The Blue Angels, until this was formally assumed by a Marine Corps KC-130F (see Chapter 5).

Returning now to VR-1 and its six-year period at Patuxent River with Hercules, between 1962 and 1968. It was at around the time that this Squadron was scheduled to receive its first GV-1Us in 1962, that the Department of Defense instructed the Director of Naval Communications to investigate and develop a highly reliable air mobile VLF (Very Low Frequency) communications system, its ultimate purpose to provide a radio link with the global deployment of the Polaris-armed submarines, whose cruise duration

Above *One of only four C-130Gs, 151891 (C/N 3878), supplied to the US Navy seen here prior to conversion to EC-130G communications aircraft, probably early in 1964 (Lockheed-Georgia, Neg No RH 4188).*

Below *The first EC-130Q, 156170 (C/N 4239), in service with VQ-4; antenna guides are fitted in the rear loading ramp and extreme tail. The aircraft carries the Unit Citation 'ribbons' painted below the cockpit windows (MAP, Neg No U-06603).*

Pre-delivery view of an EC-130Q showing the wing tip electronic pods (Lockheed-Georgia, Neg No RM 3530-1).

would take them to remote and distant areas not normally or conveniently accessible to standard Navy communications facilities. Early feasibility studies showed that such a system would be possible by employing a weight-lifting aircraft the size of the Hercules. The project was henceforth codenamed 'TACAMO', generally said to be an acronym coined from the order 'Take Charge and Move Out' (although one Navy source has indicated that its more explicit origin was Tactical Communications and Monitoring Organisation). Early breadboard investigations were followed by a rudimentary trial installation, TACAMO I, in a KC-130F early in 1963 at the Naval Air Test Center. From this was developed the second generation TACAMO II which, installed in four C-130Gs, were delivered for operational service. *151888* and *151889* were assigned to VR-1 at Patuxent River, Maryland, and *151890* and *151891* to VR-21 at NAS Barber's Point, Hawaii, in December 1964 under the operational control of the Commanders-in-Chief, US Atlantic and Pacific Fleets respectively (CINCLANTFLT and CINCPACFLT).

The TACAMO II installation comprised three equipment vans: a communications central module, accommodating four Airborne Communicators and weighing 6,000 lb; a Power Amplifier

module to provide power for the VLF transmitter, weighing 1,500 lb; and a VLF Antenna Reel Assembly module housing a drive mechanism, reel and VHF antenna wire, weighing over 13,500 lb. It should be explained that this antenna was 35,000 ft or more than six and a half miles long! These van modules were loaded through the main ramp access, bolted to the cabin floor and connected to the aircraft's power sources through the overhead 'hog's trough'. The trailing antenna passed through an aperture in the lower rear ramp by means of a conical guide which reduced the risk of damage to the aircraft structure or severing of the antenna during a turn.

The VR-21 TACAMO Detachment at Hawaii was found to be too remote from the main areas of submarine activity in the Western Pacific, so in January 1966 it was moved to NAS Agana, Guam, splitting from its parent unit and recommissioning as the TACAMO element of Airborne Warning Squadron VW-1 under Lieutenant-Commander Ron Carlson USN. After a further 30 months of operations with TACAMO II, it was decided to establish dedicated communications Squadrons and on July 1 1968 the VW-1 TACAMO element was commissioned as Fleet Air Reconnaissance Squadron (still at Agana), while VQ-4 was commissioned from the TACAMO element

Fine view of a VQ-4 EC-130Q, 159469 (C/N 4595), trailing both ramp and tail antennae; note the absence of the stabilising cones from the guides. The aerial wires are too thin to distinguish, as are the additional aerials between fuselage and tail (Lockheed-Georgia, Neg No RM 5084).

of VR-1, remaining at Patuxent River when that Squadron moved to NAS Norfolk, Virginia.

Both VQ-3 and VQ-4 retained their C-130Gs but during 1969–70 a custombuilt version of the Hercules, the EC-130Q, was delivered to the Squadrons, four new aircraft being delivered to each (*156171, 156172, 156176* and *156177* to VQ-3 and *156170, 156173, 156174* and *156175* to VQ-4). Considerable advances had been made by the manufacturers of the TACAMO equipment, Collins Radio Company, in the meantime and the new version, TACAMO III, featured increased power output to enable significantly increased signals to be transmitted over the entire VLF band, using the trailing antenna and an auto-tuned coupler. It also possessed the capability to receive and transmit signals simultaneously on all frequency bands from VLF to UHF. Other improvements in miniaturisation and integration with the aircraft structure allowed the TACAMO system weight to be reduced from 28,300 lb to 18,400 lb, as well as providing improved in-flight maintenance and crew comfort.

After working up with the new TACAMO III system, VQ-3 and VQ-4 became regularly integrated with the American World-Wide Command and Control System (WWCCS), a command network which embraces elements of the USAF to reduce the likelihood of breakdown of strategic control in the event of war, although survivable communication with the American submerged nuclear deterrent remains the *raison d'être* of the EC-130Q aircraft.

Three of the old C-130Gs (later to be redesignated

EC-130Gs after updating of their equipment) were still in service in the early 1980s, although *151890* was badly damaged by an in-flight fire at Patuxent River in January 1972; however, its communication section survived and it has since been used for ground testing and system development. Reflecting the work done by these Squadrons, VQ-3 was awarded a Meritorious Unit Commendation on January 15 1973 and followed this with a COMNAVAIRPAC Safety Award in 1981. TACAMO IV was introduced in two further EC-130Qs, *159348* and *159469*, delivered in July 1975, and was followed by TACAMO IVB in *160608, 161223, 161494, 161495, 161496* and *161531*, delivered between 1978 and 1982. Details of this new equipment have not been divulged by the US Navy.

*   *   *

Throughout all these operational deployments the US Navy's C-130 Squadrons on account of their heavy-lift, rough-field operating capabilities have been available for secondary employment for emergency relief work on behalf of civilian authorities—as witness the use of a VR-24 C-130, on deployment rotation at NAF Sigonella, Italy, to airlift food, clothing and medical supplies to the west coast of Sicily on January 19 1969 where 40,000 civilians had been made homeless by an earthquake near Montevago. Similar relief operations have been mounted at very short notice in Japan, South East Asia, Spain and South America.

Chapter 5

Leatherneck Hercules

The famous United States Marine Corps is traditionally tasked with the amphibious assault of hostile coastal areas, with the air supply and defence of first wave forces until relieved by conventional land environmental troops of the US Army and pending the seizure and control of a permanent land air base. The past 30 years have witnessed considerable expansion of the Marine Corps' duties, including air transportation by fixed-wing aircraft (as well as helicopters) and air refuelling of US Navy and Marine Corps combat aircraft.

Prior to the late 1950s in-flight refuelling of Navy and Marine Corps fighters was confined to the use of 'buddy' aircraft (accompanying fighters which would supply fuel and then return to base, allowing the replenished aircraft to continue the sortie) or to that of USAF KB-29 and KB-50 Superfortress tankers. In 1956, with the production of the C-130A accelerating,

the US Marine Corps saw in the big aeroplane the ability to double-up the tanker/transport roles and, as no work had then been done to test the Hercules in the former configuration, secured the loan from the USAF of two early C-130As (*55-0046* and *55-0048*, C/Ns 3073 and 3075) in 1957. Modifications were made to the fuel system to enable underwing reel-and-hose pods to be mounted outboard of the outer engines, the flight trials continuing for about six months. These experiments were adjudged an immediate success and, in 1958, the US Navy endorsed an initial purchase requirement with the Department of Defense for 28 tankers, to be delivered over a period of four years (1959–62). At the same time it was planned to form three dual-role transport/tanker squadrons, each with an initial establishment of eight GV-1 aircraft (seven GV-1Us being ordered by the US Navy without the air refuelling modifications), and each attached to one of

The two USAF C-130As, 55-0046 and 55-0048, loaned to the US Marine Corps in 1957 for initial air refuelling trials (US Navy, via R. Dorr).

the three Marine Air Wings (MAW-1 in the Far East, MAW-2 on the Atlantic seaboard of the USA and MAW-3 on the Pacific seaboard).

VMGR-252

Based at MCAS Cherry Point, North Carolina, for operations to the east of the United States, Marine Aerial Refueling Transport Squadron VMGR-252 took delivery of 12 of the first GV-1 aircraft (later redesignated KC-130Fs) during 1959–60. Typical of its early work was in support of Marine Attack Squadron VMA-225 when its 16 A-4C Skyhawks flew in October 1962 from Cherry Point to Bermuda and then direct to Rota in Spain, being refuelled en route by ten GV-1s, and again on their return flight. In September 1967 VMGR-252 participated in Operation Deep Furrow, flying refuelling missions from Cherry Point as far east as Turkey, in the course of

one month refuelling 31 other aircraft, carrying 548,478 lb of freight and 536 personnel; during this period the squadron was established with 14 KC-130Fs. In June the following year one of these carried listening devices and explosives to Lajes in the Azores in support of operations to locate the missing submarine *Scorpion*. Also at this time the Squadron was processing air- and ground crews for subsequent transfer to VMGR-152 and VMGR-352 which were being heavily engaged in South-East Asia so one of its KC-130Fs was transferred there to replace one shot down during the support of Khe Sanh. In 1972 one of the Squadron's aircraft (*149810*) was lost when it caught fire and burned out at Lake City, Florida, while being serviced with liquid oxygen. In June 1980 VMGR-252 received a Meritorious Unit Commendation for completing more than 234,000 accident-free flying hours in the 21 years since 1959.

Left *US Marine Corps KC-130F tanker, 149795 (C/N 3664), of VMGR-252 on the approach to the Auxiliary Landing Field, Bogue, North Carolina, on November 1 1972 (Sergeant D.H. Humble, USMC, Neg No A142152).*

Below left *An elderly KC-130F, 150684 (C/N 3727), of VMGR-252 refuelling a Sikorsky CH-53E Super Stallion amphibious assault transport helicopter in 1982 (Lockheed-Georgia).*

Above *Fine study of VMGR-252's KC-130R tanker, 160626 (C/N 4770) (MAP, Neg No U04501).*

Below *A pair of Marine Corps McDonnell Douglas F-18A Hornets refuel from a VMGR-252 KC-130R, 160626 (C/N 4770), in the early 1980s (Lockheed-Georgia, Neg No 2647).*

VMGR-152

Being permanently deployed in the Western Pacific at MCAS Futema, Okinawa, VMGR-152 was not unnaturally involved more heavily in the combat operations in Vietnam than the other two Marine Hercules squadrons. Prior to and during the early stages of the war VMGR-152 was engaged in transportation of personnel and supplies in support of American forces in South-East Asia, losing one aircraft *(149802)* in an accident when it struck a sea wall while taking off at Hong Kong on August 24 1965.

As military operations in Vietnam gradually increased the Squadron, then commanded by Lieutenant-Colonel John Urell USMC, was ordered to detach four KC-130Fs at Da Nang AB, in Vietnam itself, these combat support aircraft, together with a single aircraft detached from VMGR-352, operated under the direct control of the Commanding General, 1st Marine Air Wing. The work undertaken by the Hercules was primarily to refuel Navy and Marine Corps fighter and attack aircraft in the combat zone and to operate flare-dropping missions in support of local ground actions.

In 1967 Lieutenant-Colonel Royce M. Williams arrived to take command having been transferred from VMGR-352, the Squadron stepping up its operations, taking a greater share of the refuelling task both in reinforcement flights to the war zone and over the Gulf of Tonkin where almost daily MIGCAP flights required air refuelling. The Squadron lost an aircraft in action, *149813* being shot down in support operations at Khe Sanh on February 10 1968. In 1969, under Lieutenant-Colonel Frank R. Smoke USMC, the KC-130Fs participated in night air refuelling of attack aircraft operating in the Ashau Valley area and in Operation Bold Mariner they discharged no fewer than 4,739 flares. On another occasion a successful bid to rescue two ditched pilots from the sea at night was achieved using flares dropped by a VMGR-152 Hercules. Another KC-130F, *149814*, was lost on May 18 1969 in an air collision while refuelling two Navy F4B Phantoms.

After the war VMGR-152 remained in the Far East and assisted in the airlift of American forces out of South-East Asia during 1973–75.

VMGR-352

Marine Air (Refueling) Transport Squadron VMGR-352 received its first KC-130Fs in 1959 and, based at El Toro, California, was undoubtedly the most heavily committed Hercules squadron during the war in Vietnam, though less involved in the combat itself than VMGR-152. From 1966 the Squadron operated a forward detachment of four aircraft at Futema, Okinawa, and these, with the remaining aircraft in the United States, operated trans-Pacific (TransPac) services for combat squadrons deploying to and from

Below *A very early KC-130F tanker, 148248 (C/N 3574), of VMGR-352 at MCAS El Toro, California* (courtesy of Major John M. Elliot, USMCR(Retd)).

Right *Five KC-130Fs (from the nearest, 150688, 150687, 150686, 149816 and 149814) of VMGR-352 head out over the Pacific on October 22 1963 from MCAS El Toro, California, to rendezvous with the F-4B Phantoms of Marine Corps Fighter Attack Squadron VMFA-314 en route to their Far East destination. Refuelling the fighters 750 miles out to sea, the tankers had taken off two hours prior to the F-4Bs. Note that some of the KC-130Fs carry their serial numbers on their wings* (A. Scruggs, USMC, Neg No A146391).

the war zone. At the same time one of the Okinawa-based aircraft was required to provide combat support in the land operations themselves, being detached to Da Nang AB, Vietnam. Supporting the III Marine Amphibious Forces, these included Operation Hastings of July 1966, Operation Prairee of September that year, and Operation Chinook early in 1967, as well as supporting the Battle for Hill 881 in which no fewer than five of VMGR-352 aircraft took part and all were slightly damaged by enemy ground fire. They also flew a supply shuttle to Dong Ha and Khe Sanh, and carried construction materials and equipment during the building of Quang Tri airstrip in the latter half of 1967.

Some idea of the considerable scale of operations un-dertaken by VMGR-352 during the 1966–70 period may be gained by the following list of TransPac operations, each of which had to be meticulously planned on both sides of the ocean to achieve accurate rendezvous, despite infinitely variable conditions of weather and wind, not to mention the widely differing performance characteristics of the combat aircraft involved.

1966 (Commanding Officer, Lieutenant-Colonel Royce M. Williams, USMC)

| August | Operation File Cabinet | VMF-121 and VMF(AW)-232 |
| | Operation Holly Pine | VMAW-242, VMCJ-2, VMCJ-3 |

Left *Line-up of KC-130Fs of VMGR-352 at Takhli in November 1972 (Starliner Aviation Press, Neg No CS 901).*

Below *Two Marine Corps McDonnell Douglas F-4J Phantoms of VMFA-212 are refuelled by a KC-130R tanker of VMGR-352 over the Pacific near Hawaii on February 10 1979 (M.E. Cotton, US Navy, Neg No K-125987).*

1967 (Commanding Officer, Colonel William L. Beach, USMC)

March	Operation Long Pull	12 A6As of VMF (AW)-533
June	Operation Dancing Bear	VF-121 and VF-124
July	Operation Charlie Brown	8 F4Bs of VF-41
August	Operation White Rabbit	8 F4Bs of VF-121
August	Operation Bearing Summit	16 F4Bs and TA4Fs of VMFA-122
September	Operation Red Devil	10 F8Es of VMF(AW)-232
September	Operation Bell Buoy	10 A4Es of VA-125
November	Operation Key Bolt	10 A4Es and one A6A of VA-125
December	Operation Key Charger	4 F4Bs of VF-121
December	Operation Key Eagle	6 A4Es and 2 A6As of VA-125

1968 (Commanding Officer, Lieutenant-Colonel Williams D. Harris, USMC)

January	Operation Bearing Echo	10 EA6As of VRF-31, and 17 A6As and 9 TA4Fs of VRF-32
February	Operation Key Jump and Operation Key Lancer	8 F4Bs, 7 A3Bs and 5 F8s of Attack Carrier Air Wing 5
February	Operation Key Mover	12 F4Bs and 2 TA4Fs of VRF-31 and VRF-32
March	Operation Key Object	7 A4Es and 1 KA3B of VRF-31
April	Operation Key Steer	6 F4Bs of VF-162 and 4 F8Es of VF-124
May	Operating Bearing Butler	6 F4Js of VMFA-334 and VMFA-232
June	Operation Key Usher	6 F4Bs, 4 A4Fs, 2 RF8s, 2 A6As and 2 KA3Bs of VRF-31 and VRF-32
July	Operation Key Venture	4 F4Bs and 4 F8s of VRF-32
July	Operation Kennel Cross	2 TA4Fs of VMT-103 and 3 RF4Bs of VMCJ-3
August	Operation Key Yield I	4 F4Bs of VRF-32
August	Operation Key Yield II (Ticonderoga East	4 F4Bs of VRF-32 and 8 F8Es of VF-121
August	Operation Beige Rock	15 F4Js of VMFA-334 and 6 F4Js of VMFA-212
September	Operation Key Arrow I	4 F4Js of VRF-32 and 2 A4Es of VRF-32
September	Operation Key Arrow II (Bon Homme Richard)	4F4Js and 8 F8Es of VRF-32
October	Operation Key Champ	8 F4Js of VRF-32
November	Operation Key Dodger I	4 A4Es, 2 F4Bs, 3 TA4Fs and one RF4B of VRF-32
November	Operation Key Dodger II	2 A4Es, one A3 and one KA3B of VRF-32
December	Operation Key Elevator	4 F4Js and one A3 of VRF-32

1969 (Commanding Officer, Lieutenant-Colonel Harry D. Scott, USMC)

January	Operation Key Flight	One EA6 and 2 A3s of VRF-32
January	Operation Begonia Pod	12 A6As of VMA-225
February	Operation Key Howler	2 TA4Fs, 4 F4s and 2 A3s of VRF-32
March	Operation Key Jammer	3 A3Bs and 3 F4Js of VRF-32
March	Operation Beggar Lion	15 F4Js of VMFA-232 and 3 F4Js of VRF-32
May	Operation Key Nav I	4 F4Js of VMFA-212
June	Operation Key Quoit I	4 A6s and one A3J of VRF-32
June	Operation Key Packer	4 F4Js and 3 F8Js of VRF-32
July	Operation Key Nav II	4 F4Js of VMFA-212
July	Operation Key Quoit II	6 A6s and two A3Js of VRF-32
July	Operation Key Nav III	4 F4Js of VRF-32
July	Operation Redskin	4 F8s of VRF-32
August	Operation Key Nav IV	3 F4Js of Marine Air Group 24
August	Operation Key Nav V	3 F4Js of Marine Air Group 24
August	Operation Key Quoit IV	6 A6s of VRF-32

August	Operation Key Steeler	4 F4Js of Marine Air Group 24
September	Operation Key Nav VI	5 F4Js of Marine Air Group 24
September	Operation Key Quoit V	7 A6s of VRF-32
September	Operation Key Nav VII	3 F4Js of Marine Air Group 24
September	Operation Key Quoit VI	7 A6s of VRF-32
October	Operation Key Nav VIII	4 F4Js of Marine Air Group 24
October	Operation Key Quoit VII	8 A6s of VRF-32
October	Operation Key Quoit VIII	5 A6s and 2 A3s of VRF-32
October	Operation Key Nav IX	2 F4Js of Marine Air Group 24
October	Operation Key Nav X	3 F4Js of Marine Air Group 24
November	Operation Key Nav XI	3 F4Js of Marine Air Group 24
December	Operation Key Nav XII	6 F4Js of VRF-32

1970 (Commanding Officer, Lieutenant-Colonel Marvin P. Mann, USMC)

January	Operation Key Nav XIII	4 F4Bs of VF-121
February	Operation Key Wallop	20 A4Es of VMA-223 and 15 F4Bs of VMF(AW)-542
March	Operation Shangri-La West	12 F8Es of VF-111 VF-162
April	Operation Key Actor VI	3 F4Bs of VF-121
June	Operation Key Charm	2 F4Js of VRF-32

With only a single exception, involving a fighter which had to make an unscheduled landing owing to a mechanical defect, every one of these operations was successfully accomplished without mishap—an astonishing feat of airmanship and organisation.

By the end of 1970 VMGR-352 had completed 142,240 flying hours in 11 years and had carried over 300,000 personnel. In the five years of operating TransPac refuelling flights across the Pacific, detailed

KC-130F, 148249 (C/N 3577), with small dorsal radome or fairing, flying with VMGR-234 (Starliner Aviation Press, Neg No CS 904).

above, the Squadron had supplied nearly three million gallons of fuel to Marine and Navy combat aircraft. The Squadron earned four Meritorious Unit Commendations (in 1970, 1972, 1978 and 1981) and the Navy Unit Commendation in 1971, being permitted to emblazon the streamers on its aircraft together with the Vietnam Service Medal ribbon. By 1981 the Squadron had carried nearly two-and-a-half million pounds of freight and dispensed 7.7 million gallons of fuel to 1,278 aircraft. The Squadron was selected to convert to the extended-range KC-130R in 1975, the first four aircraft being delivered to El Toro during that year, providing an extra 18,000-lb of give-away fuel per aircraft by use of two additional tanks.

The US Marine Corps has of course undertaken numerous other tasks during the past 30 years and one other unit, VMGR-234, should be mentioned. Hitherto flying KC-130Fs from NAS Glenview, Illinois, this squadron is a constituent of the Marine Air Reserve's Air Control Group 48 of Marine Air Wing 4, and undertakes routine tanker and other crew preparation, making periodic flights overseas as part of the normal training process. As already mentioned, the improved-capacity KC-130R tanker started delivery to VMGR-352 in 1975, followed the next year by VMGR-252. In 1983 the first four of 11 Model 382C-34E KC-130T tankers were delivered to VMGR-234; this new version featuring the latest modifications, including Inertial, Omega and TACAN navigation systems, a new flight director and autopilot, and a solid state search radar. Its enhanced flight envelope with -15 engines enables refuelling to be carried out between 5,000 and 25,000 ft, and from 105 kt up to 250 kt. At full capacity as a tanker it can carry up to 11,073 Imp Gal (13,280 US Gal) of fuel and is compatible with all in-service helicopters and fixed-wing aircraft equipped for in-flight refuelling. Compatibility clearance has been achieved with the A-4, A-6, A-7, F-4, F-5, F-8, F-9, F-11, F-14, F-18, F-101, F-105, AV-8A and AV-8B, as well as such aircraft as the OV-1 Mohawk, HH-3E and CH-53E.

Other fuel supply-related work undertaken by Marine Hercules have included carriage of bulk fuel canisters (either a single 5,000-Imp Gal tank, two rubber pillow tanks each of 2,500 Imp Gal capacity, or 125×55-Imp Gall drums) for fuel farm or storage depot replenishment. Indeed the Marine Corps is the only Service that has regularly undertaken LAPES delivery of bulk fuel in palletised rubber tank components.

VMGR-234 flew this KC-130F, 148892 (C/N 3606), at NAS Glenview, Illinois; note the absence of the dorsal fairing (Starliner Aviation Press, Neg No CS 905).

The Blue Angels

Finally, in the realms of display flying, a single Marine Corps Hercules is regularly flown in support of the US Navy's formation aerobatic team, the Blue Angels, and although perhaps not as spectacular in the air as the jet fighters, the beautifully-prepared KC-130F is no less attractive on the ground.

Originally undertaken by the US Navy itself on an *ad hoc* basis (for instance using a C-130F of VR-24 when displaying in Europe during 1965), support of the team involves carrying a comprehensive spares inventory, mobile workshop, servicing personnel and reserve pilots, not to mention the fuel carried in recent years for air refuelling the display jets if necessary en route to and from display venues. The support Hercules is sometimes also required to act as a communications relay on occasions when the display aircraft themselves are not equipped to communicate direct with the radio facilities in some foreign countries.

The first Marine Corps KC-130F to be assigned to the Blue Angles in 1969 was *150690*, the last KC-130F to be built. This aircraft was originally finished in over-

all white, but in 1973 had the paint removed from its undersides; when it was dubbed *Fat Albert*. In 1974 *150690* was replaced by an earlier production aircraft, *149806*, and this was painted in the livery of the Blue Angels themselves: blue lower surfaces, white upper surfaces and golden-yellow cheat lines. The name *Fat Albert* was inscribed over the crew entry door. In the past ten years *Fat Albert (II)* has flown some five million miles in support of the Navy A-4 display team, its pilots including Major Chip Perrault, Major Ken Hines and Captain Charlie Meyer, and crewed by Sergeants Jesse Wagstaff, Herb Vogt, Dale Tinline, Dan Speaker and Dave Eckley, all of the Marine Corps. With only one abort (when an engine suffered foreign object damage), *Fat Albert* has attended well over 500 displays, usually returning to its base at NAS Pensacola, Florida, after each show, except when on foreign tour. Twice a year it has been customary for *Fat Albert* to give a public display of its own, after the stars have departed, performing a jet-assisted take-off with eight rockets attached to the rear fuselage.

Below *The US Navy's formation aerobatic team 'Blue Angels' was supported by this all-white KC-130F, 150690 (C/N 3742), of the US Marine Corps between about 1970 and 1974; later in this period the area below the aircraft's cheat line was stripped of paint and the aircraft christened 'Fat Albert' (MAP, Neg No U06632).*

Opposite page *The second 'Fat Albert' support KC-130F, 149806 (C/N 3703), in the full 'Blue Angels' blue and yellow livery.* (Lockheed-Georgia, Easton Gallant, Neg Nos RM 2680-8C, upper, and RM 2680-10C, lower).

Colour scheme of the second 'Fat Albert' was dark royal blue, with white upper surfaces and yellow cheat line and nose. All lettering on the blue sections was in yellow, that on the white in blue. The air steps in the nose entry door were painted white (Starliner Aviation Press, Neg Nos CS 906, CS 908 and CS 909).

Chapter 6

Vietnam

In any account of the Vietnam War, however brief, conventional chronology is almost impossible due to the very nature of operations undertaken by the opposing forces. There were no spectacular advances or decisive battles by established armies, only a succession of ennervating strokes and counter-strokes, pinprick strikes, politically-inspired policies and limitations and, above all, tactical innovations. There was not even a front line behind which the forces of friend and foe fought: the tactics of infiltration, employed by both sides, rendered the entire theatre a potential battlefield. Indeed, it was often difficult to distinguish friend from foe and whereas the Communist North possessed the ultimate determination to succeed in national unification, the ideologies of the South were inadequate to sustain effective resistance. Meanwhile the American forces found themselves fighting an undeclared war against an enemy possessing powerful but undeclared allies—and with one hand tied behind their back by a powerful pacifist lobby at home. To any but the blindest observer, the war—an outcome of political intrigue over the past 20 years—could have but two alternative results: escallation to world conflict or abandonment of South Vietnam to its Communist fate. The choice, inevitably deprecated by the hawkish firebrands, was no less than a victory of commonsense and one on which the United States, for all its humiliation, may reflect with pride.

The first acts of open war by the US forces in the Vietnam theatre were carried out on August 2 and 4 1964 in retaliation for attacks by North Vietnamese torpedo boats against American destroyers in the Gulf of Tonkin. At that time there were no combat elements of the USAF based in Vietnam, its most modern aircraft in that country being four RF-101C Voodoo reconnaissance aircraft; other older aircraft were in use to train the ill-equipped Vietnamese Air Force. There was also a squadron of Fairchild C-123 Provider tactical transports to contribute a tactical airlift element, and six such aircraft had been engaged in 'Ranch Hand' defoliation missions for more than two years.

The USAF's own heavy airlift element in the Far East comprised the C-130As of the 815th TCS, 315th Air Division at Tachikawa AB in Japan, and those of the 35th and 817th TCS, 374th TCW, at Naha AB, Okinawa. A few aircraft of the 315th Air Division were also detached at Naha.

Events moved swiftly as the United States began preparing for a major war in Vietnam; B-57 jet bombers were moved to Bien Hoa near Saigon, and F-100s and F-102s to Da Nang on the coast, 100 miles from the border with North Vietnam. American Army engineers were flown in by the 817th TCS to improve and enlarge the airfields throughout the country and in neighbouring Thailand, few of which were suitable for the operation of modern combat aircraft. At the beginning of the war, Military Airlift Command was short of heavy airlift capacity, so piston-engined C-124 Globemasters and C-133 Cargomasters were used to lift much of the bulky materiel to the war zone in the early months, though these big aeroplanes were by no means rough-field aircraft. As air bases in South Vietnam were quickly improved the excellent Lockheed C-141 Star Lifter jet transports took over much of the personnel transportation to Saigon, as well as most of the casualty evacuation from the theatre. However, for tactical airlift purposes, by far the most widely-used aircraft throughout the war, was to be the C-130. Soon the Squadrons were being used to fly American troops from terminal air bases in Japan and Okinawa direct to their bases at Quang Tri, Khe Sanh and Da Nang in the zone covered by the US I Corps in the north, and to Kontum, Pleiku and Na Trang in the central area occupied by the II Corps.

While regular ground operations against the North Vietnamese Army (NVA) continued to be limited to those of a strictly retaliatory nature, covert operations (which had already been in train for many months by US Special Forces) began to assume a much greater importance; small groups of highly trained personnel being lifted to remote locations by helicopter to attack and destroy key positions on the enemy's lines of communications. Air support of these small forces soon became one of the main tasks of C-130s, although the vast majority of combat troop movement was to be undertaken by the fast-growing fleet of Army heli-

Delivery of supply pallets from a 314th TAW Hercules, 62-1806, as it continues its ground roll, probably at Ching Chuan Kang ROCAB, Taiwan, (Lieutenant-Colonel Walt Evans, USAF).

copters. When called on to fly deep into North Vietnam, the C-130 crews were faced with navigation of pinpoint accuracy to locations in the featureless landscape. Often the proximity of enemy ground forces would prevent an air drop, so that recourse to a low-level delivery technique was adopted; known as the ground proximity extraction system (GPES). This simply involved dragging the loads off the Hercules' rear loading ramp as it flew a few feet above the ground, a trailing hook engaging a cable set up by the troops on the ground. Various other methods of delivery were also employed, including the low-altitude parachute extraction system (LAPES) which employed large parachutes to drag the palletised and shock-proofed loads from the rear of the freight cabin; this had the advantage of being capable of delivering very heavy items of equipment such as tanks and other armoured vehicles, or earth-moving equipment, but obviously required a fairly firm and unobstructed ground surface. On other occasions, where a firm surface existed but when speed of delivery was paramount, the Hercules would simply touch down and immediately discharge its pallets off the rear ramp in quick succession without much loss of speed, before opening up to climb away.

First Hercules casualties

During the first year of the war air combat was largely confined to medium and high altitude fighting, involv-

ing raids by American attack aircraft against targets in the north, provoking interception by the small but fast-growing fighter force of the Communists. Following vicious and highly destructive attacks by groups of Viet Cong infiltrators against a hotel in Saigon (used by US officers) on Christmas Eve 1964, a mortar attack on the newly-extended airfield at Pleiku on February 7 1965 and on Soc Trang the next day, 'Flaming Dart' retaliatory attacks by US Navy aircraft, flying from carriers in the Gulf of Tonkin, were mounted against enemy barracks at Dong Hoi and Vit Thuu in North Vietnam. The pattern of war was becoming established and on July 1 the Viet Cong, landing from the sea, struck with light artillery and mortars the base at Da Nang, which was now a key airfield and a main supply base of the US I Corps. Eight aircraft were destroyed, including two C-130As, *55-0039* and *55-0042*, of the 817th TCS.

The rigours of flying operations in these difficult conditions of heavy loads, hazardous supply delivery and unpredictable weather over a featureless landscape also began to take a toll, two C-130As (probably both from the 817th) crashing in South Vietnam during the year and another in Thailand.

By the end of the year almost a quarter of a million US personnel had arrived in Vietnam, including 3,500 US Marines airlifted into Da Nang in March. A start had been made to create an extensive network of Loran navigation stations throughout South East Asia, and

Two views of the low-altitude parachute extraction system (LAPES) delivering tanks from 317th TAW C-130Es (Lockheed-Georgia, Neg Nos RM 1865 and RL 9010).

A C-130B, 58-0752 (C/N 3551), taking part in the airlift of the 101st US Airborne Division's ('Screaming Eagles') 1st Brigade from Kontum to Phan Rang (US Air Force).

this would ultimately enable American aircraft to fix their position in the war zone with considerable accuracy, thereby reducing one of the hazards inherent in the air operations.

Another arrival was the 350th Strategic Reconnaissance Squadron (SRS) of the 100th Strategic Reconnaissance Wing (SRW), based at U Tapao AB, Thailand, with, among other aircraft, two DC-130As (*56-0527* and *57-0461*) equipped to carry a single Ryan AQM-34 (Type 147) remotely-piloted vehicle (RPV), a jet-powered reconnaissance drone. This RPV was carried under the right wing of the Hercules, could be released at any altitude—usually fairly low—and controlled by secure microwave link from the launch air-

craft to gather intelligence over difficult targets. After conclusion of the reconnaissance, which might be by photo camera, infra-red linescan, TV or radar sensing, the AQM-34 would navigate itself by reference to the Loran network to rendezvous with a retrieval HH-3E helicopter which, by means of a trapeze frame, would snag and hold a parachute deployed from the drone. No DC-130A or DC-130E (which soon arrived in Vietnam) was ever lost to enemy action, but as early as May 1965 at least eight of the drones had been shot down by ground fire over China during intelligence gathering missions over the supply routes to North Vietnam.

It was the enormous expansion of the surface-to-air missile defences in North Vietnam, which continued

During the Vietnam War US Marine Corps KC-130Fs were heavily committed to air refuelling of Navy aircraft. Here an aircraft, 148895 of VMGR-152, based at MCAS Futema, Okinawa, 'tops off' an F-8J Crusader of Navy Squadron VF-51 over the Gulf of Tonkin in August 1969 (US Navy, Neg No 1142724).

throughout the war, that brought about fundamental advances in the level of technology employed by the Americans, and it was to counter these defences that the USAF introduced all manner of special equipment, decoys and weapons. In the early stages much of the enemy SAM-site identification was performed visually by observers either flying with an attacking force or, with considerably greater hazard, in slow and vulnerable observation aircraft. Another method of observation, soon introduced, particularly of the presence and movement of enemy transport and foot personnel, was by means of remote sensors, known collectively as 'Igloo White' and including such equipment as Adsid (air-delivered seismic intrusion detector), the acoustic

buoy (Acoubuoy) and Spikebuoy. Dropped in their thousands by all types of aircraft over huge areas of the country, these expendable battery-powered sensors lay inert, part-buried in the ground or hanging from trees, until triggered by the nearby movement of a human being or vehicle, whereupon it would transmit a coded signal which could be received by a Ryan AQM-34 drone, a DC-130A or any other radio relay aircraft for relaying to the giant Infiltration Surveillance Center (ISC) near Nakhon Phanom AB, just across the border with Thailand. Many a ground or air strike was launched by the US forces on the strength of signals relayed from Igloo White sensors.

In 1966, as C-130 operations continued growing

Sequence of photographs showing an MC-130E carrying out a personnel recovery using the Fulton pick-up system at Nha Trang, Vietnam, in 1970 (Lieutenant-Colonel Walt Evans, USAF, Neg Nos 11/10 to 11/14).

both in weight and scope, losses from enemy action were held to three aircraft: a Marine Corps KC-130F (*149809*), almost certainly of Marine Corps Squadron VMGR-152, shot down while on a refuelling sortie over North Vietnam on February 1; a C-130E of an unknown unit shot down by a SAM during the audacious attack (Operation 'Carolina Moon') against the bridge at Thanh Hoa over the Song Ma river far into North Vietnam on May 31; and another C-130E, also of an unknown unit, shot down by ground fire over South Vietnam on October 2. Five other Hercules were lost in accidents during that year.

In 1967 the Special Operations Wing, whose activities had been almost exclusively associated with those of the 5th Special Forces Group in Vietnam and whose headquarters were located at Nha Trang, broadened the scope of its operational flexibility with the introduction of four specially equipped C-130Es with its 15th SOS. (Originally known as CT aircraft, said to denote Combat Talon, these aircraft were also in turn designated C-130E-I Skyhook, HC-130Es and MC-130Es). Equipped with Fulton recovery yokes in the nose and terrain-following radar, the C-130E-Is were intended to be used to recover Special Forces personnel from the ground by use of the balloon and cable snatch

system; the E-I designation also covered electronic reconnaissance and provision was made to carry an airborne command module allowing supervision and surveillance of commando-style troop injections into hostile territory. When equipped with the command module, RATOG was often used by the Hercules for take-off from restricted sites. More than half a dozen such operations were launched, seldom by more than 20 men or so, during the latter half of that year. On November 25 Viet Cong infiltration forces landed on the coast and carried out a mortar attack on Nha Trang AB, inflicting the first casualty among the C-130E-Is when *64-0563* was hit and destroyed. A second aircraft, *64-0547*, was hit during a clandestine operation over North Vietnam on December 9 and crashed in Laos. (Another, *64-0508*, was to be lost while serving with the 318th SOS, shot down over South Vietnam on April 25 1972.)

In the north of the US II Corps' area, Viet Cong infiltrators had crossed the Laotian border and carried out another mortar attack on the airfield at Dak To on November 15, destroying two C-130Es, *62-1865* and *63-7827*, of the 776th TAS, 314th TAW.

While the Special Operations Wing had been engaging in airborne command of covert offensive

Combat-employed HC-130H at Ubon RTAFB, Thailand (Lieutenant-Colonel Walt Evans, USAF, Neg No 11/33 dated November 1970).

The sinister MC-130Es. **Top** *MC-130E (C-130E-I Skyhook), with Fulton, 64-0568, with the 318th SOS, passing through Elmendorf AFB in August 1973. Note the 'droop-snoot' nose radome.* **Bottom** *This anonymous MC-130E, in Saigon during 1971, was black almost overall and was employed on Special Forces covert surveillance and recovery missions (Lieutenant-Colonel Walt Evans, USAF, Neg Nos 25/75 and 10/49).*

Above *Scene at Cam Ranh Bay. The further of the two Hercules is an electronic reconnaissance RC-130B (C-130B-II), 59-1526 (C/N 3563), of the 556th Reconnaissance Squadron, 347th Tactical Fighter Wing. The nearer aircraft is a similar example, 59-1525 (C/N 3561), though employed differently by the 7406th Combat Support Squadron* (Lieutenant-Colonel Walt Evans, USAF, Neg No 14/49).

Below *A pair of AC-130A gunships on the ramp at Ubon RTAFB early in 1970; the nearer aircraft belongs to the 35th TAS, 374th TAW, normally based at Naha AB, Okinawa; beyond, an aircraft of the 16th SOS, 8th Tactical Fighter Wing, on its home base* (Lieutenant-Colonel Walt Evans, USAF, Neg No 11/61, dated November 1970).

operations, an element of the 7th Airborne Command and Control Squadron (ACCS) had also begun operations along much the same lines with conventional forces, using two or three EC-130Es equipped as Airborne Battlefield Command Control Centres, one of these aircraft, *62-1815*, being destroyed on the ground during a Viet Cong rocket attack on Da Nang on July 15 1967, an attack which also claimed a C-130A, *55-0009*, of the 41st TAS, 374th TAW. Accidents accounted for seven other C-130s in 1967, one of them, a C-130B, being blown to pieces when its cargo of ammunition exploded on the ground at Bao Loc AB on April 16.

New Tasks
The increasing tempo of the air war posed a growing problem of rescuing downed airmen, with raids by B-52 heavy bombers and all manner of other USAF and US Navy aircraft reaching to the far north of North Vietnam, and with powerful fighter and SAM defences taking an increasing toll of the attackers. More often than not those who came down in the Gulf of Tonkin were rescued by helicopters from the American carriers using conventional search and rescue techniques. The

same applied to those who fell in the relative safety of South Vietnam, but experience showed the importance of attempting rescue of American airmen who fell in hostile territory and who could expect little in the way of humane treatment by the North Vietnamese.

As previously recorded, the only C-130H version adopted by the USAF when it first entered production at Marietta in the mid-1960s was the HC-130H, ordered for the Air Rescue Service. Early in 1966 the 3d Aerospace Rescue and Recovery Group (ARRG) set up headquarters at Tan Son Nhut AB, its 38th Squadron bringing 12 HC-130Hs with it. The following year the 39th ARRS received a similar number of HC-130Ps which were capable of refuelling HH-3 and HH-53 helicopters, the latter often being required to fly long-endurance missions on rescue or Igloo White monitoring work. Two of the HC-130Ps, *66-0214* and *66-0218*, were destroyed by explosive satchel charges planted in a Viet Cong attack on Tuy Hoa on July 29 1968. Equipped with the Fulton recovery gear the HC-130s effected a number of outstanding rescues over both land and water on occasions when the use of helicopters was impractical.

Fairly well-known, yet nonetheless dramatic photo of an AC-130A Spectre gunship firing its 40 mm Bofors guns (Lockheed-Georgia, Neg No RM 3563).

C-130Es of the 317th Tactical Airlift Wing on the ramp at Pope AFB, North Carolina. Fort Bragg and Smoke Bomb Hill, head-quarters of the 7th Special Forces Group, are just beyond (Lieutenant-Colonel Walt Evans, USAF, Neg No 25/44).

The arrival in Vietnam of the AC-47 gunships, already referred to in Chapter 2, was followed by AC-119s and, early in 1967, the first AC-130A Spectre gunship. Armed with four 7.62-mm Miniguns, and later with four 20-mm cannon or two 40-mm Bofors, the first aircraft were evaluated under operational conditions by the 14th SOW's 16th SOS at Nha Trang AB early in 1967, and the aircraft entered full service later the same year; the 16th SOS being transferred to the 8th Tactical Fighter Wing ('The Wolf Pack'), at Ubon RTAFB, Thailand. The aircraft were widely employed, despite their relatively small numbers (16 AC-130As and ten AC-130Es were delivered to the war zone), and made frequent attack sorties along the Ho Chi Minh trail, often being launched as the result of Igloo White signals; however their value at night, when they were most used, was limited until fitted with low-light television sensors in 1968.

Gunship casualties were fairly heavy, the first air-craft, *54-1629*, being badly damaged by ground fire over Laos and written off after crash landing at Ubon on May 24 1969. Another, *54-1625*, was shot down over the Ho Chi Minh trail on April 21 1970, but in 1972 four were lost, *55-0044* shot down by an SA-2 south-east of Tchepone in Laos on March 28, *69-6571* (an AC-130E) near An Loc on March 30, *55-0043* by an SA-7 south-west of Hue on June 18 and *56-0490* at An Loc on December 21.

Brief mention above of the bombing campaigns by the B-52 heavy bombers prompts reference to another form of bombing undertaken by C-130s in Vietnam, although little detailed information has been made available as to the unit involved, or the occasions on which it occurred. Indeed the largest bomb explosions in the war were caused, not by B-52s but by Hercules! Such was the density of jungle in parts of Vietnam and Laos that, when required for the landing of helicopters, large spaces were cleared of trees and other obstacles by the use of huge charges of explosives. Up to 15,000 pounds of explosives were packed on to a pallet, together with parachutes, and loaded in a C-130 which would simply discharge it along the rear loading ramp

Rescue Hercules at Elmendorf AFB, Alaska, during the latter stages of the War. **Top** *HC-130H, 69-5824, of the 71st ARRS without Fulton gear.* **Bottom** *HC-130H, 64-14865 (C/N 4098), complete with Fulton, of the 303d ARRS* (Lieutenant-Colonel Walt Evans, USAF, Neg Nos 25/76 and 25/61).

at medium altitude over the required spot. An extended detonator or barostatic fuse would ensure that the explosion occurred well above the ground surface, thereby ensuring maximum blast effect without cratering.

One other job was undertaken by Hercules in Vietnam, that of weather reconnaissance. A small number of WC-130Bs was located at Ubon RTAFB from 1967 onwards with Overseas Location Alpha of the 1st Weather Group, whose operational element was based at Tan Son Nhut AB. A total of four aircraft was deployed during the war, their crews providing weather data required for forecasting prior to deep penetration air operations.

*   *   *

The heaviest losses among Hercules in Vietnam occurred during 1968, a total of 16 aircraft being destroyed, including three C-130As, six C-130Bs, a KC-130F tanker of VMGR-152 and four C-130Es, (including a special mission aircraft which crashed at Cam Ranh Bay on March 3 following an electrical fire in the air) and the two HC-130Ps already mentioned. One of the C-130As, *56-0477*, was shot down on May 22 while flying a Blind Bat flare operation over Laos, while the 463d TAW lost a couple of C-130Bs at Tan Son Nhut, the first being destroyed on the ground in a rocket attack on February 17 and the other shot down as it was taking off on May 12.

1969 saw Hercules losses drop to seven, a total which included a second Blind Bat casualty over Laos on November 24 and another VMGR-152 KC-130F which collided while refuelling a pair of F-4 Phantoms. In 1970 losses dropped further to three, of which the AC-130A shot down over the Ho Chi Minh trail was the only direct combat casualty, and in the following year only a single C-130B was destroyed in a Viet Cong rocket attack at Da Nang.

In 1972, the year when four gunships were lost, a

US Army forces await boarding of 314th TAW C-130s (nearest aircraft is 62-1859), probably towards the end of the War (Lieutenant-Colonel Walt Evans, USAF).

total of 11 Hercules was lost, of which nine were destroyed in action. The only other C-130 lost by direct enemy action in Vietnam was a C-130E of the 314th TAW, destroyed by a Viet Cong rocket on the ground at Tan Son Nhut AB on April 28 1975, literally hours before the last American evacuation aircraft left the stricken country.

It was perhaps ironic that it was a C-130E which landed first at Hanoi after the truce of January 27 1973, and a C-130A that made the last evacuation flight out of Saigon on April 28 1975—carrying an astonishing com-plement of 437 people desperate to escape the clutches of the Communists.

Total losses from all causes among C-130s in the Vietnam War amounted to 66 aircraft, plus about six aircraft lost in accidents just outside the war theatre (over Taiwan for instance). To this should be added some 23 aircraft, among those previously turned over to the South Vietnamese Air Force but which were not returned to the USAF, and which were either destroyed or fell into the hands of the Communists in April 1975.

Chapter 7

Hercules the Coastie

The United States Coast Guard is a constituent part of the US Armed Forces, its tasks including search and rescue (SAR), enforcement of immigration and sea traffic laws and treaties (ELT)—this embracing the fast increasing role of illegal drug traffic interdiction—marine environmental protection (MEP, the watch for and reporting of illegal fishing and oil dumping at sea), iceberg patrol and tracking, and cargo and personnel transportation. Its aircraft are normally funded through the US Navy Appropriations, the Coast Guard District Commanders being Rear Admirals of the US Navy.

There are five Coast Guard stations at which C-130s are based: Elizabeth City, North Carolina, which also includes an engineering facility where modification

and salt corrosion control is carried out; Clearwater, Florida (St Petersburg until 1979), responsible for surveillance of the Gulf of Mexico and the Caribbean; Sacramento (McClelland AFB), California (since 1978; prior to that year the station was San Francisco), responsible for the Pacific seaboard of the United States; Kodiak, Alaska, responsible for the northern Pacific Aleutian Islands; and Barber's Point, Hawaii, responsible for the central Pacific area. The aircraft at each Coast Guard station differ in a number of minor respects according to the emphasis of work undertaken.

It was in 1957 that the choice of the Hercules to equip the Coast Guard was first made, the basis of the selection being on account of the aircraft's long-range capability at low altitude, its mission endurance (up to

One of 12 HC-130Bs, CG1344 (C/N 3594), of the US Coast Guard, variously designated R8V-1G, SC-130B and HC-130G; this aircraft served its entire life at Elizabeth City, North Carolina (Lockheed-Georgia, Neg No RL 9296-C).

The sole Coast Guard EC-130E, CG1414 (C/N 4158), used for calibration of the Loran network, being deployed to the various Coast Guard stations between 1966 and 1981 (MAP, Neg No U03833).

18 hours and more than 2,600 nautical miles) and its ability to conserve fuel and increase time-on-station by shutting down two engines. Early evaluation trials demonstrated the C-130's excellent low-speed handling qualities when required to fly 'low and slow' over target areas.

In 1958 four aircraft (C/Ns 3529, 3533, 3542 and 3548) were ordered under the designation R8V-1G (G for Guard), these aircraft receiving the Guard numbers *CG1339* to *CG1342*, and being delivered for service at Elizabeth City, Barber's Point, San Francisco and St Petersburg respectively. In due course they were redesignated SC-130Bs as being derivatives of the C-130B with T56A-7 engines. Two identical aircraft were authorised in 1960 (C/Ns 3594 and 3595), *CG1344* and *CG1345*, both going to Elizabeth City initially, all six aircraft at that time being redesignated the HC-130G.

In March and April 1962 the next three aircraft, *CG1346* to *CG1348* (C/Ns 3638, 3641 and 3650), were delivered, the first being allocated to San Francisco while the others went to Argentia in Newfoundland for work in the North Atlantic. Later CG1347 moved to

Elizabeth City and in 1979 it was equipped with side-looking radar pods on the undercarriage fairings and with sensor pods under the wings.

The last three C-130B-based aircraft (now yet again redesignated HC-130Bs) were delivered during the winter of 1962–63 as *CG1349* to *CG1351* (C/Ns 3745, 3763 and 3773). These completed the initial Coast Guard procurement, all 12 aircraft remaining in service throughout the last 20 years. It has been customary to maintain two aircraft at each station on rotation with two aircraft which have been periodically due for re-engineering, corrosion and fatigue inspection and control. As would be expected, they have had to operate in some of the most testing of all operating conditions, being based at coastal stations and flying in turbulent air at low level as well as in constant salt air. Distinctively finished in all-over white with broad red and narrow blue chevrons around the front fuselage and red panels on the vertical fin, the Coast Guard Hercules carry the American national insignia on the tail rather than the rear fuselage, as is customary on other aircraft. Internal accommodation is provided for an extra radio operator, two search

A Kodiak-based HC-130H, CG1602 (C/N 4762), seen in Britain in 1979; ordered in 1977, this aircraft had the conventional nose shape without Fulton yoke attachment (Starliner Aviation Press, Neg No CS 910).

equipment operators and between 22 and 44 passengers. The rear paratroop doors incorporate large clear vision panels for visual search.

A typical sortie pattern flown by the Coast Guard HC-130B would be to fly out 1,000 miles at 370 mph at 25,000 ft, descend to 5,000 ft, cruise for eight hours' search duty at 145 mph on two engines, restart two engines and return to base at 300 mph, leaving a 25 min fuel reserve.

A special aircraft, a Model 382-4B EC-130E, *CG1414*, (C/N 4158), was delivered for equipment installation at Elizabeth City on August 23 1966. (This new-built aircraft should not be confused with and bore no relationship to the 19 converted electronic warfare EC-130Es produced for the USAF which were undergoing conversion at about this time.) The Coast Guard EC-130E was employed to calibrate Guard LORAN (long-range navigation) equipment and has gone the rounds of the Coast Guard stations, being usually based at Elizabeth City. As shown in the accompanying photograph, it featured a styled nose panel and fin panels in high-visibility red, and carried the stars-and-bars insignia on the rear fuselage.

Soon after the first C-130Hs had been delivered (as the extended-range HC-130H) to the USAF's Aerospace Rescue and Recovery Service, the US Navy gained Appropriation authority on behalf of the Coast Guard for three of these T56A-15-powered aircraft, and *CG1452 to CG1454* were delivered during the spring of 1968 (the second of them being the 1,000th Hercules produced). Five Model 382C-27D HC-130H Hercules, *CG1500* to *CG1504*, followed in 1973–74; these completed the second ten-year procurement of Coast Guard Hercules. Unlike the USAF ARRS HC-130Hs, the Coast Guard aircraft possessed no provision for the Fulton ground-air recovery system. With a further procurement due for ratification in the late 1970s, purchase orders were divided between four Model 382C-70D HC-130Hs, *CG1600* to *CG1603*, delivered in the last three months of 1977 (for service at Kodiak, Alaska), and five Model 382C-37E HC-130H-7s, *CG1700* to *CG1704*, in 1983; two of the latter were scheduled in the production line during 1983 as Model 383Gs and two as 382Ts (being intended for other customers at the time), and it is not known at the time of writing in what form they have been delivered.

Top *The first Model 382C-37E, HC-130H-7, CG1700 (C/N 4947), to be delivered to the US Coast Guard, seen flying over the Florida Coast in 1983 (Lockheed-Georgia, Neg No RM 2683-12C).* **Above** *CG1700 over Tampa Bay, Florida, with the Saraseta-St Petersberg Sunshine Skyway bridge in the distance (Lockheed-Georgia, Neg No RM 2683-27C).*

At the hand-over ceremony of the first HC-130H-7 at Clearwater on May 31 1983 Admiral Donald C. Thompson, commanding Coast Guard Seventh District, stated that four of the latest five aircraft would be based at Clearwater, replacing 25-year-old HC-130Bs, but that they would utilise the -7 engines from the old veterans. The 1984 fiscal Appropriations are scheduled to include five further HC-130H-7s, and 11 more aircraft are planned. Indeed the Coast Guard has stated its intention to continue flying the Hercules at least until, and probably well beyond, the end of the century.

Chapter 8

Early Hercules abroad

With C-130A production for the USAF's Tactical Air Command well underway and accelerating during the mid-1950s, a number of overseas nations, whose air forces had substantial transport responsibilities, began to take an interest in the Hercules, particularly in its ability to operate from second-grade airfields. The Second World War had, after all, been over for little more than a decade and had been followed by the dis-

establishment of many bases, and the pressure to repair national economies had deprived the military in most countries of finance with which to lavish elaborate facilities on their peacetime armed forces.

At a unit cost (including spares) of something under $2 million—in those days about £800,000—the C-130A was certainly not inexpensive, yet measured by its long-range and heavy-lifting capacity a single

Australian C-130A, the first delivered, A97-205 (C/N 3205), and C-130H, also the first delivered, A97-001 (C/N 4780), both of which served with No 36 Squadron, RAAF (Lockheed-Georgia).

Hercules was, in fact, well able to accomplish what at least two of any other aircraft type then available on the world market could manage, with all the attendant savings in cost of maintenance facilities, crew training, base establishments and fuel. The United States government on the other hand had to balance the requirements of the USAF and its overseas responsibilities (the spectres of McCarthyism and the war in Korea still loomed in many minds) with the determination to maintain a substantial export trade to nations in the West. Dominating its pre-occupation overseas at that time were the tensions and problems in South-East Asia which refused to lie down or go away.

Australia

Heavily committed to the war in Korea, the Royal Australian Air Force had been dependent almost exclusively on elderly Dakotas for its transport requirements, carrying some 120,000 troops and evacuating 15,000 casualties. With its commitment to the SEATO Pact and the British Commonwealth Strategic Reserve in Malaya, the need to modernise its transport force was obvious and the contributions to maintaining stability, and supporting British anti-terrorist operations in Malaya provided the necessary stimulus to the negotiations to purchase 12 C-130As.

These Australian aircraft were located in the Marietta production line immediately after the last USAF C-130As and C-130Ds and before the 15 RC-130As, being allotted serial numbers concurrent with those of the 1957 Appropriations. Delivered to Australia in 1958, they entered service with No 36 Squadron, RAAF, replacing the old Dakotas and accompanying the new No 86 Transport Wing to its new base at Richmond, New South Wales. Target task for the Squadron was to be capable of transporting an entire combat Squadron's personnel, spares and equipment from Australia to Butterworth in Malaya within 48 hours.

So successful was the Hercules deemed to be in early Australian service that in 1964 a second Squadron, No 37 (also at Richmond), was planned to equip with the aircraft, and 12 Model 382C-2D C-130Es were delivered in 1966. These 24 Hercules provided valuable support for Australian forces committed to the war in Vietnam, delivering war materiel and mail, and evacuating casualties; they continued in service without serious mishap until 1978 when (as told in Chapter 10) a dozen C-130Hs were purchased to replace the 20-year-old C-130As which were then offered for sale on the world market by the Australian government. The C-130Es remain in service, at least two aircraft being operated on behalf of the International Red Cross for relief flights into Kampuchea during 1980; it is to be assumed that these aircraft will become due for replacement in the mid-1980s.

At the time of writing only two of the old C-130As have as yet been sold, one (and possibly both) purchased by the French *Securité Civile* for transport work in Chad; the first aircraft (ex-*A97-208*, C/N 3208) is registered *TT-PAA*.

Serving with No 37 Squadron, RAAF, this Model 382C-2D C-130E, A97-180 (C/N 4180), operated relief flights in Kampuchea for the Red Cross in mid-1980 (Marshall of Cambridge (Engineering) Ltd, Neg No 54/9229).

Indonesia

While Australia remained the only overseas purchaser of new-built C-130As, Indonesia was the first to negotiate purchase of C-130Bs, its strategic proximity to South East Asia weighing heavily in US government considerations; indeed the first aircraft was diverted from Tactical Air Command's 1958 production allocation.

It may well have been the 1958 communist-inspired rebellion in Sumatra that lent urgency to the delivery of ten C-130Bs during 1958–59, and these entered service with the *Angkatan Udara Republik Indonesia*'s No 31 Squadron at Halim, Jakarta, in Java. Two of them were subsequently lost, one being missing from a flight over the Malayan west coast in September 1964 and the other crashing in Malaysia in September the following year. Another aircraft was cannibalised for spares and these three were replaced by three ex-USAF C-130Bs in 1975. The last two aircraft of the original new-build batch were subsequently converted into air refuelling tankers (KC-130Bs), the only two such adaptations of the C-130B to be produced.

Canada

Sharing many of the warning and defence responsibilities of the North American continent with the United States, as well as being a full member of NATO, Canada has for many years had to sustain a substantial air transport force and in the mid-1950s the Royal Canadian Air Force operated close on 3,000 air-

craft, its Air Transport Command possessing a heterogeneous collection of such aircraft as the Fairchild C-119F, Bristol Type 170, Canadair DC-4M North Star, de Havilland DHC-3 Otter, de Havilland Comet 1A and, inevitably, the C-47 Dakota. None of these could be classified as heavy-lift aircraft, none could transport worthwhile freight loads to Canadian forces across the Atlantic and all required fairly sophisticated base operating facilities.

An initial order for four C-130Bs was placed in 1959, these aircraft being intended to serve alongside the C-119F/Gs of No 435 Squadron, RCAF, at Edmonton, providing a heavy-lift capability. Their value was quickly confirmed and a further order for 20 C-130Es was placed for delivery in 1964–65, it being intended to resell the original C-130Bs back to Lockheed-Georgia when the new aircraft were established in service. Unfortunately however one of these crashlanded wheels-up in Saskatchewan after the forward cargo door opened in flight, striking the port inner propeller which threw it over the fuselage. En route it severed the tail control cables before striking both the starboard propellers. The other three C-130Bs arrived back at Marietta in 1967 and were sold to Colombia two years later (see below).

The C-130Es (Model 382-15Bs) were delivered in 1964–65, the majority equipping No 437 Squadron and some later being passed on to the Air Navigation School at Winnipeg; most are currently serving with the Canadian Armed Forces transport squadrons. At least two have been lost, one being written off at

Second Indonesian C-130B, T-1302 (C/N 3578), to be delivered; it served with No 31 Squadron, Angkatan Udara Republik Indonesia (Lockheed-Georgia, Neg No RF 6518-3).

Background photograph *A C-130E, 10320 (C/N 4096), of the Royal Canadian Air Force (Lockheed-Georgia).*

Inset *Canadian troops disembarking in the snow from a C-130B, 10304 (C/N 3590); this was the aeroplane which came to grief spectacularly when its forward cargo door opened in flight (Lockheed-Georgia, Neg No RL 7509).*

Trenton, Ontario, as long ago as April 1967, and one which crashed after stalling in a low-level turn while searching for a missing civilian helicopter in Western Quebec in October 1980. In 1968 four further C-130Es (Model 382C-7Ds) were also purchased, and all these are believed to have joined No 436 Squadron.

Iran

With no likely external military threat evident and under the authoritarian rule of Mohammad Reza Shah Pahlevi (himself a pilot), Iran's air force possessed no long-term policy to replace its fleet of surplus American C-47 transports until 1960 when, in an atmosphere charged with international intrigue, the entire Middle East became more sharply aligned with the super powers, a distillation that stemmed from the growing militancy of Egypt and Israel and the inevitable closing of Arab ranks. Anxious to perpetuate political and economic ties, on account of Iran's oil supplies to the West, the American administration of the day agreed to support the modernisation of the Shah's air force, *Nirou Havai Shahanshahiye Iran*, an initial batch of four C-130Bs (C/Ns 3698 to 3701) being offset against the USAF's 1962 Appropriations under the Military Assistance Programme (MAP). These aircraft served for about four years with No 5 Air Transport Squadron at Mehrabad before being sold to neighbouring Pakistan on arrival of Iran's first C-130Es.

The Imperial Iranian Air Force was to become the largest foreign user of the C-130E, its first order for eight Model 382C-1Ds being delivered in 1965–66; four Model 382C-6Ds and five -10Ds followed in 1968, 12 of these aircraft equipping No 5 Squadron until the mid-1970s when five more were sold to Pakistan; one of the -1D aircraft had been destroyed following a lightning strike in April 1967. The last order, for 11

C-130Es, was delivered in 1971–72 and was of interest solely on account of its Lockheed Model number, 382C-17D, a designation shared with 30 subsequent C-130Hs (see Chapter 10), the only occasion on which a single Model number covered both T56A-7 and -15 Hercules supplied to a single customer. At least four of these C-130Es were lost in accidents between 1973 and 1975.

Pakistan

Pakistan's air force, since self-determination within the British Commonwealth and separation from India in 1947, has flown relatively large numbers of aircraft obtained from Britain, the United States, Communist China, Western Germany, France, Libya, the Soviet Union and Sweden, as well as a number of smaller nations. To this list was added Iran when in 1966–67 that country disposed of its four C-130Bs (see above). Pakistan itself had however already entered the Hercules market some five years earlier by acquiring two new C-130Bs in 1961 under MAP, one of which had already been written off in August 1965. The remaining five aircraft served with No 6 Squadron, PAF, at Chaklala; three of the ex-Iranian aircraft were, however, to be written off in accidents in 1969, 1970 and 1979 (the last of these also involving the destruction of another ex-Iranian Hercules, delivered later, in a ground collision). Four more new C-130Bs were delivered in about 1963–64, also under MAP, and all served with No 6 Squadron. Five further ex-Iranian aircraft, all C-130Es, were acquired in 1975, and to the surviving fleet of ten military Hercules should be added two commercial L-100s (see Chapter 11), which were purchased by the Pakistan government in 1966 for Pakistani International Airlines but have also been periodically flown by the PAF.

Third C-130B (C/N 3700) supplied to the Imperial Iranian Air Force under the Mutual Assistance Programme; it flew with the IIAF's No 5 Air Transport Squadron before being sold to Pakistan where it was written off in 1969 (Lockheed-Georgia, Neg No RH 2275-2).

Top *C-130B, 23491 (C/N 3701), of the Pakistan Air Force wearing military insignia only* (W.F. Wilson, MCE, dated June 6 1974).
Above *L-100, 64144 (C/N 4144), of the Pakistan Air Force also carrying the civil registration* AP-AUT; *see also Chapter 11* (W.F. Wilson, MCE, dated February 13 1974).

Saudi Arabia

Another nation of the Middle East whose alliance and favours are constantly nurtured by successive American administrations is the Kingdom of Saudi Arabia, one of the richest oil-producing areas in the world. The supposed alienation of British influence in the Middle East, following its decline in the 1950s, resulted in greater dependence on arms supplies from the United States and in 1964 was delivered the first of many Hercules to be purchased over the next 20 years.

In all, 11 C-130Es were acquired for the Royal Saudi Air Force, the first four Model 382-15Bs being delivered for service with No 4 Squadron, RSAF, in 1964 and 1965. One of these was lost in a New Year's Day crash at Le Bourget in 1969 but the others continued giving excellent service for 15 years until, on September 14 1980, another was destroyed following an engine fire during take-off at Medina in Saudi Arabia and the pilot feathered the wrong propeller. A single Model 382C-3D was delivered in 1967, followed by a final order for six C-130Es which entered RSAF service in 1969–70, all of which joined a second Squadron, No 16 at Jeddah. Later, with the arrival of C-130Hs and KC-130Hs, the RSAF's transport force was re-organised somewhat, No 16 Squadron equipping largely with the tankers, and the transports being taken over by No 4.

South Africa

Air Transport Command of the South African Air Force continues to fly seven C-130B (Model 382-11B) Hercules, originally ordered in 1962 and delivered the following year. These aircraft have completed an enormous amount of flying in the past 20 years, being seen during frequent visits to Europe in support of aircraft of the SAAF purchased mainly from manufacturers in Britain and France. Such are the manufacturing facilities available in South Africa that the Hercules themselves have been little affected by the 1977 United Nations arms embargo on sales to South Africa which has significantly reduced the supply of spares from Lockheed, although it is known that the South Africans are particularly adept at international shopping. However, it is not known to what extent the aircraft have been affected by limitations imposed by the lack of fatigue and corrosion control — a service normally afforded to other overseas Hercules operators.

The C-130Bs have served continuously on No 28 Squadron, SAAF, at Waterkloof.

Turkey

The *Turk Hava Kuvvetleri* (Turkish Air Force) was the next customer for the C-130E, eight aircraft being delivered under MAP provisions between 1964 and 1974 for service with Air Transport Command at Erkilet. Apart from the loss of one aircraft in 1968 this small fleet has been fully employed on numerous air transportation duties, ranging from support of the 6th Allied Tactical Air Force of NATO Allied Air Forces Southern Europe and support of the Turkish invasion forces in Cyprus during 1974, to relief operations in the wake of natural disasters—of which earthquakes are the most frequent phenomena.

Indeed deliveries of Hercules were being made at the time the United States announced an arms sale embargo on Turkey following the invasion of Cyprus and it has never been stated publicly whether this embargo prematurely halted continuing deliveries of C-130s.

Sweden

The acquisition of C-130s by Sweden started with the lease—followed by its purchase—of a single C-130E (a Model 382-8B, C/N 4039) from Lockheed at short notice in 1965, the aeroplane being diverted from the USAF's 1964 Appropriation production for Tactical Air Command. Allocated to the *Flygvapnet's Flygflottilj 7* at Såtenäs, this aircraft was also commercially registered *SE-XBT* for use by the Swedish Red Cross in 1968.

Both this and a second C-130E (C/N 4332), which was delivered to F 7 at Såtenäs in May 1969, were flown in natural metal finish until camouflaged in 1974. Much later, in 1982, both were re-engineered to bring them up to full C-130H level so as to standardise operation and maintenance with six C-130Hs purchased by Sweden between 1975 and 1981 (see Chapter 10).

Lockheed Model 282-11B C-130B, 403 (C/N 3750), of the South African Air Force's No 28 Squadron, which was delivered in 1963 (MAP, Neg No 98/132).

Top *Delivery view of Turkish C-130E (C/N 4011), Hercules which served with No 221 Squadron of the* Turk Hava Kuvvetleri *at Erkilet* (Lockheed-Georgia, Neg No RK 8757-1).

Above and below *First Swedish Hercules was this C-130E (C/N 4039) which was leased by Lockheed to the* Flygvapnet *in September 1965 and served with F7. It was later sold to Sweden and registered* SE-XBT *for use with the Swedish Red Cross (upper photo) in 1968. It was camouflaged in 1975 and carried the numeral 841 on the tail, as shown below in September 1981; in 1982 it was modified to become a C-130H* (Lieutenant-Colonel Lars Olausson, FV).

Top *Flying view of Brazilian C-130E, 2455 (C/N 4202)* (Lockheed-Georgia). **Above** *2457 (C/N 4290), a Brazilian C-130E, with the familiar 'arrow' marking omitted from the tail* (MAP, Neg No 100/3).

Brazil

The *Fôrça Aérea Brazileira* operated a total of 11 C-130Es. The first three (Model 382-16Bs) were delivered for transport duties with *1° Esquadrão, 1° Grupo*, at Galeao in 1966, but one of these was written off before the end of that year and another in 1969. Two more C-130Es arrived in 1967 together with a replacement for the first aircraft lost and two in August 1969.

In November that year, following a trial installation carried out by Lockheed, Brazil purchased three C-130Es equipped for maritime reconnaissance and search-rescue duties, each of the rear parachute doors being interchangeable with three transparent panels. These aircraft served with *6° Grupo de Aviacão* at Recife, often but incorrectly being referred to as RC-130Es—for they carried no fixed camera reconnaissance equipment.

Argentina

Last overseas purchaser of new-built C-130Es was Argentina, that country purchasing three consecutive aircraft on the production line (Model 382C-12Ds, C/Ns 4308 to 4310) for delivery late in 1969.

Military operations by the *Fuerza Aérea Argentina* to combat depredations by communist-inspired guerilla forces in the north-west region of the country were a constant responsibility and these operations dominated much of the military activity in the early 1970s, the Hercules being used for transport and support of the ground forces. One of the C-130s was destroyed in the course of these operations on August 28 1975 when guerillas detonated a bomb beside the runway at Tucumán just as it was taking off. The third of the C-130Es to be delivered, serving with the 1 *Brigada Aerea*, was to be lost during the 1982 Falkland Islands campaign when Argentine aircraft successfully operated an air bridge between the mainland and Port Stanley. On June 1 that year the Hercules (*TC-63*) was intercepted by a British Sea Harrier flown by Commander Nigel Ward AFC RN and shot down by a Sidewinder missile; among the seven occupants killed were Vicecomodoro Meisner and two other senior officers.

Colombia

Following the re-sale by Canada of her three surviving C-130Bs back to Lockheed in 1967, the aircraft were offered for sale abroad and, in January 1969, were purchased by Colombia for the *Fuerza Aérea Colombiana* and were based at Techa. One, however, crashed the following August and another was written off in July 1978.

Vietnam (Saigon and Hanoi governments)

The increasing involvement of American forces in the war of Vietnam brought about the deployment of large numbers of USAF Hercules in the war zone, including C-130As and their derivatives. In the early stages of the war virtually all transportation of Saigon and American forces by fixed-wing aircraft was undertaken by US aircraft but at the end of 1972, with the formulation of plans to achieve self-sufficiency within the South Vietnamese Air Force, large numbers of American aircraft, including Hercules, were handed over to the Saigon government. A total of 30 C-130As (including a single C-130A-II) was handed over in November 1972,

followed by three more in August 1973.

With no evidence of any willingness by the communists to accommodate a compromise solution to the war, a massive evacuation of large numbers of South Vietnamese troops and civilians to neighbouring states was started in 1973, involving all manner of available aircraft ranging from Hercules to helicopters. In the last flight out of Saigon one Hercules took off with no fewer than 437 refugees on board!

By April 1975 the possibility of continuing any sort of organised resistance to the forces of the North had disappeared and the South Vietnamese Air Force ceased to exist, so as many of the C-130s as were immediately serviceable (19 in all, including the C-130A-II) were handed back to the USAF. The other 14 aircraft, of which some may have been destroyed already, fell into the hands of the forces of the Hanoi government. Contrary to suggestions elsewhere, no ex-USAF AC-130A gunships passed into communist hands, although it is believed that some of the Hercules which were subsequently flown by the North Vietnamese Air Force (sic) were employed as bombers in raids on targets in Kampuchea during the invasion late in 1978. They were also used to fly troop reinforcements to the north when, in February 1979, the Chinese invaded North Vietnam. Any aircraft that survived the campaigns of 1978–79 were probably kept airworthy for some time by use of the large quantity of spares left behind by American forces in Vietnam (as well as cannibalisation of damaged and crashed aircraft), but it is thought that few, if any Hercules survive in a flyable condition today.

One of the ex-USAF C-130As, 55-0045 (C/N 3072), transferred to the South Vietnam Air Force in November 1972, seen at Seletar, Singapore, on February 7 1974; it was not, however, one of those Hercules recovered by the USAF a year later (W.F. Wilson, MCE).

Ex-USAF C-130B supplied to Jordan as 140 (C/N 3612), seen at Lyneham, England, on June 21 1973 (W.F. Wilson, MCE).

Jordan

With the start of deliveries of C-130Hs to USAF airlift squadrons beginning in 1972, increasing numbers of C-130Bs and Es were being declared surplus to American requirements (although this was soon to be seen as premature). As always, a number of favoured overseas governments were seeking to acquire military equipment from the United States as a price of political alignment and the Hashemite Kingdom of Jordan obtained two C-130Bs (C/Ns 3610 and 3612) in 1973 and two more (3611 and 3620) in 1976. They were based at King Abdullah Air Base, Amman, during the period of their service, but two were sold in 1977 to the Republic of Singapore (see below).

Israel

Faced with hostile states to the north, east and southwest of her territories, Israel had always had to cope with pressing problems of troop and materiel movement at short notice between likely war zones, a task undertaken for many years by such venerable aeroplanes as the C-47 and Nord Noratlas, as well as a large force of helicopters. Two new C-130Hs had been purchased in 1971 (see Chapter 10), but during the vicious Yom Kippur War of October 1973, when the Israeli Air Force (*Heyl Ha'Avir*) faced the reality of heavy fighting in the north and south simultaneously, impassioned pleas to America for assistance brought forth the immediate supply of 12 C-130Es, all aircraft recently

disposed of by the 313th, 316th and 516th Tactical Airlift Wings of the USAF.

Employed for purely military purposes in the aftermath of the 1973 war, the Hercules were soon given dual military/commercial registration to obviate any political difficulties in moving aircraft abroad and it became customary to remove the national markings from the C-130s when flown to Athens for servicing purposes in view of the international targeting of Israeli interests by members of the Palestine Liberation Organisation and other hostile factions.

Singapore

Following the eventual British withdrawal from Singapore in March 1976 (the RAF's No 48 Squadron with Hercules had returned home in August 1971), the Republic of Singapore Air Force undertook a contribution to the tri-national Integrated Air Defence System of the Malaysian peninsula and late in 1977 set about acquiring a small fleet of transport aircraft; the heavy-lift element of this comprised two ex-USAF C-130Bs (C/Ns 3519 and 3557) and two from Jordan (3611 and 3620), these being delivered in October that year to form part of No 121 Squadron, RSAF. An ex-US Marine Corps KC-130F (C/N 3573) was for sometime to be seen at Seletar in a much-cannibalised state and this aircraft may have been acquired to provide spares for the C-130Bs.

Chapter 9

Britain and the Hercules

By a short head Britain comes second among the nations after the United States in the field of major users of the Hercules, with a total of 66 C-130Ks delivered between December 1966 and May 1968 (ahead of Iran which received 64). However, as will become apparent, Britain's involvement in the Hercules saga reaches considerably further than simply as a military customer.

The Royal Air Force

Experience in recent decades has suggested that the future planning by the operational requirements authorities both in the British Air Ministry (sic) and more recently in the Ministry of Defence has been constantly characterised by shortsightedness, if not incompetance. This lack of efficiency has been compounded on the one hand by fundamentally conflicting political dogmas reflected by the two government ideologies—the one paying lip service to priority of national defence and the other, if not blind to it, deft at producing excuses to avoid paying for it—and on the other by the RAF's outmoded system of staff rotation wherein a precarious and constantly fluctuating tenure of office has resulted in a lack of continuity of ideas, downright reversal of policies and an absence of the 'fire in the belly' approach to vital needs.

The problem facing Britain's Royal Air Force for much of the time since the Second World War has been that of acquiring aircraft which, on account of conflicting world-wide operational requirements, have for reasons of financial strictures resulted in supposedly-justifiable mediocrity and design compromise. For something like a dozen years after the War, including, in particular, the period of the Berlin Airlift to which Britain made a considerable contribution, Royal Air Force Transport Command progressed from the use of such aircraft as the Dakota, Lancastrian, York, Valetta and Hastings (at best troop transports of very limited capacity and at worst capable of carrying nothing of much positive value to a battlefield) to a tacit acceptance that the delivery of awkward military loads to a combat area demanded specialist aircraft whose loading and unloading facilities were far more stringent

than those existing in commercial aircraft. The first heavy specialist transport to join the RAF was the Beverley, a big, robust aeroplane which gave sterling service with five squadrons at home and overseas for the 11 years between 1956 and 1967, but which, on account of aging piston engines, was slow in the air and perpetuated awkward servicing problems on the ground in an air force that was still being 'dragged screaming' into the all-jet age. The piston-engine Hastings—which had been developed in parallel with a suspect commercial airliner, the Hermes—equipped a total of 15 RAF squadrons, entered service in 1948 and soldiered on for 20 years.

It was in the early 1960s that three new but conventional RAF transports were approaching their Service debut, two of them adaptations of commercial aircraft, the Argosy and Andover, and the third a very large freight-lifter, the Belfast. All were powered by British turboprops. The Argosy, having been originally conceived for the relatively undemanding task of ferrying motor vehicles across the North Atlantic, proved too fragile for the military tasks demanded of it, while the Belfast, of which only ten examples were ordered by a Labour government, despite state ownership of the manufacturer, ran out as such a costly aeroplane that it was prematurely sold by another cost-cutting Labour administration for commercial use, albeit maintaining a military availability.

Thus in the 20-year period between 1945 and 1965 the Royal Air Force flew 19 different types of transport aircraft of which only one, the Hastings, served with more than about half a dozen squadrons for any length of time. Standardisation of equipment, spares, powerplant, training and maintenance had been impossible. And when in 1964 the British government summarily cancelled the one specialist tactical transport then being developed, the Hawker Siddeley AW 681 V/STOL aircraft, there remained no indigenous project that could conceivably replace the aging Beverley in the heavy semi-tactical transport role in the foreseeable future.

It was in 1964, at the time that the Wilson administration was terminating every imaginative

Above left *The heavy-lift Beverley gave good service in the RAF, particularly during the period of redeployment in, and eventual withdrawal from, the Middle East. No 84 Squadron, one of whose aircraft is shown here, was based at Khormaksar, Aden, from 1958 until 1967 (MAP, Neg No 99/93).*

Left *Early photo of a Hercules C 1, XV186, of No 242 OCU, showing the high gloss paint scheme, black undersurfaces, red-white-and-blue markings and RAF TRANSPORT COMMAND inscription (MAP, Neg No 99/118).*

Above *Standard Hercules C 1, XV196, with sand camouflage and black undersides, and red-and-blue markings (Starliner Aviation Press, Neg No CS 809).*

project then being pursued by the British aircraft industry, that Lockheed sales representatives were present in the United Kingdom offering such aircraft as the Orion maritime patrol aircraft and the C-130 Hercules. In opting to purchase the C-130K (sufficient to re-equip the five squadrons of Beverleys at a cost, with spares, said to be around £300 million) the Air Staff, of course with Treasury sanction, advanced the tactical airlift capacity of the Royal Air Force to a truly global capability, and it must be acknowledged that, if nowhere else in this dismal chapter of government mishandling and misunderstanding of Britain's defence needs in the mid-1960s, this represented a lone instance of circumstantial good fortune, if not indeed imaginative planning.

The version selected for supply to the Royal Air Force was the then-current C-130H with Allison T56-15 turboprops—although there was a short-lived lobby for the use of Rolls-Royce Tynes—the fairly wide divergence from standard engendered by specification

of British equipment meriting the new designation C-130K. Subcomponent manufacture would be undertaken in Britain and elsewhere, the components being shipped to Marietta for final assembly and factory flight test before the complete aircraft would be delivered by air back to Britain. Simultaneously the Ministry of Defence appointed the company Marshall of Cambridge (Engineering) Ltd as 'Designated Firm' to be responsible for the support and co-ordination of all engineering development of the RAF's C-130Ks (of which more is said below). Indeed all new C-130Ks were delivered from Marietta direct to Marshall for final preparation for RAF service.

The prototype C-130K, *XV176*, was first flown at Marietta on October 19 1966 and remained for continuing flight trials in the USA for about six months; the second aircraft however, was delivered to Marshall on December 16 and, together with the third, underwent Service trials and handling to prepare Pilots' Notes at the Aircraft and Armament Experimental

Left *An RAF Hercules C 1, XV200, of the Lyneham Transport Wing, at the Greenham Common Tattoo. This was to be the first Hercules to receive a refuelling probe* (Starliner Aviation Press, Neg No CS 812).

Below *A pristine Hercules C 3, XV305, of the Lyneham Transport Wing. At the time of writing the Lyneham squadrons carried no individual unit markings, the aircraft being pooled* (MAP, Neg No 99/268).

Below right *A pair of RAF Hercules, XV189 and XV217 (C/Nos 4207 and 4244), undergoing the -30 stretch for conversion to C Mark 3s at Marshall of Cambridge (Engineering) Ltd. Thirty of the RAF aircraft were scheduled for conversion* (Marshall of Cambridge, Neg No 54/9357).

Establishment (A&AEE), Boscombe Down, early in 1967.

In the event the Hercules C Mark 1, as it was officially designated in the RAF, did not replace the Beverley exactly as planned, it being found necessary to remove the latter fairly abruptly from service during 1968 before deliveries of the Hercules had been completed. The first squadron to re-equip was No 36 which gave up Hastings at Colerne and moved to Lyneham in August 1967 to become the first component of what was to emerge as the 'Lyneham Wing', fully equipped with Hercules. In the meantime a special Hercules Operational Conversion Unit, No 242, had taken

delivery of half a dozen aircraft and was working to produce pilots and crews for the Squadrons. Second of these, also an ex-Hastings unit, was No 48 Squadron whose new aircraft were flown out to its base at Changi, Singapore, in October 1967. By coincidence these two Squadrons were destined to relinquish their Hercules much sooner than the other RAF units, the former being disbanded in November 1975 and the latter only two months later, having returned home in 1971.

In 1968 three further Squadrons converted to Hercules. In January the veteran transport Squadron, No 24, took delivery of its new aircraft, and the following month joined No 36 at Lyneham. Also in February No

47 Squadron (an ex-Beverley unit) became the first component of a new Hercules Wing at Fairford in Gloucestershire, being joined by No 30 (also ex-Beverley) in June. The decision in 1970 to concentrate all Hercules in a single Wing at Lyneham was taken in order to assemble on one station all equipment, spares, on-base servicing and air terminal facilities as well as to co-ordinate specialist flying training and achieve a central pooling of aircraft among the Squadrons.

Thereafter frequent excercises were flown in conjunction with the Army in the United Kingdom, Norway and Germany, and considerable use of the Hercules was made in the redeployment of other RAF squadrons between overseas bases, the big aircraft being ideal for the movement of bulky spares and servicing equipment. Also in 1970 a sixth Squadron, No 70 at Akrotiri, Cyprus, started receiving Hercules in November, although it also continued to fly Argosys for a further 15 months. In January 1975 this Squadron returned to England for the first time in 55 years—having been based in the Middle East and Mediterranean continuously since 1920. Today it is part of the Lyneham Wing, trained specifically in the tactical supply role.

During the past 15 years RAF Hercules of the Lyneham Wing have also been called on to render assistance overseas, delivering food, clothing, medical aid and other vital loads to drought, flood, earthquake and famine afflicted areas of Europe, Asia and Africa, work that has often involved long flights to and operation from the most primitive of landing grounds—usually at very short notice.

Bearing in mind the very demanding nature of these operations the RAF's Hercules fleet has enjoyed an excellent safety record, one aircraft being lost at Fairford in 1969, one at Melovia, Italy, one at Tromsø, Norway, in 1971 and one at Colerne in 1973. Several others have suffered lesser accidents, but all have been repaired and returned to service.

Marshall of Cambridge (Engineering) Ltd

The selection of Marshall of Cambridge (Engineering) Ltd (MCE) as Designated Firm in preference to a major aircraft manufacturer to sustain the RAF Hercules fleet may appear strange on the face of it, especially as the appointment was made so soon after the swingeing cancellations forced on the British aircraft industry in 1964–65.

It was, however, recognised that by being privately-owned and wholly independent of the mainstream manufacturing industry a firm such as Marshall, with its long experience in the field of in-service aircraft support, established user-liaison organisation and trouble-shooting administration exactly suited it to the demands of a transport fleet likely to be deployed world-wide at short notice. For MCE is an old-established company that has been in existence since 1909 and entered the field of aviation in 1929. Since then it has engaged in tasks as multifarious as wartime

pilot training, repair and modification of countless RAF and other aircraft, subcontracted design, development and manufacture of numerous components of modern aircraft. For example, in recent years the company has undertaken major component design and production for such aircraft as Concorde, HS 146 and Airbus, with full CAA, FAA and MoD approval. Its manufacturing, finishing, fitting out, structural test, research, flight and design facilities are comparable with those of many a major aircraft manufacturer. Moreover, the Company wholly owns the airfield and plant facilities at Cambridge, even to the extent of providing its own fuel reserves for the stand-by power so as to remain independent of national utilities for periods of up to three months at a time. Its industrial relations have always been second to none, a situation that has been well reflected in the continuity of professional and manufacturing employment.

Apart from the initial preparation of all C-130K aircraft on arrival in Britain, prior to their delivery to the RAF from 1967 onwards, the first major task that

The manufacture of all C-130 fuselage centre sections is sub-contracted to Scottish Aviation, Ayrshire (via Starliner Aviation Press).

The first conversion of an RAF Hercules to C Mk 3 was undertaken by Lockheed-Georgia on this aircraft, XV223 (C/N 4253). Subsequent conversions were carried out by Marshall of Cambridge from 1980 onwards (Lockheed-Georgia, Neg No RL 6441-2C).

confronted MCE cropped up in 1969 when it was discovered that, following the use of contaminated fuel, a fairly large number of RAF aircraft had suffered corrosion of their integral wing tanks, caused by the chemical action of a fungus (*cladisporium resinae*) on the wing planks. This necessitated the withdrawal of 11 aircraft from service, each requiring either complete or partial replacement of these huge (48-ft long) components by newly-manufactured items which had to be shipped from Marietta to Cambridge.

Following normal manufacturing practice, each aircraft which emerged from Lockheed's manufacturing plant incorporates the latest modifications aimed at extending the fatigue life of the aircraft, according to the latest research information. The aircraft destined for the RAF included all such modifications produced up to 1966, and were officially termed C-130H–130-LG when located in the production line. However, as illustrated elsewhere, individual customer utilisation and tasking programmes impose widely differing fatigue characteristics which are not simply a function of flying hours, particularly in the case of freight-carrying aircraft operating from unpaved surfaces. In 1968 Lockheed introduced a redesigned wing centre-section for the USAF's C-130A, E and HC-130H aircraft to ensure a substantially enhanced fatigue life; at the same time changes in materials gave improved resistance to corrosion. In order to discover whether the nature of RAF employment of the Hercules justified adoption of the new wing section, a standard

RAF wing specimen was subjected to a lengthy structural test programme and when, in January 1975, a major failure of this specimen occurred it was decided to modify every Hercules with the new centre-section—an undertaking that was eventually completed by MCE in 1979. Yet another life-extension programme, this time involving considerable modification to the outer wing structure, wing joints and engine truss mounts was initiated in 1972 and is due for completion in 1985.

In 1978, following the successful development of the commercial -20 and -30 fuselage extensions by Lockheed (see Chapter 11), the British Ministry of Defence opted to introduce the larger fuselage 'plugs' in 30 of its Hercules C Mk 1s, thereby increasing the available cabin volume by 37 per cent. Accordingly an RAF aircraft, *XV223*, (C/N 4255), was flown back to Marietta late in 1979 to undergo prototype conversion, and was back in the United Kingdom with 'B' Flight at the A&AEE in January 1980 undergoing Service trials as the first Hercules C Mark 3. Thereafter newly-manufactured fuselage 'plugs' were shipped to MCE for insertion into RAF aircraft as and when they became due for routine engineering work. By the end of 1983 only one or two aircraft remained to complete modification.

As well as these undertakings Marshall has, since 1976, carried out all major servicing of the 62 remaining RAF Hercules, each on a three-year cycle, and between 1976 and 1979 all aircraft underwent an anti-

corrosion programme at Cambridge, necessitating complete paint strip, corrosion control, protection and repaint; and a repeat of this process will again be scheduled before 1986.

The Hercules W Mark 2

Relatively little experimental work has been undertaken by British Establishments on the Hercules, although one or two have been deployed at the A&AEE, Boscombe Down. One aircraft was, however, flown with sensing antennae on the fin and rear

fuselage (believed to be for radar warning receivers, RWR) in 1980–81.

Another aircraft, *XV208*, previously of No 48 Squadron, was taken out of RAF service in 1972 and delivered to MCE for extensive modification as the Hercules W Mark 2 for weather reconnaissance and research by the Royal Aircraft Establishment's Meterological Research Flight at Farnborough. The most prominent external features of this modification included the substitution of the nose radome by a huge instrumentation boom and relocation of the weather

radar in a pod located above the cockpit. It was first flown in this guise on March 31 1973.

Hercules in the Falkland Islands campaign

At the beginning of April 1982 Great Britain was faced with assembling and sailing a large naval task force (Task Force 317) to repossess the Falkland Islands which had just been seized illegally by Argentina. A major commitment undertaken by the RAF was the establishment of an air supply route from Britain to Wideawake airfield on the island of Ascension, and subsequently to provide an air bridge to the Falkland Islands, a distance of some 3,400 miles further south. The route south from Lyneham to Wideawake was already familiar to many of the RAF Hercules pilots who had previously flown training flights to the island, refuelling at Dakar in West Africa (and Gibraltar on southbound flights owing to prevailing headwinds).

At the time the campaign (Operation 'Corporate') was mounted, the RAF's home-based transport force, the Lyneham Transport Wing, comprised a total of 50 Hercules, distributed between Nos 24, 30, 47 and 70 Squadrons; of these aircraft, 14 were the lengthened C Mark 3 version and the remainder standard C Mark 1s. Nos 24 and 30 Squadrons were not trained for air dropping, thus being assigned the task of carrying stores to Ascension, leaving Nos 47 and 70 to perform the tactical supply operations in the South Atlantic.

On April 3 the first Hercules set out for Ascension carrying a six-man team from the UK Mobile Air Movements Squadron (UK MAMS) whose job it was to set up an airhead to off-load subsequent Hercules arriving from England. To begin with it was anticipated that about a dozen aircraft would be landing, but it transpired that no fewer than 163 flights were made in the first three weeks, bringing with them almost 1,500 tons of stores and equipment required by Task Force 317 when it arrived on its way south. By mid-April the average number of daily movements to Ascension had reached 20; in addition some ex-RAF Belfasts and two chartered Boeing 707s also joined the airlift, as did No 10 Squadron's VC-10 aircraft which later undertook the movement of Argentine prisoners-of-war and repatriation of casualties. It therefore became necessary to despatch further teams from the UK MAMS to Wideawake.

So long as the Hercules was required to fly the supply route to Ascension, with ground refuelling at Dakar and Gibraltar when necessary, no problems arose. From the outset, however, it was recognised that if subsequent support of Task Force 317 was to be provided as far as the Falkland Islands themselves—where landing would probably be out of the question—the range performance of Nos 47 and 70 Squadrons' Hercules would have to be considerably increased, and provision made for in-flight refuelling. As an initial expedient the Engineering Wing at Lyneham adapted and fitted a pair of auxiliary fuel tanks in the forward cabin of the Hercules (using some ex-store surplus tanks originally produced for the Argosy) thereby increasing the aircraft's fuel capacity by 1,650 Imp gal and its still-air range by about 1,000 miles. Starting on April 16, this adaptation was completed in five days. This version became known (for convenience) as the LR2. A further range extension was affected by a four-tank installation, but this restricted the payload to no more than 10,000 lb and thus was only of value when a Hercules was required to make an air drop to the task force as it approached the Falkland Islands; it was referred to as the Hercules LR4, the first being deployed to Wideawake on May 4.

It was on the afternoon of April 15 that Marshall of Cambridge was first instructed to design, develop, install and flight test an in-flight refuelling probe in the Hercules. No precedent existed (other than in a small number of special USAF EC-130E aircraft which featured underwing probes) and, despite no previous experience in air refuelling techniques, MCE started round-the-clock working; using an aircraft already at Cambridge for routine engineering, the Company completed the first installation (Mod 5308) within ten days. The aircraft, *XV200*, made its first flight thus fitted on April 28 and was delivered the following day to the A&AEE, making its first 'wet' coupling with a Victor on May 2; three days later it was delivered to Lyneham—the result of outstanding dedication and hard work that was to be a feature of so many aspects of the Falkland Islands campaign.

The probe installation consisted of a ready-made Vulcan-type probe, with Mark 8 nozzle, fitted in the upper forward fuselage and offset to starboard, the refuelling pipe leading thence along the top of the fuselage to enter the wing trailing edge fillet to connect with the vertical ground refuelling pipe; a non-return valve was included to avoid fuel spillage in the event of probe failure that might occur due to excessive side loads during air refuelling. Subsequent aircraft sent to Marshall for the probe modification were those equipped with the two internal auxiliary tanks (LR2s), and when fitted with probes came to be referred to temporarily as Hercules PLR2s.

Marshall had just finished the first probe installation in *XV200* when, on April 30, the Company was asked to introduce CMA 771 Omega navigation equipment to RAF Hercules, similar to that employed in the standard USAF C-130H. This installation (Mod 5309) involved mounting the display and control panel in the navigator's station and the small antenna on the upper rear fuselage on the port side abaft the fin. A second Hercules, *XV179*, had been delivered for the probe modification and this aircraft was also used for the first installation of Omega, being first flown for CA Release on May 12. Indeed it was the very long distances likely to be flown by air-refuelled Hercules that lent urgency for the Omega equipment and all subsequent probe-equipped Hercules were modified to include it. Also on April 30 the hard-worked Marshall company was asked to prepare a trial installation in a Hercules to incorporate a standard Flight Refuelling Ltd hose-drum unit (HDU) Mark 17B. The following day one of Lyneham's 'LR4' Hercules, *XV296*, arrived at Cambridge to undergo modification (Mod 5310). The HDU was mounted on the rear loading ramp with the auxiliary carriage and drogue deployment box on the cargo door; this allowed the Hercules to remain pressurised while not refuelling; however, to have devised a system to retain pressurisation during refuelling would have been more complex and time-consuming (such a system has been undertaken by Marshall more

Fourth of the Hercules C 1 (K) tankers to be converted by Marshall, XV192, also equipped with refuelling probe. Just visible are the added strakes under the rear fuselage (MAP, Neg No 98/370).

recently). Fuel supply to the HDU was taken from the tanker's main tanks (and not from the cabin auxiliary tanks), refuelling pressure being provided by a bleed-air turbine-driven fuel pump. To provide cooling for the HDU components two ram-air intakes and exhaust ducts were mounted in the sides of the pressure hull. Normal external tanker lights were fitted, together with their switches adjacent to the air-refuelling panel above the navigator's station.

On June 8 *XV296* successfully deployed its drogue, and three days later was flown to the A&AEE where it made a dry coupling with a Harrier. However, some buffeting was experienced caused by the HDU projecting from the loading ramp, as well as overheating of the HDU oil cooler. *XV296* was therefore returned to Cambridge where, following wooltufting of the rear fuselage, strakes were attached to the loading ramp, and a third ram-air intake added to provide additional cooling. On June 21 a successful 'wet' coupling with a Buccaneer was carried out, and the next day *XV296* returned to Boscombe Down where 'prods' by Hercules, Nimrod, Sea Harrier and Phantom aircraft were made successfully at various weights and altitudes. *XV296* was delivered to Lyneham on July 5, with three more aircraft (*XV201, XV204* and *XV192*), termed Hercules C Mark 1(K), following on the 12th, 21st and 26th. The Company's feat of achieving design, manufacture, installation, flight testing and delivery of these four aircraft, all in the space of 87 days, was recognised by the award of the OBE to Roy O. Gates, Marshall's Executive Director, Engineering.

Returning to the progress of Operation Corporate, the arrival of the first probe-equipped Hercules at Lyneham was followed by a number of trial 'prods' with RAF Victor tankers during which a new refuelling technique was evolved. Because the Victor's minimum speed at 23,000 ft (the Hercules' best range-height with load) was 264 mph, compared with the Hercules' maximum speed at high all-up weight—the internal auxiliary tanks were not used until the return leg of a sortie—of 242 mph, a procedure was adopted by which the Victor tanker would approach the Hercules from above and astern, the latter beginning a 500 fpm descent as soon as visual contact was made. The Victor would slowly overtake, allowing the Hercules to move into the low six o'clock position to engage the drogue; the descent would continue at about 500 fpm for some 15 min at a speed of 270 mph.

The first long-range operational air-refuelled flight by a Hercules was made by Flight Lieutenant Harold Burgoyne of No 47 Squadron on May 16 with a journey to the Total Exclusion Zone (TEZ), imposed by the British around the Falkland Islands, where he air-dropped 1,000-lb of special stores and eight parachutists who, having regard to Flight Lieutenant Burgoyne's specialist training for clandestine operations, were

In-flight refuelling of one RAF Hercules from another; this view through the hose aperture clearly shows the probe of the receiving aircraft offset to starboard (D.K. McCarthy, MCE).

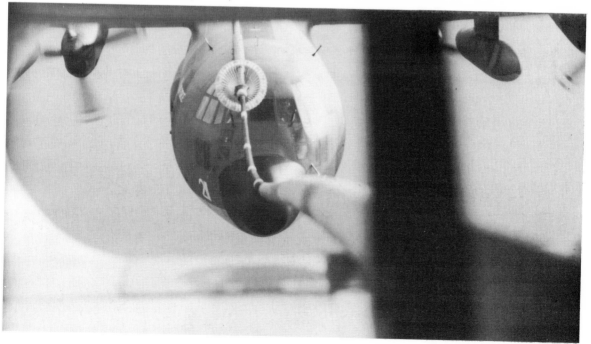

probably members of the Special Air Service. The citations accompanying the award of the Air Force Cross to this pilot and another, Squadron Leader Arthur Roberts, for these long-distance flights did not indicate the nature of any clandestine operations undertaken. Flight Lieutenant Burgoyne's first flight covered 7,247 miles in 24 h 5 min. On June 3 the Hercules recorded their 10,000th flying hour since the launching of Operation Corporate.

Long distance support flights continued to be made by Nos 47 and 70 Squadrons to Task Force 317 throughout the land battle for the Falkland Islands, and of course the supply route between England and Wideawake was as busy as ever. The UK MAMS teams at Ascension handled over 18,000 tons of freight, as well as 42,000 passengers in 14 weeks, all without a single mishap.

The first operational use of the Hercules C 1(K) tanker was made early in August, some seven weeks after the Argentine surrender at Port Stanley. Before the Islands' airfield at the capital could be made ready to receive aircraft, RAF Hercules flew frequent round trips to the Falklands, usually refuelling about four times en route and often remaining aloft for about 26 hours at a time. (The Argentine Air Force had operated their C-130s in and out of Port Stanley throughout the campaign, but during the final battles some damage and obstruction had been caused to the runway). On June 28 an RAF Hercules, flown by Flight Lieutenant Terry Locke of No 70 Squadron, established a new world duration record for the C-130 with a flight lasting 28 h 4 min.

To enable a single Hercules to reach Port Stanley after the arrival in service of the C 1(K)s it was customary to fly off the primary Hercules from Wideawake in company with a Hercules tanker, followed by two Victor tankers; the primary Hercules would be refuelled by the Victors before they returned to Ascension to be refuelled themselves; the Hercules tanker would then refuel the primary Hercules which would fly on to Port Stanley, while the tanker also returned. The Victors would then take off and rendezvous with the primary Hercules on its return flight.

When, on June 24, the first Hercules landed at Stanley it brought with it the first three members of a UK MAMS airhead team that was to handle the considerable quantity of material needed to sustain the islands' war-torn economy. The next day a Hercules flown by Flight Lieutenant Burgoyne returned the former governor of the Falkland Islands, Mr Rex Hunt, to his capital. Between August 15 and 28 the single runway at Stanley was closed for landing while it underwent repairs and extension; during this period the Hercules were forced to make the very long return flights without landing, making air drops of mail and supplies, and picking up mail using an air snatch technique devised at Brize Norton six weeks earlier. This involved trailing a grappling hook from the Hercules' lowered ramp and engaging a nylon rope, suspended between two 22 ft poles on the ground, to which the mailbag was attached.

Ever since the end of the Falkland Islands campaign a large proportion of the Hercules fleet has been deployed at Ascension, tasked with maintaining the air bridge to the South Atlantic. All four Hercules C 1(K) tankers have been assigned to the route south from Wideawake, thereby alleviating the workload of the Victor squadrons. At the time of writing work is nearing completion to equip about 30 of the C 1s (including the tankers) with refuelling probes, while almost all the remaining 30 aircraft have completed conversion to C Mark 3s. It is not currently intended to fit the latter for air refuelling (although there is no technical objection to this) and all Mark 3 Hercules

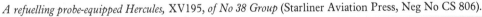

A refuelling probe-equipped Hercules, XV195, *of No 38 Group* (Starliner Aviation Press, Neg No CS 806).

The Royal Air Force Parachute Display Team, the Red Devils, spill from the ramp of an RAF Hercules C 1, XV214. *This remarkable picture was taken by the leader, free-falling ahead of the team* (via Lockheed-Georgia).

remain based at Lyneham.

Among the lessons learned in the highly successful mounting of Operation Corporate was that dependence on conveniently situated staging airfields, once strung out over the globe during the years of the Empire, was a thing of the past. The extraordinary adaptability of the RAF's Hercules (though brilliantly exploited by the engineers both at Lyneham and Cambridge) was fortuitous, but then so much that characterised the assembly and support of Task Force 317 was a matter of good fortune, and by no means the result of competent strategic planning either by successive British governments or the Ministry of Defence. Too many facets of the Falkland Islands campaign—the chance survival of two aircraft carriers, the existence of a minimum viable force of Sea Harriers, and the availability and adaptability of a fleet of heavy-lift Hercules transports—can only be ascribed to sheer coincidence and luck. The exploitation of good fortune and the final victory of arms was due solely to the professionalism of those who fought, sailed and flew—and the men and women who worked so hard to support them at home.

Authorised Service Centre

Stemming from, but entirely independent of MCE's nomination as Designated Firm for the support of Royal Air Force Hercules, Marshall was, in 1975, also appointed by Lockheed as an authorised Hercules Service Centre. As well as being an FAA-approved repair authority for the Hercules, this appointment gave MCE the authority to undertake the engineering support of any Hercules operator, and in practice has already involved the Company in the scheduled and unscheduled maintenance and repair of C-130 and L-100 aircraft belonging to about 30 overseas operators. For example, all six C-130s of the Royal Norwegian Air Force have paid three visits to Cambridge for IRAN (Inspection and Repair as Necessary) programmes; during the second the opportunity was taken to include the latest wing strengthening modifications and installation of the Brooks and Perkins Cargo Handling System. Three C-130s of the Swedish Air Force have made a total of 20 visits to MCE for corrosion control, IRAN and repainting.

In all, C-130s and L-100s from Abu Dhabi, Algeria, Angola, Belgium, Cameroon, Dubai, France, Gabon, Great Britain, Jordan, Kuwait, Morocco, Niger, Nigeria, Norway, Pakistan, Philippines, Portugal, Saudi Arabia, Sweden, Uganda, the USA, Zaïre and Zambia have made regular visits to Cambridge for routine maintenance and engineering up-dating. On other occasions foreign-operated C-130s have suffered accidents involving fairly serious damage and, rather than invoke lengthy delays with 'AOG Awaiting Spares', MCE has sent out engineering teams to patch up the aircraft adequately to allow it to be flown to Cambridge for major repair work. Such is the scope of engineering expertise at the Cambridge facility that MCE had justifiably assumed a status at least equal to that of the USAF's own C-130 facility at the Warner Robins Air Logistic Center, Georgia, a status that seems unlikely to diminish for many years to come.

Chapter 10

Hercules the cosmopolitan

As already recorded the USAF transport squadrons were not the first to receive the more powerful C-130H version of the Hercules with T56A-15 turboprops. Indeed, the first such aircraft, an HC-130H (C/N 4036) rescue and recovery aircraft equipped as an air tanker, was destined for the USAF's Aerospace Rescue and Recovery Service. It made its first flight on November 30 1964. However, following only 14 aircraft behind the first three HC-130Hs on the Marietta production line was the first of three C-130H transport aircraft for the Royal New Zealand Air Force (C/N 4052). This aeroplane was in fact completed and flown *before* the HC-130Hs, first flying on November 19. On this aircraft was performed much of the flight testing of the H-Series and therefore it was not delivered to New Zealand until March 24 1965. Not for a further nine years was the USAF's Tactical Air Command destined to receive its first C-130H transport. In the meantime 161 examples of this version were sold to

Argentina, Belgium, Chile, Great Britain (as the C-130K), Iran, Israel, Italy, Libya, New Zealand, Norway, Peru, Saudi Arabia, Spain, Turkey, Venezuela and Zaïre.

The servicing of these orders is traced in chronological sequence, according to the commencement of the first order, together with the fortunes of some of the Hercules involved.

New Zealand

As just remarked, New Zealand ordered the C-130H first, taking delivery of the first three Model 382-14Bs early in 1965 and two Model 382C-13Ds late in 1968. All served with No 40 Squadron, RNZAF, at Whenuapai, Auckland, one of them attending the Hercules anniversary gathering at Greenham Common, England, in 1979.

Typical of the tasks undertaken by No 40 Squadron was the supply of a 12-ton earth-mover to the tiny

Below left *Second C-130H,* NZ7002 *(C/N 4053, Model 382-14B), delivered to the RNZAF for service with No 40 Squadron at Whenuapai* (Starliner Aviation Press, Neg No CS 836).

Below right *Flying shot of* NZ7002 *of the RNZAF* (Starliner Aviation Press, Neg No CS 837).

Loading the bulldozer into an RNZAF C-130H for Pitcairn. Note the six massive parachutes (Lockheed-Georgia, Neg No RM 5006).

island of Pitcairn, 900 miles out in the Pacific. The islanders' existing bulldozer was approaching the end of its useful life and, following an appeal through the British government and owing to the infrequency of a shipping service, the RNZAF undertook to supply a replacement. Packed on a shock-absorbing honeycomb platform and lashed to a pallet, the new bulldozer was dragged off the Hercules' ramp by a 30-ft parachute and descended 1,100 ft under six 90-ft parachutes to the marked-out dropping zone.

The RNZAF Hercules have also made numerous supply flights to Antarctica although, not being equipped with skis (as on the US Navy's LC-130s), their contribution to the Antarctic Development Programme has been of a more limited nature.

Great Britain

See Chapter 9.

Norway

Six Model 382C-14Ds were delivered to the Royal Norwegian Air Force in June and July 1969 for service with No 335 Squadron (*Skv 335*) of the *Kongelige Norske Luftforsvaret* based at Gardermoen, replacing eight Fairchild C-119s and three Douglas C-47s. At one time the first two Hercules also bore the civil markings *LN-SUW* and *LN-SUR*, as well as their military marks. In service they carried the names *Odin, Tor, Balder, Fröy, Ty* and *Brage*, and all have been frequent visitors to NATO bases throughout Europe during the past 15 years.

Above *Norwegian C-130H* Fröy, UN-955, BW-D *(C/N 4337), of No 335 Squadron* (Starliner Aviation Press, Neg No CS 838).

Below *Seen during a routine visit to Cambridge is Norway's C-130H* Brage, UN-957 *(C/N 4339)* (Marshall of Cambridge, Neg No 54/9234).

Bottom *One of the early Libyan C-130Hs,* 112 *(C/N 4369), that were delivered before the arms embargo, seen here at RAF Lyneham on August 18 1972* (W.F. Wilson, MCE).

Libya

The Libyan government ordered a total of 16 C-130Hs (eight Model 382C-18Ds and eight Model 382C-30Ds), the first eight aircraft being delivered in 1970–71, but following the deterioration of relations between the Libyan pro-Soviet administration and the West in the early 1970s no export licence was authorised by the US State Department for the remainder and, although manufacture was completed, the last eight aircraft have been stored under embargo at Marietta ever since. The eight aircraft already serving with the Libyan Arab Republic Air Force have led a fairly active life although the embargo on spares must have created mounting problems and at least one aircraft (C/N 4401) was destroyed by fire at Entebbe, Uganda, on April 8 1979, presumably during overt support operations by the LARAF for the Amin regime in that country.

Venezuela

The original order for the *Fuerza Aérea Venezolana*, placed in 1969, was for six C-130Hs, four to be delivered in 1970 and two in 1975. These were Model 382C-20Ds and -42Ds respectively and all served with *Escuadron de Transporte 1* at Caracas. However, one of the -20Ds was lost when it crashed in bad visibility while approaching to land at Lajes in the Azores on August 27 1976 and a replacement was ordered from Lockheed. This, a C-84D, was delivered in December 1978. Unfortunately another -20D was lost the following month when it suffered loss of power during take-off from Caracas.

Below *Last of the seven C-130Hs purchased by Venezuela, this Model 382C-84D, 3134 (C/N 4801) was delivered in December 1978 to replace the aircraft that had crashed in the Azores two years previously* (Lockheed-Georgia, Neg No RL 3674-23C).

Bottom *A Venezuelan C-130H, 4224 (C/N 4556) seen at the Greenham Common Air Tattoo in 1979* (Starliner Aviation Press, Neg No CS 847).

Zaïre

After the bitter warfare that accompanied the acquisition of independence from Belgium the *Forces Aériennes Congolaises* were established to embrace the various factions that existed in the Congo and by the end of the 1960s were being strengthened by aircraft supplied largely by the United States. In 1971 an initial batch of three C-130Hs (Model 382C-21Ds) were delivered and carried the civil markings *9T-TCA, 'B* and *'D* despite being in all respects military aircraft. Two years later Zaïre (thus renamed in 1972) ordered three more, Model 382C-36Ds, *9T-TCE, 'F* and *'G* (the latter being changed later to *9T-TCC*). These aircraft, less *9T-TCD* which crashed at Kisangani on August 18 1974, were heavily engaged in the movement of troops and arms during the war of 1977 which followed the invasion of Shaba by foreign mercenaries. All the C-130Hs, including a replacement -66D delivered in May 1977, equipped No 19 Wing, *1 Groupement Aérien* of the *Force Aérien Zaïroise* based at Kinshasa.

Israel

For a dozen years Israel has maintained a sizeable fleet of Hercules aircraft, all carrying quasi-commercial markings to facilitate their movement abroad but all are in fact, on the inventory of the *Heyl Ha'Avir* (the Israeli Defence Force/Air Force, IDFAF). Starting in October 1971 the IDFAF took delivery of the first of ten C-130Hs (two Model 382C-24Ds, two -34Ds and six -52Ds) and two -53D KC-130H tankers. The final delivery was made in September 1976. A dozen ex-USAF C-130Es were also acquired during the early 1970s. Although much of the tactical transportation of personnel in the IDFAF is undertaken by helicopters, most of the heavy-lift task is performed by the fleet of C-130s, of which the tankers are employed for purely military purposes. It is also known that a small number of the aircraft double-up on electronic countermeasure duties and as airborne tactical command stations. IDFAF Hercules transports were involved in the audacious operation to secure the release of Israeli nationals being held hostage by the Amin regime at Entebbe, Uganda, an operation which involved a long night flight and a commando-style assault by troops at the distant airport as well as a return flight with the liberated hostages to Israel.

Israeli C-130s undergo periodic maintenance at Athens, for which purpose and for political expediency all national markings are removed.

Second of the C-130Hs, 9T-TCB *(C/N 4416), supplied to the* Force Aérienne Zaïroise *in 1971; signs of the removal of the USAF tail markings can still be seen* (Air and General Photos).

Above *Israeli C-130H,* 4X-FBW *(C/N 4686),* *at Greenham Common* (Starliner Aviation Press, Neg No CS 832).

Below *Last of Israel's C-130Hs to be delivered was* 4X-FBX *(C/N 4692), alias IDF/AF* 428 (Lockheed-Georgia, Neg No RL 0043).

Iran

Iran was at one time, the third-largest user of the Hercules (after the United States and Great Britain), having purchased no fewer than a total of 64 aircraft. The embargo on the supply of military equipment to the country since the late 1970s and the long-running war with Iraq has unquestionably resulted in a considerable deterioration of this fleet, most surviving aircraft presumably being maintained in an operational condition by cannibalisation of damaged aircraft. Latest estimates suggest that no more than about 24 aircraft are still airworthy.

The first C-130H was delivered to the *Nirou Havai*

Shahanshahiye Iran (Imperial Iranian Air Force, IIAF) on November 11 1971, one of 30 Model 382C-17Ds whose delivery continued until mid-1973. Two further aircraft, -37Ds, were delivered in May 1975. All were based at Shirah and Mehrabad. During the final years of political alignment with the West four of the IIAF's C-130Hs were modified for covert signal monitoring and electronic reconnaissance along the Iranian border with the Soviet Union as part of the Ibex Elint-gathering network; the electronic equipment was installed in pods carried outboard of the outer engines. Such operations were presumably discontinued when war broke out with Iraq, if not before.

Above *One of the Ibex Elint-gathering C-130Hs, 5-136 (previously 5-142, C/N 4454) of the Imperial Iranian Air Force photographed at Cambridge in November 1974 (W.F. Wilson).*

Below *TC-67 (C/N 4576), a C-130H of the* Fuerza Aerea Argentina *which was delivered in April 1975 for service at El Palomar* (Lockheed-Georgia).

Argentina

Following the purchase of three C-130Es the *Fuerza Aerea Argentina* took delivery of two Model 382C-23D C-130Hs in 1972–73, two -48Ds in 1975 and two -82D KC-130H tankers in 1979, all these aircraft being flown by the *1 Escuadron de Transporte, 2 Grupe, 1 Brigada Aerea*, at El Palomar, Buenos Aires. All were presumably employed in heavy-lift operations during the invasion of the Falkland Islands in 1982 and the subsequent air bridge flights into and out of Port Stanley; it is also reported that at least one C-130H was employed as a makeshift bomber, 1,000-lb bombs being rolled off the rear loading ramp in an attack on British ships of Task Force 317 in the South Atlantic.

Italy

The *Aeronautica Militare Italiana* (AMI) had been persevering for many years with elderly Fairchild C-119 transports when, early in 1972, it started converting to C-130Hs, a total of 14 Model 382C-22Ds being delivered over a period of about a year. These flew with the *50° Grupo, 46ᵃ Aerobrigata Trasporti Medi* at Pisa-San Guisto. Three of them were employed on firefighting duties during 1978, and two were lost in accidents; one was totally destroyed when it flew into a mountainside on March 3 1977, and on January 23 1979 another was cannibalised for spares after a ground collision when it jumped its chocks during an engine run-up.

Top right *An Argentine KC-130H, TC-70 (C/N 4816), which took part in the Greenham Common 'rally' of Hercules in 1979* (Starliner Aviation Press, Neg No CS 821). **Above right** *Close-up of the Argentine KC-130H* (Starliner Aviation Press, Neg No CS 822).
Below *Italian C-130H,* 46-09, MM61995 *(C/N 4491), of the 46ᵃ* Aerobrigata, *50° Gruppo* (MAP, Neg No 98/267).

Chile

The *Fuerza Aérea de Chile*, also a new Hercules customer, purchased two Model 382C-28D C-130Hs in 1972 and 1973, these aircraft serving alongside three Douglas DC-6As and other aircraft on *Escuadrilla No 40* of *Grupo No 10* at Santiago-Los Cerillos, the centralised base of all military transport operations.

Belgium

A dozen C-130Hs (Model 382C-25Ds) were the first Hercules purchased by the *Force Aérienne Belge (Belgische Luchtmacht)* in 1972–73, replacing Fairchild C-119Gs and equipping No 20 Squadron, No 15 Wing, at Melsbroek. They regularly participate in support operations for NATO exercises.

Above left *The second Chilean C-130H, 996 (C/N 4496), at Greenham Common in 1979 (MAP, Neg No 98/245).*

Left *Belgian C-130Hs served with No 20 Squadron, Force Aérienne Belge, at Melsbroek; the first to be delivered, CH-01 (C/N 4455), is shown here (Lockheed-Georgia, Neg No RK 2587-3).*

Above *Saudi Arabian C-130Hs carry numerals on the nose indicating Squadron and individual aircraft identity. Shown here is 1609 (C/N 4311) of No 16 Squadron, RSAF (Starliner Aviation Press, Neg No CS 840).*
Right *Close-up view of another Saudi C-130H, 1619 (C/N 4756) (Starliner Aviation Press, Neg No CS 843).*

Saudi Arabia

Continuing the substantial build-up of the *Al Quwwat Aljawwiya Assa'udiya* (Royal Saudi Air Force, RSAF), Saudi Arabia purchased four KC-130Hs (Model 382C-29Ds) in 1973. The first two were delivered in November and December that year and the others the following May, these being used to air refuel the air

force's large number of Northrop F-5 fighter-bombers and serving with No 4 Squadron, RSAF, at Jeddah.

Thereafter orders continued to flow in at Marietta, four C-130Hs (-39Ds) arriving at Jeddah for Nos 4 and 16 Squadrons before the end of 1974; ten -46s followed in 1975, of which the first, a VIP transport (VC-130H) with square windows, served with the Royal Flight of No 1 Squadron in company with a luxuriously

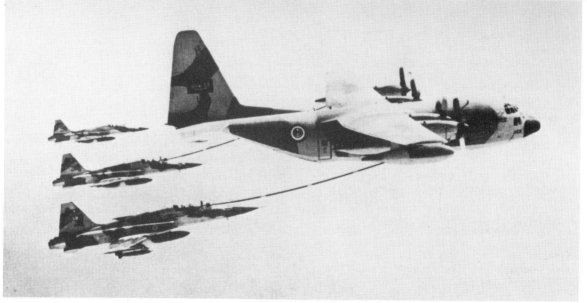

Top *Saudi Arabia was one of several overseas buyers of the KC-130H tanker, this example, 458 (C/N 4532), serving with No 4 Squadron, RSAF (Lockheed-Georgia, Neg No RK 5452-2).*

Above *A Saudi KC-130H refuelling RSAF F-5 fighter-bombers (via R. Dorr).*

Top right *KC-130H, 301-07 (C/N 4652), of Spain's EdA, in the marking of Escuadron 301 (Starliner Aviation Press, Neg No CS 844).*

Above right *C-130H, (C/N 4742), of the Royal Maroc Air Force, normally based at Kenitra (MAP, Neg No 98/492).*

furnished Boeing 707-320. Nine Model 382C-60Ds were delivered in 1977 (of which one was also converted to a VC-130H by Lockheed Aircraft Service), together with two more KC-130Hs (Model 382C-61Ds). In July 1980 two Model 382C-4Es were delivered to the RSAF modified as passenger-limousine aircraft, being flown by the airline Saudia (as *HZ-HM5* and *HZ-HM6*) on behalf of the Saudi Royal Flight and were followed the next month by a special hospital aircraft (a -93D), modified by Lockheed Air-

craft Service at Ontario, Canada, to accommodate an entire operating theatre and ward rest room. Two further -96D KC-130H tankers were delivered to Jeddah in December the same year.

The most recent Saudi purchases were a pair of Autopax aircraft (-26Es) incorporating provision for removable passenger cabin-packs and a further hospital aircraft (a -32E) delivered in March 1982 bringing the total number of C-130s of all versions delivered to Saudi Arabia to 48.

Spain

The Spanish *Ejército del Aire* (EdA) received its first C-130Hs (Model 382C-31Ds) in December 1973 and early 1974, these aircraft being initially delivered to *Escuadron 301* of the *Mando Aviacion Tactica* (Tactical Air Command) at Valenzuela-Zaragoza. In Spanish service they were designated T-10s.

Early in 1976 the EdA took delivery of three KC-130H tankers (Model 382C-55Ds) which also joined *Escuadron 301*, but in 1978 all Hercules were transferred to *Escuadron 311*, the tankers (designated TK-10s) being affiliated to the McDonnell-Douglas F-4C(S) Phantom Wing at Torrejon. Three more C-130Hs (-92Ds) and two KC-130Hs (-98Ds) were delivered in 1979 and 1980 respectively, the tanker element then being segregated to form *Escuadron 312*. One aircraft, the first aircraft delivered, crashed into a mountain on Gran Canaria while operating from Las Palmas on May 28 1980 and was destroyed.

Morocco

Reflecting the fluctuating influences in North Africa and periodic alignment with the West, the *Al Quwwat Aljawwiya Almalakiya Marakishiya* (Royal Maroc Air Force, RMAF) operates a cosmopolitan transport force which includes about 20 C-130Hs, the first of which (six Model 382C-35Ds) started delivery in May 1974 for deployment to Kenitra, replacing elderly C-119s. Like the C-130s of a number of other air forces the Moroccan aircraft carried civil registration markings to ease traffic movement between international airports. These were followed by six more C-130Hs (-67Ds) in 1977 and five -11Es in 1981. Two C-12E KC-130H tankers were also delivered in November 1981, but three further C-130Hs completed for a Moroccan order in 1982 were not delivered according to plan, two being diverted to the Algerian Air Force and one to Jordan during the summer of that year.

Several Moroccan Hercules have been lost, the first being written off in December 1976; a second aircraft suffered fairly severe damage during a landing accident at Lag Youn on December 5 1979. One of the -67Ds was shot down by Polisario forces at Guelta Zemmour in the Western Sahara in January 1981, apparently using a SAM-6 ground-to-air missile.

Canada

Canada followed earlier orders for C-130Bs and Es with the purchase of five C-130Hs (four -33Ds and a -51D), diverted from the USAF's 1973 Appropriations for Tactical Air Command and delivered between October 1974 and February 1975. Referred to in Canadian Armed Forces service as CC-130Hs, these Hercules served at CAFB Edmonton and all were still believed to be in service early in 1984.

Brazil

The *Fôrca Aérea Brasileira*, which had already acquired 11 C-130Es but had written off several, ordered a C-130H (a -45D) as a replacement, this being delivered for service with the *1° Esquadrao, 1° Grupo*, at Galeao in March 1975. Another -45D followed in November that year at about the same time as a pair of KC-130H tankers (-47Ds), which apparently joined the *Grupo de Transporte de Tropas* at Camp dos Afoncos to support the air force's F-5E fighter force.

Denmark

Only three C-130Hs have as yet been purchased for the *Kongelige Danske Flyvevaben* (Royal Danish Air Force, RDAF). All Model 382C-38Ds, these aircraft were delivered between April and July 1975 and have served with *Eskadrille 721* of the *Flyvertaktisk Kommando* (Tactical Air Command) at Værlöse, replacing C-47s and C-54s.

Abu Dhabi

Twenty years ago the purchase by a small Arab state of four multi-million-dollar aircraft would have been unthinkable, yet Abu Dhabi, one of the oil-rich Arab Emirates, has purchased four C-130Hs in the past nine years (two-40Ds being delivered early in 1975 and two -14Es in 1981) to contribute the heavy-lift element to the United Emirates Air Force, which has undertaken to assist in securing freedom of passage by international oil shipping in the Persian Gulf, as well as self-defence tasks. All the C-130Hs are normally based at Abu Dhabi.

Nigeria

Following more than a decade of internal strife, during which the Federal Nigerian Air Force came under the influence of East and West alike and flew aircraft supplied by West Germany, France, Czechoslovakia, Algeria and Egypt, Nigeria began to establish itself on a more peaceful footing at the beginning of the 1970s. Despite receiving new equipment from the Soviet Union, the country balanced its political alignment by announcing a $47 million order in 1974 placed with Lockheed for six C-130Hs with spares. These aircraft Model 382C-49Ds, were delivered between September 1975 and February 1976, serving with the Nigerian Air Force at Lagos. A further order, this time for three 'stretched' C-130H-30s (Model 382Ts), was announced in 1980 but at the time of writing the aircraft are believed to be still awaiting signature of contract prior to delivery.

Brazilian KC-130H, 2461 (C/N 4625), the first of two tankers purchased for the support of the FAB's F-5E force (via R. Dorr).

Top *Danish C-130H, 678 (C/N 4572), one of three which equipped 721 Eskadrille at Værløse* (Starliner Aviation press, Neg No CS 831).

Above *First of four C-130Hs, 1211 (C/N 4580), delivered to the Abu Dhabi Air Force between 1975 and 1981* (Lockheed-Georgia, Neg No RK 6565).

Below *Customarily based at Lagos, this Nigerian Air Force C-130H, its first Hercules, NAF910 (C/N 4619), is seen at Marshall's airfield at Cambridge* (Marshall of Cambridge, Neg No 54/9374).

Greece

Greece was another nation which might have been expected to opt for the Hercules sooner than it did but which continued to use such aeroplanes as the C-47 and Noratlas for many years. An initial order for four C-130Hs (Model 382C-54s) was delivered to the *Elliniki Aéroporia* (Hellenic Air Force) between September 1975 and June 1976 for service with *356 Mira* (Squadron) of Air Material Command, but thereafter relations with the United States became strained after Greece's withdrawal from NATO following Turkey's

invasion of Cyprus and it was not until 1977 that President Carter sanctioned the resumption of arms sales to the Hellenic Air Force. Included in a $410 million arms package was $71 million for eight further C-130Hs (-59Ds) which were to be diverted from the 1975 USAF Appropriations.

Several of these aircraft are believed to have been modified for electronic reconnaissance as part of the Ibex Elint-gathering network on NATO's southern flank in south-east Europe; other aircraft in this batch began replacing the Noratlas on *355 Mira* at Eleusis.

Left *First C-130H purchased by the Royal Hellenic Air Force, 741 (C/N 4622). These aircraft served with Nos 355 and 356 Squadrons at Eleusis* (Lockheed-Georgia, Neg No RJ 8371-3C).

Below left *The Government of Malaysia ordered a total of nine Hercules for transport and maritime patrol duties. The first to be delivered, in March 1976, was this Model 382C-57D C-130H FM2401 (C/N 4656)* (Lockheed-Georgia, Neg No RL 6736).

Above *Egyptian C-130H, SU-BAK (C/N 4797), seen in the United Kingdom* (MAP, Neg No 98/488).

Malaysia

The Government of Malaysia in 1974 ordered six C-130Hs (-57Ds) for delivery to the *Tentera Udara Diraja Malaysia* (Royal Malaysian Air Force) in 1976 at a cost, to include spares, of $47 million. Replacing Handley Page Heralds, these aircraft joined No 14 Squadron at Kuala Lumpur. They were joined in 1980 by three Model 382C-97D C-130H-MP maritime patrol Hercules which are engaged in operations over coastal waters to combat the depredations of pirates and smugglers whose activities have steadily increased in recent years.

Philippines

The Government of the Republic of the Philippines has for many years continued to receive regular military aid from the United States, acting in some respects as a leasing agent for transport aircraft, dividing their utilisation between commercial development organisations and the Philippines Air Force. In the latter the 220th Heavy Airlift Wing at Mactan Air Base is established with three squadrons, of which No 222 flies Hercules. Replacing a number of L-100s (on temporary lease from the Government), three C-130Hs were ordered in 1975, the first two, Model 382C-63Ds, being delivered in November 1976 and August 1977 respectively and a -77D in November that year.

Egypt

Following the Camp David negotiations and the establishing of acquiescent tolerance between Egypt and Israel, there has been a considerable flow of military equipment from the United States to Egypt and in the past eight years no fewer than 23 C-130Hs have been supplied to *Al Quwwat Alijawwiya Ilmisriya* (the Air Force of the Republic of Egypt, EAF).

The first six aircraft, Model 382C-64Ds, were diverted from the USAF's 1976 Appropriations and were delivered during December 1976 and January 1977, carrying both commercial and military registration markings. The first aircraft delivered (*SU-BAA*) was to be destroyed during Egypt's commando-style assault against terrorist hijackers who had taken hostage a number of Egyptian nationals at Larnaca airport in Cyprus on February 19 1978. Two other aircraft of this batch were said to have been delivered equipped to perform radio/radar countermeasures duties with the EAF, although their identity is not known. Four more aircraft (-81Ds) arrived in Egypt in October and November 1978 and once again the first to be delivered, *SU-BAH*, was to be lost when it struck the ground soon after taking off from Cairo-West airport with a load of ammunition aboard in May 1981. Ten C-130Hs (also -81Ds) were delivered from the USAF's 1978 Appropriations. Finally three -24Es were delivered in September and October 1982.

Background photograph *Surely one of the most aesthetically pleasing liveries carried by a Hercules was that of this L-100-30, a model 382G-55C TR-KKD (C/N 4895) ordered for the President of Gabon and named N'tem; it is seen here at Cambridge (Marshall of Cambridge, Neg No 54/9230).*

Inset *Peru first ordered three L-100-20 transports, the first of which, FAP 396 (C/N 4450), was delivered in April 1972; it was written off after an emergency night landing in Peru on April 24 1981 (D.K. McCarthy, MCE).*

Peru

Reflecting Peru's constant struggle against the ravages of natural disaster and the perpetual privations of remote populations, the nation's relatively well-equipped *Fuerza Aérea Peruana* (Peruvian Air Force, FAP) includes a large transport element, of which one squadron of its *Grupo 41* at Jorge Chavez is equipped with Hercules. The first three aircraft, all L-100-20 aircraft, had been purchased between 1970 and 1972 and were followed by three more at the end of 1976. The first military-style Hercules, two Model 382E-47C C-130Hs, were completed early in 1980 but were not delivered to the FAP until March 1981 when financial arrangements had been concluded through the Lockheed Financing Corporation. In the meantine one of the original L-100-20s had been destroyed in a take-off accident at Tarapota on February 19 1978.

The Republic of Gabon

Gabon, formerly part of French Equatorial Africa, has slowly built up a small, well-equipped air force *(Force Aérienne Gabonaise)* whose transport fleet of about a dozen aircraft currently includes four Hercules. However, the first aircraft, an L-100-30 delivered in April 1975, has recently been loaned to Indonesia to assist in that nation's transmigration programme (see pages 168-9). The second aircraft, an L-100-20 delivered in December 1976, together with a military C-130H (a Model 382C-79D) delivered in December 1977, have been flown by the air force in support of the Trans Gabon Railway construction project, being used mainly in the transportation of personnel and equipment to remote airstrips at the advancing railhead. The fourth aircraft is an L-100-30, delivered in July 1981, and is set aside for the use of the President of the Republic.

Ecuador

One of South America's most modern air forces, the *Fuerza Aérea Ecuatoriana* (FAE) has purchased three C-130Hs, the first two (-74Ds) being delivered for service with *Escuadrilla 11* in July and August 1977; however the second of these was destroyed when it

Left *Third and last C-130H ordered by Ecuador was this Hercules,* FAE-812 *(C/N 4812), delivered in April 1979* (MAP, Neg No 99/C236).

Below left *Bolivia's first C-130H,* CP-1375 *(C/N 4744) was operated by the* Transporte Aereo Militar *as* TAM-90; *it was written off when the pilot crashed during a night take-off at Panama in September 1979* (via R. Dorr).

Top right *Fine air shot of the C-130H, a Model 382C-69D,* TJ-XAD *(C/N 4752), of the* Armée de L'Air du Cameroun, *delivered in 1977 and based at Douala* (Lockheed-Georgia, Neg No RL 1376-6).

Above right *Last of five C-130Hs,* 6805 *(C/N 4778), was delivered in 1978 for service with the FAP's* Esquadra 501; *it was one of Greenham Common's visitors in 1979* (Starliner Aviation Press, Neg No CS 839).

struck a mountain in Ecuador on July 12 1978. A replacement (a -87D) was delivered in April 1979.

Bolivia

A similar pattern of history attended the C-130s acquired by Bolivia for the *Fuerza Aérea Boliviana* (FAB). Two -72s were delivered in July and October 1977 for operation by the FAB's *Transportes Aéreos Militares* at La Paz. The first of these was lost when its pilot became disorientated during a night take-off at Panama-Tacuman airport on September 28 1979 and flew into the water beyond the runway. In this instance an L-100-30 was leased to the FAB by Lockheed Aircraft Corporation, though it is not known whether outright purchase is anticipated.

Cameroon

The Cameroon Republic possesses a small air force whose title (*l'Armée de l'Air du Cameroun*) reflects its French origins. Its two Model 382C-69D C-130Hs, delivered in August and September 1977, are based at Douala and are employed to carry equipment between the airstrips at Batouri, Garoua and the headquarters at Yaounde in support of the Army's frequent counter-insurgency operations.

Portugal

Portugal purchased two Model 382C-73D C-130Hs for delivery in August and September 1977 and three more (-78Ds) which arrived in May and June the following year. Equipping *Esquadra 501* of the *Forca*

Top *One of Sudan's C-130Hs during delivery in 1978, still bearing USAF markings; this aircraft, 78-0745 (C/N 4766), became ST-AHR and 1100 in Sudanese service* (Lockheed-Georgia, Neg No RL 1970-2C).

Above *C-130H, 344 (C/N 4779), of the Royal Jordanian Air Force* (Lockheed-Georgia, Neg No RL 2490-2).

Left *Latest of Jordan's C-130Hs, 347 (C/N 4929), was delivered in August 1982. Seen here in the United Kingdom, it carried the inscription GUTS AIRLINE on each side of the nose* (MAP, Neg No 98/242).

Aérea Portuguesa and replacing Douglas DC-6s and Noratlas transports, they are based at Lisbon. Specially modified with a new auxiliary generating power unit, improved air conditioning and a new weather radar, the C-130Hs have assumed fishery protection and search-and-rescue duties, previously undertaken by Lockheed Neptune aircraft.

Sudan

The strained international relations that pervaded the Middle East in the late-1960s brought about a period of political alignment by the Sudan with the Soviet Union and Communist China. By the mid-1970s however, following the example of neighbouring Egypt, relations between the Sudan and the United States moderated, and President Numeiri was able to secure purchase of six C-130Hs (Model 382C-76Ds), these aircraft being delivered to Khartoum between January and May 1978 carrying diminutive USAF markings during the delivery flights. One or two of the aircraft were subsequently also flown by Sudan Airways on freighting operations. Incidentally, the third C-130H delivered was the 1,500th Hercules completed by Lockheed.

Jordan

Never overawed by the hostile and powerful air force of neighbouring Israel, the Royal Jordanian Air Force (*Al Quwwat Aljawwiya Almalakiya*) has always struggled to maintain a high level of efficiency balanced with deliberately-imposed financial limitations.

Following the acquisition of three ex-USAF C-130Bs in 1973, Jordan purchased new a single C-130H (a -89D) in April 1979, and another (a -28E) in May 1982. Yet another aircraft (a -31E) was delivered in August 1982 having been diverted from a contract placed by Morocco. All these aircraft served with No 3 Squadron at King Abdullah Air Base, Amman.

Australia

After the earlier purchases of 12 C-130As in 1958 and 12 C-130Es in 1966 the Royal Australian Air Force received a dozen C-130Hs (Model 382C-71Ds) during the latter half of 1978, and straightway put its 20-year-old C-130As up for disposal on the world market, so that the new aircraft could take their place on No 36 Squadron at Richmond.

The RAAF Hercules force recently reached a total of 331,000 flying hours free of accident, an achievement that embraced operations by both Nos 36 and 37 Squadrons in Vietnam, support missions to Australian United Nations forces in Pakistan and Egypt and a courier service to the Australian contingent of the multi-national force's observers group in El Gorah. It has flown resupply sorties to Antarctica and made frequent air drops over such places as Macquarie Island. Disaster relief flights have been made in Australia, New Zealand, Indonesia, Malaysia and Singapore, and self-contained medical teams have been dropped in Fiji and Papua New Guinea, while a year-round search and rescue service has been provided over all Australian waters.

Australia took delivery of a dozen C-130Hs in 1978 to replace her 20-year-old C-130As. A97-008 (C/N 4788), visited the United Kingdom bearing the badge of No 36 Squadron, RAAF (Starliner Aviation Press, Neg No CS 823).

Above *Spanning 20 years of C-130 flying, the RAAF staged this flight by a C-130A, C-130E and C-130H* (Lockheed-Georgia, Neg No RL 4070-2).

Below *Bush fire-fighting at very low level, an RAAF Hercules,* A97-011 *(C/N 4791), discharges its load of fire-retardant slurry* (via Lockheed-Georgia, Copy Neg No RM 3593).

In the recent gigantic bush fires an RAAF C-130H from No 36 Squadron was quickly converted for fire-fighting duties by installation of a modular airborne fire fighting system (MAFFS), comprising five modular tank pallets locked to the cabin floor. Flying at 200 ft the Hercules laid a pressurised stream of fire retardant slurry, 90 ft wide and a quarter mile long, successfully fireproofing trees and scrub in the path of the fires and saving considerable tracts of property from destruction.

Indonesia

For about ten years after 1965 the Indonesian Air Force (*Angkatan Udara Republik Indonesia*, AURI) continued to fly its C-130Bs on heavy-lift duties and in 1975 acquired three similar ex-USAF aircraft to make

good losses from attrition. In 1977 it was decided to gradually modernise the entire force serving with what had been renamed the *Tentara Nasional Indonesia: Angkatan Udara* (TNI-AU) by the purchase of the new generation of Hercules, starting with a VIP-appointed L-100-30 (Model 382G-41C). This was delivered in December 1978 for use by the Presidential Flight. Two C-130Hs (-93Ds) followed at the end of 1979, and in September and October five 'stretched' C-130H-30s were delivered to Halim for service with No 31 Squadron; these Model 382T-3Es were the first stretched military Hercules to be delivered direct from the production line. A -15E and two -21Es followed in 1981 and 1982, as well as a C-130H-MP (a -9E) maritime patrol aircraft, though it is not known what squadron flies the latter.

Above *Lockheed Model 382C-9E C-130H-MP maritime patrol aircraft (C/N 4898), of the Indonesian Air Force, seen here paradropping stores; note the large transparent panels in the rear door (Lockheed-Georgia, Neg No RM 823-8C).*

Below *The 1,600th Hercules completed, this Indonesian Model 382T-3E, C-130H-30, A-1321 (C/N 4870), was one of the relatively small number of stretched military C-130s built as such from new (Lockheed-Georgia, Neg No RL 7479-2).*

Yemen Arab Republic

Both the People's Democratic Republic of Yemen (PDRY) and the Yemen Arab Republic (YAR) have engaged in arms purchasing from East and West alike. However, at least as yet, only the latter has acquired Hercules. Two Model 382C-86D C-130Hs were delivered new from Lockheed in August 1979, and it has been suggested that two C-130Es have been supplied from Royal Saudi Air Force stocks, although these may have been on temporary loan pending the arrival of the new aircraft.

Niger

The *Force Aérienne du Niger* is wholly tasked with transport duties, responsible for support of the land-locked nation's Army. Until the late 1970s its equipment comprised a Douglas C-54B, two C-47s and three Noratlas aircraft, but in September and October 1979 two Model 382C-90D C-130Hs arrived at the airport at Niamey with civil registrations to perform both military and commercial land development work, as well as continuing the Army support role.

Dubai

Another of the constituent arms of the United Arab Emirates' Air Force is Dubai, a state which purchased for military use a single L-100-30 in November 1979 (a Model 382G-44C). It is based at Dubai, but on April 30 1981 suffered fairly extensive damage in a tropical hailstorm requiring repair by Marshall of Cambridge (Engineering) Ltd in England.

Singapore

After operating two ex-USAF C-130Bs and a pair of ex-Jordanian C-130Es for some years, the Republic of Singapore Air Force purchased new four C-130Hs (two -2Es and two -6Es) for service with No 121 Squadron, RSAF; these were delivered between January and May 1980.

Thailand

Although the Royal Thai Air Force had flown predominantly American aircraft for many years, it was not until mid-1980 that the first Hercules featured in

Above left *Pre-delivery view of Yemeni C-130H,* 1150 *or* 1160 (Lockheed-Georgia, Neg No RL 4636-5C).

Left *First of two Model 382C-90D C-130Hs,* 5U-MBD *(C/D 4829), to be delivered to the* Force Aérienne du Niger *in September 1979* (Lockheed-Georgia, Neg No RL 5452-5).

Below left *Dubai's single Hercules is this stretched Model 382G-44C C-130H-30,* 311 *(C/N 4834), seen at Cambridge after repair of damage suffered in a tropical hailstorm in 1981* (Marshall of Cambridge, Neg No 54/9002).

Below *After obtaining four second-hand C-130Bs from the USA and Jordan in 1977, Singapore purchased four new Model 382C C-130Hs in 1980; the first, a Model 382C-2E,* 730 *(C/N 4842), is shown here* (Lockheed-Georgia, Neg No RL 4649-3C).

One of three C-130Hs, 60101 *(C/N 4861), supplied to the Royal Thai Air Force in 1980* (W.F. Wilson, MCE).

its large inventory when three Model 382C-1E C-130Hs were delivered to the RTAF's main base at Don Muang.

Oman

Shouldering ever-increasing responsibilities in the Persian Gulf area, the Sultan of Oman's Air Force has undertaken to secure the Straits of Hormuz for international oil shipping with a small but modern aircraft inventory provided by the United States and Britain. A Model 382C-13E was purchased in February 1981, followed by a -19E in February 1982 and a -33E in January 1983, for operations based at Seeb and Salalah.

Sweden

Both of Sweden's C-130Es, purchased during the 1960s, underwent conversion to C-130H in 1982, while a new C-130H (a -56D) has been acquired in 1975. However, during the first half of 1981 five 'new generation' C-130Hs (Model 382C-8E) joined *Flygflottilj 7* at Såtenäs, carrying both military and commercial marks.

Following an appeal to the United Nations Commissioner for Refugees late in 1982, three of the Swedish Hercules took part in an operation in southern Sudan to deep-drill 100 wells to alleviate the sufferings of the peoples forced to live in that drought-stricken area. Flying from Sweden via Crete, one Hercules delivered a truck with a nine-ton compressor and five tons of other equipment, while the other two aircraft carried two trucks and about 20 tons of drilling units, drilling tower, pipeline and hand pumps.

Algeria

After some years of Soviet domination of the *Force Aérienne Algérienne*, which included transports such as the Il-14, Il-18 and An-12, Algeria began purchasing military Hercules in 1981, starting with two 'stretched' C-130H-30s (-16Es) at the end of that year. It was perhaps significant that they carried commercial registration marks in addition to military insignia, the former running almost consecutively with the three commercial L-100-30s operated by *Air Algerie*. Seven Model 382C-25Es followed in 1982, as well as two -30Es and three -31Es, the latter diverted from a contract originally placed for the Royal Maroc Air Force.

Chad

This former French colony in central Africa has been wracked by civil war for many years, a situation considerably exacerbated by constant border action with Communist Libya to the north. This erupted into full-scale war in 1983, a war that brought support for the tiny *Escadrille Tchadienne* from France's *Armée de l'Air*. To provide a more permanent airlift capability for the movement of civilian communities displaced by the fighting, France's *Securité Civile* purchased an ex-Australian C-130A (*A97-208*), C/N 3208), and possibly another (*A97-215*, C/N 3215), both of which were seen at Ford & Vhahos, San Francisco, in October 1983, en route from Richmond, Australia. There are other reports that two ex-USAF C-130As, *57-0517* and *57-0523* (C/Ns 3224 and 3230) may also be supplied to Chad.

Above *By 1981 the Sultan of Oman Air Force had ordered three C-130Hs, the first, C/N 4878, shown here, carrying the marks N4138M before delivery in March that year* (Lockheed-Georgia, Neg No RL 9081-2).

Below *Sweden's* Flygvapnet *took delivery of five C-130Hs in 1981, 846 (C/N 4885), being delivered in May that year* (Lieutenant-Colonel Lars Olausson).

Above *The surviving Lockheed L-100-20, 318 (C/N 4412), of the Kuwait Air Force, seen here undergoing maintenance at Cambridge* (Marshall of Cambridge, Neg No 54/9626).

Left *Second Model 382C-27E C-130H (C/N 4980), of the Japanese contract, completed in November 1983* (Lockheed-Georgia, Neg No RM 4576-26).

Kuwait

Following the conclusion of the Kuwaiti Air Force's seven-year modernisation programme between 1973 and 1980, four L-100-30s (Model 382G-59Cs) were purchased early in 1983 to join the one remaining L-100-20 that had been delivered a dozen years earlier.

Iraq

The Iraq Air Force, which has depended to a great extent on transport aircraft from the Soviet Union for some years, placed an order for five L-100-30 Hercules intended for delivery in 1983, but the contract had not been signed early in 1982 and it is not known whether the aircraft were granted an export licence, having regard to the Iraqi-Iranian War and the sensitive political aspects of arms supply to the two nations.

Japan

Latest recipient of C-130Hs (Model 382C-27Es), at the time of writing, is the Japanese Air Self Defence Force (*Koku Jieitai*) which has ordered four aircraft. The first aircraft (the 1,700th Hercules to be completed) was flown towards the end of 1983 and, with the second, is being flown temporarily at Marietta for training purposes but with the last two aircraft of the order will be delivered to Japan late in 1984, based at Komaki.

★   ★   ★

The Hercules production line continues to build about 36 new aircraft yearly and, although some of this effort will probably go on new versions for the US Services for some time to come, follow-up orders seem certain to be placed by existing customers overseas, for the fact is that, in its heavy-lift category, the Hercules remains supreme. The long-term investment in airframe extension and fatigue resistance will bear fruit during the next 20 or 30 years—all programmes that have been amortised and which would have to be amortised in the future in any new aircraft. So long as Hercules remain in service and on the world market there will be ready customers for them.

Chapter 11

Hercules the civilian

Throughout the 1960s and 1970s aviation commentators have constantly expressed some surprise at the relatively small proportion of the total Hercules production that has been sold to commercial operators. To some extent this has resulted from the slow build-up in the demand for international air freighting—contrary to widespread forecasts in the early 1960s. Moreover, among the smaller nations, wherein demands for air freighting were and have continued to be sporadic it has been the nature of such demands—as well as economically essential—to employ military aircraft. In numerous instances of natural disaster, whether by flood, fire, famine or earthquake, a military presence has been decreed for purposes of restoring order out of chaos. Thus the provision of military air transportation of police, administrative personnel, medical and food supplies and evacuation of refugees has been essential rather than fortuitous.

Nevertheless Lockheed was not slow to anticipate a perceptible slackening in American military orders for the Hercules in the mid-1960s, resulting in a growing availability of spare production capacity that might be taken up by the commercial sale of suitably certificated Hercules aircraft, particularly to potential operators in the North American continent where the forecast exploitation of natural resources could well benefit from the use of such a rugged workhorse as the Hercules with its proven range, load-carrying and rough-field performance.

The first stage in generating commercial interest in the aircraft was to prepare a demonstrator for the company and to gain for it FAA certification under commercial operating conditions. Accordingly a Model 382 airframe, equivalent to the current military C-130E, was located in the production line at Marietta partway through the USAF's 1963 Appropriations at No 3946. Commercially-rated Allison 501-D22 (equivalent to the military T-56A-7) turboprops were installed and, termed Lockheed L-100, the prototype made its first flight on April 20/21 1964. After customary manufacturers' flight trials the aircraft, registered *N1130E*, undertook a series of demonstration flights to generate interest among potential customers.

Certification under FAA conditions was achieved on February 16 1965 and the following month Lockheed leased the prototype to Alaska Airlines, one of the likely customers for future production orders. Already the exploration for and exploitation of the rich mineral resources of that state was demanding considerable movement of personnel and equipment from the industrial centres of the USA, and Alaska Airlines, and later Alaska International Air, were seeking an aircraft with the performance offered by the Hercules.

Before going on to complete the history of the L-100 prototype, it is worth describing the proposed means of leasing and selling future commercial Hercules aircraft, bearing in mind the speculative nature of air freighting demands. After all, an aircraft of the Hercules' size is not inexpensive and represents considerable financing and/or capital outlay for a company which, unlike a regular passenger airline, is wholly dependent upon constant but often short-term contracts. To compound the problem further, for the very reason that air freighting contracts are usually of a short-term nature, the market can be quickly saturated with aircraft being offered for disposal at amortised prices (a problem not unfamiliar among bulk-cargo shipping companies).

To overcome this Lockheed planned to adopt the dual sale/lease policy to meet customer demand, a policy already adopted by passenger airliner manufacturers though at a lower level in relation to the size of their markets. Put simply, the manufacturer would continue to stimulate and encourage the outright sale of new aircraft to freighting companies, but at the same time pursue leasing agreements both with the company itself and with external leasing and financing corporations. By so doing, Lockheed would exercise some small but significant control of the 'second hand' market and prevent saturation of that market with outmoded aircraft, would be able to refurbish, update and re-lease aircraft returned on lease expiry, would be able to satisfy short-notice sale or leasing contracts and exercise control over fatigue-life extension improvements in the Hercules as operating experience accumulated. As already stated such a policy was by no means

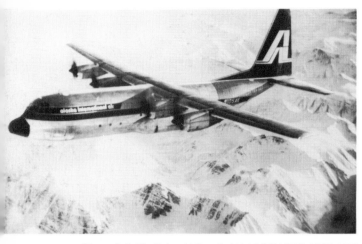

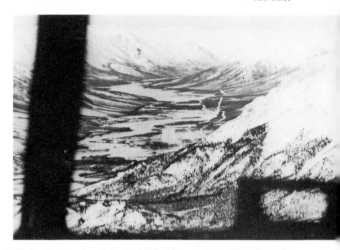

Above left *Ex-Delta Airlines L-100-20, N105AK (C/N 4176), of Alaska International Air in 1976.* **Above right** *View from the cockpit of an L-100 on the approach to a typical Alaskan airfield.* **Below left** *Take-off from an airstrip amidst the northern mountains.* **Below right** *Loading oil rig equipment aboard an L-100 of AIA.* **Bottom** *An L-100, N7999S, leased to AIA by National Aircraft Leasing on an Alaskan airstrip in 1976* (via Lockheed-Georgia).

Above *Model 382B-2C, L-100-20, CF-PWN (C/N 4129), sold to Pacific Western Airlines in 1977 (Starliner Aviation Press, Neg No CS 911).*

Below *Although a government purchase for Pakistan International Airlines in 1966, this L-100, AP-AUT, was periodically flown by the Pakistan Air Force on military duties (Lockheed-Georgia, Neg No RH 2551-4).*

innovatory, yet such was the load-carrying and range performance offered by the Hercules that flexibility of this aircraft opened up far wider horizons among potential operators than had been evident among airline operators whose passenger airliners are more exactly tailored to specific travel densities and staging distances, thereby limiting the scope for disposing of 'hand-me-down' aircraft.

For the reasons already outlined, the commercial world did not immediately beat a path to Lockheed's door when the L-100 first flew in April 1964, so that pursuit of the civil project continued relatively slowly at first. After all the company had plenty of work spread among its plants: the Model 185 Orion maritime reconnaissance aircraft was at the height of its production and the new C-141 Starlifter was approaching its first Service deliveries. Moreover, American involvement in Vietnam—although hitherto of a limited nature—was increasing, with a result that the USAF appropriations for 1964 would still demand the production of 100 C-130s, as well as 27 outstanding military orders from overseas customers.

The second and third L-100s (designated Model 382B-1Cs) therefore, did not fly until late in 1965. Meanwhile the first aircraft continued in service with Alaska Airlines until returned to Lockheed in 1967 for conversion to a Model 382E (see below). It was thereafter leased to Delta Airlines for four months and

to Airlift International in May 1969. In 1978 it was sold to the Philippine Aerospace Development Corporation. The first Model 382B-1C was flown on September 30 1965 and after a brief production checkout (commercial certification having already been granted), the aircraft was leased by Lockheed to Continental Air Services and sold the following year to the Government of Zambia. The second B-1C, which flew in October 1965, followed the same pattern.

Nine production L-100s (together worth about $50 million) were produced in 1966, two early aircraft (B-2Cs) being sold to Zambian Air Cargoes. Lockheed leased a Model 382B-3C to Pacific Western, a Canadian carrier that operated scheduled and nonscheduled freight and passenger services throughout British Columbia, Alberta and the North West Territories, as well as a world-wide freight charter service. The Government of Pakistan purchased two Model 382B-4Cs for Pakistan International Airlines, but they were made available for military use and carried either military or commercial insignia, or both; the latter aircraft crashed near Chaklala in 1968. A B-5C was delivered to International Aerodyne and leased by the Bank of America to Alaska Airlines. The last three commercial aircraft (B-6Cs) produced in 1966 were bought by Delta Airlines, but these were returned to Lockhed for modification to Model 382Es in 1968. The first of these three aircraft was to become

L-100-10 (C/N 4209), during its lease to Interior Airways Inc as N921NA *between 1969 and 1972. It was later destroyed while flying with Alaska International when its cargo exploded at Galbraith Lake on August 30 1974 (MAP, Neg No 12887).*

the first of any Hercules to reach 30,000 flying hours, in February 1977. Indeed five of the commercial aircraft produced in 1966 were still flying regularly 17 years later.

Nine L-100s were also completed in 1967. Three were produced for Lockheed leasing, a B-8C to Pacific Western and two B-14Cs to Interior Airways, an American company operating in Alaska and Canada. The second of these Hercules crashed on the approach to the Old Man 'n Camp, Alaska, on October 27 1974 following wing separation while on lease to Alaska International Air. Alaska Airlines bought its first new aircraft in 1967, a B-7C, and the Government of Zambia took delivery of its third aircraft, a B-9C. The remaining four aircraft, all B-10Cs, were purchased by Airlift International, an American company operating military freight charters throughout the Pacific as well as world-wide commercial charters; the last of these L-100s was lost in an accident at Prudhoe Bay on Christmas Eve 1968, and was temporarily replaced by leasing the first prototype in 1969.

Early in 1968 Lockheed was at work introducing a new variation of the L-100, the 'Dash 20' which, on account of the Hercules' parallel-contoured fuselage, involved a straightforward insertion of fuselage 'plugs' to extend the freight cabin volume, the fuselage length of the L-100-20 being increased by approximately 100 in. No further Model 382Bs were produced after 1967,

and the opportunity was taken to return the prototype to the Georgia plant for modification to the new standard, not only extending the fuselage but also replacing the 4,050-eshp Allison 501-D22 turboprops by 4,510-eshp 501-D22A engines (the commercial equivalent to the T56A-15s then being fitted in the first military C-130Hs for overseas customers and the RAF's C-130Ks). Now designated Model 382E, the first prototype took the air again (still registered *N1130E*) on April 19 1968, flight trials and recertification occupying four months. Meanwhile six other Model 382Bs were returned to Marietta for modification during 1968–69, either at the end of a leasing term or on repurchase by the manufacturers. (The identifying sub-variant designation remained unchanged, a Model 382B-6C, for instance, simply becoming a 382C-6C.)

Three of the conversions were sold to Air Finance and three to Saturn Airways; the latter was an American air charter company operating freight and passenger services throughout the world and was to become the third-largest operator of commercial Hercules (after Alaska International Air and Safair Freighters), taking on purchase or lease a total of 13 L-100 variants.

Five new L-100-20s were completed during the latter half of 1968, and all of them had long and interesting lives. Two were Model 382E-11Cs, one of which was leased by Air America to Southern Air Transport in

One of the 1968 L-100-20s, N7951S (C/N 4301), originally leased then sold to Southern Air Transport by Air America. Seen here at Cambridge in about 1970, it was given the -30 stretch in 1971. (Marshall of Cambridge, Neg No 54/3003).

Originally delivered for the Girard Trust in 1968, this L-100-20 (C/N 4302), flew with Red Dodge Aviation as N30FW *between December 1969 and February 1973, when it was sold to Southern Air Transport* (MAP, Neg No 18172).

November; this American Florida-based domestic operator also flew freight services in Central and South America, the Bahamas and across the Pacific. The following month the company bought outright the other -11C from Lockheed; after a further fuselage stretch (see below) this aircraft was damaged in a heavy landing in Ecuador and, after repair, was leased in turn to Alaska International, Air Algerie, Cassair and, in 1981, to Cargolux.

The next aircraft, a Model 382E-11C, was sold to the First National Bank of Chicago for a four-year lease to Interior Airlines, while the last two aircraft, E-15Cs, went to the Girard Trust for leasing to Flying 'W' Airways. The first of these remained with FWA for six months as *N7952S*, transferring to Red Dodge Aviation as *N30FW* in December 1969. In February 1973 it was sold to Southern Air Transport but soon afterwards was again sold, this time to the Philippine Government as *PI-99*, which then leased it to the Philippine Air Force and the Philippine Aerospace Development Corporation for heavy freighting. In 1981 it was sold to United African Airlines as *5J-DJR*.

The saga of *Smokey Heel*

Last of the new-built 1968 L-100-20s was perhaps the most famous of all commercial L-100s. Second of the Girard Trust -15Cs, its early life was much the same as the first, arriving with Red Dodge as *N40FW* in October 1969. It also went to the Philippines but only remained two months before returning to North America for sale to Canada's James Bay Energy Corporation as *CF-DSX* in September 1973 and a lease to

Quebecair, a passenger and freight carrier based at Dorval and operating in Quebec, Labrador and Ontario. James Bay Energy Corporation was at that time engaged in building a huge hydro-electric generation complex in Northern Quebec and *CF-DSX* came to represent the sole supply line to 12,000 construction engineers, making an average of 24 landings every day and carrying roughly 4,500 tons of freight every month on a one-way airlift of plant, food and fuel. At one dam site the Hercules was the only means of reaching the engineers.

During this period *CF-DSX* was leased to Echo Bay Mines Limited, a company that had started up in 1964 at Edmonton, Alberta, to develop the silver mine at Port Radium, North West Territories. Initial flying had been confined to a single DC-3 for some years until the lease of *CF-DSX*, the object of which was to explore the possibility of 'total air supply' between the company's base at Yellowknife and the ice/gravel strips in the barren Arctic wastes far to the north. So impressed was the management with the potentialities of this aircraft that in 1980 the purchase of *CF-DSX* from James Bay was negotiated, not only to operate 'total air supply' to the silver mine at Port Radium but to commence operations in the construction of a gold mine at Lupin on the western shore of Contwoyto Lake, 250 miles northeast of Yellowknife. In charge of these operations were Bill Granley (aviation manager), Bob Beaton (chief pilot, who had come with *CF-DSX* from James Bay Energy) and Don Switzer (flying training manager). Outstanding among these was Beaton, a pilot with 34 years' flying experience and

The long and eventful life of the L-100-20 (C/N 4303), included a spell with the Canadian James Bay Energy Corporation as CF-DSX from September 1973; it later became Echo Bay Mines' famous Smokey Heel (Lockheed-Georgia, Neg No RL 2943-3).

over 10,000 hours on Hercules behind him. In recruiting pilots for the job, Granley waived any need for previous Hercules experience but insisted instead on familiarity with flying in the unforgiving conditions of 'the North'.

To start with, the Hercules was landed on the frozen Contwoyto Lake, bringing to the virgin tract a bulldozer and other equipment with which to carve out a 5,000-ft landing strip nearby. Previous studies had established that, using surface transport, the Lupin mine complex would take up to five years to build but that, with the single Hercules, this might be reduced to little over one year. And so the Hercules went to work, christened *Smokey Heel* in memory of a legendary Candian pioneer pilot of the remote tundra territories, hauling freight to the north, its flying being limited to daylight hours until lighting could be installed beside the strip at Lupin. One hundred early loads comprised huge worker dormitories, each of which measured 48 ft × 9 ft 2 in × 8 ft 7 in, weighed 14,260 lb and included two living rooms and bath; these were followed by Caterpillars, tandem dump trucks, drilling equipment, diesel generators, fuel and food for 500 employees. As the mine became operational with an ore crusher, smelter and power unit (all lifted in by *Smokey Heel*), the airlift entered its two-way phase, bringing gold out of Lupin and silver from Port Radium, making an average of four round trips every 24 hours, six days a week (the seventh being maintenance day). Bob Beaton and his pilots soon mastered the knack of landing on Port Radium's 4,800 ft gravel/ice strip, although this involved 'dropping in' over the surrounding moun-

tains, often in strong cross winds and in temperatures invariably down to minus 50°. Not surprisingly the pilots welcomed the onset of winter when the smooth lake waters froze to a depth of 60 in—sufficient to bear the weight of a Hercules putting down with heavy loads—and the mine workers could mark out an 8,000-ft strip for landing.

Between October 1980 and October 1981 *Smokey Heel* flew 1,989.6 hours, made 2,083 landings and carried no less than 47 million pounds of freight; roughly a fifth of this consisted of food, fuel and general cargo being lifted to Port Radium and float-crushed ore brought out, the remainder being construction components, accommodation units, plants and supplies flown in to Lupin. By comparison—though not strictly relevant—the entire Canadian Armed Forces' fleet of 24 C-130s carried 24 million pounds in the same period. By April 1982 Lupin was in full operation with a 700-ft mine shaft, a thousand-ton-a-day ore crusher, smelter, offices, garages and domestic site; every nut, bolt and steel plate having been hauled 250 miles by a single Hercules. And every gold ingot was shipped out the same way.

Sadly, soon after the major operation was completed in the spring of 1983 Bob Beaton died—not a young man by flying standards but one universally popular and respected in those northern skies—and his faithful Hercules was renamed in his memory. Today, as lesser aeroplanes cope with the task of flying out the precious metals from the mines, *Bob Beaton*, with more than 20,000 flying hours to its credit, is employed for other work on lease by Echo Bay to Worldways Canada,

Opposite page *Loading a custom-designed housing unit, specially tailored to fit the cabin of* Smokey Heel, *for lifting to one of Echo Bay's stations* (Lockheed-Georgia).

Above *Amid clouds of powdered snow,* Smokey Heel *on a typical landing strip in northern Canada* (Lockheed-Georgia, Neg No RL 8625).

Below Smokey Heel *at rest on Lake Contwoyto; because the aircraft included the -20 stretch there was never any question of equipping it with wheel-ski landing gear, as on the C-130D* (Echo Bay Mines Ltd).

Above Smokey Heel *taxying on Lake Contwoyto* (Echo Bay Mines Ltd).

Left *The object of it all: a gold bar from Lupin* (Echo Bay Mines Ltd).

Top right and centre right *Huge items of cargo lifted by* Smokey Heel (Echo Bay Mines Ltd).

Right *Unorthodox loading position adopted by* Smokey Heel *to enable long, low and heavy items to be transferred from a low-bed truck (Echo Bay Mines Ltd).*

Above left *The bleak environment of Echo Bay Mines, with* Smokey Heel *on a gravel/ice strip* (Echo Bay Mines Ltd).

Left & top Smokey Heel *on a snow strip in northern Canada* (Echo Bay Mines Ltd).

Above CF-DSX *in James Bay Energy livery.* **Below** *The livery of* CF-DSX *initially unchanged after transfer to Echo Bay Mines Ltd; it was later painted with a red cheat line* (Echo Bay Mines Ltd).

though still managed and often flown by Bill Granley and his crews.

*　　　*　　　*

Smokey Heel was followed by five new L-100-20s at Marietta in 1969, all built speculatively for sale or lease by Lockheed. The company leased the first of them, a Model 382E-21C, *N7957S*, to the US Navy in May for undisclosed trials which lasted for about six months before the aircraft was returned to Marietta; it was then leased, and eventually sold to Saturn Airways as *N17ST* who christened it *Wimpey*. The next, an E-16C, was sold to the Kuwait Air Force; it was to crash near Montelimar in France on September 5 1980 after being struck by lightning. An E-19C was sold to the Canadian brokers, Maple Leaf Leasing, in November who leased it and then sold it to Pacific Western as *CF-PWR*; purchased by Cargolux as *LX-GCV* (which was, however, not painted on the aircraft), it was leased as *5A-DHJ* to United African Airlines in 1981 who later changed it to *5A-DHI* on purchasing the aircraft outright. The final aircraft completed in 1969 was an E-20C sold to Southern Air Transport in December.

Production of the Model 382E continued for the next ten years, and in 1969 the first of two similar conversions was completed on one of the two Model 382B-2Cs which was returned to Marietta after being damaged in an accident at Eureka in Canada's Northwest Territories while on lease to Pacific Western. This aircraft was rebuilt with the -20 fuselage stretch but without changing to the -D22A engines, and was redesignated Model 382F-2C; it was leased to Alaska International Air as *N109AK* in December 1969 and eventually returned to Pacific Western in 1977 as *C-FPWN*.

The Big Stretch

The success of the '-20' stretch became immediately obvious from reports received by Lockheed's customer liaison departments, together with confirmation of its performance forecasts. Lockheed was therefore encouraged to progress to a further fuselage stretch, this time the two fuselage 'plugs' extending the length by some 180 in. Among the important motivations for this increased freight volume was the intention to increase the number of standardised freight container pallets capable of being carried from five to seven in common with the long-haul Boeing 747 freighters, so as to enable the new L-100-30 to operate as a feederline freighter.

Sometimes dubbed the 'Super Hercules', the L-100-30 retained the -20's D522A turboprops driving 13 ft 6 in diameter Hamilton Standard 54H60-117 hydromatic reversing-pitch propellers and on certification was shown at maximum gross take-off weight of 155,000 lb to comply with all FAR 36 Stage 2 noise requirements, and with slight trade-off on take-off the Stage 3 requirements as well. (As with other Hercules versions currently being offered in 1984, the L-100-30 may also incorporate the drag reduction ventral strakes.) Such was the obvious appeal of the -30 (the Model 382G) that up to mid-1983 59 aircraft had been built—more than the other versions combined. To these were added four converted from Model 382Bs and seven from 382Es. As described elsewhere, the -30 stretch was specified in a number of overseas orders for C-130Hs and roughly half the RAF's fleet of Hercules C 1s (C-130Ks) are, at the time of writing, in the process of being converted to C 3s by Marshall of Cambridge (Engineering) Ltd.

The first L-100-30, a Model 382G-23C, *N7988S*, was flown on August 14 1970 and this was employed

N1OST *(ex-Saturn) in Transamerica livery in the late 1970s* (Lockheed-Georgia, Neg No RZ 29299-2).

Top *The L-100-30 (C/N 4562) (Safair's ZS-RSF) leased to Canada's Northwest Territorial Airways as* C-FNWF *in 1978 (Lockheed-Georgia, Neg No RL 4968).*

Above *This L-100-20,* RP-C101 *(C/N 4593), was purchased by the Government of the Philippines and leased to Philippine Aerotransport in 1975 (Lockheed-Georgia, Neg No RJ 9464-2C).*

for certification purposes during the autumn of that years. It was then sold to Saturn Airways in December, the long red nose accentuated by the company's livery giving rise to the aircraft being christened *Schnozz* (after the famous veteran American comedian 'Schnozzle' Durante). Two Model 382E-22Cs, which had only been delivered to Saturn in mid-1970, *(N10ST* and *N11ST)* were returned to Marietta to be converted to -30s, being named *Rudolf* and *W.C. Fields* for similar associations. Saturn received another brand-new G-23C, *N15ST*, in June 1971, and this became *Barney G.*

No further new -30s were completed for 18 months, although in August 1970 the South African carrier, Safair Freighters, took delivery of a -20, as did the Kuwait Air Force in April 1971 and Peru (for the *Fuerza Aérea Peruana*) in April 1972. Then in December 1972 Safair purchased three new -30s (all Model 382G-28Cs, ZS-RSB, 'C and 'D), leasing the first two to South African Airways two years later and the third to Alaskan International Air shortly after. Saturn purchased two more in 1974 and 1975, but by far the largest number went to Safair: three in 1974, three in 1975 and eight in 1976. The last of these, *ZS-*

Above *L-100-30*, F-FGDAQ *(C/N 4600)*, *leased to SF Air by Safair Freighters, seen on a visit to Cambridge* (Marshall of Cambridge, Neg No 54/9220).

Below *The South African cargo carrier Safair Freighters operated a total of 17 Hercules at one time or another. This L-100-30, ZS-RSH (C/N 4590), was delivered in May 1975* (MAP, Neg No 15811).

Above right *Uganda Airlines took delivery of this L-100-30, 5X-UCF (C/N 4610), in August 1975, passing it to Uganda Air Cargoes late in 1981* (MAP, Neg No 7237).

Right *First of two L-100-30s, A2-ABZ (C/N 4691), leased to Air Botswana by Safair Freighters in 1979* (Lockheed-Georgia, Neg No RM 1195-3).

JVM, delivered in December 1976, was leased to Air Botswana as *A2-ACA* in October 1979, retaining the Safair livery in red but with 'AB' in red on the vertical tail. The following year it was chartered by the International Red Cross and in June and July 1982 was used to lift relief supplies to the Lebanon following the Israeli invasion.

Certainly the commercial Hercules found plenty of work in Africa during the 1970s. Construction of the Trans-Gabon Railway prompted the purchase first of a

Model 382G-30C, *TR-KKA*, in April 1975, then an E-36C, *TR-KKB*, in December 1976, and a C-130H, *TR-KKC*, exactly a year later. A fourth aircraft, a G-55C, *TR-KKD*, was delivered in July 1981 as the Presidential aeroplane and named *N'tem*. The second -30 for Gabon, *TR-KKB*, was in 1982 leased to the Jakarta-based Pelita Air Service in Indonesia, a company which had already leased three new Model 382G-43Cs from the Mitsui Corporation in 1979 (*PK-PLU*, 'V and 'W, named *Bina, Hanonen* and *Sentiaki*

Second of Air Botswana's L-100-30s, A2-ACA (C/N 4701), leased from Safair Freighters in 1979. It was employed by the International Red Cross in 1980 and also flew relief supplies to the Lebanon during June and July 1982 (Starliner Aviation Press, Neg No BW1272).

respectively) and purchased a G-52C *(PK-PLR)*, a G-57C *(PK-PLS)* and a Model 382T-57C C-130H-30 *(PK-PLT)* in 1982. These seven aeroplanes were to be employed in one of the world's greatest airlifts, yet one that is scarcely known of in the Western Hemisphere.

Indonesia is the fifth highest populated area in the world and for decades past has suffered all the economic and social problems of over-concentration of population in a small number of connurbations. It therefore became a matter of Presidential priority to embark on a programme of 'transmigration', using Hercules aircraft to redistribute about one and a half million inhabitants from the over-populated regions of Java, Bali and Lombok to the fertile new settlements on Sumatra, at Kalimantan in Borneo, at Sulawesi in Celebes and Irian Jaya; the object being, by achieving much improved division of labour and exploitation of the nation's natural resources, to improve the standard of living of the entire population. The original target was to resettle 12,000 families (of 60,000 men, women and children) every month, the Hercules being ideal aircraft to operate high-density flights involving landings on short, unpaved airstrips close to the new settlements, usually carrying about 128 passengers. Flying the 'airbridge' 24 hours a day, seven days a week, the Hercules have at the time of writing

transferred almost three-quarters of a million 'transmigrants', the half-millionth passenger being carried in the Gabon -30, *TR-KKB*.

In recent years production of the L-100-30 has accelerated, interspersed in the production line by the stretched military C-130H-30. The freight feederline service, originally foreshadowed when the -30 was conceived, is operated by a number of carriers, including American Airlines, a Dallas/Texas-based company which contracts with Transamerica Airlines to operate an L-100-30 in the north-eastern States to feed its Boeing 747 long-haul freighters at Chicago and New York. In a similar operation Southern Air Transport operates an L-100-30 for American Airlines in the Caribbean, feeding a daily Boeing 747 at San Juan, Puerto Rico.

One of the most recent additions to the list of L-100-30 operators is Cargomasters Pty, Ltd, in Australia, which purchased a Model 382G-38C *(N108AK)* from Alaska International Air in August 1982 as *VH-CYO* to perform support operations for Australia's resource industry, regularly carrying loads of 50,000 lb into and out of short dirt strips in remote areas of the outback. Typical of other work performed by L-100s in remote areas is that of SF Air which was

Transmigration in Indonesia. Pelita Air Service employs a number of L-100s in the huge task of relocating about one and a half million inhabitants from the overpopulated regions of Java and elsewhere. The aircraft shown on this page is the L-100-30, TR-KKB *(C/N 4710), leased from Gabon in 1982* (via Lockheed-Georgia).

recently required to lift a large palletised container of electronic equipment to an installation in the Mali desert; the only truck available to accept the big load was one with an abnormally high bed level and it was necessary to bulldoze a trench to allow the truck to back up to the Hercules' rear ramp; the -30 flown by SF Air on this occasion was *F-GDAQ*, leased from Safair Freighters.

Early in 1983 the Government of Kuwait took delivery of four Model 382G-59Cs for its air force, their primary role being to lift military stores; however, purchased at the same time were conversion kits which comprised seven pallets containing seating for 91 passengers in addition to a lavatory and self-contained galley. When required for passenger carrying, the aircraft can be converted in less than an hour by inserting the pallets into the cabin on the integral loading rollers and then locking them in place.

Above *A pair of superbly-appointed Hercules flown by Saudia. The nearest aircraft, a Model 382C-4E, N4101M, HZ-HM5 (C/N 4843), although attached to the Saudi Royal Flight, was also operated by Saudia with passenger/limousine modifications. Colour scheme is pale grey lower surfaces, white upper, and blue-green panels on wings and vertical tail (Lockheed-Georgia, Neg No RL 4662-2C).*

Fare-paying passengers

Under the terms of previous Federal Aviation Agency certification the L-100 has been permitted to carry a limited number of passengers on a not-for-hire basis. In the autumn of 1983 Lockheed-Georgia applied to the FAA for a supplemental type certificate to permit the L-100-30 to carry up to 101 fare-paying passengers. To conform to safety requirements, new 28 × 48 in emergency exit doors will be included in all -30s being completed after April 1984, providing a total of six passenger exits, the option including additional emergency exits in the fuselage extension 'plugs',

enabling operators to conform to fare-paying passenger-carrying regulations when converting Model 382Bs and Es to Model 382Gs. Other requirements for fare-passenger type certification call for increased life raft installation, an increased oxygen distribution system and a revised public address system. According to customer requirements the passenger seating, galley and lavatory may either be built integrally with the aircraft from new or, as in the case of the Kuwait aircraft described above (wherein the passenger-carrying was not intended for fare-paying purposes), palletised for *ad hoc* conversion.

Above *This L-100-30, XC-EXP (C/N 4851), was purchased by* Petroléos Mexicanos *(Pemex) late in 1980, and is seen here at Nairobi, Kenya* (Author's collection, Neg No 5187/8).

SCIBE-Zaïre ordered a pair of L-100-30s (C/Nos 4796 and 4881), the first being registered 9Q-CBJ, the second N4170M prior to delivery. The latter was delivered on June 16 1981 but was subsequently sold to LADE, Argentina, as LQ-FAA. **Left** *The photograph shows 9Q-CBJ taking off in high humidity, the broad propeller blades creating vortex streams, a fairly commonplace phenomenon with Hercules.* **Below** *Photo shows the colour scheme of the SCIBE-Zaïre L-100-30 9Q-CBJ, which was white overall with dark maroon cheat line* (Lockheed-Georgia, Neg Nos RL 3568-49 and RL 4199-1C).

Chapter 12

The unrewarded labours

As much a postscript as a tidying up of loose ends, it is necessary to mention a number of C-130 projects and other ideas which either remained stillborn or contributed to wider research that quickly passed beyond the scope of the Hercules itself.

The Super Hercules

From time to time Lockheed designers have come up with projects fondly referred to as the 'Super Hercules', a name perhaps only justifiably applicable to the '-30' stretched version of relatively recent years.

However, as long ago as 1959 it was announced that, under the designation GL-207, Lockheeds were studying a somewhat enlarged version of the C-130 with a gross weight of 200,000 lb and powered by four 5,000-eshp Allison T61 turboprops. Length of the fuselage was to be extended by 23 ft and the span by some 13 ft, the 7,500-cu ft freight cabin being capable of accommodating a payload of 77,000 lb.

The design was initiated at a time when great hopes of a boom in air freighting were being nurtured, the project being primarily intended to interest the commercial market. Indeed, speculative orders for 12 aircraft were being discussed with Pan American World Airways, as well as six for Slick Airways, when funds for development of the T61 turboprop began to dry up, and at the end of 1959 the USAF lost all interest in the engine. Some unsuccessful efforts were made to keep the project alive by use of the British Rolls-Royce Tyne turboprop, but already the turbofan and swept wings were seen as the ultimate answer to the large super-freighter, a concept that was to materialise as Lockheed's own C-141 StarLifter.

Extending the concept

Throughout its life studies have been carried out to examine means of enhancing the Hercules' short-field performance, particularly in its ability to support battlefield troops right up at the firing line. Mention has already been made of the various methods of discharging the aircraft's considerable payload— ranging from palletised stores to complete armoured fighting vehicles—without the aircraft landing or coming to a halt on the ground. In these respects the C-130 excelled.

However, initiating a long series of investigations to further improve the short take-off and landing (STOL) characteristics of the Hercules, a new version, the C-130C, had been proposed in 1959 to meet a US Army requirement, employing boundary layer control. The seventh production C-130B, *57-0712*, was accordingly modified to feature a pair of Allison YT-56A-6 turbojets under the outer wings (as gas generators) to augment airflow at low airspeed over the flaps and ailerons. This and the broadening of the chord of the control surfaces enhanced control at low speeds and thereby reduced the stalling speed at maximum landing weight to 60 mph and, by use of a 22 ft diameter drag chute, reduced the landing roll at this weight to less than 500 yd. However, further interest in the operational applications of these trials seems to have waned, and the BLC Hercules was handed over to NASA for general research (later taking part in the Administration's Earth Survey 2 programme).

Notwithstanding this apparent loss of interest in STOL-enhancement, the Vietnam War rekindled efforts to exploit the Hercules' short-field performance and in mid-1966 a new battlefield version, the C-130J powered by 4,590-eshp T56A-15s, was proposed. The idea of energising the boundary layer by enhanced airflow circulation was dropped on the grounds of excessive weight; instead the aileron chord would be increased by 30 per cent and that of the rudder by 40 per cent so as to provide improved low speed handling; an improved anti-skid braking system and faster-operating engine reverse thrust would be included, these refinements allowing the aircraft to land with a 20,000-lb payload in 250 yd ground roll, discharge the load and take off again in a mere 130 yd. The wheel track was to be increased from 14 ft 3 in to 20 ft to enable the aircraft to traverse 10 in gulleys. For increased protection from small arms fire when operating within the ground combat zone, flak armour would protect all crew stations and the fuel tanks would include an explosion suppression system and self-sealing blankets. An assault tanker (the AK-130J),

Above *The first C-130B, 57-0525 (C/N 3501), undergoing STOL tests in 1962; note the instrumentation booms at the wing tips. The following year it was modified as a JC-130B for satellite recovery (Lockheed-Georgia, Neg No RG 659-8).*

Below *Crew members board the boundary layer control NC-130B, 58-0712 (C/N 3507), during its service with Air Force Systems Command in 1960 (Lockheed-Georgia, Neg No RG 1034-9).*

Opposite page *Short landing demonstrations by the boundary layer control NC-130B, 58-0712. The additional Allison YT-56A-6 turbojets under the outer wings and the much-increased rudder chord are clearly visible* (Lockheed-Georgia, Neg Nos RG 659-10, RG 659-14 and RF 7822-16).

Above *The NC-130B (ex-Boundary Layer Control aircraft), 58-0712, after transfer to NASA as N929NA for participation in Earth Survey 2. Note the altered profile of the nose radome, additional fairings on the underside of the fuselage and below the tail* (Lockheed-Georgia, Neg No NL 6643).

capable of delivering 60,000 lb of fuel to a combat zone, as well as the ability to refuel and be refuelled in the air, was also put forward.

The continuing exploitation of quick discharge of freight techniques, tested so successfully under combat conditions, seems to have caused the USAF to abandon this interesting project which, after all, would have been time consuming and expensive, as well as disruptive of Hercules production at a time when work on other C-130s was particularly urgent.

Hercules on water

Having regard for the general configuration of the C-130, a four-engine shoulder-wing aircraft with high-set tailplane, it does not require much imagination to picture a version of the Hercules with boat hull. However, half a century of flying-boat design has seldom produced aircraft which have successfully combined good aerodynamics and hydrodynamics without considerable development, and too often a boat hull that has 'looked good' on paper has proved to be quite unmanageable in practice.

When, in 1968, the US Navy Air Systems Command, through its Advanced Systems Concept Division, approached Lockheed to investigate the feasibility of a 175,000 lb amphibious version of the C-130, design studies went ahead led by Mr Rollo G. Smethers

for an aircraft with a boat-hull fairing extending 66 ft aft from the nose, and employing an hydraulically-retracting 21 ft hydroski which could extend 10 ft down during water take-off; wing-tip floats would be added and the wheel undercarriage would be retained. Manufacture of a one-sixteenth scale model was subcontracted to Lanier Industries, Gainesville, Georgia. At a cost of $9,000 this 32 lb model, constructed of laminated plastic-covered stryofoam, was powered by four Italian Super Tigre engines which produced a total thrust of 10.5 lb and were radio-controlled by a single throttle. More than 40 flights were carried out on Lake Lanier, controlled by Jack Dunn, Lockheed-Georgia test pilot, during September 1968, confirming that the idea was practical (the spray not reaching and 'killing' the engines, nor enveloping the tail), the model becoming airborne in 200 ft.

Although the US Navy did not persevere with the project, Lockheed went ahead in attempts to extend the scope of the Hercules-on-water (HOW) project, pointing to its potential both in commercial use as a commuter aircraft able to land passengers at river terminals in cities and for such military duties as a sea search and rescue aircraft. Yet it seems that to far too many people the era of the large 'flying boat', however attractive, had vanished, and no further development funding was forthcoming.

Take-off and alighting views of the HOW model. The former shows the hydro-ski and the fully-cowled, 'inverted' engines; the latter picture illustrates the considerable nose-up attitude necessary during alighting to ensure that spray passed clear of the engines (Lockheed-Georgia, Neg Nos RK 1538 and RJ 1314-19C).

Chapter 13

The Hercules described

The Lockheed C-130 Hercules is a four turboprop high-wing medium/long range transport aeroplane incorporating rear freight-loading capability through centreline under-tail ramp aperture.

Wings The cantilever wing has a root of NACA 64A613 section, becoming NACA 64A412 at the tip. Dihedral is 2° 30' on the outboard section only. Root incidence is 3° and nil at the tip. The centresection planform is rectangular and the outer sections are tapered towards the tips; there is no sweepback on the quarter-chord (front spar line). The wing is a stressed-skin two-spar structure with integrally-stiffened tapered machined skins up to 48 ft 0 in (14.63 m) long. Internal fuel is carried in six integral wing tanks. Aluminium alloy fabricated ailerons are operated by tandem-system hydraulic boost with either of two independent hydraulic systems and each aileron carries a trim tab. Lockheed-Fowler trailing edge aluminium alloy fabricated landing flaps extend from the wing root to the ailerons. The wing leading edge incorporates anti-icing ducts for engine-bled hot air.

Fuselage The fuselage is a semi-monocoque structure fabricated of aluminium and magnesium alloy and is of near-circular cross section, flattened at the bottom. As well as numerous secondary frames the structure comprises primary joint double frames at the rear of the flight deck, at the forward and rear wing box attachment points and at the forward end of the rear loading ramp station. 'Stretched' versions of the Hercules incorporate extension 'plugs' inserted immediately aft of the rear flight deck frame and immediately forward of the rear loading ramp frame. Longitudinal and torsional loads are carried through primary longerons and secondary stringers as well as through the longitudinal members of the strengthened cabin floor structure. Personnel access is through a base-hinged door with integral airstairs on the port side of the nose, a pair of paratroop exit doors at the rear of the undercarriage fairings and up the rear loading ramp; crew emergency exit is through a forward hatch in the top of the flight deck section and the main cabin emergency exit is via a roof escape hatch amidships. The rear fuselage tapers rearwards to wide elliptic section, flattened laterally.

The main loading ramp, hinged on its forward edge, is lowered hydraulically and incorporates detachable vehicular end ramps; to the rear of the main ramp the undersurface of the rear fuselage is hydraulically retractable to increase the height of loading aperture.

Tail unit The tail unit is a conventional all-metal stressed-skin structure, the single fin being a three-spar structure and the fixed-incidence tailplane a two-spar structure. Elevators and rudder carry trim tabs and the control surfaces operate through tandem-piston hydraulic boost. The tailplane incorporates leading-edge anti-icing with engine hot air.

Landing gear The nosewheel tricycle landing gear is hydraulically retractable and comprises twin nosewheels and tandem mainwheel units, the latter retracting into fairings on the sides of the fuselage. The nosewheel unit is steerable through 60° on each side of centre and incorporates an oleo shock-absorber. The main units retract vertically by means of twin long-stroke screw jacks. Anti-skid hydraulic wheelbrakes are fitted. Ski-equipped versions incorporate retractable wheel-ski combination units. Tyre pressures vary between 45 and 95 lb/sq in (3.16 - 6.68 kg/cm²) depending on mission operating surfaces. When fitted, the ski surfaces are coated with a Teflon composite to reduce ice accretion.

Powerplant and fuel system The C-130 is powered by four Allison T56 turboprops driving four-blade Hamilton-Standard propellers (see below). Internal fuel (6,960 US gal, 26,344 l) is carried in six integral wing tanks and external fuel in two underwing pylon tanks (each with 1,360 US gal, 5,146 l); total, 9,680 US gal, 36,636 l. Single pressure refuelling point in starboard main landing gear fairing (also overwing gravity refuelling fillers). Oil capacity 46 US gal, 182 l. Provision on some versions of the C-130 for eight Aerojet-General 15KS-1000 solid fuel rockets for assisted take-off (each of 1,000 lb, 454 kg, thrust for 15 sec).

Other systems AiResearch gas turbine auxiliary power unit (APU) for engine starting, engine pre-heat, ground air conditioning and to drive air-turbine motor with alternator. Air conditioning and pressurisation system with maximum pressure differential of 7.5 lb/sq

The Lockheed C-130 with the U.S. Navy, U.S. Marine Corps and U.S. Coast Guard

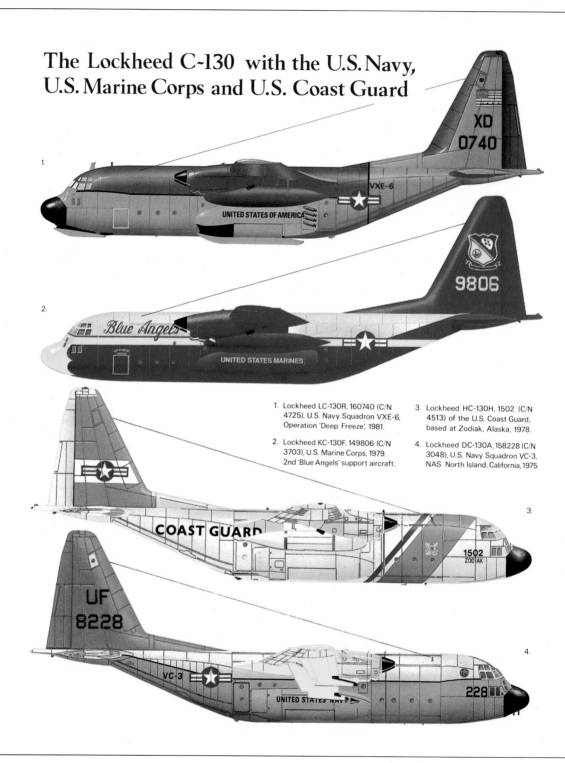

1. Lockheed LC-130R, 160740 (C/N 4725), U.S. Navy Squadron VXE-6, Operation 'Deep Freeze', 1981.

2. Lockheed KC-130F, 149806 (C/N 3703), U.S. Marine Corps, 1979. 2nd 'Blue Angels' support aircraft.

3. Lockheed HC-130H, 1502 (C/N 4513) of the U.S. Coast Guard, based at Zodiak, Alaska, 1978.

4. Lockheed DC-130A, 158228 (C/N 3048), U.S. Navy Squadron VC-3, NAS North Island, California, 1975.

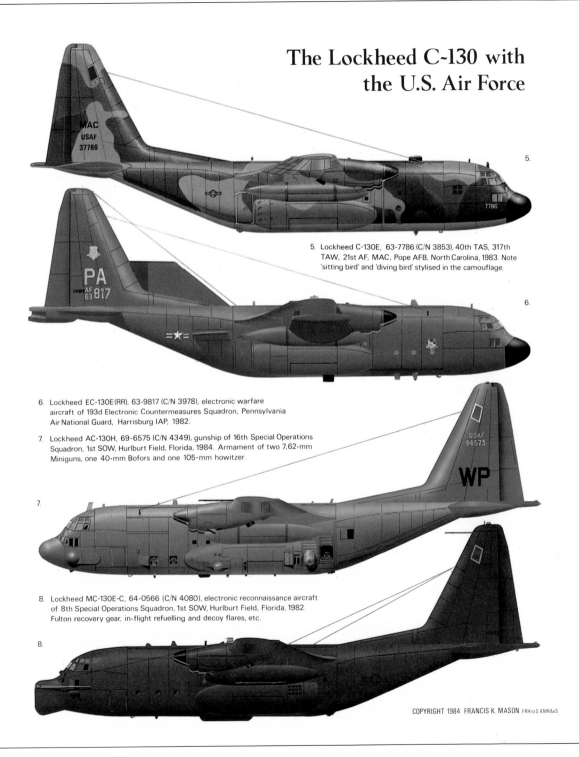

The Lockheed C-130 with the U.S. Air Force

5. Lockheed C-130E, 63-7786 (C/N 3853), 40th TAS, 317th TAW, 21st AF, MAC, Pope AFB, North Carolina, 1983. Note 'sitting bird' and 'diving bird' stylised in the camouflage.

6. Lockheed EC-130E(RR), 63-9817 (C/N 3978), electronic warfare aircraft of 193d Electronic Countermeasures Squadron, Pennsylvania Air National Guard, Harrisburg IAP, 1982.

7. Lockheed AC-130H, 69-6575 (C/N 4349), gunship of 16th Special Operations Squadron, 1st SOW, Hurlburt Field, Florida, 1984. Armament of two 7,62-mm Miniguns, one 40-mm Bofors and one 105-mm howitzer.

8. Lockheed MC-130E-C, 64-0566 (C/N 4080), electronic reconnaissance aircraft of 8th Special Operations Squadron, 1st SOW, Hurlburt Field, Florida, 1982. Fulton recovery gear, in-flight refuelling and decoy flares, etc.

LOCKHEED MODEL 382-19B C-130K

1 Weather radar scanner
2 Radar tracking unit
3 Radome
4 Radome hinge
5 Radar mounting structure
6 Front pressure bulkhead
7 Pitot heads (both sides)
8 Instrument panels
9 Instrument panel shroud
10 Front windscreens
11 Downward vision panels
12 Upward vision panels
13 Cockpit floor
14 Pilot's seat
15 Second pilot's seat

34 Crew entry door
35 Integral airstairs
36 UHF antenna
37 Forward emergency escape hatch
38 Control cable runs behind bulkhead
39 Fire extinguisher
40 Front cabin bulkhead
41 Double frame joint
42 Intercommunicating hatch
43 Front fuselage extension (100 inches) 'plug' section
44 Secondary frame structure
45 Cargo-handling roller system

46 Overhead stowage rack
47 Stretcher installation
48 Stretcher/seat mounting beam
49 Troop carrier seating shown stowed
50 Underfloor structure
51 Double frame joint
52 Fuselage aerial lead-in fairings (both sides)
53 Cabin wall trim panels
54 Cabin window skin panel
55 Primary longeron structure
56 Cargo cabin floor; maximum load, 51,819 lb., in seven standard pallets
57 Emergency exit break-out window panel
58 Cabin air conditioning system in starboard main landing gear fairing

59 Wing inspection light
60 Foreign object damage rein-forced protection panel
61 Air conditioning ducting
62 Main hydraulic system components
63 Booster hydraulic reservoir
64 Cabin handrail
65 Port main landing gear and equipment bay fairing
66 Gas turbine APU
67 APU air intake
68 APU equipment gearbox
69 Landing lamp
70 Tandem twin mainwheels
71 Main landing gear oleos
72 Gear retraction screw jacks
73 Port landing gear bay
74 Mainwheel door
75 Gear retraction hydraulic motor and torque shaft
76 Wing root fairing fillet
77 Engine bleed air ducts
78 Fuselage/main wing spar attachment joint
79 Detachable leading edge

16 Nose gear wheel bay
17 Ground telecom socket
18 Twin nosewheels
19 Nose gear wheel door
20 Battery compartment
21 Portable oxygen bottle
22 Port side console
23 Electrics switch panel
24 Systems manager's station
25 Navigator's station
26 Overhead switch panel
27 VHF Antenna
28 Navigator's instrument panel
29 Crew's rest bunks
30 Crew's closet
31 Crew's galley unit
32 Electronic unit racks
33 Flight deck access ladder

80 Engine jetpipe
81 Allison T56-A-15 turboprop
82 Engine oil tank
83 Propeller reduction gearbox
84 Hamilton Standard constant-speed reversible-pitch four-blade propeller

HERCULES C.MK.3

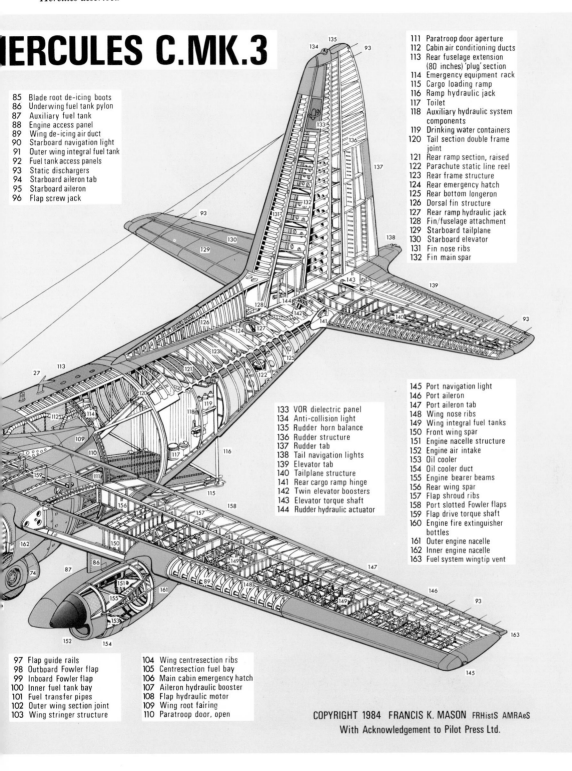

85 Blade root de-icing boots
86 Underwing fuel tank pylon
87 Auxiliary fuel tank
88 Engine access panel
89 Wing de-icing air duct
90 Starboard navigation light
91 Outer wing integral fuel tank
92 Fuel tank access panels
93 Static dischargers
94 Starboard aileron tab
95 Starboard aileron
96 Flap screw jack

111 Paratroop door aperture
112 Cabin air conditioning ducts
113 Rear fuselage extension (80 inches) 'plug' section
114 Emergency equipment rack
115 Cargo loading ramp
116 Ramp hydraulic jack
117 Toilet
118 Auxiliary hydraulic system components
119 Drinking water containers
120 Tail section double frame joint
121 Rear ramp section, raised
122 Parachute static line reel
123 Rear frame structure
124 Rear emergency hatch
125 Rear bottom longeron
126 Dorsal fin structure
127 Rear ramp hydraulic jack
128 Fin/fuselage attachment
129 Starboard tailplane
130 Starboard elevator
131 Fin nose ribs
132 Fin main spar

133 VOR dielectric panel
134 Anti-collision light
135 Rudder horn balance
136 Rudder structure
137 Rudder tab
138 Tail navigation lights
139 Elevator tab
140 Tailplane structure
141 Rear cargo ramp hinge
142 Twin elevator boosters
143 Elevator torque shaft
144 Rudder hydraulic actuator

145 Port navigation light
146 Port aileron
147 Port aileron tab
148 Wing nose ribs
149 Wing integral fuel tanks
150 Front wing spar
151 Engine nacelle structure
152 Engine air intake
153 Oil cooler
154 Oil cooler duct
155 Engine bearer beams
156 Rear wing spar
157 Flap shroud ribs
158 Port slotted Fowler flaps
159 Flap drive torque shaft
160 Engine fire extinguisher bottles
161 Outer engine nacelle
162 Inner engine nacelle
163 Fuel system wingtip vent

97 Flap guide rails
98 Outboard Fowler flap
99 Inboard Fowler flap
100 Inner fuel tank bay
101 Fuel transfer pipes
102 Outer wing section joint
103 Wing stringer structure
104 Wing centresection ribs
105 Centresection fuel bay
106 Main cabin emergency hatch
107 Aileron hydraulic booster
108 Flap hydraulic motor
109 Wing root fairing
110 Paratroop door, open

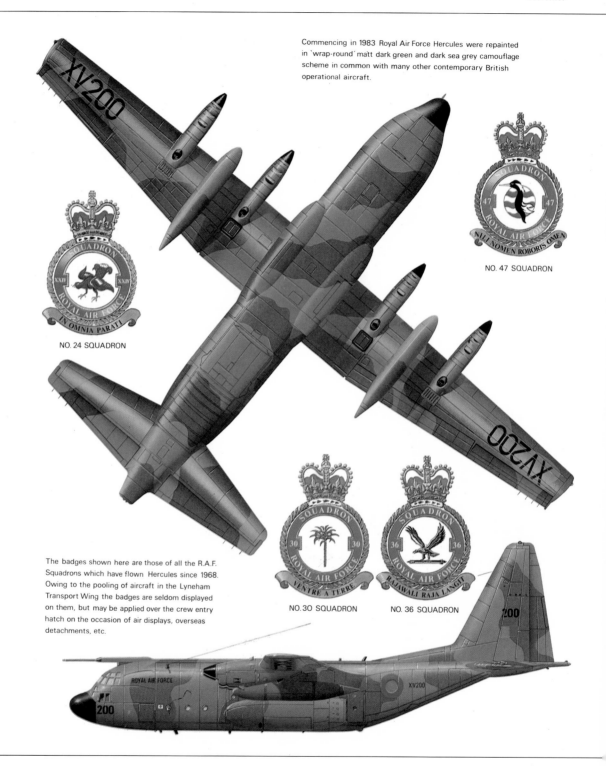

Commencing in 1983 Royal Air Force Hercules were repainted in `wrap-round' matt dark green and dark sea grey camouflage scheme in common with many other contemporary British operational aircraft.

NO. 47 SQUADRON

NO. 24 SQUADRON

The badges shown here are those of all the R.A.F. Squadrons which have flown Hercules since 1968. Owing to the pooling of aircraft in the Lyneham Transport Wing the badges are seldom displayed on them, but may be applied over the crew entry hatch on the occasion of air displays, overseas detachments, etc.

NO. 30 SQUADRON   NO. 36 SQUADRON

LOCKHEED C-130K HERCULES C Mark 1P
LYNEHAM TRANSPORT WING, 1984

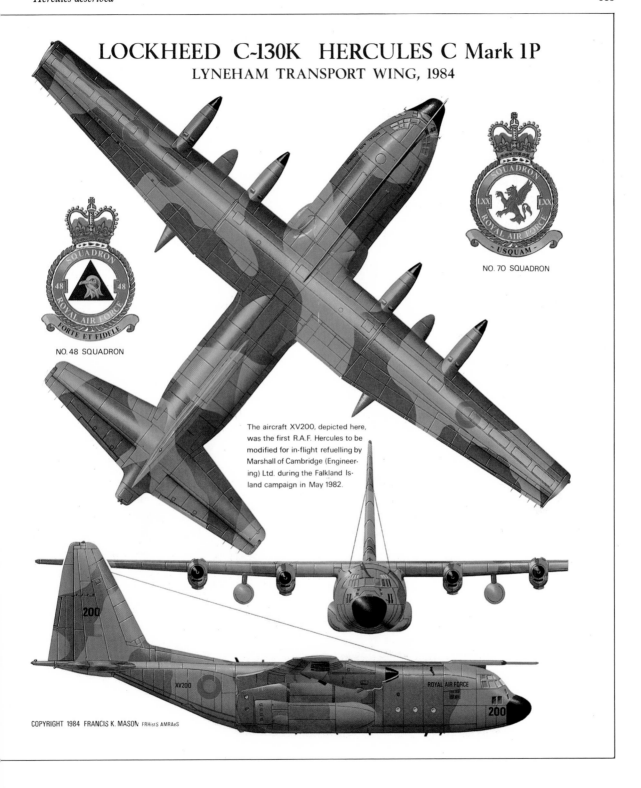

NO. 70 SQUADRON

NO. 48 SQUADRON

The aircraft XV200, depicted here, was the first R.A.F. Hercules to be modified for in-flight refuelling by Marshall of Cambridge (Engineering) Ltd. during the Falkland Island campaign in May 1982.

COPYRIGHT 1984 FRANCIS K. MASON FRHistS AMRAeS

ROYAL AIR FORCE

in (0.53 kg/cm²). Two independent hydraulic systems, pressure 3,000 lb/sq in (210 kg/cm²). Electrical system supplied by four 40 kVA AC generators driven by Allison T56 turboprops and one 20 kVA auxiliary generator driven by APU.

Crew, accommodation and freight Basic flight crew of four on flight deck, comprising pilot, second pilot, navigator and systems manager; provision also for fifth man (loadmaster). Galley and sleeping accommodation for relief crew. Flight deck and main cabin is pressurised and air conditioned. Accommodation for military personnel is (in the C-130E and H) a maximum of 92 combat troops, or 64 paratroops; alternatively 74 litter cases and two medical attendants. When employed for transport of freight or other military equipment, a maximum payload of 43,449 lb (19,704 kg) may be carried by standard-length aircraft, or 53,600 lb (24,312 kg) by maximum-stretched versions. Alternative representative loads may include:

a) Three Douglas MGR-1A Honest John missiles (each 5,820 lb, 2,640 kg), or one missile together with launch vehicle.

b) Two Western Electric MIM-14A Nike Hercules missiles (each 10,400 lb; 4,720 kg) including boosters.

c) Two Sperry MGM-29A Sergeant missiles (each 10,000 lb, 4,580 kg).

d) One Boeing MIM-1OB Super Bomarc missile (16,032 lb, 7,272 kg).

e) One Martin MGM-81A Pershing missile (10,000 lb, 4,540 kg) together with five-ton EL articulated launcher.

f) 200 Philco AIM-9 Sidewinder air-to-air missiles in containers.

g) One 155-mm howitzer and its associated high-speed tractor.

h) One Type 6 refuelling trailer (26,640 lb, 12,080 kg).

j) Up to six standard pre-loaded air freight pallets in standard-length versions of the C-130.

k) Up to seven 88 × 118-in pre-loaded air freight pallets plus 470 cu ft ramp container in maximum-stretched C-130 versions.

l) Single cargo pallet for paradropping of 41,740 lb (18,950 kg).

m) Bulk fuel delivery in drums and bladder tanks of 7,350 gal.

n) Maximum of 4,720 US gal carried in air refuelling tanker versions.

Basic avionics Scarcely any two air forces specify identical avionic fits in their C-130s and variations exist even within individual Services. The following list of equipment represents the basic standard fit in the majority of Tactical Airlift Command C-130Hs as delivered:

Dual 618M-3A VHF communications
Dual 628T-1 UHF communications
AN/ARC-164 UHF communications
AN/AIC-13 Public Address System
AN/AIC-18 Intercom
Dual 621A-6A ATC transponders
DF-301E UHF navigation system
Dual 51RV-4B VHF navigation system
CMA 771 Omega navigation system
LTN-72 Inertial navigation system
Dual DF-206 ADF
51Z-4 marker beacon receiver
Dual 86OE-5 distance measuring equipment
AL-101 radio altimeter
RDR-1F weather radar
Dual C-12 compass systems
AP-105V autopilot
Dual FD-109 flight directors

Leading particulars

Dimensions

Wings (all versions). Wing span, 132 ft 7 in, 40.57 m; wing root chord, 16 ft 0 in, 4.90 m; mean wing chord, 13 ft 8½ in, 4.19 m; wing aspect ratio, 10.09 m. *Length overall* (all versions except HC-130H, L-100-20 and -30, and C Mk 3), 97 ft 9 in, 29.91 m; (HC-130H, recovery system folded), 98 ft 9 in, 30.22 m; (HC-130H, recovery system extended), 106 ft 4 in, 32.54 m; (L-100-20), 106 ft 0½ in, 32.45 m; (L-100-30 and C Mk 3), 112 ft 8½ in, 34.49 m. *Height overall* (all versions, unloaded), 38 ft 3 in, 11.70 m. *Tailplane span* (all versions), 52 ft 8 in, 16.12 m. *Wheel track* (all versions), 14 ft 3 in, 4.36 m. *Wheelbase* (all versions except L-100-20 and -30, and C Mk 3), 32 ft 0¾ in, 9.81 m; (L-100-20), 37 ft 1¼ in, 11.35 m; (L-100-30 and C Mk 3), 40 ft 4¾ in, 12.36 m.

Aerodynamic surface areas

All versions. *Gross wing area*, 1,745 sq ft, 162.285 m²; *total aileron area*, 110 sq ft, 10.23 m²; *total landing flap area*, 342 sq ft, 31.81 m²; *gross fin area*, 225 sq ft, 20.925 m²; *rudder area* (including tab), 75 sq ft, 6.975 m²; *gross tailplane area*, 381 sq ft, 35.43 m²; *total elevator area* (including tabs), 155 sq ft, 14.415 m²

Cabin and loading dimensions

Main cargo loading door, rear (all versions). Height, 9ft 1 in, 2.78 m; width, 10 ft 1 in, 3.085 m; height of sill above ground, 3 ft 5 in, 1.045 m. *Paratroops doors, each* (military troop transports). Height, 6 ft 0 in, 1.84 m; width, 3 ft 0 in, 0.92 m; height of sill above ground, 3 ft 5 in, 1.045 m. *Main accommodation cabin, excluding flight deck:* Length, excluding rear ramp (all military versions, except C Mk 3), 41 ft 5 in, 12.67 m; (L-100-20), 49 ft 1½ in, 15.03 m; (L-100-30 and C Mk 3), 55 ft 5¼ in, 16.96 m. Length, including rear ramp (all military versions, except C Mk 3), 51 ft 8½ in, 15.82 m; (L-100-20), 62 ft 0 in, 18.97 m; (L-100-30 and C Mk 3), 65 ft 8¾ in, 20.11 m. Maximum width (all versions), 10 ft 3 in, 3.14 m. Maximum height (all military versions), 9 ft 2¾ in, 2.82 m; (all commercial versions), 9 ft 0 in, 2.75 m. Floor area, excluding ramp (all military versions except C Mk 3), 425 sq ft, 39.525 m²; (L-100-10), 413 sq ft, 38.41 m²; (L-100-20), 499 sq ft, 46.41 m²; (L-100-30 and C Mk 3), 563 sq ft, 52.36 m². Main cabin volume, including ramp (all military versions except C Mk 3), 4,300 cu ft, 121.7 m³; (L-100-20), 5,307 cu ft, 150.28 m³; (L-100-30 and C Mk 3), 6,057 cu ft, 171.5 m³). *Ramp floor area* (all versions), 103 sq ft, 9.58 m².

Weights and loadings

Military versions. *Weight empty, equipped* (C-130E), 75,693 lb, 33,063 kg; (C-130H), 72,892 lb, 33,063 kg; (C Mk 1), 72,367 lb, 32,825 kg; (C Mk 3), 73,400 lb, 33,324 kg. *Maximum payload* (C-130E), 45,000 lb, 20,412 kg; (C-130H), 45,000 lb, 20,412 kg; (C Mk 1), 45,525 lb, 20,650 kg; (C Mk 3), 46,525 lb, 21,122 kg. *Maximum normal take-off weight* (all military versions), 155,000 lb, 70,310 kg. *Maximum overload take-off weight* (all military versions), 175,000 lb, 79,380 kg. *Maximum zero fuel weight* (C-130E, C-130H and C Mk 1), 119,142 lb, 54,032 kg. *Design landing weight* (all versions), 130,000 lb, 58,970 kg. *Maximum wing loading* (all versions), 89 lb/sq ft, 434.5 kg/m². *Maximum power loading* (C-130E), 9.6 lb/eshp, 4.35 kg/eshp; (C-130H and RAF versions), 8.6 lb/eshp, 3.90 kg/eshp.

Commercial versions. *Weight empty, equipped* (L-100-10), 67,336 lb, 30,543 kg; (L-100-20), 70,837 lb, 32,131 kg; (L-100-30), 71,400 lb, 32,386 kg. *Maximum payload* (L-100-10), 48,758 lb, 22,116 kg; (L-100-20), 49,163 lb, 22,300 kg; (L-100-30), 53,600 lb, 24,312 kg. *Maximum take-off weight* (all versions), 155,000 lb, 70,308 kg. *Maximum ramp weight* (L-100-10), 155,000 lb, 70,308 kg; (L-100-20 and -30), 155,800 lb, 70,670 kg. *Maximum landing weight* (L-100-10 and -20), 130,000 lb, 58,970 kg; (L-100-30), 135,000 lb, 61,235 kg. *Maximum wing loading* (all versions), 88.8 lb/sq ft, 433.5 kg/m². *Maximum power loading* (L-100-10), 9.6 lb/eshp, 4.35 kg/eshp; (L-100-20 and -30), 8.6 lb/eshp, 3.90 kg/eshp.

Performance

Military versions (Maximum take-off weight except where otherwise stated). *Maximum level speed* (C-130E, C-130H, HC-130H, HC-130P and C Mk 1), 384 mph, 333 kts, 618 km/h, at 20,000 ft, 6,100 m. *Maximum cruising speed* (C-130E), 368 mph, 320 kts, 592 km/h; (C-130H and C Mk 1), 375 mph, 326 kts, 603 km/h; (HC-130H), 366 mph, 318 kts, 589 km/h. *Economical cruising speed* (all versions), 340 mph, 295 kts, 547 km/h. *Typical stalling speed* (all versions), 115 mph, 100 kts, 185 km/h).
Rate of climb at sea level (C-130E), 1,830 ft/min, 558 m/min; (C-130H and C Mk 1), 1,900 ft/min, 579 m/min; (HC-130H), 1,820 ft/min, 555 m/min.
Service ceiling (C-130E at 155,000 lb, 70,310 kg, AUW), 23,100 ft, 7,010 m; (C-130H and C Mk 1 at 130,000 lb, 58,970 kg, AUW), 33,000 ft, 8,075 m. *Service ceiling (one engine out)* (C-130E at 130,000 lb, 58,970 kg, AUW), 21,500 ft, 6,550 m; (C-130H and C Mk 1 at same AUW), 26,500 ft, 8,075 m.
Minimum ground turning radius (all versions), 85 ft, 26 m. *Runway LCN* at 155,000 lb, 70,310 kg, AUW, 37 on asphalt, 42 on concrete.
Take-off ground run (C-130E), 3,800 ft, 1,160 m; (C-130H, HC-130H and C Mk 1), 4,700 ft, 1,432 m. *Take-off to clear 50 ft, 15 m* (C-130E), 5,580 ft, 1,700 m; (C-130H, HC-130H, HC-130P and C Mk 1), 4,500 ft, 1,372 m.
Landing from 50 ft, 15 m, at 100,000 lb, 45,360 kg, AUW (all versions), 2,700 ft, 823 m. *Landing from 50 ft, 15 m*, at maximum landing weight (all versions), 3,750 ft, 1,143 m. *Landing ground run* at maximum landing weight (all versions), 2,130 ft, 650 m.
Range with maximum payload, 5 per cent reserve and allowance for 30 min loiter at sea level: (C-130E), 2,420 miles, 2,101 nautical miles, 3,895 km; (C-130H and C Mk 1), 2,450 miles, 2,127 nautical miles, 3,943 km. *Range with maximum fuel*, with two 1,360 US gal external tanks, 20,000 lb (9,070 kg) payload, reserves of 5 per cent and allowance for 30 min loiter at sea level: (C-130E), 4,700 miles, 4,081 nautical miles, 7,560 km; (C-130H and C Mk 1), 4,770 miles, 4,142 nautical miles, 7,675 km.

Commercial versions (Maximum take-off weight except where otherwise stated). *Maximum cruising speed*, at 20,000 ft, 6,100 m, at 120,000 lb, 54,430 kg, AUW: (L-100-10), 357 mph, 310 kts, 575 km/h; (L-100-20 and -30), 377 mph, 327 kts, 607 km/h. *Typical landing speed* (all versions), 145 mph, 126 kts, 233 km/h.
Rate of climb at sea level (L-100-10), 1,830 ft/min, 588 m/min; (L-100-20 and -30), 1,900 ft/min, 579 m/min. *Minimum ground turning radius* (L100-10 and -20), 85 ft, 26 m; (L-100-30), 90 ft, 27.5 m.
FAA-defined take-off field length (L-100-10), 6,640 ft, 2,024 m; (L-100-20 and -30), 6,000 ft, 1,829 m. *FAA-defined landing field length*, at maximum landing weight (L-100-10 and -20), 4,760 ft, 1,450 m; (L-100-30), 4,830 ft, 1,472 m.
Range with maximum payload, 45 min fuel reserves (L-100-10), 2,230 miles, 1,936 nautical miles, 3,588 km; (L-100-20), 2,560 miles, 2,223 nautical miles, 4,120 km; (L-100-30), 2,130 miles, 1,850 nautical miles, 3,435 km. *Range with nil payload*, 45 min fuel reserves (L-100-10), 3,220 miles, 2,796 nautical miles, 5,182 km; (L-100-20), 4,840 miles, 4,203 nautical miles, 7,789 km; (L-100-30), 4,740 miles, 4,120 nautical miles, 7,630 km.
Field operating noise characteristics (L-100-30). Take-off noise level at 4 miles, 3.5 nautical miles, 6.5 km, from

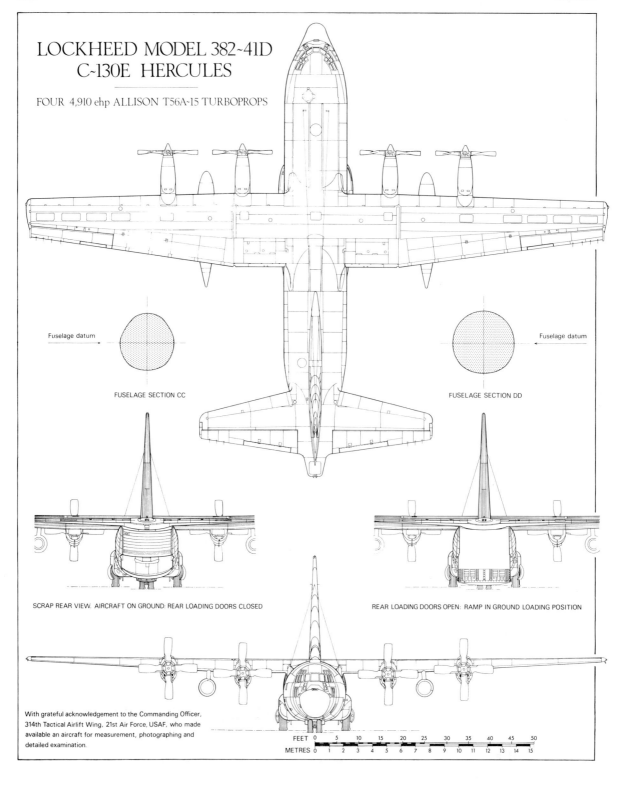

LOCKHEED MODEL 382-41D
C-130E HERCULES

FOUR 4,910 ehp ALLISON T56A-15 TURBOPROPS

Fuselage datum

FUSELAGE SECTION CC

Fuselage datum

FUSELAGE SECTION DD

SCRAP REAR VIEW. AIRCRAFT ON GROUND: REAR LOADING DOORS CLOSED

REAR LOADING DOORS OPEN: RAMP IN GROUND LOADING POSITION

With grateful acknowledgement to the Commanding Officer, 314th Tactical Airlift Wing, 21st Air Force, USAF, who made available an aircraft for measurement, photographing and detailed examination.

FEET 0   5   10   15   20   25   30   35   40   45   50
METRES 0 1 2 3 4 5 6 7 8 9 10 11 12 13 14 15

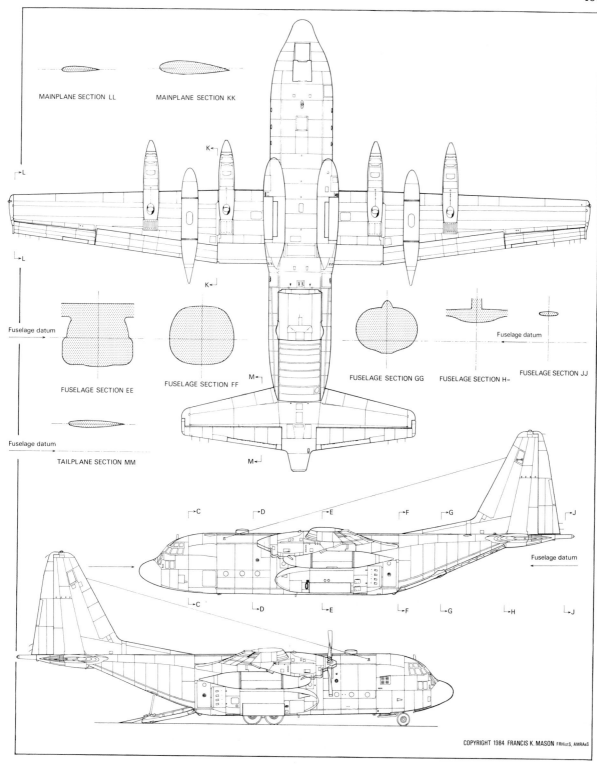

MAINPLANE SECTION LL

MAINPLANE SECTION KK

K←

L←

└→L

K←┘

Fuselage datum

Fuselage datum

FUSELAGE SECTION EE

FUSELAGE SECTION FF

M←

FUSELAGE SECTION GG

FUSELAGE SECTION H–

FUSELAGE SECTION JJ

Fuselage datum

TAILPLANE SECTION MM

M←┘

┌→C   ┌→D   ┌→E   ┌→F   ┌→G   ┌→J

Fuselage datum

└→C   └→D   └→E   └→F   └→G   └→H   └→J

COPYRIGHT 1984 FRANCIS K. MASON FRHistS, AMRAeS

start of take-off roll, 95.0 EPNdB; approach noise level at 1.15 miles, 1.0 nautical mile, 1.85 km, from landing threshold on 3° glidepath, 101.5 EPNdB. Sideline noise level at 0.40 miles, 0.35 nautical miles, 0.65 km, from runway centreline, 97.8 EPNdB.

Powerplant: Allison T56

General description. The Allison T56 axial-flow turboprop as installed in the Lockheed C-130 drives Hamilton Standard 54H60 four-blade constant-speed, fully-feathering, reversible-pitch propellers of 13 ft 6 in (4.11 m) diameter. *Propeller drive,* combination spur/planetary gear type, primary step-down by spur, secondary by planetary; overall gear ratio, 13.54:1; power section rpm, 13,820; reduction gear contained in cast magnesium casing; gearbox assembly supported from power assembly by main drive shaft casing 28 in (71.1 cm) long and two inclined strut members. Weight of gearbox assembly, approx 550 lb (249 kg). *Air intake,* circular duct on engine face with thermal anti-icing. *Compressor,* 14-stage axial-flow with series of 14 discs and low-creep alloy rotor blades dovetailed into perimeters and locked by adjacent discs. Rotor assembly tie-bolted to shaft which runs in one ball and one roller bearing. Fifteen rows of stator blades, welded in rings. Disc, rotor and stator blades, and four-piece cast casing of stainless steel. Compressor inlet area, 155.65 sq in (1,004 cm^2). Pressure ratio, 9.25:1; mass flow 32.4 lb (14.70 kg)/sec. *Combustion section,* six stainless steel cannular-type perforated combustion liners within one-piece stainless steel outer casing; fuel nozzles at forward end of each combustion liner; primary ignition by two igniters in diametrically opposite liners. *Fuel system,* high pressure type with Bendix system control; fuel grade JP-4 or JP-5 (Spec MIL-J-5624). *Power section,* hollow air-cooled nozzle guide vanes of high-temperature alloy. Four-stage turbine comprising rotor assembly with four stainless-steel discs with first stage having hollow air-cooled high-temperature alloy blades (introduced in A-15) secured in discs by 'fir-tree' roots; discs splined to rotor shaft running in front and rear roller bearings. Steel outer casing. Gas temperature at turbine entry, 1,975°F (1,076°C). *Jet pipe,* stainless steel, fixed. *Lubrication,* low pressure system with dry sump. Pesco dual-element oil pump; oil supply pressure, 55 lb/sq in (3.87 kg/cm^2); oil specification, MIL-L-7808. *Starting,* air turbine mounted on gearbox.

Appendices

1 Glossary of abbreviations

AA Air America.
AAC Alaskan Air Command.
A & AEE Aircraft and Armament Experimental Establishment, UK.
AB Air Base.
ABS/W/G Air Base Squadron/Wing/Group.
ACCS/W Airborne Command and Control Squadron/Wing, USAF.
AAS/W/G Aeromedical Airlift Squadron/Wing/ Group, USAF.
ACGS Aerospace Cartographic and Geodetic Squadron/Service, USAF.
AD Air Division, USAF.
ADAF Abu Dhabi Air Force.
ADTC Armament Development & Test Center, USAF.
AFCOM Aerospace Defense Command, USAF.
ADW Air Defense Wing, USAF.
ADWC Air Defense Weapons Center, USAF.
AEWS/W/G Airborne Early Warning Squadron/Wing/Group, USAF.
AFARE Air Force of the Arab Republic of Egypt.
AFB Air Force Base.
AFCS Air Force Communications Service, USAF.
AFFTC Air Force Flight Test Center, USAF.
AFM Air Force Museum.
AFMDC Air Force Missile Development Center, USAF.
AFRES Air Force Reserve, USAF.
AFSC Air Force Systems Command, USAF.
AFSWC Air Force Special Weapons Center, USAF.
AFTC Air Force Test Center, USAF.
AIA Alaska International Air.
AII Airlift International Inc.
Ak(AK) Alaska.
Al (AL) Alabama.
AMC Air Materiel Command, USAF.
ANG Air National Guard, USAF.
ANGB Air National Guard Base, USAF.
AOG Aircraft on ground.
AP Airport.
APCS Air Photographic and Charting Service, MATS, USAF.
ARDC Air Research & Development Center, USAF.
ARPS Aerospace Research Pilots' School, USAF.
ARRS/W Aerospace Rescue & Recovery Squadron (Service)/Wing, USAF.

ARS/W Air Refuelling Squadron/Wing, USAF.
ASA Alaska Airlines.
ATC Air Training Command, USAF.
ATO Assisted Take-off.
ATTW Aircrew Training and Test Wing, USAF.
AURI *Angkatan Udara Republik Indonesia* (Indonesian Air Force). Later TNI-AU.
Az (AZ) Arizona.
BAF Belgian Air Force (*Force Aérienne Belge*).
BLC Boundary Layer Control.
BoLAF Bolivian Air Force (*Fuerza Aérea Boliviana*).
BuAer Bureau of Aeronautics, USA.
CAF Canadian Armed Forces (previously Royal Canadian Air Force).
CAS Continental Air Services.
CAML Cargo Aircraft Minelaying System.
CCK Ching Chuan Kang ROCAB, Taiwan.
Ca (CA) California.
CCRS Combat Crew Replacement Squadron, USAF.
CCTW Combat Crew Training Wing, USAF.
CDS Container Delivery System.
CIA Central Intelligence Agency.
C/N Constructor's Number.
Co(CO) Colorado.
CS/W Composite Squadron/Wing.
CSS/G/W Combat Support Squadron/Group/Wing, USAF.
Ct (CT) Connecticutt.
CTA *Consorcio Technice de Aeronautica*, Luanda, Angola.
Cz (CZ) Canal Zone.
DC District of Columbia, USA.
Deld Delivered
Det Detached or Detachment.
De (DE) Delaware.
DoC Department of Commerce, USA.
EA *Elliniki Aéroporia* (Hellenic Air Force).
EAF Egyptian Air Force (see also AFARE).
ECM Electronic Countermeasures.
ECS Electronic Countermeasures Squadron, USAF.
EdA *Ejercito del Aire* (Spanish Air Force).
ELINT Electronic Intelligence.
ESD Electronic Systems Division, AFSC, USAF.
FAA *Fuerza Aérea Argentina* (Argentine Air Force); Fleet Air Arm.
FAB *Forca Aérea Brasileira* (Brazilian Air Force).
FABol *Fuerza Aérea Boliviana* (Bolivian Air Force).
FAC *Fuerza Aérea Colombiana* (Columbian Air Force).
FAE *Fuerza Aérea Ecuatoriana* (Ecuador Air Force).

FAP *Fuerza Aérea Peruana* (Peruvian Air Force).
FAV *Fuerza Aérea Venezolana* (Venezuelan Air Force).
FAZ *Force Aérienne Zaïroise* (Zaïre Air Force).
FCS Facility Checking Squadron, USAF.
FDS Flight Demonstration Squadron, ('The Blue Angels'), US Navy.
FEWSG Flight Electronic Warfare Support Group, US Navy.
Fl (FL) Florida.
FNAF Federal Nigerian Air Force.
FNB First National Bank of Chicago.
FTS Flying Training Squadron, Flight Transport Squadron, USAF.
FV *Flygvapnet* (Swedish Air Force).
FWS Fighter Weapons School, NAS Miramar, US Navy.
FY Fiscal Year.
Ga (GA) Georgia.
Gelac Lockheed-Georgia Company, Marietta, Georgia, USA.
GOM Government of Malaysia.
GRZ Government of Republic of Zambia.
Hi (HI) Hawaii.
Ia (IA) Iowa; also International Aerodyne.
IAI Interior Airways Inc.
IAP International Airport.
Id (ID) Idaho.
IDF/AF Israel Defence Force/Air Force.
IIAF Imperial Iranian Air Force.
Il (IL) Illinois.
In (IN) Indiana.
JATO Jet-assisted Take-off.
La (LA) Louisiana.
LAC Lockheed Aircraft Corporation.
LAPES Low Altitude Parachute Extraction System.
LAS Lockheed Aircraft Service.
LFC Lockheed Financing Corporation.
Ma (MA) Massachusetts.
MAC Military Airlift Command, USAF.
MAFFS Modular Airborne Firefighting System.
MAP Mutual Assistance Program; Municipal Airport.
MARTD Marine Air Reserve Training Detachment, USMC.
MAS/G Military Airlift Squadron/Group, USAF.
MASDC Military Aircraft Storage & Disposition Center, Davis Monthan AFB, USAF.
MATS Military Air Transport Service, USAF.
MAW Marine Air Wing, USMC.
MCAS Marine Corps Air Station, USMC.
MCS Mapping and Charting Squadron, USAF.
Md (MD) Maryland.
Me (ME) Maine.
Mi (MI) Michigan.
Mn (MN) Minnesota.
Mo (MO) Missouri.
MCE Marshall of Cambridge (Engineering) Ltd, UK.
Mod Modified or modification.
MoD Ministry of Defence, UK.
Mt (MT) Montana.
NAF Nigerian Air Force (see also FNAF); also Naval Air Facility, USN.
NAL National Aircraft Leasing.
NAS Naval Air Station, USN.
NASA National Aeronautics & Space Administration, USA.

NATC Naval Air Test Center, USN.
NATO North Atlantic Treaty Organisation.
Nc (NC) North Carolina.
Nd (ND) North Dakota.
Nh (NH) New Hampshire.
Nj (NJ) New Jersey.
Nm (NM) New Mexico.
NOAA National Oceanic and Atmospheric Administration, USA.
NSF National Science Foundation, USA.
NSW New South Wales, Australia.
Nv (NV) Nevada.
NWT Northwest Territorial Airways.
Ny (NY) New York.
OCU Operational Conversion Unit, RAF.
Oh (OH) Ohio.
Ok (OK) Oklahoma.
Or (OR) Oregon.
Pa (PA) Pennsylvania.
PACAF Pacific Air Forces, USAF.
PADC Philippine Aerospace Development Corporation.
PAF Pakistan Air Force.
PhAF Philippine Air Force.
PIA Pakistan International Airways.
PLADS Parachute Low Altitude Delivery System.
PMW Photo Mapping Wing, USAF.
PortAF Portuguese Air Force.
PTW Pilot Training Wing, USAF.
PWA Pacific Western Airlines.
Pr (PR) Puerto Rico.
RAAF Royal Australian Air Force.
RAF Royal Air Force.
RCAF Royal Canadian Air Force.
RDA Red Dodge Aviation.
RDAF Royal Danish Air Force, *Flyvevabnet*.
RHAF Royal Hellenic Air Force (see also *Elliniki Aéroporia*).
Ri (RI) Rhode Island.
RJAF Royal Jordanian Air Force.
RMAF Royal Moroccan Air Force.
RNoAF Royal Norwegian Air Force.
ROCAB Republic of China Air Base.
RSAF Royal Saudi Air Force; also Republic of Singapore Air Force.
RTAF(B) Royal Thai Air Force (Base).
RWRW Rescue and Weather Reconnaissance Wing, USAF.
SAAF South African Air Force.
SAR/R Search and Rescue/Reconnaissance.
SAT Southern Air Transport.
Sc (SC) South Carolina.
Sd (SD) South Dakota.
SAM Surface-to-Air Missile.
SKE Station-Keeping Equipment (AN/APN-169).
SOS/G/W Special Operations Squadron/Group/Wing, USAF.
SOTS/G Special Operations Training Squadron/Group, USAF.
SpAF Spanish Air Force (see also *Ejercito del Aire*).
Sqn Squadron.
SRS/W Strategic Reconnaissance Squadron/Wing, USAF.
SS Support Squadron, USAF.
SVAF South Vietnamese Air Force.
SwAF Swedish Air Force (see also *Flygvapnet*).

TAB *Transporte Aereo Boliviano.*
TAC Tactical Air Command, USAF.
TAF Turkish Air Force (see also *Turk Hava Kuvvetleri*).
TAS/W/G Tactical Airlift Squadron/Wing/Group, USAF.
TATS Tactical Airlift Training Squadron, USAF.
TCS Troop Carrier Squadron, Tactical Control Squadron, USAF.
TCW Troop Carrier Wing, Tactical Control Wing, USAF.
TDS Tactical Drone Squadron, USAF.
TFS/W Tactical Fighter Squadron/Wing, USAF.
TGR Trans-Gabon Railway.
THK *Turk Hava Kuvvetleri* (Turkish Air Force).
Tn (TN) Tennessee.
TNI-AU *Tentara Nasional Indonesia-Angkatan Udara* (Indonesian Air Force).
TRS Tactical Reconnaissance Squadron, USAF.
TS/W Test Squadron/Wing, USAF.
TTC Tactical Training Center, USAF.

Tx (TX) Texas.
UA Uganda Airlines.
UAC Uganda Air Cargo.
UEAF United Emirates Air Force.
USAF United States Air Force.
USAFRES United States Air Force Reserve.
USCG United States Coast Guard.
USFS United States Forestry Service.
USMC United States Marine Corps.
USN United States Navy.
Ut (UT) Utah.
Va (VA) Virginia.
Vt (VT) Vermont.
Wa (WA) Washington.
Wi (WI) Wisconsin.
WRS Weather Reconnaissance Squadron, USAF.
Wv (WV) West Virginia.
Wy (WY) Wyoming.
ZAC Zambian Air Cargoes.

2 Production, allocation and service

Hercules aircraft did not pass through the Marietta plant in strictly numerical order of Constructors' Numbers, therefore nothing is gained by listing them in this order. The order presented here indicates the approximate chronological sequence and grouping by which designs and contracts were initiated and is therefore a logical compromise of the order of demand and supply.

The Lockheed system of aircraft nomenclature
The original Hercules project identification was Model 82. When afforded official recognition and became subject of a preliminary production order it became the Model 182 (USAF designation C-130A and derivatives). The USAF's C-130B and derivatives became the Model 282; design derivatives of the C-130B were identified in the Lockheed Model designation by 'dashed suffixes' (eg, the HC-130B was Model 282-2B).

The introduction of the USAF's C-130E was identified in the Lockheed Model 382 and all Hercules, military and civil, have since then carried the Model 382 nomenclature. Initially the 'dashed suffix' system continued as before, simply identifying variants by a 'dashed B' suffix (eg, the C-130E for the USAF's MAC being Model 382-4B and for the USAF's TAC being Model 382-8B).

The Lockheed system became complicated by the introduction of the civil Hercules. Henceforth, from September 1965, the 'dashed suffix' number was followed by the letter C, indicating 'civil' where appropriate. Civil aircraft also carried a separate Lockheed nomenclature, the Hercules being the L-100; the basic aircraft was the L-100-10; with the 2.5 m fuselage stretch it became the L-100-20 and with 4.6 m stretch became the L-100-30.

It also became necessary to identify the powerplant application to the various Hercules versions (apart from slightly differing military and commercial certification requirements, the military Allison T56A-7 corresponded to the Civil Allison 501-D22 and the rerated T56A-15 to the 501-D22A). This identification by powerplant was introduced by adding a letter to the Model 382 designation, the 382B having 501-D22 (civil) engines, the 382E having -D22A engines (2.5 m stretch), and the 382G having -D22A engines (4.6 m stretch). Models 382C and 382D were Lockheed designations for military Hercules, and the Model 382T was the 'stretched' military transport that originated on the production line (as distinct from being converted later in life).

In most instances each overseas contract has been identified by a new 'dashed-suffix' number and the numerical order of these 'dashed-suffixes' has usually dictated the order in which aircraft histories are presented here. To complicate matters, military and civil Hercules have followed each other down the production line apparently at random, their position in fact being planned to meet conflicting customers' delivery date requirements.

Commercial and sales leasing
During recent years the demand for commercial L-100s has been generally constant, particularly in the international market. Due, however, to the financial condition of many nations and the consequent reluctance of major lenders to accept sovereign risk or asset-based financing, a few aircraft have been made available on an immediate delivery basis. Innovative financing techniques have been employed to obviate sovereign risk and hard currency requirements—including, but not limited to, consideration of barter/countertrade and tax incentive lease structuring. The Hercules has thus not only avoided long and unprofitable periods, awaiting the disposal of existing aircraft, but has avoided re-purchase agreements and other sweetening of transactions for lenders —a phenomenon that has plagued the manufacturers of many passenger airliners. In several instances an aggressive trade-in policy has resulted in acquisition of used L-100s for re-sale to satisfy an active customer requirement. The continuing product demand, product improvement and innovative financing, together with the aggressive trade-in policy, have resulted in a projected production of Hercules at least to the end of the century.

LOCKHEED MODEL 82 YC-130 (C/Ns 1001 and 1002) Two prototype aircraft, *53-3396* and *53-3397*. Second aircraft flown first on August 23 1954. Built at Burbank, Los Angeles, California. APS-42 radar.

53-3396 Deld Edwards AFB, 26-8-55; Logistics Command, Marietta, Georgia, 23-3-56. Powerplant development, Allison Motors, 12-56. Became NC-130. Warner Robins AFB, AMC, 10-60; dismantled 10-60.

53-3397 To Lockheed-Georgia, Marietta, 18-12-55; experimental engine trials, Allison Motors, 2-7-59. Became NC-130. Stored Warner Robins AFB, 1960. Further trials, Allison, 10-61; dismantled 4-62.

LOCKHEED MODEL 182 C-130A HERCULES (C/Ns 3001 to 3007) Seven development aircraft, *53-3129* to *53-3135*. First flight by production aircraft *(53-3129)*, 7-4-55. APS-42 radar. All aircraft served with TAC.

53-3129 (C/N 3001) Caught fire on landing from third flight, port wing destroyed; repaired at Marietta. Became JC-130A, 9-57. ARC, Hanscom Field, Massachusetts, 10-59. AFMC, 4-60. Majors Field, Texas, 12-61; 6650th SW, 8-62. Became AC-130A, 4413th CCTS; 415th SOTS; 16th SOS (Vietnam and Thailand) up to 11-70. 711th SOS, 1976-81.

53-3130 (C/N 3002) Trials at Marietta. Became JC-130A, 9-57. Proof strength tested to destruction, 2-58.

53-3131 (C/N 3003) Deld, 31-7-56. Became JC-130A, 8-56. Edwards AFB 1-4-57; 314th TCW, 12-3-58. Became C-130A, 3-58. Edwards AFB, 8-59. Returned to JC-130A, 3-60; 6550th SW, Patrick AFB, 31-7-62; 6515th TS, 9-62; Edwards AFB, 10-75. Ground trainer at Sheppard TTC, 10-78.

53-3132 (C/N 3004) Deld, 19-1-57, to Wright Patterson AFB. Became JC-130A, 1-57. Cambridge ARC, 2-4-58; AFDD, 1-4-60; 3245th ABW, 5-62. Returned to C-130A, 10-62; 6515th TS, 14-10-62. Returned to JC-130A, 1-63; 704th TS, 1974; 64th TAS, 1977; 105th TAS, 1977; 155th TAS, 1978-80; 64th TAS, 1981.

53-3133 (C/N 3005) Deld, 13-1-56, to 3206th TW, Eglin AFB; Wright Patterson AFB, 10-56. Became JC-130A, 12-56; Cambridge ARC, 1-58; AFDC, 4-60; EDD, Hanscom Field, 6-61; 3245th ABW, 7-62. Became NC-130A. 4900th TS, 1973-75; AFSWC, AFSC, Kirtland AFB, 1975-76; MASDC, 1976-81.

53-3134 (C/N 3006) Deld, 18-12-57, to 314th TCW; 6200th ABW, Clark AB, Philippines, 12-58; AFTC, El Centro, 6-59. Became JC-130A, 9-61; 6511th TG, 6-62. Returned to C-130A. 327th TAS, c1967; 155th TAS, Memphis MAP, Tennessee, 1975; MASDC, 1976-81.

53-3135 (C/N 3007) Deld, 9-7-57, to 314th TCW; Edwards AFB, 5-59. Became JC-130A, 4-60. 6515th TS, 7-62; 31st AD, 1-64. Returned to C-130A. 704th TAS, 1971; 327th TAS, 1971-74; 185th TAS, 1977-79; 69th TAS, 1981.

LOCKHEED MODEL 182 C-130A HERCULES (C/Ns 3008 to 3027) 20 production aircraft, *54-1621* to *54-1640*. APS-59 radar. All aircraft for USAF TAC.

54-1621 (C/N 3008) Became trainer, TC-130A. Eventually used as ground instruction aircraft, GC-130A; Sheppard TTC, c1969-77. SOC 1978.

54-1622 (C/N 3009) Became NC-130A. 4900th TS, AFSWC, 1973; 185th TAS, Oklahoma ANG, 1975; MASDC, 1976-81.

54-1623 (C/N 3010) Became AC-130A. 16th SOS, 8th TFW, Ubon RTAFB, Thailand, 1971-72(*Ghost Rider*); 711th SOS, 1978-80

54-1624 (C/N 3011) 39th TCS, c1967. Edwards AFB, 1971; 47th TAS, Forbes AFB, Kansas, 1972; 185th TAS, 1975-76; MASDC, 1976-81.

54-1625 (C/N 3012) Became JC-130A; AFSC. Became AC-130A; 4413th CCTS, 4410th CCTW, Lockbourne AFB, Ohio, 1968-9; 16th SOS, 8th TFW, Ubon RTAFB, Thailand, 1969 (*War Lord*). Shot down, Ho Chi Minh Trail, 21-4-70.

54-1626 (C/N 3013) AFTC, El Centro, 1956. Became prototype AC-130A, 1967. 4950th TW, 1966-67; 16th SOS, 14th SOW, Nha Trang AB, Vietnam, 1968; crashed and damaged, Vietnam, 3-72, but repaired. 711th SOS, 1979. USAF Museum, 1980.

54-1627 (C/N 3014) Became JC-130A, thence AC-130A. 16th SOS, 8th TFW, Ubon RTAFB, Thailand, 1969-72 (*Gomer Grinder*); 415th SOTS, 1st SOW, Hurlburt Field, Florida, 1973-74; 711th SOS, 1975; MASDC, 1976-81.

54-1628 (C/N 3015) Became JC-130A. 6550th SW, Patrick AFB. Became AC-130A; 16th SOS, 8th TFW, Ubon RTAFB, Thailand, 1969-73 (*The Exterminator*); 711th SOS, 919th SOG, Duke Field, Florida, 1977-80.

54-1629 (C/N 3016) Became JC-130A; AFSC; 6550th SW, 1964. Became AC-130A; 16th SOS, 8th TFW; suffered damage from ground fire over Laos and written off after crash landing, Ubon RTAFB, Thailand, 24-5-69.

54-1630 (C/N 3017) Became JC-130A, thence AC-130A; 16th SOS, 8th TFW 1970-71 (*Mors de Callis*); 415th SOTS, 1st SOW, 1971-76; 711th SOS, 1977-81.

54-1631 (C/N 3018) 18th TCS, 64th TCW, c1962; 704th TAS, c1969; to South Vietnamese Air Force, 11-72, but returned to USAF. 327th TAS, 1976; 143d TAS, Rhode Island ANG, 1977; 180th TAS, Missouri ANG, 1977-81.

54-1632 (C/N 3019) Became prototype for proposed TC-130A trainer, thence prototype RC-130A; 1370th Photo Mapping Wing, c1968; returned to C-130A. 706th TAS, 1974-75; 704th TAS, 1976; MASDC, 1976-81.

54-1633 (C/N 3020) 327th TAS, 403d TAW, Willow Grove NAS, Pennsylvania, c1972-77; 180th TAS, Missouri ANG, 1977-80.

54-1634 (C/N 3021) 327th TAS, 403d TAW, Willow Grove NAS, Pennsylvania, 1972. To South Vietnamese Air Force, 11-72, but returned to USAF, 4-75. 327th TAS, 1975-76; 180th TAS, Missouri ANG, 1977-80.

54-1635 (C/N 3022) Became NC-130A; AFRL. Returned to C-130A, 5-63; 327th TAS, 913th TAG, 1972-77; 185th TAS, Oklahoma ANG, 1978-79; 142d TAS, Delaware ANG, 1979-81.

54-1636 (C/N 3023) 327th TAS, 913th TAG, 1972-77; 64th TAS, 1978-81.

54-1637 (C/N 3024) 7406th CSS; Rhein-Main ABW, c1970; 109th TAS, Minnesota ANG, 1974-75; 155th TAS, Tennessee ANG, 1976-81.

54-1638 (C/N 3025) 327th TAS, 913th TAG, 1972-77; 64th TAS, 1978-79; 155th TAS, Tennessee ANG, 1979-80; 64th TAS, 1980-81.

54-1639 (C/N 3026) Became JC-130A. 704th TAS, 1970-71. Returned to C-130A. 327th TAS, 1971-77; 155th TAS, Tennessee ANG, 1977-81.

54-1640 (C/N 3027) 704th TAS, 1970. To South Vietnamese Air Force, 11-72, but returned to USAF, 1974. 327th TAS, 1974-77; 143d TAS, Rhode Island ANG, 1977-78; 105th TAS, Tennessee ANG (*Nashville*), 1979-81.

LOCKHEED MODEL 182 C-130A HERCULES (C/Ns 3028 to 3075) 48 aircraft, *55-0001* to *55-0048*. Four 3,750 eshp Allison T56A-1 turboprops driving three-blade propellers (all modified to four-blade propellers, 1978-79). All standard transports for USAF's TAC.

55-0001 (C/N 3028) 815th TCS, 483d TCW, 315th AD, Tachikawa AB, Japan, 1968–69; to South Vietnamese Air Force, 11-72; SOC 4-75.

55-0002 (C/N 3029) 815th TCS, Tachikawa AB, Japan, 1968–69; 706th TAS, 926th TAG, New Orleans NAS, 1972. To South Vietnamese Air Force, 11-72, but returned to USAF, 11-74; 167th TAS, West Virginia ANG, 11-74; crashed and destroyed, 4-75.

55-0003 (C/N 3030) 815th TCS, Tachikawa AB, Japan 1967–68; 706th TAS, New Orleans NAS, 1972; 63d TAS, 1975–80; AFRES, 1981.

55-0004 (C/N 3031) 41st TAS, 374th TAW, Naha AB, Okinawa, 1969; 109th TAS, 133d TAW, Minneapolis-St Paul IAP, Minnesota, 1972–73; 195th TAS, California ANG, 1973–74; 185th TAS, Oklahoma ANG, 1975–79; 105th TAS, Tennessee ANG, 1979–81.

55-0005 (C/N 3032) 322d Air Division, 1960; 139th TAS, New York ANG, 1972. To South Vietnamese Air Force, 11-72; written off, 4-75.

55-0006 (C/N 3033) 64th TAS, 440th TAW, 1971. To South Vietnamese Air Force, 11-72; written off, 4-75.

55-0007 (C/N 3034) 167th TAS, West Virginia ANG, 1972–73; 711th SOS, 1978–82.

55-0008 (C/N 3035) 815th TCS, Tachikawa AB, Japan, 1968–70; 35th TAS, 374th TAW, Naha AB, Okinawa, 1972. To South Vietnamese Air Force, 11-72, but returned to USAF, 1974. AFRES, 1975. 64th TAS, 440th TAW, 1976; 711th SOS, 1978–79.

55-0009 (C/N 3036) 322d AD, 1959; 41st TCS, 1964–66; destroyed during North Vietnamese rocket attack on Da Nang, 15-7-67.

55-0010 (C/N 3037) 815th TCS, Tachikawa AB, Japan, 1967–70; 64th TAS, 440th TAW, O'Hare IAP, Chicago, Illinois, 1972–76; 95th TAS, 440th TAW, 1977–80.

55-0011 (C/N 3038) 40th TAS, 1968. Became AC-130A. 4413th CCTS, 4410th CCTW, 1970; 415th SOTS, 1st SOW, 1971; 16th SOS, 8th TFW, Ubon RTAFB, Thailand, 1972; 711th SOS, 919th SOG, Duke Field, Florida, 1976–81.

55-0012 (C/N 3039) 815th TCS, Tachikawa AB, Japan, 1967–c1969; 63d TAS, 403d TAW, Selfridge Field ANGB, Michigan, 1972. To South Vietnamese Air Force, 11-72, but returned to USAF, c1974. MASDC, 1976–81.

55-0013 (C/N 3040) 815th TCS, Tachikawa AB, Japan, 1969; 115th TAS, California ANG, 1971–72. To South Vietnamese Air Force, 11-72; written off, 4-75.

55-0014 (C/N 3041) 815th TCS, Tachikawa AB, Japan, 1967; 40th TAS, 1968. Became AC-130A. 16th SOS, 8th TFW, Ubon RTAFB, Thailand, 1973; 711th SOS, 1973–80.

55-0015 (C/N 3042) 40th TCS, 1958; 39th TAS, 1968; 115th TAS, 146th TAW, 1972–73; 195th TAS, California ANG, 1973–74; 155th TAS, Tennessee ANG, 1974–80.

55-0016 (C/N 3043) 815th TCS, Tachikawa AB, Japan, 1968; 39th TAS, 317th TAW, 1969. To South Vietnamese Air Force, 11-72; written off, 12-74.

55-0017 (C/N 3044) 41st TCS, c1958; 39th TAS, 1968. To South Vietnamese Air Force, 11-72; written off, 4-75.

55-0018 (C/N 3045) 40th TCS (later TAS), 1966–68; 115th TAS, 1971; 167th TAS, West Virginia ANG (*City of Martinsburg*), 1974–76. 180th TAS, Missouri ANG, 1977–81.

55-0019 (C/N 3046) 21st TAS, 374th TAW, Naha AB, Okinawa, 1971; 109th TAS, Minnesota ANG, 1972–76; MASDC, 1976–81.

55-0020 (C/N 3047) 40th TCS, 1958; written off, 5-62.

55-0021 (C/N 3048) Became C-130D, 1-57; ff 29-1-57; AFSC, 1968–69. Became DC-130A. 1969. To US Navy as *158228*, 1969; VC-3/'UF-28' (with four-blade propellers), 1974–78; MASDC, 1979–81.

55-0022 (C/N 3049) Became NC-130A. 4950th TW, Wright Patterson AFB, 1974–81.

55-0023 (C/N 3050) 363d TCW, 12-56 (*City of Ardmore*); 374th TCW, 1968; damaged by enemy action, Vietnam, 3-68; repaired and became NC-130A; 21st TAS, Naha AB, Okinawa, 2-71; 142d TAS, 1972; 64th TAS, O'Hare IAP, Chicago, 1973–81.

55-0024 (C/N 3051) AFSC, 4950th TAW (*Local Yokel*), 1963–81; air missile trials, 4-75.

55-0025 (C/N 3052) 815th TCS; 706th TAS, 442d TAW, New Orleans NAS, Louisiana, 1971; 328th TAS, 403d TAW, 1972–74; 63d TAS, 1979–82.

55-0026 (C/N 3053) 40th TCS, 1958, 109th TAS, Minnesota ANG, 1972–76; 105th TAS, Tennessee ANG, 1977–81.

55-0027 (C/N 3054) 815th TCS, 1958; 167th TAS, West Virginia ANG, 1972. To South Vietnamese Air Force, 11-72, but returned to USAF, c1974. 63d TAS, 6-76; 328th TAS, 1977; 63d TAS, 1979–82.

55-0028 (C/N 3055) 772d TCS, 463d TCW, 1957-8; 815th TCS, 1958; 115th (and later 195th) TAS, California ANG, 1971–74; 185th TAS, Oklahoma ANG, 1976–79; 105th TAS, Tennessee ANG, 1979–82.

55-0029 (C/N 3056) 815th TCS, 1958. Became AC-130A. c1970. 16th SOS, 8th TFW, Ubon RTAFB, Thailand, 1972–73; 711th SOS, 1977–81.

55-0030 (C/N 3057) 817th TCS, 815th TCS, 1958–c1960; 115th and 195th TAS, California ANG, 1971–72; 139th TAS, New York ANG, 1973–75; 167th TAS, West Virginia ANG, 1976–77; 180th TAS, Missouri ANG, 1977–81.

55-0031 (C/N 3058) 815th TCS, 1958–61; 63d TAS, 1972–81.

55-0032 (C/N 3059) 815th TCS, 1958–61; 63d TAS, 1972–82.

55-0033 (C/N 3060) 815th TCS, 1958–61; 105th TAS, Tennessee ANG, 1973–81.

55-0034 (C/N 3061) 815th TCS, 1958–c1962. To South Vietnamese Air Force, 11-72, but returned to USAF, c1974. MASDC, 1976–81.

55-0035 (C/N 3062) 815th TCS, from 1958; 64th TAS, 1972–81.

55-0036 (C/N 3063) 815th TCS, 463d TCW (four-blade propellers) from 1958; 35th TAS, 374th TAW, Naha AB, Okinawa, 1970, 63d TAS, 1972–82.

55-0037 (C/N 3064) 773d TCS, 463d TCW, c1968; 815th TAS, Tachikawa, Japan, c1969; 35th TAS, Naha AB, Okinawa, c1970; 109th TAS, Minnesota ANG, c1972 167th TAS, West Virginia ANG, 1975–77; 180th TAS, Missouri ANG, 1977–82.

55-0038 (C/N 3065) Crashed and written off, South Vietnam, 9-65.

55-0039 (C/N 3066) Destroyed in North Vietnamese attack on Da Nang, 1-7-65.

55-0040 (C/N 3067) Became AC-130A. 16th SOS, 8th TFW, Ubon RTAFB, Thailand, 1972–73; 711th SOS, 1975–76; MASDC, 1976–81.

55-0041 (C/N 3068) 817th TCS, 1959; 63d TAS, 1972–80.

55-0042 (C/N 3069) 817th TCS, 1959. Destroyed in North Vietnamese attack on Da Nang, 1-7-65.

55-0043 (C/N 3070) 463d TCW, 3-58. Became AC-130A, C1970. Shot down by SA-7, Shan Valley, SW Hue, 18-6-72.

55-0044 (C/N 3071) Became AC-130A, c1970. 16th SOS, 8th TFW, Ubon RTAFB, Thailand (*Prometheus*); damaged by ground fire, 12-71; repaired but shot down by SA-2, Tchepone, Laos, 28-3-72.

55-0045 (C/N 3072) 463d TCW, 3-58. To South Vietnamese Air Force, 11-72; written off, 4-75.

55-0046 (C/N 3073) Delivered on loan to US Marine Corps, 1957, for air refuelling trials. Became AC-130A, c1969. 21st TAS, Naha AB, Okinawa, 1970; 16th SOS, 8th TFW, Ubon RTAFB, Thailand, 1972-74; 711th SOS, 1976-81.

55-0047 (C/N 3074) 815th TCS, 1958. 195th TAS, California ANG, 1971; 167th TAS, West Virginia ANG, 1972-75; 155th TAS, Tennessee ANG, 1974-78; 185th TAS, Oklahoma ANG, 1978-79; 105th TAS, Tennessee ANG, 1979-81.

55-0048 (C/N 3075) Delivered on loan to the US Marine Corps, 1957, for air refuelling trials; 35th TAS, Naha AB, Okinawa, 1970; 133d TAS, New Hampshire ANG, 1973; 105th TAS, Tennessee ANG, 1973-76; MASDC, 1976-81.

LOCKHEED MODEL 182 C-130A HERCULES (C/Ns 3076 to 3159) 84 aircraft, *56-0468* to *56-0551*. Four 3,750 eshp Allison T56A-1 turboprops driving three-blade propellers (all modified with four-blade propellers in 1978-79). All built as standard transports for USAF's TAC.

56-0468 (C/N 3076) 195th TAS, California ANG, 1972-74; 185th TAS, Oklahoma ANG, 1975-79; 105th TAS, Tennessee ANG, 1979-81.

56-0469 (C/N 3077) Became AC-130A; 16th SOS, 8th TFW, Ubon RTAFB, Thailand, 1970-73; 711th SOS, 1976-81.

56-0470 (C/N 3078) 314th TCW, 1961; 115th TAS, California ANG, 1970-72; 167th TAS, West Virginia ANG, 1974-76; 180th TAS, Missouri ANG, 1977-82.

56-0471 (C/N 3079) 463d TCW; 35th TAS, Naha AB, Okinawa, c1969; 139th TAS, New York ANG, 1972-75; 105th TAS, Tennessee ANG, 1976; 142d TAS, Delaware ANG, 1976-77; 105th TAS, 1977-81.

56-0472 (C/N 3080) Shot down during landing in South Vietnam, 27-5-69.

56-0473 (C/N 3081) 35th TAS, Naha AB, Okinawa, c1969-70; 303d TAS, 442d TAW, 1973-74; 64th TAS, 1975-82.

56-0474 (C/N 3082) 35th TAS; caught fire during refuelling and destroyed, Naha AB, 8-63.

56-0475 (C/N 3083) 314th TCW, 1961; 35th TAS, 1969-70; 303d TAS, 1972-74; 95th TAS, 1975-81.

56-0476 (C/N 3084) 133d TAS, New Hampshire ANG, 1972; 304th TAS, 10-72. To South Vietnamese Air Force, 11-72; SOC, 4-75.

56-0477 (C/N 3085) Shot down over Laos, 22-5-68, during Blind Bat flare operation.

56-0478 (C/N 3086) 815th TAS, Tachikawa AB, Japan, 1968; 39th TAS, 1969-70; 133d TAS, New Hampshire ANG, 1972-75; 143d TAS, Rhode Island ANG, 1976-82.

56-0479 (C/N 3087) 314th TCW, 1960-61; 95th TAS, 440th TAW, 1970-72. To South Vietnamese Air Force, 11-72, but returned to USAF, c1974; 95th TAS, 1977-82.

56-0480 (C/N 3088) 96th TAS, 1968; crashed in South Vietnam, 16-4-68.

56-0481 (C/N 3089) 35th TAS, Naha AB, Okinawa, 1969; 303d TAS, 1972. To South Vietnamese Air Force, 11-72, but returned to USAF, c1974; 328th TAS, 1977-80.

56-0482 (C/N 3090) 463d TCW, 1957; 817th TAS, Naha AB, Okinawa, 1969. To South Vietnamese Air Force, 11-72; SOC, 4-75.

56-0483 (C/N 3091) 21st TAS; 105th TAS, Tennessee ANG, c1970; 142d TAS, Delaware ANG, 1971-72. To South Vietnamese Air Force, 11-72, but returned to USAF, c1974; 167th TAS, West Virginia ANG, 1976-77; 180th TAS, Missouri ANG, 1977-81.

56-0484 (C/N 3092) Became C-130A-II for electronic reconnaissance; 7406th CSS, 1959; 109th TAS, Minnesota ANG, 1973-74; 105th TAS, Tennessee ANG, 1974-76; 109th TAS, Minnesota ANG, 1979-82.

56-0485 (C/N 3093) 40th TAS; 133d TAS; 105th TAS, Tennessee ANG, 1973-81.

56-0486 (C/N 3094) 21st TAS, Naha AB, Okinawa, 1970; 95th TAS, 1971; 711th TAS, 1972; 95th TAS, 1973-82.

56-0487 (C/N 3095) 314th TCW, 1961; 21st TAS, c1968; 115th TAS, California ANG, 1971-72; 142d TAS, Delaware ANG, 1973-81.

56-0488 (C/N 3096) Crashed and written off, 10-62.

56-0489 (C/N 3097) 374th TAW, Naha AB, Okinawa, 1968-70; 115th TAS, California ANG, 1972. To South Vietnamese Air Force, 11-72; SOC, 4-75.

56-0490 (C/N 3098) 817th TCS, 1958-59. Became JC-130A, thence AC-130A. 16th SOS, 8th TFW, Ubon RTAFB, Thailand (*Thor*), 1972; shot down over An Loc, Laos, 21-12-72.

56-0491 (C/N 3099) 817th TCS, 1957-59; 314th TCW, 1961; AFSC, 1967. Became DC-130A; To US Navy as *158229*; VC-3 'UF-29', 1969-79; MASDC, 1979-81.

56-0492 (C/N 3100) Crashed and written off, 5-64.

56-0493 (C/N 3101) 817th TCS, 1958-59. Became JC-130A, thence RC-130S reconnaissance aircraft with searchlights; 704th TAS, 1970-72; 155th TAS, Tennessee ANG, 1975-81.

56-0494 (C/N 3102) 39th TAS, 1968-69; 133d TAS, 1972; 139th TAS, New York ANG, 1974-75; 142d TAS, Delaware ANG, 1976-81.

56-0495 (C/N 3103) 817th TAS, Naha AB, Okinawa, 1967-c1970; 303d TAS, 1972. To South Vietnamese Air Force, 11-72, but returned to USAF, c1974; 142d TAS, Delaware ANG, 1973-81.

56-0496 (C/N 3104) 95th TAS, 440th TAW, 1972-82.

56-0497 (C/N 3105) 817th TCS, 1958-59. Became JC-130A, thence RC-130S reconnaissance aircraft; returned to C-130A. 142d TAS, Delaware ANG, 1974-81.

56-0498 (C/N 3106) 115th TAS, California ANG, 1971-74; MAFFS trials; 155th TAS, Tennessee ANG, 1974-75; 115th TAS, California ANG, 1975-81.

56-0499 (C/N 3107) 315th AD, 1967; 815th TAS, Tachikawa AB, Japan, 1967-69; crashed on take-off, Okinawa, 13-12-69.

56-0500 (C/N 3108) 35th TAS, 1968-70; 105th TAS, Tennessee ANG, 1972. To South Vietnamese Air Force, 11-72, but returned to USAF; 64th TAS, 1977-81.

56-0501 (C/N 3109) 815th TAS, Tachikawa AB, Japan, 1969; 817th TAS, Naha AB, Okinawa, 1969-70; 303d TAS, 1972-74; 711th SOS, 1977; 95th TAS, 1977; 64th TAS, 1977-81.

56-0502 (C/N 3110) Crashed in South Vietnam, 8-12-65.

56-0503 (C/N 3111) 314th TCW, 1967; 139th TAS, New York ANG, 1972-75; 105th TAS, Tennessee ANG, 1975-81.

56-0504 (C/N 3112) 139th TAS, New York ANG, 1972-75; 105th TAS, Tennessee ANG, 1975-80; crashed at McMinnville, near Nashville, Tennessee, 2-10-80, following loss of wing leading edge.

56-0505 (C/N 3113) 39th TAS, 1968; 328th TAS, 1972; To South Vietnamese Air Force, 11-72; SOC, 4-75.

56-0506 (C/N 3114) Crashed on landing, Tuy Hoa, 3-66, and written off.

56-0507 (C/N 3115) 322d Air Division, 1960; 706th TAS, 1971; 328th TAS, 1972-81.

56-0508 (C/N 3116) 328th TAS, 1972-76; 711th SOS, 1977; 63d TAS, 1979-81.

56-0509 (C/N 3117) Became AC-130A; 16th SOS, 8th TFW, Ubon RTAFB, Thailand (*Raid Kills Um Dead*), 1972-74; damaged at An Loc, 23-12-72, but repaired; 711th TAS/SOS, 1977-81.

56-0510 (C/N 3118) Crashed 10-4-70 (either off Okinawa or in central Laos; see also *56-0516*).

56-0511 (C/N 3119) 21st TAS, 1971; 142d TAS, Delaware ANG, 1971-81.

56-0512 (C/N 3120) 322d AD, 1958; 21st TAS, 1971; 105th TAS, Tennessee ANG, 1973; 142d TAS, Delaware ANG, 1974-76; MASDC, 1976-81.

56-0513 (C/N 3121) 40th TAS, 1968; 328th TAS, 1972-80.

56-0514 (C/N 3122) Became DC-130A; 6514th TS, 1973; 11th TDS, 1977-79; MASDC, 1979. To US Navy as *560514*; VC-3 'UF-0514', 1980-81.

56-0515 (C/N 3123) Written off, 12-65.

56-0516 (C/N 3124) Crashed 10-4-70 (either off Okinawa or in central Laos; see also *56-0510*).

56-0517 (C/N 3125) 21st TAS, 1971; 139th TAS, New York ANG, 1972-75; 185th TAS, Oklahoma ANG, 1975-79; 105th TAS, Tennessee ANG, 1979-81.

56-0518 (C/N 3126) 328th TAS, 1972. To South Vietnamese Air Force, 11-72; carried 437 refugees on last Saigon-Thailand flight. Returned to USAF, *c*1974. 185th TAS, Oklahoma ANG, 1977-79; 105th TAS, Tennessee ANG, 1979-82.

56-0519 (C/N 3127) Based at Udorn RTAFB, Thailand, 1967-70; 64th TAS, 1971-72; To South Vietnamese Air Force, 11-72; SOC, 4-75.

56-0520 (C/N 3128) 50th TCS; 303d TAS, 1972; 704th TAS, 1976; MASDC, 1976-81.

56-0521 (C/N 3129) 40th TCS, 1958; 39th TAS, 1969; 704th TAS, 1972. To South Vietnamese Air Force, 11-72; SOC, 4-75.

56-0522 (C/N 3130) 40th TCS, 1958; based at Udorn RTAFB, Thailand, 1967-70; 64th TAS, 1971-81.

56-0523 (C/N 3131) 40th TCS, 1958; 21st TAS; 142d TAS, Delaware ANG, 1971-74; 109th TAS, Minnesota ANG, 1975-82.

56-0524 (C/N 3132) 40th TCS, 1958. Became C-130A-II; 7406th CSS, 1959; returned to C-130A. 40th TAS, 1968; 115th TAS, California ANG, 1971-72. To South Vietnamese Air Force, 11-72, but returned to USAF, *c*1974. 115th TAS, California ANG, 1975-81.

56-0525 (C/N 3133) Became C-130A-II; 7406th CSS, 1959-69; returned to C-130A; 115th TAS, California ANG, 1971-73; 109th TAS, 1973-81.

56-0526 (C/N 3134) Destroyed in air collision, 9-58.

56-0527 (C/N 3135) 40th TCS, 1958. Became DC-130A; 350th SRS; 11th TDS, 1977-79; MASDC, 1979-81.

56-0528 (C/N 3136) May have become C-130A-II; 7406th CSS, 9-58; shot down by Soviet fighters, 2-9-58, Yerevan, Soviet Armenia.

56-0529 (C/N 3137) 40th TAS, 1968-71; 133d TAS, 1972; 105th TAS, Tennessee ANG, 1973-81.

56-0530 (C/N 3138) Became C-130A-II; 7406th CSS, 1959-70; returned to C-130A. 195th TAS, 1974; 155th TAS, Tennessee ANG, 1974-75; 180th TAS, Missouri ANG, 1976-81.

56-0531 (C/N 3139) 39th TAS, 1968; 133d TAS, 1972-75; 167th TAS, West Virginia ANG, 1975-76; 180th TAS, Missouri ANG, 1977-81.

56-0532 (C/N 3140) 39th TAS, 1968-69; 142d TAS, Delaware ANG, 1971-72; 139th TAS, New York ANG, 1972. To South Vietnamese Air Force, 11-72; SOC, 4-75.

56-0533 (C/N 3141) 40th TCS, 1958-65; 374th TCW, 1967; 21st TAS, Naha AB, Okinawa, 1968. Shot down, 24-11-69, over Laos during Blind Bat flare operation.

56-0534 (C/N 3142) Became C-130A-II; 7406th CSS, 1959; returned to C-130A. 711th TAS, 1972-73; 109th TAS, Minnesota ANG, 1976-81.

56-0535 (C/N 3143) Became C-130A-II; 7406th CSS, 1960-68; 314th TAS, *c*1970; 109th TAS, Minnesota ANG, 1973-81.

56-0536 (C/N 3144) 39th TAS, 1969; 64th TAS, 1972; 314th TAS, 1972; 328th TAS, 1975-80.

56-0537 (C/N 3145) Based at Udorn RTAFB, Thailand, 1967-70. Became C-130A-II; 7406th CSS, *c*1970. Returned to C-130A; 64th TAS, 1972-81.

56-0538 (C/N 3146) Became C-130A-II; 7406th CSS, 1959-69. Returned to C-130A; 109th TAG, 1971-72; damaged in force landing, Minneapolis, 4-73, but repaired; 133d TAS, 1973; 109th TAS, Minneapolis ANG, 1975-81.

56-0539 (C/N 3147) 40th TAS, 1969; 95th TAS, 1972; 314th TAS, 10-72; 94th TAS, 1973-76; MASDC, 1976; aircraft partly dismantled for ground training, Little Rock AFB, 1981.

56-0540 (C/N 3148) Became C-130A-II; 7406th CSS, 1959. Returned to C-130A. 167th TAS, West Virginia ANG, 1972; 109th TAS, Minnesota ANG, 1973-81.

56-0541 (C/N 3149) Became C-130A-II; 7406th CSS, 1959; 109th TAS, 1973-81.

56-0542 (C/N 3150) 21st TAS; 142d TAS, Delaware ANG, 1972. To South Vietnamese Air Force, 11-72; SOC, 4-75.

56-0543 (C/N 3151) 463d TCW; 483d TCW (*Ashiya Queen*), 1968; 21st TAS, Naha AB, Okinawa, 1970; 195th TAS, California ANG, 1971. To South Vietnamese Air Force, 11-72, but returned to USAF, 1974; 142d TAS, 1975-81.

56-0544 (C/N 3152) 322d Air Division, 1959; 39th TAS, 1968; 317th TAW, 1970; 142d TAS, Delaware ANG, 1971-72; 167th TAS, West Virginia ANG, 1972-76; 180th TAS, 1977-81.

56-0545 (C/N 3153) 39th TAS, 1968; 317th TAW, 1970. To South Vietnamese Air Force, 11-72, but returned to USAF, 1974; MASDC, 1976-81.

56-0546 (C/N 3154) 40th TCS, 1958; 322d AD, 1962. Written off, 5-62.

56-0547 (C/N 3155) 40th TCS/TAS, 1958-69; 115th TAS, California ANG, 1971-73; 185th TAS, Oklahoma ANG, 1977-79; 105th TAS, Tennessee ANG (*Nashville*), 1979-81.

56-0548 (C/N 3156) 41st TCS; shot down at Kham Duc, South Vietnam, 12-5-68.

56-0549 (C/N 3157) 322d AD; 21st TAS, Naha AB, Okinawa; written off, 3-68.

56-0550 (C/N 3158) 40th TCS, 1958; 30th TCS, 1968; 133d TAS, 1972-75; 167th TAS, West·Virginia ANG, 1975-76; 180th TAS, Missouri ANG, 1977-81.

56-0551 (C/N 3159) 40th TCS/TAS, 1958-68; 374th TAW,

1970–71; 142d TAS, Delaware ANG, 1971–81.

LOCKHEED MODEL 182 C-130A HERCULES (C/Ns
3160 to 3190) 31 production aircraft. Four 3,750 eshp Allison
T56A-1 turboprops driving three-blade propellers (most
modified to four-blade propellers in 1978–79). Production
1957–58 as standard transports for USAF's TAC.

57-0453 (C/N 3160) 41st TCS, 1958; 39th TAS, 1965–68;
155th TAS, Tennessee ANG, 1976–81.

57-0454 (C/N 3161) 41st TCS, 1958; 322d Air Division,
1960; 39th TCS/TAS, 1966–69; 304th TAS, 1972; 303d TAS,
1973–75; crashed after propeller failure, 27-7-75, near
Selfridge ANGB, Michigan.

57-0455 (C/N 3162) 40th TCS/TAS, 1958–68; 304th TAS,
1972–74; 63d TAS, 1975–77; 328th TAS, 1979–81.

57-0456 (C/N 3163) 40th TCS, 1958; 39th TAS, 1968; 304th
TAS, 1972–74; 303d TAS, 1974–75; 95th TAS, 1975–81.

57-0457 (C/N 3164) 40th TAS, 1968; 314th TAS, 1974; 64th
TAS, 1975–81.

57-0458 (C/N 3165) 322d Air Division, 1962; 40th TAS,
1968; 304th TAS, 1972–73; 303d TAS, 1975; 95th TAS,
1975–81.

57-0459 (C/N 3166) 39th TAS, 1968; 17th TAS, 21st CW,
(*Miss Sparrevohn*) 1975; 155th TAS, Tennessee ANG,
1975–81.

57-0460 (C/N 3167) 322d Air Division, 1960; 40th TAS,
1968; 304th TAS, 1972. To South Vietnamese Air Force,
11-72, but returned to USAF, *c*1974. 63d TAS, 1977–81.

57-0461 (C/N 3168) Became DC-130A. 350th SRS; 11th
TDS, 1977–79; MASDC, 1981.

57-0462 (C/N 3169) 40th TCS/TAS, 1958–68; 39th TAS,
1969; 17th TAS, 21st CW, 1975; 167th TAS, West Virginia
ANG, 1976; MASDC, 1976–81.

57-0463 (C/N 3170) 40th TCS/TAS, 1958–68; 39th TAS,
1969; 17th TAS, 21st CW, 1975; 155th TAS, Tennessee
ANG, 1975–81.

57-0464 (C/N 3171) 40th TAS, 1967–69; 105th TAS, Tennessee ANG, 1973–81.

57-0465 (C/N 3172) 317th TCW, 1966; 39th TAS, 1969. To
South Vietnamese Air Force, 11-72; SOC, 4-75.

57-0466 (C/N 3173) 322d AD, 1962; 40th TAS, 1968–69;
704th TAS, 1975–76; 95th TAS, 1979–81.

57-0467 (C/N 3174) Collided with truck at Dak To AB,
12-10-67, and written off.

57-0468 (C/N 3175) 815th TCS; crashed at Ashiya, Japan,
5-59, on training flight.

57-0469 (C/N 3176) 41st TCS, 1958; 95th TAS, 1972–82.

57-0470 (C/N 3177) 35th TAS, Naha AB, Okinawa, 1969;
95th TAS, 1971–77; 711th SOS, 1978; 95th TAS, 1978–81.

57-0471 (C/N 3178) 21st TAS; 142d TAS, Delaware ANG,
1972–82.

57-0472 (C/N 3179) 115th/195th TAS, California ANG,
1971–72. To South Vietnamese Air Force, 11-72, but returned
to USAF, *c*1974; NASDC, 1976–81.

57-0473 (C/N 3180) Became C-130D, but returned to
C-130A; 17th TAS, 1975; 155th TAS, Tennessee ANG;
185th TAS, Oklahoma ANG, 1976–78; 143d TAS, Rhode
Island ANG, 1978–81.

57-0475 (C/N 3182) Crashed in Thailand, 24-4-65, and
written off.

57-0476 (C/N 3183) 815th TAS, Tachikawa AB, Japan,
1968; 304th TAS, 1972; 303d TAS; 96th TAS, 1973–80.

57-0477 (C/N 3184) 815th TAS, Tachikawa AB, Japan,
1968; 96th TAS, 1972–81.

57-0478 (C/N 3185) 815th TAS, Tachikawa AB, Japan,
1968; 328th TAS, 1975–80.

57-0479 (C/N 3186) 815th TAS, Tachikawa AB, Japan,
1968–70; 96th TAS, 1975–81.

57-0480 (C/N 3187) 815th TAS, Tachikawa AB, Japan,
1968; 96th TAS, 1971–81.

57-0481 (C/N 3188) 815th TAS, Tachikawa AB, Japan,
1968–69; 96th TAS, 1972–81.

57-0482 (C/N 3189) 815th TAS, Tachikawa AB, Japan,
1968; 96th TAS, 1972–81.

57-0483 (C/N 3190) 815th TAS, Tachikawa AB, Japan,
1968–70; 706th TAS, 1972–76; 96th TAS, 1977–80.

LOCKHEED MODEL 182 C-130D HERCULES (C/Ns
3191 to 3202) 12 ski-equipped transports built as such from
new for USAF's TAC in 1958–59; *57-0484* to *57-0495*. Four
Allison T56A-1 turboprops driving three-blade propellers.

57-0484 (C/N 3191) 61st TCS, 1959; 17th TCS, 1961.
Became C-130D-6, 1962–63. 17th TCS, AAC, 1964–75;
139th TAS, New York ANG (skis removed), 1975–81.

57-0485 (C/N 3192) 61st TCS, 1959; 17th TCS, 1961.
Became C-130D-6, 1962–63. 17th TCS, AAC, 1964–67;
139th TAS, New York ANG (skis removed), 1975–76;
MASDC, 1976–81.

57-0486 (C/N 3193) 61st TCS, 1959; 17th TCS, 1961.
Became C-130D-6, 1962–63. 17th TCS, AAC, 1964–66;
139th TAS, New York ANG (skis removed), 1975–81.

57-0487 (C/N 3194) 61st TCS, 1959; 17th TCS, 1961.
Became C-130D-6, 1962–63. 17th TCS, AAC, 1964–75;
(*Hustling Husky*); 139th TAS, New York ANG (skis
removed), 1975–81.

57-0488 (C/N 3195) 61st TCS, 1959; 17th TCS, 1961.
Became C-130D-6, 1962–63. 17th TCS, AAC, 1964–75;
139th TAS, New York ANG (skis removed), 1975–81.

57-0489 (C/N 3196) 61st TCS, 1959; 17th TCS, 1961.
Became C-130D-6, 1962–63. 17th TCS, AAC, 1964–75;
139th TAS, New York ANG (skis removed), 1975–81.

57-0490 (C/N 3197) 61st TCS, 1959; 17th TCS, 1961; 17th
TAS, AAC, 1964–75; 139th TAS, New York ANG (skis
retained), 1975–81.

57-0491 (C/N 3198) 61st TCS, 1959; 17th TCS, 1961; 17th
TCS/TAS, AAC, 1964–75; 139th TAS, New York ANG
(skis retained), 1975–81.

57-0492 (C/N 3199) 61st TCS, 1959; 17th TCS, 1961; 17th
TCS/TAS, AAC, 1964–75; 139th TAS, New York ANG
(skis retained), 1975–81.

57-0493 (C/N 3200) 61st TCS, 1959; 17th TCS, 1961; 17th
TCS/TAS, AAC, 1964–75; 139th TAS, New York ANG
(skis retained), 1975–81.

57-0494 (C/N 3201) 61st TCS, 1959; 17th TCS, 1961; 17th
TCS/TAS, AAC, 1964–75; 139th TAS, New York ANG
(skis retained), 1975–81.

57-0495 (C/N 3202) 61st TCS (*Frozen Assets*), 1959; 17th
TCS/TAS, 1961–72 (*The Harker*, 1970); damaged 200 miles
east of Sondrestrom, 5-6-72, and written off.

LOCKHEED MODEL 182 C-130A HERCULES (C/Ns
3203 and 3204) Two special aircraft, *57-0496* and *57-0497*, as
CG-130A and GC-130A respectively (preliminary designations). Drone launchers with chin radomes. Allison T56A-1
turboprops driving three-blade propellers.

57-0496 (C/N 3203) 3225th Drone Squadron, 1958. Became
DC-130A, 1962; 4453d CCTW, 1969; 4472d CCTS, 4453d

CCTW, 1970; 11th Tactical Drone Sqn, 355th TFW, 1971-79; MASDC, 3-79. To US Navy as '*570496*'; VC-3 'UF-0496', 1980. (VC-3 disbanded 30-9-81).

57-0497 (C/N 3204) 3225th Drone Sqn, 1958. Became DC-130A, 1962; 4453d CCTW, 1969; 4472d CCTS, 4453d CCTW, 1970; 11th Tactical Drone Sqn, 355th TFW, 1971-79; MASDC, 3-79. To US Navy as '*570497*'; VC-3 'UF-0497', 1980-81. (VC-3 disbanded 30-9-81.)

LOCKHEED MODEL 182 C-130A HERCULES (for Australia) (C/Ns 3205 to 3216) 12 production transport aircraft (USAF Nos *57-0498* to *57-0509*), for Royal Australian Air Force, delivered in 1958; equipped No 36 Squadron, RAAF, serving in Vietnam, late 1960s. Allison T56A-1 turboprops. All aircraft offered for resale, 12-78.

A97-205 (C/N 3205, *57-0498*) No 36 Sqn, Richmond, 1959-78; stored at Laverton. Victoria, 1981.

A97-206 (C/N 3206, *57-0499*) No 36 Sqn, Richmond, 1959-78; stored at Laverton, Victoria, 1981.

A97-207 (C/N 3207, *57-0500*) No 36 Sqn, Richmond, 1959-78; stored at Laverton, Victoria, 1981.

A97-208 (C/N 3208, *57-0501*) No 36 Sqn, Richmond, 1959-78; stored at Laverton, Victoria, 1981; sold to Chad, October 1983, as *TT-PAA*, via *Securité Civile*.

A97-209 (C/N 3209, *57-0502*) No 36 Sqn, Richmond, 1959-78; used for loadmaster training at Richmond, 1979-81.

A97-210 (C/N 3210, *57-0503*) No 36 Sqn, Richmond, 1959-78; stored at Laverton, Victoria, 1979-81.

A97-211 (C/N 3211, *57-0504*) No 36 Sqn, Richmond, 1959-78; stored at Richmond, Victoria, 1979; used as ground instruction airframe at RAAF School of Technical Training, Wagga, New South Wales since 1980.

A97-212 (C/N 3212, *57-0505*) No 36 Sqn, Richmond, 1959-78; stored at Laverton, Victoria, 1979-81.

A97-213 (C/N 3213, *57-0506*) No 36 Sqn, Richmond, 1959-78; stored at Laverton, Victoria, 1979-81.

A97-214 (C/N 3214, *57-0507*) No 36 Sqn, Richmond, 1959-78; stored at Laverton, Victoria, 1979-81.

A97-215 (C/N 3215, *57-0508*) No 36 Sqn, Richmond, 1959-79; stored at Laverton, Victoria, 1979-81.

A97-216 (C/N 3216, *57-0509*) No 36 Sqn, Richmond, 1959-79; stored at Laverton, Victoria, 1979-81.

LOCKHEED MODEL 182 RC-130A HERCULES (C/Ns 3217 to 3231) 15 photo reconnaissance/mapping aircraft, *57-0510* to *57-0524*, for USAF's Military Air Transport Service. Most aircraft eventually modified to standard C-130A, *c*1973. Allison T56A-1 turboprops driving three-blade propellers (most changed to four-blade propellers, 1978-79).

57-0510 (C/N 3217) 1375th Mapping and Charting Sqn, *c*1960-68; 711th TAS, 1972. Became C-130A; 63d TAS, 1974-76; 328th TAS, 1977-80; 143d TAS, Rhode Island ANG, 1980-81.

57-0511 (C/N 3217) 1375th Mapping and Charting Sqn, *c*1960-68. Became C-130A; 711th TAS, 1972; 63d TAS, 1974-76; 328th TAS, 1977-80; 143d TAS, Rhode Island ANG, 1980-81.

57-0512 (C/N 3219). 1375th MCS, *c*1960-68; 1st ACGS, 1968-73. Became C-130A; 185th TAS, Oklahoma ANG, 1974-75; 143d TAS, Rhode Island ANG, 1976-81.

57-0513 (C/N 3220). 1375th MCS, *c*1960-68; 1st ACGS,

1968-73. Became C-130A; 143d TAS, Rhode Island ANG, 1976-81.

57-0514 (C/N 3221) 1375th MCS, *c*1960-68; 1st ACGS, 1972. Became C-130A; 143d TAS, Rhode Island ANG, 1976-81.

57-0515 (C/N 3222) 1375th MCS, *c*1960-68; 1866th FCS, 1971-72; 1st ACGS, 1972. Became C-130A; 143d TAS, Rhode Island ANG, 1977-81.

57-0516 (C/N 3223) 1375th MCS, *c*1960-68. Became C-130A; 704th TAS, 1975-76. 143d TAS, Rhode Island ANG, 1977-78; 96th TAS, 1978-81.

57-0517 (C/N 3224) 1375th MCS, *c*1960-68; 1866th FCS, 1971-73. Became C-130A; 704th TAS, 1975-76; MASDC, 1976-81. Carried civil registration, *N9539G*, 1981.

57-0518 (C/N 3225) 1375th MCS, *c*1960-68; 1st ACGS, 1972. Became C-130A; 704th TAS, 1975-76; MASDC, 1976-81.

57-0519 (C/N 3226) 1375th MCS, *c*1960-68. Became C-130A, *c*1970; 924th TAG, 1970; 711th TAS, 1972; 314th TAS, 1972-73; 95th TAS, 1973-74; 96th TAS, 1976-81.

57-0520 (C/N 3227) 1375th MCS, *c*1960-68. Became C-130A, *c*1970; 704th TAS, 1970; 711th TAS, 1972; 328th TAS, 1973-80.

57-0521 (C/N 3228) 1375th MCS, *c*1960-68. Became C-130A, *c*1970; 711th TAS, 1972-73; 704th TAS, 1975-76; 328th TAS, 1979-81.

57-0522 (C/N 3229) 1375th MCS, *c*1960-68. Became C-130A, *c*1970; 711th TAS, 1972-73; 304th TAS, 1974; 303d TAS, 1974-75; 328th TAS, 1975-81.

57-0523 (C/N 3230) 1375th MCS, *c*1960-68; 1866th FCS, 1971-73. Became DC-130A; 11th TDS, 1977; MASDC, 1978-81.

57-0524 (C/N 3231) 1375th MCS, *c*1960-68. Became C-130A, 1866th FCS, 1971-74; 167th TAS, West Virginia ANG, 1974-75; 143d TAS, Rhode Island ANG, 1976-81.

LOCKHEED MODEL 282 C-130B HERCULES (C/Ns 3501 to 3528, 3530 to 3532, 3534 to 3541, 3543 to 3545, 3547, 3549 to 3553 and 3556 to 3559, USAF Nos *57-0525* to *57-0529*, *58-0711* to *58-0747*, *58-0749* to *58-0758* respectively) 52 production aircraft. Standard transport for USAF's TAC. Four 4,050 eshp Allison T56A-7 turboprops driving four-blade propellers; external tanks (when carried) mounted outboard of outer engines; forward cargo door.

57-0525 (C/N 3501) Underwent STOL trials, 1962. Became JC-130B, *c*1963; 6593d TS, AFSC. Returned to C-130B; 705th TATS, 433d TAW, 1-76, 167th TAS, West Virginia ANG, 1978-81

57-0526 (C/N 3502) Became JC-130B, *c*1963; 6593d TS, AFSC, *c*1965-81.

57-0527 (C/N 3503) Became JC-130B, *c*1963; 6593d TS, AFSC, *c*1965-80.

57-0528 (C/N 3504) Became JC-130B, *c*1963; 6593d TS, AFSC, *c*1965-80.

57-0529 (C/N 3505) Became JC-130B, *c*1963; 6593d TS, AFSC, *c*1964-80.

58-0711 (C/N 3506) Became C-130B-II, *c*1963. 6091st RS, 1965-67; 556th RS, 1967-68. Returned to C-130B, 1969; 7406th CSS, 1970-71; 337th TAS, 1972-73; 815th TAS, 1973-75; 115th TAS, California ANG, 1976-80; 135th TAS, Maryland ANG, 1980-81.

58-0712 (C/N 3507) Modified as C-130BLC, for trials at NACA with boundary layer control, 1959. Became NC-

Above left *View at Marietta in 1954 as the front fuselage of a 'short-nose' C-130A, 54-1639 (C/N 3026), is lifted over the production line. In the background are Boeing B-47 Stratojet six-jet bombers (Lockheed-Georgia).*

Above right *Marietta in 1974-75. In the foreground is a C-130H destined for Venezuela, 4224 (C/N 4556) (Lockheed-Georgia, Neg No RK 8398).*

Below *Another production line view, this time showing a C-130H, 1212 (C/N 4584), scheduled for Abu Dhabi in 1975 (Lockheed-Georgia, Neg No RK 6671).*

Above *Centre fuselage, largely built in Scotland, being lowered into the Marietta line to mate up with a C-130H, 7T-WHJ (C/N 4928), for the Algerian Air Force in 1982* (Lockheed-Georgia, Neg No 9832-68).

Below *The aircraft, C/N 4928, shown in the previous photograph, nears completion at Marietta; in the background can be seen five C-141 four-jet transports of the USAF—emphasising the vast size of Lockheed's assembly plant in Georgia* (Lockheed-Georgia).

130B, 2-60; carried NACA civil registration *N929NA*. Employed for NASA Earth Survey 2, 1974–80.

58-0713 (C/N 3508) Became JC-130B, *c*1963; 6593d TS, AFSC, 1964–80.

58-0714 (C/N 3509) Became JC-130B, 1963; 6593d TS, AFSC, 1964–73; 904th TAG, 1973. Returned to C-130B; 711th TAS, 1974; 336th TAS, 1974; 187th TAS, Wyoming ANG, 1975–81.

58-0715 (C/N 3510) Became JC-130B, 1963; 6593d TS, AFSC, 1964–*c*1966. Became VC-130B VIP transport; 1174th SS, MAC, Norton AFB, 1969–73. Returned to C-130B, 1974–75; 115th TAS, California ANG, 1976–80; 135th TAS, Maryland ANG, 1980–82.

58-0716 (C/N 3511) Became JC-130B, 1963; 6593d TS, AFSC, 1964–80.

58-0717 (C/N 3512) Became JC-130B, 1963; 6593d TS, AFSC, 1964–80. Became NC-130B; AFSC, 1981.

58-0718 (C/N 3513) 773d TAS, 463d TAW, Clark AB, Philippines, 1961–69; destroyed in mid-air explosion over Philippines, 6-10-69.

58-0719 (C/N 3514) Became JC-130B, 1963; 6593d TS, AFSC, 1964–65; 313d TAW, 1965; ground looped during engine run-up and collided with *58-0730*, Forbes Field, Kansas, 1-65, and destroyed.

58-0720 (C/N 3515) 773d TAS, Clark AB, Philippines, 1961–70; 187th TAS, Wyoming ANG, 1973–81 (damaged in tornado, Cheyenne, 16-7-79, but repaired).

58-0721 (C/N 3516) 773d TAS, Clark AB, Philippines, 1961–69; 556th RS, Yokoto AB, Japan, 1971; 756th TAS, 1972; 706th TAS, 1974–75; crashed and written off, New Orleans, 2-75.

58-0722 (C/N 3517) 773d TAS, Clark AB, Philippines, 1961; 29th TCS, *c*1965–67; aircraft destroyed when ammunition load exploded, Bao Loc, South Vietnam, 16-4-67.

58-0723 (C/N 3518) 773d TAS, Clark AB, Philippines, 1961. Became C-130B-II; 556th RS, Yokota AB, Japan, 1971–72. Returned to C-130B, 1972; 756th TAS, 1972–75; 337th TAS, 1975–80.

58-0724 (C/N 3519) 774th TAS, Clark AB, Philippines, *c*1962; 67th TAS, 1972–*c*1974; 314th TAS, 1976. Sold to Singapore Government, 1977; No 121 Squadron, RSAF, as *720*.

58-0725 (C/N 3520) Became WC-130B weather reconnaissance aircraft; 53d WRS, 1971. Returned to C-130B; 706th TAS, 1974; 314th TAS, 1975–76; 167th TAS, West Virginia ANG, 1977–81.

58-0726 (C/N 3521) 47th TAS, *c*1967. Became WC-130B, *c*1969; 53d WRS, 1971. Returned to C-130B; 756th TAS, 1974–75; 164th TAS, Ohio ANG, 1977–81.

58-0727 (C/N 3522) 774th TAS, Clark AB, Philippines, *c*1962–71; 756th TAS, 1972–75; 337th TAS, 1976–79; 181st TAS, Texas ANG, 1979–81.

58-0728 (C/N 3523) 756th TAS, 1973–74; 156th TAS, North Carolina ANG, 1975–81.

58-0729 (C/N 3524) 774th TAS, Clark AB, Philippines, *c*1961; 463d TAW, *c*1962. Became WC-130B, 1969–70, then returned to C-130B, 1971. 756th TAS, 1972; 706th TAS, 1974–75; 337th TAS, 1975–76; 704th TAS, 1977–78; 181st TAS, Texas ANG, 1978–81.

58-0730 (C/N 3525) 313th TCW, 1964–65; aircraft burned and destroyed after ground collision with *58-0719*, Forbes Field, Kansas, 1-65.

58-0731 (C/N 3526) 774th TAS, Clark AB, Philippines, *c*1961. Became WC-130B; carried civil registration *N6541C* (US Department of Commerce, *N8037*, 1972–80) and operated by National Oceanic and Atmospheric Administration, Miami, Florida.

58-0732 (C/N 3527) 556th RS; 337th TAS, 1973–74; 167th TAS, West Virginia ANG, 1977–81.

58-0733 (C/N 3528) 772d TAS, Clark AB, Philippines, 1962–68; damaged in South Vietnam, 1968, but repaired. Became WC-130B, 1969–70; 53d WRS, 1971–72. Returned to C-130B, 1973; 711th TAS, 1973–75; 164th TAS, Ohio ANG, 1977–81.

58-0734 (C/N 3530) 772d TAS, Clark AB, Philippines, 1962–68. Became WC-130B, 1969–70; 53d WRS, 1971–72; 815th WRS, 1974–75. Returned to C-130B; 706th TAS, 1975–78; 181st TAS, Texas ANG, 1978–81.

58-0735 (C/N 3531) 316th TAW, 1971; 756th TAS, 1972–73; 314th TAS, 1973–76; 164th TAS, Ohio ANG, 1978–81.

58-0736 (C/N 3532) 463d TAW, 1968; 756th TAS, 1972–73; 314th TAS, 1973–76; 164th TAS, Ohio ANG, 1977–81.

58-0737 (C/N 3534) Crashed in South Vietnam, 9-6-67, and written off.

58-0738 (C/N 3535) 313th TAW, 1966–68; 67th TAS, 1972–73; 706th TAS, 1973–78; 337th TAS, 1978–80.

58-0739 (C/N 3536) 773d TAS, Clark AB, Philippines, 1961–68; 772d TAS, 1968–70; 156th TAS, North Carolina ANG, 1973–81.

58-0740 (C/N 3537) 774th TAS, Clark AB, Philippines, 1962–69. Became WC-130B, 1969–70; 53d WRS, 1971–73; 815th WRS, 1974. Returned to C-130B, 1976; 68th TAS, 1977–78; 181st TAS, Texas ANG, 1978–81.

58-0741 (C/N 3538) 772d TAS, Clark AB, Philippines, *c*1963–68. Became WC-130B, 1969–70; 53d WRS, 1971–73. Returned to C-130B; 336th TAS, 1975–76; 167th TAS, West Virginia ANG, 1976–81.

58-0742 (C/N 3539) 711th TAS; 337th TAS, 1972–77; 181st TAS, Texas ANG, 1977–81.

58-0743 (C/N 3540) 772d TAS, Clark AB, Philippines, *c*1963–68; destroyed in rocket attack on Tan Son Nhut, 17-2-68.

58-0744 (C/N 3541) 772d TAS, Clark AB, Philippines, *c*1963–69; 756th TAS, 1972–76; 187th TAS, Wyoming ANG, 1977–81.

58-0745 (C/N 3543) Crashed and written off, 10-61.

58-0746 (C/N 3544) 772d TAS, Clark AB, Philippines, *c*1963–69; 756th TAS, 1971–76; 156th TAS, North Carolina ANG, 1976–77; 181st TAS, Texas ANG, 1978; 156th TAS, North Carolina ANG, 1979–81.

58-0747 (C/N 3545) 772d TAS, Clark AB, Philippines, *c*1963–69. Became WC-130B, 1969–70; 54th WRS, 1972–73. Returned to C-130B; 68th TAS, 1976; 167th TAS, West Virginia ANG, 1976–81.

58-0749 (C/N 3547) 756th TAS, 1972–76; 164th TAS, Ohio ANG, 1977–81.

58-0750 (C/N 3549) 772d TAS, Clark AB, Philippines, *c*1963–69. Became JC-130B; 6593d TS, 1977–80.

58-0751 (C/N 3550) 463d TCW; 772d TAS, Clark AB, Philippines, *c*1965–68; 67th TAS, *c*1971; 68th TAS, 1975–78; 181st TAS, Texas ANG, 1978–81.

58-0752 (C/N 3551) Became WC-130B; 53d WRS, 1972–74. Returned to C-130B; 711th TAS, 1974; 68th TAS, 1975–76; 705th TATS, 433d TAW, 1976; 181st TAS, Texas ANG, 1978–81.

58-0753 (C/N 3552) 773d TAS, Clark AB, Philippines, *c*1963–69; 68th TAS, 1973–76; 705th TATS, 1976; 167th TAS, West Virginia ANG, 1976–81.

58-0754 (C/N 3553) 774th TAS, Clark AB, Philippines, *c*1963–69; 187th TAS, Wyoming ANG, *c*1972–81.

58-0755 (C/N 3556) 337th TAS; 156th TAS, North Carolina ANG, 1972; 115th TAS, California ANG, 1973–80; 187th TAS, Wyoming ANG, 1980; 135th TAS, Maryland ANG, 1981.

58-0756 (C/N 3557) Became JC-130B; 6593d TS. Returned to C-130B; 756th TAS, 1974; 711th TAS, 1974; 756th TAS, 1975–76; 337th TAS, 1976. Sold to Singapore Government, 10-77; No 121 Sqn, RSAF, as *721*.

58-0757 (C/N 3558) 774th TAS, Clark AB, Philippines, *c*1969; 336th TAS, 1972–76; 337th TAS, 1976–80;

58-0758 (C/N 3559) Became WC-130B; 53d WRS, 1971–72. Returned to C-130B; 336th TAS, 1973; 68th TAS, 1977; 181st TAS, Texas ANG, 1978–81.

LOCKHEED MODEL 282-2B HC-130B HERCULES
(C/Ns 3529, 3533, 3542 and 3548) Four aircraft (Serial Nos *58-5396, 58-5397, 58-6973* and *58-6974*) purchased for service with the US Coast Guard, redesignated R8V-1G.

58-5396 (C/N 3529) Based at Elizabeth City, North Carolina, 1964; San Francisco, California, 1971; Barbers Point, Hawaii, 1975; Elizabeth City, 1976. Registered *CG1340*.

58-5397 (C/N 3533) Based at Barbers Point, Hawaii, 1970; Elizabeth City, North Carolina, *c*1975. Registered *CG1341*.

58-6973 (C/N 3542) Based at San Francisco, California, *c*1969; Elizabeth City, North Carolina, 1976; Barbers Point, Hawaii, 1981. Registered *CG1342*.

58-6974 (C/N 3548) Based at San Francisco, California, 1971; Barbers Point, Hawaii, 1975; Elizabeth City, North Carolina, 1980; Barbers Point, 1981. Registered *CG1343*.

LOCKHEED MODEL 282 C-130B HERCULES (C/Ns 3560, 3561, 3563, 3568 to 3571, 3576, 3579, 3581, 3584 to 3586, 3588 and 3589.) 15 aircraft, USAF Nos *59-1524* to *59-1537* and *59-5957* (not respectively). Standard transport for USAF's TAC. Four 4,050 eshp Allison T56A-7 turboprops driving four-blade propellers; external tanks (when carried) outboard of outer engines; forward cargo door.

59-1524 (C/N 3560) Became C-130B-II; 556th RS, 347th TFW, Yokota AB, Japan, 1967; 7406th CSS, 1971–73. Returned to C-130B; 711th TAS, 1974; 337th TAS, 1976; 704th TAS, 1977–81.

59-1525 (C/N 3561) Became C-130B-II; 556th RS, 347th TFW, 1968–71. Returned to C-130B; 336th TAS, 1972; 815th TAS, 1973–74; 164th TAS, Ohio ANG, 1977–81.

59-1526 (C/N 3563) Became C-130B-II; 556th RS, 347th TFW, 1968–71; 7406th CSS, 1971–73. Returned to C-130B; 68th TAS, 1974–81.

59-1527 (C/N 3568) Became C-130B-II; 556th RS, 347th TFW, 1967; 7406th CSS, 1971–73. Returned to C-130B; 68th TAS, 1975–81.

59-1528 (C/N 3571) 315th AD, 1967. Became C-130B-II; 556th RS, 347th TFW, 1969; 7406th CSS, 1971–73. Returned to C-130B; 314th TAS, 1974; 67th TAS, 1975; 156th TAS, North Carolina ANG, 1976–81.

59-1529 (C/N 3569) 774th TAS, Clark AB, Philippines, *c*1969; 337th TAS, 1970–73; 314th TAS, 1975–76; 167th TAS, West Virginia ANG, 1976–81.

59-1530 (C/N 3576) Became C-130B-II; 556th RS, 347th TFW, 1967–69; 7406th CSS, 1971–73. Returned to C-130B;

337th TAS, 1974–75; 68th TAS, 1977–81.

59-1531 (C/N 3579) Became C-130B-II; 556th RS, 347th TFW, 1969; 7406th CSS, 1971–73. Returned to C-130B; tests with E-Systems Inc, Greenville, Texas, 1977–80.

59-1532 (C/N 3581) Became C-130B-II; 556th RS, 347th TFW, 1970–71; 7406th CSS, 1971–73. Returned to C-130B; 706th TAS, 1975–76; 442nd TAW, 1977–81.

59-1533 (C/N 3586) Became C-130B-II; 556th RS, 347th TFW, 1970; 7406th CSS, 1971–73. Returned to C-130B; 187th TAS, Wyoming ANG, 1976–80 (damaged in tornado at Cheyenne, Wyoming, 16-7-79, but repaired).

59-1534 (C/N 3570) 773d TCS, 1961; written off, 5-61.

59-1535 (C/N 3585) Became C-130B-II; 556th RS, 347th TFW, 1967–70; 7406th CSS, 1971–73. Returned to C-130B; 706th TAS, 1974–76; 442d TAW, 1977–81.

59-1536 (C/N 3588) 772d TCS/TAS, 1963; 187th TAS, Wyoming ANG, 1972–73; 115th TAS, California ANG, 1973–80; 135th TAS, Maryland ANG, 1980–81.

59-1537 (C/N 3589) Became C-130-II; 556th RS, 347th TFW, 1969; 7406th CSS, 1971–73. Returned to C-130B; 67th TAS, 1975; 68th TAS, 1975–81.

59-5957 (C/N 3584) Replaced *58-0748* (C/N 3546, supplied to Indonesia). 773d TAS, Clark AB, Philippines, 1969; 706th TAS, 1973; 187th TAS, Wyoming ANG, 1974–81.

LOCKHEED MODEL 282-3B KC-130F (GV-1) HERCULES (C/Ns 3554, 3555, 3566, 3573, 3574, 3577, 3592, 3605 to 3608, 3619, 3623, 3627, 3631, 3632, 3640, 3644, 3657, 3658, 3664, 3665, 3680, 3684 and 3685) 25 aircraft, US Navy Nos *147572, 147573, 148246* to *148249, 148890* to *148899, 149788, 149789, 149791, 149792, 149795, 149796, 149798* to *149800*. Built as air refuelling tankers for the US Marine Corps as GV-1s.

147572 (C/N 3554) VMGR-152, Marine Air Wing 1, MCAS Futema, Okinawa, *c*1966–78.

147573 (C/N 3555) VMGR-152, MAW-1, MCAS Futema, Okinawa, *c*1966–76; VMGR-352, MAW-3, MCAS El Toro, California, 1978.

148246 (C/N 3566) VMGR-352, MAW-3, MCAS El Toro, California, *c*1970; VMGR-152, MAW-1, MCAS Futema, Okinawa, *c*1976; VMGR-234, Marine Air Reserve Training Detachment, (MARTD)/MAW-4, NAS Glenview, Illinois.

148247 (C/N 3573) VMGR-352, MAW-3, MCAS El Toro, California, *c*1966; VMGR-152, MAW-1, MCAS Futema, Okinawa, 1969–80; dismantled at Seletar, Singapore, 1981.

148248 (C/N 3574) VMGR-352, MAW-3, MCAS El Toro, California, *c*1966; VMGR-152, MAW-1, MCAS Futema, Okinawa, 1969–80.

148249 (C/N 3577) VMGR-234, MATD/MAW-4, NAS Glenview, Illinois, 1978–81.

148890 (C/N 3592) VMGR-352, MAW-3, MCAS El Toro, California, *c*1970; VMGR-152, MAW-1, MCAS Futema, Okinawa, *c*1976–77; VMGR-352, MAW-3, 1979–80.

148891 (C/N 3605) VMGR-152, MAW-1, MCAS Futema, Okinawa, *c*1970; VMGR-352, MAW-3, MCAS El Toro, California, *c*1974; VMGR-252, MAW-2, MCAS Cherry Point, North Carolina, 1976–81.

148892 (C/N 3606) VMGR-152, MAW-1, MCAS-Futema, Okinawa, *c*1970; VMGR-352, MAW-3, MCAS El Toro, California, *c*1974; VMGR-234, MARTD/MAW-4, NAS Glenview, Illinois, 1976–81.

148893 (C/N 3607) VMGR-152, MAW-1, MCAS Futema, Okinawa, *c*1970; VMGR-252, MAW-2, MCAS Cherry

Point, North Carolina, 1976; attached VQ-4, NAS Patuxent River, Maryland, 1978–79; Naval Air Test Center, NAS Patuxent River, 1979.

148894 (C/N 3608) VMGR-152, MAW-1, MCAS Futema, Okinawa, 1966–70; VMGR-352, MAW-3, MCAS El Toro, California, 1972–78; VMGR-152, 1978–80; VMGR-252, MAW-2, MCAS Cherry Point, North Carolina, 1980–81.

148895 (C/N 3619) VMGR-152, MAW-1, MCAS Futema, Okinawa, c1965; VMGR-352, MAW-3, MCAS El Toro, California, 1967; VMGR-234, MAW-4, NAS Glenview, Illinois, 1975–81.

148896 (C/N 3623) VMGR-252, MAW-2, MCAS Cherry Point, North Carolina, 1978–81.

148897 (C/N 3627) VMGR-252, MAW-2, MCAS Cherry Point, North Carolina, 1976–81.

148898 (C/N 3631) VMGR-252, MAW-2, MCAS Cherry Point, North Carolina, 1976–81.

148899 (C/N 3632) VMGR-252, MAW-2, MCAS Cherry Point, North Carolina, 1974–81.

149788 (C/N 3640) VMGR-352, MAW-3, MCAS El Toro, California, 1972; VMGR-152, MAW-1, MCAS Futema, Okinawa, 1976–81.

149789 (C/N 3644) VMGR-152, MAW-1, MCAS Futema, Okinawa, 1968; VMGR-252, MAW-2, MCAS Cherry Point, North Carolina, 1976–81.

149791 (C/N 3657) VMGR-252, MAW-2, MCAS Cherry Point, North Carolina, c1968; VMGR-152, MAW-1, MCAS Futema, Okinawa, c1974; VMGR-234, MARTD/MAW-4, NAS Glenview, Illinois, 1977–81.

149792 (C/N 3658) VMGR-152, MAW-1, MCAS Futema, Okinawa, c1970; VMGR-352, MAW-3, MCAS El Toro, California, 1977; VMGR-252, MAW-2, MCAS Cherry Point, North Carolina, 1981.

149795 (C/N 3664) VMGR-252, MAW-2, MCAS Cherry Point, North Carolina, 1976–81.

149796 (C/N 3665) VMGR-152, MAW-1, MCAS Futema, Okinawa, 1964; VMGR-234, MARTD/MAW-4, NAS Glenview, Illinois, 1977–81.

149798 (C/N 3680) Carrier suitability trials aboard USS *Forrestal*, 30-10-63. VMGR-252, MAW-2, MCAS Cherry Point, North Carolina, 1978–81.

149799 (C/N 3684) VMGR-152, MAW-1, MCAS Futema, Okinawa, 1969; VMGR-252, MAW-2, MCAS Cherry Point, North Carolina, 1980–81.

149800 (C/N 3685) VMGR-252, MAW-2, MCAS Cherry Point, North Carolina, c1970; VMGR-352, MAW-3, MCAS El Toro, California, 1975; VMGR-152, 1978–80; VMGR-352, 1981;

LOCKHEED MODEL 282-6B LC-130F (C-130BL) HERCULES (C/Ns 3562, 3564, 3565 and 3567, US Navy Nos *148318* to *148321*, (ex-USAF) *59-5922* to *59-5925*). Four aircraft, ski-equipped transports for US Navy.

148318, *59-5922* (C/N 3562) VX-6, NAS Point Mugu, California (*City of Christchurch*); burned at McMurdo after hitting snow wall, 15-2-71.

148319, *59-5923* (C/N 3564) VX-6, NAS Point Mugu, California ('JD-19', 1969); damaged at Dome Charlie, Antarctica, 15-1-75, when JATO unit broke loose during take-off; repaired and flown out, 25-12-76; VXE-6, Christchurch, New Zealand ('XD-07', 1980–81).

148320, *59-5924* (C/N 3565) VX-6, NAS Point Mugu, California, 1969; crashed at Dome Charlie, Antarctica, 4-11-75; repaired and flown out, 26-12-76; VXE-6,

Christchurch, New Zealand ('XD-6', 1981)

148321, *59-5925* (C/N 3567) VX-6, NAS Point Mugu, California, 1969; force landed at Care Four, 750 miles from McMurdo after JATO unit broke loose and struck aircraft, 4-12-71; repaired 1972.

LOCKHEED MODEL 282 C-130B HERCULES (for Canada) (C/Ns 3572, 3575, 3587 and 3590) Four aircraft, USAF Nos *60-5450* to *60-5453*. Standard transports for Royal Canadian Air Force (RCAF Nos *10301* to *10304*). Completed in 1960.

10301, *60-5450* (C/N 3572) No 435 Sqn, RCAF. Repurchased by Lockheed-Georgia, 7-67, and civil registered *N4652*. Sold to Colombia (FAC) as *1003*, 1-69. Ditched 180 miles SE of Cape May, New Jersey, USA, 16-10-82.

10302, *60-5451* (C/N 3575) No 435 Sqn, RCAF. Repurchased by Lockheed-Georgia, 7-67, and civil registered *N4653*. Sold to Colombia (FAC) as *1001*, 1-69

10303, *60-5452* (C/N 3587) No 435 Sqn, RCAF. Repurchased by Lockheed-Georgia, 7-67, and civil registered *N4654*. Sold to Colombia (FAC) as *1002*, 1-69; crashed and destroyed, 26-8-69.

10304, *60-5453* (C/N 3590) No 435 Sqn, RCAF; crash-landed in Saskatchewan after forward cargo door broke loose and struck propellers.

LOCKHEED MODEL 282-7B C-130B HERCULES (for Indonesia) (C/Ns 3546, 3578, 3580, 3583, 3598, 3599, 3601, 3615 and 3616) Ten aircraft. Standard transports for *Angkatan Udara Republik Indonesia* (AURI, Indonesian Air Force). Note: First aircraft (C/N 3546) originally part of USAF contract as *58-0748* and replaced by C/N 3584, *59-5957*, qv; Indonesian Nos *T1301 to T1310*.

T1301 (C/N 3546) No 31 Sqn, AURI, based at Halim

T1302 (C/N 3578) No 31 Sqn, AURI; damaged during landing at Malacca, Malaysia, 9-7-78. (Probably written off for spares.)

T1303 (C/N 3580) Civil registered by Lockheed-Georgia, *N9298R*, *1963*–65; No 31 Sqn, AURI, Halim, 1966–80.

T1304 (C/N 3582) Civil registered by Lockheed-Georgia, *N9297R*, 1963–65; No 31 Sqn, AURI, Halim, 1966–80.

T1305 (C/N 3583) Civil registered by Lockheed-Georgia, *N9296R*, 1963–65; No 31 Sqn, AURI, Halim, 1966–80.

T1306 (C/N 3598) No 31 Sqn, AURI, Halim; shot down in Malaysia, 9-65.

T1307 (C/N 3599) No 31 Sqn, AURI, Halim; shot down in west coastal area of Malayan peninsula, 9-64.

T1308 (C/N 3601) No 31 Sqn, AURI, Halim. Leased to Penas Aerial Survey, 1969, as *PH-VHA*.

T1309 (C/N 3615) No 31 Sqn, AURI, Halim. Became KC-130B tanker for AURI, c1980.

T1310 (C/N 3616) No 31 Sqn, AURI, Halim. Became KC-130B tanker for AURI, c1980.

LOCKHEED MODEL 282-2B HC-130B HERCULES (C/Ns 3594, 3595, 3638, 3641 and 3650, USAF Nos *60-0311*, *60-0312*, and *61-2081* to *61-2083*) Five aircraft purchased for service with the US Coast Guard, also designated SC-130B. Completed 1961–62.

60-0311, *CG1344* (C/N 3594) Based at Elizabeth City, North Carolina, 1969–80.

60-0312, *CG1345* (C/N 3695) Based at Elizabeth City, North Carolina, 1966–71; San Francisco, California, 1973–79.

61-2081, *CG1346* (C/N 3638) Delivered 23-3-62; based at San Francisco, California, c1967–68; Elizabeth City, North Carolina, 1969–75.

61-2082, *CG1347* (C/N 3641) Delivered 1-3-62; based at Elizabeth City, North Carolina, 1977–80; equipped with sensor units on undercarriage fairings and under wings.

61-2083, *CG1348* (C/N 3650) Delivered 19-4-62; based at Barbers Point, Hawaii, 1975–81.

LOCKHEED MODEL 282-10B C-130F (GV-1U) HERCULES (C/Ns 3636, 3645, 3660, 3661, 3666, 3686 and 3696) Seven aircraft, US Navy Nos *149787, 149790, 149793, 149794, 149797, 149801* and *149805*. Standard transports purchased for the US Navy. Completed 1961–62.

149787 (C/N 3636) VR-1, NAS Norfolk, Virginia, 1965; VRC-50 'RG-787', NAS North Island, California (with detachment to Atsugi, Japan), 1969–81.

149790 (C/N 3645) VR-24, 'JM-790', NAS Naples, Italy (with detachment to NAS Rota, Spain), 1981.

149793 (C/N 3660) VR-24, 'JM-793', NAS Naples, Italy, *c*1971; VRC-50, 'RG-793', NAS North Island, California, 1977–81.

149794 (C/N 3661) VR-1, NAS Norfolk, Virginia, 1965; VR-24 'JM-794', NAS Naples, Italy, 1973–82.

149797 (C/N 3666) VR-24 'JM-797', NAS Naples, Italy (with detachment to NAS Rota, Spain), 1970–82.

149801 (C/N 3686) VR-24 'JM-801', NAS Naples, Italy, 1969–80.

149805 (C/N 3696) VR-1, NAS Norfolk, Virginia, *c*1967; VRC-50 'RG-805', NAS North Island, California (with detachment to NAS Atsugi, Japan), 1975–80.

LOCKHEED MODEL 282 C-130B HERCULES (C/Ns 3591, 3593, 3596, 3597, 3600, 3602 to 3604, 3610 to 3614, 3617, 3618 and 3620 to 3622) 18 aircraft, USAF Nos *60-0293* to *60-0310* (not respectively). Standard transports for USAF's TAC. Four Allison T56A-7 turboprops driving four-blade propellers; external tanks outboard of outer engines; forward cargo door. Completed in 1961–62.

60-0293 (C/N 3591) 463d TAW, 1964; overshot runway at An Khe AB, 17-6-67, and written off.

60-0294 (C/N 3593) 775th TCS, 1964; 773d TAS, 1969; 337th TAS, 1972–80.

60-0295 (C/N 3596) 772d TAS, 1967; 337th TAS, 1972–81.

60-0296 (C/N 3597) 772d TAS, 1967; 756th TAS, 1972; 337th TAS, 1972–80.

60-0297 (C/N 3600) 314th TCW, 1962; 773d TAS, 1967–68; shot down during take-off at Tan Son Nhut, 12-5-68.

60-0298 (C/N 3602) 733d TAS; shot down over South Vietnam, 26-4-68.

60-0299 (C/N 3603) 29th TAS, 1967; 337th TAS, 1971–80.

60-0300 (C/N 3604) 772d TAS, 1967–68; 337th TAS, 1972–74; 68th TAS, 1975–81.

60-0301 (C/N 3610) 68th TAS, 1972. Sold to Royal Jordanian Air Force as No *141* in 1973; re-registered *341* in 1979.

60-0302 (C/N 3611) 711th TAS, 1967; 67th TAS, 1970; 68th TAS, 1975–76. Sold to Royal Jordanian Air Force as No *142* in 1976. Resold to Singapore Government as '*724*' in 1977.

60-0303 (C/N 3613) 774th TAS, 1968; 711th TAS, 1973; 67th TAS, 1973–74; 68th TAS, 1974–81.

60-0304 (C/N 3612) 774th TAS, 1968; 67th TAS, c1973. Sold to Royal Jordanian Air Force as No *140* in 1973; re-registered *340* in 1979.

60-0305 (C/N 3614) 773d TAS, 1969–72, 68th TAS, 1973. Sold to Indonesia, 1975, as *T1311*; No 31 Sqn, AURI, based at Halim.

60-0306 (C/N 3617) 711th TAS, 1973; 337th TAS, 1974. Sold to Indonesia, 1975, as *T1312;* No 31 Sqn, AURI, based at Halim.

60-0307 (C/N 3618) 463d TAW, 1966–67; crashed in South Vietnam, 17-2-67.

60-0308 (C/N 3620) 67th TAS, 1972; 68th TAS, 1976. Sold to Royal Jordanian Air Force, 1976, as No *143*. Resold to Singapore Government in 1977 as *725*.

60-0309 (C/N 3621) 774th TAS, *c*1970; 67th TAS, 1973. Sold to Indonesia, 1975, as *T1312;* No 31 Sqn, AURI, based at Halim.

60-0306 (C/N 3617) 711th TAS, 1973; 337th TAS, 1974. Sold to Indonesia, 1975, as *T1312*; No 31 Sqn, AURI, based at Halim.

60-0307 (C/N 3618) 463d TAW, 1966–67; crashed in South Vietnam, 17-2-67.

60-0308 (C/N 3620) 67th TAS, 1972; 68th TAS, 1976. Sold to Royal Jordanian Air Force, 1976, as No *143*. Resold to Singapore Government in 1977 as *725*.

60-0309 (C/N 3621) 774th TAS, *c*1970; 67th TAS, 1973. Sold to Indonesia, 1975, as *T1313*; No 31 Sqn, AURI, based at Halim.

60-0310 (C/N 3622) 317th TAW, 1967; 67th TAS, 1973; 68th TAS, 1975–81; extensively damaged by fire in flight, 20-11-78, but repaired.

LOCKHEED MODEL 282 C-130B HERCULES (1961 USAF Appropriations) (C/Ns 3624 to 3626, 3628 to 3630, 3633 to 3635, 3637, 3639, 3642, 3643, 3646 to 3649, 3652-3656, 3667 to 3679, 3682, 3683, 3590 and 3692) 39 aircraft, USAF Nos *61-0948* to *61-0972, 61-2634* to *61-2645, 61-2647* and *61-2649*. Standard transports for USAF's TAC. Completed in 1962.

61-0948 (C/N 3624) 773d TAS, 1968–72; 756th TAS, 1972–74; 711th TAS, 1974–75; 706th TAS, 1975–78; 337th TAS, 1978–80.

61-0949 (C/N 3625) 313th TAW, 1968–69; 156th TAS, North Carolina ANG, 1972–81.

61-0950 (C/N 3626) 772d TAS, 1968–72; 156th TAS, North Carolina ANG, 1975–81.

61-0951 (C/N 3628) 314th TAW, 1968; 711th TAS, 1972; 336th TAS, 1972–76; 433d TAW, 1977–80.

61-0952 (C/N 3629) 773d TAS, 1968; 314th TAS, 1973–76; 164th TAS, Ohio ANG, 1977–82.

61-0953 (C/N 3630) 463d TAW, 1966; crashed in South Vietnam, 29-3-66.

61-0954 (C/N 3633) 773d TAS, 1968; 336th TAS, 1972; 711th TAS, 1973–75; 706th TAS, 1975–78; 68th TAS, 1978–81.

61-0955 (C/N 3634) 463d TAW, 1965–66; crashed off Kam Ranh Bay, 10-66.

61-0956 (C/N 3635) 772d TAS, *c*1967; 337th TAS, 1972–73; 711th TAS, 1974–75; 67th TAS, 1975; 68th TAS, 1975–81.

61-0957 (C/N 3637) 47th TAS, 1964–68; 336th TAS, 1973–74; 187th TAS, Wyoming ANG, 1974–75; 336th TAS, 1975–76; 68th TAS, 1977–81.

61-0958 (C/N 3639) 47th TAS, 1967–72; 711th TAS, 1974–75; 68th TAS, 1975–81.

61-0959 (C/N 3642) 774th TAS, 1969; 109th TAS, Minnesota ANG, 1972; 336th TAS, 1972–73; 314th TAS, 1976; 433d TAW, 1977–80.

61-0960 (C/N 3643) 711th TAS, 1968; 336th TAS, 1972–76; 68th TAS, 1977–81.

61-0961 (C/N 3646) 773d TAS, *c*1967; 156th TAS, North

Carolina ANG, 1972; 115th TAS, California ANG, 1973–76; 164th TAS, Ohio ANG, 1977–81.

61-0962 (C/N 3647) Became JC-130B; 6593d TS, 6594th ABG, 1977–80.

61-0963 (C/N 3648) Delivered 21-9-61. Became JC-130B; 6593d TS, 1964. Returned to C-130B; 711th TAS, 1968–74; 756th TAS, 1974–76; 164th TAS, Ohio ANG, 1977–81.

61-0964 (C/N 3649) 774th TAS, 1969; 67th TAS, 1973; 68th TAS, 1976–79; 337th TAS, 1979–81.

61-0965 (C/N 3652) 773d TAS, 1967–69; shot down over South Vietnam, 23-6-69.

61-0966 (C/N 3653) 463d TAW, 1970–72; 187th TAS, Wyoming ANG, 1975–81.

61-0967 (C/N 3654) 774th TAS, 1966–68; crashed in South Vietnam, 13-4-68.

61-0968 (C/N 3655) 773d TAS, 1967–70; 336th TAS, 1972–74; 706th TAS, 1975–78; 68th TAS, 1978–81.

61-0969 (C/N 3656) 756th TAS, 1972; 711th TAS, 1973–75; 706th TAS, 1975–78; 68th TAS, 1978–81.

61-0970 (C/N 3667) 314th TCW, 1965–66; destroyed in landing crash, South Vietnam, 9-1-66.

61-0971 (C/N 3668) 313th TCW, 1966–68; 336th TAS, 1972–76; 704th TAS, 1977–81.

61-0972 (C/N 3669) 314th TCW, 1965–66; crashed (possibly shot down), South Vietnam, 6-1-66.

61-2634 (C/N 3670) 4442d CCTW, 1962–63; 64th TCW, 1966; 316th TCW, 1966–*c*1968; 29th TAS, 1969; 187th TAS, Wyoming ANG, 1973; 115th TAS, California ANG, 1973–80; 135th TAS, Maryland ANG, 1980–81.

61-2635 (C/N 3671) 774th TAS, 1966–68; 187th TAS, Wyoming ANG, 1972–81.

61-2636 (C/N 3672) 47th TCS, 1965–68; 156th TAS, North Carolina ANG, 1973–81.

61-2637 (C/N 3673) 29th TAS, 1967–68; 711th TAS, 1969; landed at Loc Ninh, South Vietnam, 29-4-69, with fire in wheel fairing, and written off.

61-2638 (C/N 3674) 774th TAS, 1966–68; 156th TAS, North Carolina ANG, 1972–81.

61-2639 (C/N 3675) 772d TAS, 1968; 187th TAS, Wyoming ANG, 1972; 156th TAS, North Carolina ANG, 1973; 115th TAS, California ANG, 1975–80; 135th TAS, Maryland ANG, 1980–81.

61-2640 (C/N 3676) 314th TCW, 1968; 156th TAS, North Carolina ANG, 1973–81.

61-2641 (C/N 3677) 313th TCW, 1964–66; written off in Norway, 19-3-66.

61-2642 (C/N 3678) 463d TAW, 1969–71; damaged in rocket attack on Da Nang, South Vietnam, 21-2-71, and written off; tail unit used to repair AC-130.

61-2643 (C/N 3679) 711th TAS, 1972–73; 187th TAS, Wyoming ANG, 1973–81.

61-2644 (C/N 3682) 772d TAS, 1965–68; crashed in South Vietnam, 28-11-68.

61-2645 (C/N 3683) 773d TAS, 1968–70; 156th TAS, North Carolina ANG, 1973; 115th TAS, California ANG, 1973–80; 135th TAS, Maryland ANG, 1980–81.

61-2647 (C/N 3690) 337th TAS, *c*1969; 68th TAS, 1971–73; 815th TAS, 1973–75; 433d TAW, 1977–80; 68th TAS, 1981.

61-2649 (C/N 3692) 463d TCW, 1966–67; crashed between Phu Bai and Cam Ranh, 8-10-67.

LOCKHEED MODEL 282 C-130B HERCULES (for Pakistan) (C/Ns 3689, 3691, 3751, 3766, 3768 and 3781) Six

aircraft, offset under Mutual Assistance Programme from USAF blocks, USAF Nos *61-2646*, *61-2648*, and *62-4140* to *62-4143*. Standard transports for Pakistan Air Force. Completed in 1962–63.

61-2646 (C/N 3689) Mutual Assistance Programme. No 6 Sqn, PAF, based at Chaklala; at one time civil registered, *AK-MOB*.

61-2648 (C/N 3691) MAP. No 6 Sqn, PAF; written off, 8-65.

62-4140 (C/N 3751) MAP. No 6 Sqn, PAF, Chaklala; aircraft 'B'.

62-4141 (C/N 3766) MAP. No 6 Sqn, PAF, Chaklala; aircraft 'F', later 'A'.

62-4142 (C/N 3768) MAP. No 6 Sqn, PAF; written off, 7-66.

62-4143 (C/N 3781) MAP. No 6 Sqn, PAF, Chaklala; aircraft 'O'. At one time civil registered *AS-HFO*.

LOCKHEED MODEL 282-3B KC-130F (GV-1) HERCULES (C/Ns 3693 to 3695, 3703 to 3705, 3709 to 3711, 3718, 3719, 3723, 3725 to 3728, 3733, 3734 and 3740 to 3742) 21 aircraft, US Navy Nos *149802* to *149804*, *149806* to *149816* and *150684* to *150690*, built as air refuelling tankers for the US Marine Corps. Completed in 1961–63.

149802 (C/N 3693) VMGR-152, MAW-1, MCAS Futema, Okinawa; struck sea wall on take-off from Hong Kong, 24-8-65, and destroyed.

149803 (C/N 3694) VMGR-252, MAW-2, MCAS Cherry Point, North Carolina, 1976–81.

149804 (C/N 3695) VMGR-152, 1976–77; VMGR-352, MAW-3, MCAS El Toro, California, 1977–79.

149806 (C/N 3703) NATC, Patuxent River, 1964; US Navy Sqn VR-1, NAS Norfolk, Virginia, 1967; VMGR-352, MAW-3, MCAS El Toro, California; Blue Angels aerobatic team support aircraft, 1974–80.

149807 (C/N 3704) VMGR-252, MAW-2, MCAS Cherry Point, North Carolina, *c*1968–70; US Navy Squadron VQ-3, NAS Agana, Guam, 1979.

149808 (C/N 3705) VMGR-152, MAW-1, 1964–68; VMGR-352, MAW-3, 1975–78; VMGR-152, 1978–80; VMGR-252, MAW-2, 1980–81.

149809 (C/N 3709) Shot down over South Vietnam, 1-2-66.

149810 (C/N 3710) VMGR-252, MAW-2; destroyed in fire while being serviced with liquid oxygen, 2-72, Lake City, Florida.

149811 (C/N 3711) VMGR-352; VMGR-152; VMGR-234, MAW-4, 1978–81.

149812 (C/N 3718) VMGR-352, MAW-3; VMGR-152, MAW-1, 1973–80.

149813 (C/N 3719) VMGR-152 'QD-813', MCAS Futema, Okinawa, 1967; crashed in South Vietnam, 10-2-68.

149814 (C/N 3712) VMGR-352, MAW-3, *c*1965; VMGR-152, 1968; crashed in South Vietnam, 18-5-69, after collision while refuelling two F-4 Phantoms.

149815 (C/N 3725) VMGR-252, MAW-2, MCAS Cherry Point, North Carolina, 1976–80.

149816 (C/N 3726) VMGR-352, MAW-3, *c*1968; VMGR-152, MAW-1, 1976–80.

150684 (C/N 3727) VMGR-352, MAW-3, 1969; VMGR-152, MAW-1, 1976–79; VMGR-252, MAW-2, 1981.

150685 (C/N 3728) VMGR-352, MAW-3, 1966–67; VMGR-152, MAW-1, 1967; destroyed by fire, El Toro, California, 7-70.

150686 (C/N 3733) VMGR-352, MAW-3, *c*1965–68; VMGR-152, MAW-2, 1976–77.

150687 (C/N 3734) VMGR-352, MAW-3, c1965; VMGR-152, MAW-1, 1976–78. VMGR-252, MAW-2, 1981.

150688 (C/N 3740) VMGR-352, MAW-3, 1968–69; VMGR-152, MAW-1, 1978–80; VMGR-252, MAW-2, 1981.

150689 (C/N 3741) VMGR-152, MAW-1, MCAS Futema, Okinawa, 1968–80.

150690 (C/N 3742) VMGR-252, MAW-2, 1967–69; Blue Angels aerobatic team support aircraft, '*Fat Albert*', 1970–74; VMGR-352, MAW-3, 1974–80.

LOCKHEED MODEL 282 C-130B HERCULES (1962 Appropriations) (C/N 3697) One aircraft, USAF No *62-3487*. Standard transport for USAF's TAC. Completed in 1963.

62-3487 (C/N 3697) 29th TAS, 1964-65; 68th TAS, 1969–70; 706th TAS, 1973–76; 433d TAW, 1978–81.

LOCKHEED MODEL 282 WC-130B HERCULES (C/Ns 3702, 3707, 3708, 3721 and 3722) Five aircraft, USAF Nos *62-3492* to *62-3496*, for weather reconnaissance duties with USAF's TAC. Completed in 1963.

62-3492 (C/N 3702) 53d WRS, 1969; 55th WRS, c1972; 53d WRS, 1975–80. Became C-130B; 156th TAS, North Carolina ANG, 1979–80. (Photo, page 00.)

62-3493 (C/N 3707) 53d WRS, 1969; 54th WRS, 1972–73; 53d WRS, 1974–77. Became C-130B; 433d TAW, 1978–81.

62-3494 (C/N 3708) 53d WRS, 1969; 54th WRS, 1972–74; 53d WRS, 1974–75; 57th WRS, 1975. Became C-130B; 68th TAS, 1975–80; 135th TAS, Maryland ANG, 1981.

62-3495 (C/N 3721) 53d WRS, 1969–73. Became C-130B; 115th TAS, California ANG, 1977–81.

62-3496 (C/N 3722) 54th WRS, 1964; 53d WRS, 1969; 55th WRS, 1970; 54th WRS, 1972–73. Became C-130B; 68th TAS, 1975–81.

LOCKHEED MODEL 282 C-130B HERCULES (for Iran) (C/Ns 3698 to 3701) Four aircraft, offset under Mutual Assistance Programme from USAF blocks, USAF Nos *62-3488* to *62-3491*. Standard transports for Imperial Iranian Air Force. Completed in 1963. (All subsequently resold to Pakistan.)

62-3488 (C/N 3698) MAP. No 5 ATS, IIAF, Mehrabad, as *5-101*. Resold to Pakistan; No 6 Sqn, PAF, Chaklala, aircraft 'P'; also civil registered *AQ-ACP* and *AS-HFP*. Aircraft overran chocks during engine run and was destroyed in collision with C-130E (C/N 4117), 3-79.

62-3489 (C/N 3699) MAP. No 5 ATS, IIAF, Mehrabad, as *5-102*. Resold to Pakistan; No 6 Sqn, PAF, Chaklala, aircraft 'D'. Written off, 3-70.

62-3490 (C/N 3700) MAP. No 5 ATS, IIAF, Mehrabad, as *5-103*. Resold to Pakistan; No 6 Sqn, PAF, Chaklala, aircraft 'Q'; also civil registered AS-HFQ. Written off, 7-69. (Photo, page 00.)

62-3491 (C/N 3701) MAP. No 5 ATS, IIAF, Mehrabad, as *5-104*. Resold to Pakistan; No 6 Sqn, PAF, Chaklala, aircraft 'V'; also civil registered AQ-ACV; Transport Conversion School, Chaklala, aircraft 'W'.

LOCKHEED MODEL 282-11B C-130B HERCULES (for South Africa) (C/Ns 3724, 3749, 3750, 3764, 3765, 3767 and 3769; South African Nos *401* to *407*) Seven aircraft, standard transports for South African Air Force. Completed and delivered in 1963–64.

401 (C/N 3724) No 28 Sqn, SAAF, Waterkloof, Transvaal, 1965–80.

402 (C/N 3749) No 28 Sqn, SAAF, Waterkloof, Transvaal, 1965–80.

403 (C/N 3750) No 28 Sqn, SAAF, Waterkloof, Transvaal, 1965–80.

404 (C/N 3764) No 28 Sqn, SAAF, Waterkloof, Transvaal, 1965–80.

405 (C/N 3765) No 28 Sqn, SAAF, Waterkloof, Transvaal, 1965–80.

406 (C/N 3767) No 28 Sqn, SAAF, Waterkloof, Transvaal, 1965–80.

407 (C/N 3769) No 28 Sqn, SAAF, Waterkloof, Transvaal, 1965–80.

LOCKHEED MODEL 282-2B HC-130B (HC-130G) HERCULES (C/Ns 3745, 3763 and 3773) Three aircraft, USAF Nos *62-3753* to *62-3755*, purchased for service with the US Coast Guard. Completed 1962–63.

62-3753, CG1349 (C/N 3745) Delivered 14-12-62. Based at Elizabeth City, North Carolina, 1972; St Petersburg/Clearwater, Florida, 1979–81.

62-3754, CG1350 (C/N 3763) Delivered 31-1-63. Based at San Francisco, California, 1968; Barbers Point, Hawaii, 1973; Clearwater, Florida, 1981.

62-3755, CG1351 (C/N 3773) Delivered 22-2-63. Based at San Francisco, California, 1966; Elizabeth City, North Carolina, 1974–76; Clearwater, Florida, 1981.

LOCKHEED MODEL 382-4B C-130E HERCULES (1961 USAF Appropriations) (C/Ns 3609, 3651, 3659, 3662, 3663, 3681, 3687, 3688, 3706, 3712 to 3717 and 3720) 16 aircraft, USAF Nos *61-2358* to *61-2373*. Standard transports; eight for Tactical Air Command and eight for Military Airlift Command. Four 4,050 eshp Allison T56A-7 turboprops driving four-blade propellers; enlarged external tanks mounted between engines; forward cargo doors. MAC aircraft equipped with station-keeping equipment (SKE, with radome on front fuselage); all MAC aircraft transferred to TAC during 1964-66.

61-2358 (C/N 3609) Served as prototype for MAC; first flight, 15-8-61. Tests at Lockheed-Georgia, 1961–62. Became JC-130E; AFTC, El Centro, 1966. Became C-130E; 183d TAS, Mississippi ANG, 1972–80; 115th TAS, California ANG, 1980–81.

61-2359 (C/N 3651) Served as prototype for TAC. 4442d CCTG, Sewart AFB, Tennessee, 1964–68; 183d TAS, Mississippi ANG, 1972–80; 115th TAS, California ANG, 1980–81.

61-2360 (C/N 3654) TAC. 4442d CCTG, 1964. Became WC-130E; 54th WRS, 1965–81.

61-2361 (C/N 3662) TAC. 4442d CCTG, 1964; 64th TCW, 1966; 316th TCW, 1966. Became DC-130E, 1968; AF Missile Development Center, Holloman AFB, 12-68; 350th SRS, c1971; 11th TDS, 1977; 22d TDS, 1978–79. Became C-130E; 314th TAW, 1979–81.

61-2362 (C/N 3663) TAC. 4442d CCTG, 1964–65; AF MDC, Holloman AFB, 1967. Became DC-130E; 350th SRS, 1971; 11th TDS, 1977; 22d TDS, 1978. Became C-130E, 314th TAW, 1979–81.

61-2363 (C/N 3681) TAC. 4442d CCTG, 1964; 64th TCW, 1966; 313th TCW, 11-66. AF MDC, Holloman AFB, 1967–68. Became DC-130E; 350th SRS, 1971–74; 11th TDS, 1977; 22d TDS, 1978–79. Became C-130E; 314th TAW, 1979–81.

61-2364 (C/N 3687) TAC. 4442d CCTW, 1966; 314th TCW, 1967. Became DC-130E; 350th SRS, 1973–74;

6514th TS, 1975–80. Became C-130E, 314th TAW, 1981.

61-2365 (C/N 3688) TAC. Became WC-130E; 54th WRS, 1966–72; 53d WRS, 1975–80. Chartered to International Technical Supply Co, 1980, and civil registered *N5024E*.

61-2366 (C/N 3706) TAC. 4442d CCTG, 1964. Became WC-130E; 54th WRS, 1966–81.

61-2367 (C/N 3712) MAC. 1608th ATW, 1964; 437th MAW, 1965; 464th TCW, 1966; 316th TCW, 1966–68; 464th TAW, 1968; 314th TAW, 11-68; 779th TAS, 12-68; 374th TAW, 1971; 183d TAS, Mississippi ANG, 1975–80; 115th TAS, California ANG, 1980–81.

61-2368 (C/N 3717) MAC. 1608th ATW, 1964; 437th MAW, 1965; 4442d CCTW, 1966. Became DC-130E; 350th SRS, 1966–72; 11th TDS, 1977; 22d TDS, 1978–79. Became C-130E; 314th TAW, 1980–81.

61-2369 (C/N 3714) MAC. 1608th ATW, 1964; 437th MAW, 1965; 4442d CCTW, 1966. Became C-130E; 314th TAW, 1980–81.

61-2370 (C/N 3715) MAC. 1608th ATW, 1964; 4442d CCTW, 1966; 183d TAS, Mississippi ANG, 1972–80; 115th TAS, California ANG, 1980–81.

61-2371 (C/N 3716) MAC. 1608th ATW, 1964; 437th MAW, 1965; 316th TCW, 1966. Became DC-130E, 1966; 350th SRS, 1972–73; 11th TDS, 1977–78; 22d TDS, 1978–79. Returned to C-130E; 314th TAW, 1979–81.

61-2372 (C/N 3717) MAC. 1608th ATW, 1964; 437th MAW, 1965; 316th TCW/TAW, 1966–67; 779th TAS, 1968; 776th TAS, Ching Chuan Kang ROCAB, Taiwan, 1970; 347th TAS, *c*1972; 183d TAS, Mississippi ANG, 1974–80; 115th TAS, California ANG, 1980–81.

61-2373 (C/N 3720) MAC. 1608th ATW, 1964; 4462d CCTW, 1966; 183d TAS, Mississippi ANG (*City of Jackson*), 1972–79; 115th TAS, California ANG, 1980–81.

LOCKHEED MODEL 382-4B C-130E HERCULES (1962 USAF Appropriations for MAC) (C/Ns 3729 to 3732, 3735 to 3739, 3743, 3744, 3746 to 3748, 3752 to 3762, 3770 to 3772, 3774 to 3777, 3782 to 3785, 3787, 3790 to 3793, 3800 to 3803, 3810 to 3812, 3814 and 3815) 50 standard transports, USAF Nos *62-1784* to *62-1815*, *62-1819* to *62-1822*, *62-1824*, *62-1827* to *62-1830*, *62-1837* to *62-1840* and *62-1847* to *62-1851*). Details as for 1961 Appropriations, except no forward cargo door. Completed in 1963.

62-1784 (C/N 3729) 1608th ATW, 1964; 316th TAW; 314th TAW, 1968; 345th TAS, Ching Chuan Kang ROCAB, Taiwan, 1969–70; 374th TAW, 1972–73; 130th TAS, West Virginia ANG, 1976–81.

62-1785 (C/N 3730) 1608th ATW, 1964; 314th TAW, 1968; shot down over South Vietnam, 6-9-68.

62-1786 (C/N 3731) 1608th ATW, 1964; 314th TAW, 1968–69; 776th TAS, Ching Chuan Kang ROCAB, Taiwan, 1970; 36th TAS, 1972–74; 158th TAS, Georgia ANG, 1975–81.

62-1787 (C/N 3732) 1608th ATW, 1964; 314th TAW, 1968–69; 776th TAS, Ching Chuan Kang ROCAB, Taiwan, 1970; 374th TAW, 1972–73; 314th TAW, 1974; 139th TAS, New York ANG, 1976; 130th TAS, West Virginia ANG, 1977–81.

61-1788 (C/N 3735) 1608th ATW, 1964; 316th TAW, 1966; 314th TAW, 1968–69; 374th TAW, 1973; 130th TAS, West Virginia ANG, 1977–82.

62-1789 (C/N 3736) 1608th ATW, 1964; 464th TAW, 1968–70; 314th TAW, 1972–75; 303d TAS, 1976–81.

62-1790 (C/N 3737) 1608th ATW, 1964; 316th TAW, 1966; 314th TAW, 1968–71; 374th TAW, 1973; 130th TAS, West Virginia ANG, 1976–81.

62-1791 (C/N 3738) 1608th ATW, 1964. Became EC-130E, 1967; 7th ACCS, 1971–80, Korat RTAFB, Thailand, and later Clark AB, Philippines. Became EC-130H in *c*1978.

62-1792 (C/N 3739) 1608th ATW, 1964; 346th TAS, 1969; 348th TAS, 1970; 183d TAS Mississippi ANG (*Jackson, Mississippi*), *1975–80*; 115th TAS, California ANG, 1980–81.

62-1793 (C/N 3743) 1608th ATW, 1964; 464th TAW, 1968–70; 314th TAW, 1971; 183d TAS, Mississippi ANG, 1972–80; 115th TAS, California ANG, 1980–81.

62-1794 (C/N 3744) 1608th ATW, 1964; 314th TAW, 1968–74; 303d TAS, 1975–81.

62-1795 (C/N 3746) 1608th ATW, 1964; 437th MAW, 1965; 345th TAS, 1970–71; 374th TAW, 1973; 130th TAS, West Virginia ANG, 1976–81.

62-1796 (C/N 3747) 1608th ATW, 1964; 778th TAS, 1968–69; 779th TAS, 1969. Sold to Israel as *4X-FBE*, 10-73.

62-1797 (C/N 3748) 1608th ATW, 1964; 314th TAW, 1968; 374th TAW, Naha AB, Okinawa, 1971; shot down at An Loc, 5-72.

62-1798 (C/N 3752) 1608th ATW, 1964; 314th TAW, 1968; 374th TAW, 1971–73; 130th TAS, West Virginia ANG, 1976–81.

62-1799 (C/N 3753) 1608th ATW, 1964; 779th TAS, 1968; 777th TAS, 1969–70; 16th TATS, 314th TAW, 1974; 115th TAS, California ANG, 1974–81.

62-1800 (C/N 3754) 1608th ATW, 1964; 464th TAW, 1967–68; 50th TAS, 314th TAW, Ching Chuan Kang ROCAB, Taiwan, 1969; written off, 12-69.

62-1801 (C/N 3755) 18th TCS, 516th TCW, *c*1967; 115th TAS, California ANG, 1976–81.

62-1802 (C/N 3756) 4442d CCTG, 1964; crashed at Piggott, Arkansas, 31-7-70.

62-1803 (C/N 3757) 36th TAS, 316th TAW, *c*1972; 303d TAS, 1975–81.

62-1804 (C/N 3758) 4442d CCTG, 1964; 314th TAW, 1970; 374th TAW, 1973; 130th TAS, West Virginia ANG, 1976–81.

62-1805 (C/N 3759) 1501st ATW, 1964; 316th TAW, 1967–70; crashed in South China Sea, 5-6-72.

62-1806 (C/N 3760) 1501st ATW, 1964; 1611th ATW, 1964; 438th MAW, 1969?; 4442d CCTW, 1970; 374th TAW, 1973; 115th TAS, California ANG, 1974–75; 756th TAS, 1975–80.

62-1807 (C/N 3761) 1501st ATW, 1964; 4442d CCTW, 1970; 314th TAW, 1970–71; 374th TAW, 1973; 314th TAW, 1974; 303d TAS, 1975–81.

62-1808 (C/N 3762) 4442d CCTG/CCTW, 1964–71; 316th TAW, 1975; 303d TAS, 1975–81.

62-1809 (C/N 3770) Became EC-130E, *c*1970; 7th ACCS, 432d TRW, 1971; 388th TFW, Korat RTAFB, Thailand, 1973; 7th ACCS, 374th TAW, 1974–75; given air refuelling facility, 1976; 7th ACCS, 552d AEWG, 1977–80. Took part in rescue attempt of US hostages, Iran, 24-4-80; collided with RH-53D helicopter at Posht-i-Badam, Iran, and destroyed.

62-1810 (C/N 3771) 4442d CCTG, 1964–66; 316th TAW, 1970–71; 303d TAS, 1975–81.

62-1811 (C/N 3772) 4442d CCTG, 1964–66; 316th TAW, 1970–71; 115th TAS, California ANG, 1974–81.

62-1812 (C/N 3774) 4442d CCTG, 1964–66; 374th TAS,

*c*1969; 314th TAW, *c*1972; 158th TAS, Georgia ANG, 1974–81.

62-1813 (C/N 3775) 1501st ATW, 1964; 1608th ATW, 1965; 1501st ATW, 1965; 4442d CCTG, 1965; 1611th ATW, 1966; 438th MAW, 1967. Written off in collision at Little Rock, Arkansas, 19-2-72.

62-1814 (C/N 3776) 1501st ATW, 1964; 41st ATS, 1608th ATW, 1964–65. Special missions aircraft, South Vietnam, 1966–68; crashed at Cam Ranh Bay, 3-3-68, after electrical fire in the air.

62-1815 (C/N 3777) 1501st, ATW, 1964; 1608th ATW, 1965. Became EC-130E, 1965–66; destroyed on ground during rocket attack on Da Nang, 15-7-67.

62-1819 (C/N 3782) 1501st ATW, 1964–65; 464th TAW, 1967–69; 316th TAW, 1971–78; 7405th SS, 435th TAW, Rhein-Main AB, Germany, 1978–82.

62-1820 (C/N 3783) 1501st ATW, 1964; 4442d CCTW, 1965. Became EC-130E, 1965; 374th TAW, 1971; 314th TAW, 1974–75; 303d TAS, 1976; 7th ACCS, 1976. Returned to C-130E, 1977; 303d TAS, 1979–81.

62-1821 (C/N 3784) 1501st ATW, 1964–65; 316th TAW, 1969–72; 314th TAW, 1975–82.

62-1822 (C/N 3785) 1501st ATW, 1964–65; 316th TCW/TAW, 1966–75; 314th TAW, 1976–80; 435th TAW, 1981–82.

62-1824 (C/N 3787) 516th TCW, 1965; 314th TCW/TAW, 1965–70; 374th TAW, 1973; 130th TAS, West Virginia ANG, 1976–81.

62-1827 (C/N 3790) 1501st ATW, 1964–65; 60th MAW, 1965–66; 464th TCW, 1966; 316th TCW/TAW, 1966–75; 314th TAW, 1975–81.

62-1828 (C/N 3791) 60th MAW, 1965–66; 316th TAW, 1969–70; 313th TAW, 1970; 7405th SS, 435th TAW, Rhein-Main AB, Germany, 1977–81.

62-1829 (C/N 3792) 1501st ATW, 1964; 316th TAW, 1969–70; 516th TAW, 1970–72; 158th TAS, Georgia ANG, 1974–81.

62-1830 (C/N 3793) 1501st ATW, 1964; 437th MAW, 1965; 316th TAW, 1969; 464th TAW, 1969–70; 316th TAW, 1970–72; 303d TAS, 1975–81.

62-1837 (C/N 3800) 4442d CCTW, 1970; 314th TAW, 1972; 303d TAS, 1973; 158th TAS, Georgia ANG, 1975–81.

62-1838 (C/N 3801) 316th TAW, 1970–74; 303d TAS, 1975–81.

62-1839 (C/N 3802) 1501st ATW, 1964; 4442d CCTW, 1968–69; 314th TAW, 1975; 756th TAS, 1975–80.

62-1840 (C/N 3803) Shot down over South Vietnam, 2-10-66.

62-1847 (C/N 3810) 345th TAS, 314th TAW, Ching Chuan Kang ROCAB, Taiwan, (*Deanna Sue*), 1967–73; 374th TAW, 1973; 756th TAS, 1976–80.

62-1848 (C/N 3811) 345th TAS, 1968–72; 374th TAW, 1972–73; 756th TAS, 1977–80; 459th TAW, 1981.

62-1849 (C/N 3812) 314th TAS, 1968; 316th TAW, 1970–72; 303d TAS, 1975–80.

62-1850 (C/N 3814) 316th TAS, 1969–73; 303d TAS, 1975–81.

62-1851 (C/N 3815) 777th TAS, 1968–70; 115th TAS, California ANG, 1974–81.

LOCKHEED MODEL 382-8B C-130E HERCULES (1962 USAF Appropriations for TAC) (33 standard transports without SKE or forward cargo door,) (C/Ns 3778 to 3780, 3786, 3788, 3789, 3794-3799, 3804 to 3809 and 3816 to 3830) USAF Nos *62-1816* to *62-1818*, *62-1823*, *62-1825*,

62-1826, *62-1831* to *62-1836*, *62-1841* to *62-1846* and *62-1852* to *62-1866*. Completed in 1963.

62-1816 (C/N 3778) 464th TCW, 1964; 4442d CCTW, 1965–71; 316th TAW, 1973–75; 303d TAS, 1976–81.

62-1817 (C/N 3779) 464th TCW, 1964; 516th TCW, 1965; 314th TCW, 1965–70; 158th TAS, Georgia ANG (*City of Savannah*), 1974–81.

62-1818 (C/N 3780) 516th TCW, 1964; 314th TCW/TAW, 1965–68. Became EC-130E, 1972; 7th ACCS, 1974–81; given air refuelling facility, 1977. Became EC-130H, *c*1978. Took part in attempted rescue of US hostages, Tabas, Iran, 25-4-80.

62-1823 (C/N 3786) 464th TCW, 1864; 4442d CCTW, 1965–69; 316th TAW, 1972–74; 303d TAS, 1975–81.

62-1825 (C/N 3788) 516th TCW, 1964; 4485th TW, Eglin AFB, 1964–65; 4442d CCTW, 1965; 314th TCW, 1965–67. Became EC-130E, 1967; 7th ACCS, 1970–80; given air refuelling facility, 1977. Became EC-130H, *c*1979.

62-1826 (C/N 3789) 464th TCW, 1964; 4442d CCTW, 1965; 464th TCW/TAW, 1965–70; 16th TATS, 314th TAW, 1971; 115th TAS, California ANG, 1975–81.

62-1831 (C/N 3794) 516th TCW, 1964–65; 314th TCW, 1966; written off, 2-69.

62-1832 (C/N 3795) 464th TCW, 1964; 4442d CCTW, 1965–66. Became EC-130E, 1966; 7th ACCS, 1969–79; 115th TAS, California ANG, 1979–80.

62-1833 (C/N 3796) 464th TCW, 1964; 4442d CCTW, 1965–66; 316th TAW, 1968; 115th TAS, California ANG, 1974–81.

62-1834 (C/N 3797) 314th TCW, 1966–68; 374th TAW, 1973; 756th TAS, 1975–80.

62-1835 (C/N 3798) 516th TCW, 1964; 464th TCW, 1964–65; 4442d CCTW, 1966–67; 314th TAW, 1970; 374th TAW, 1973; 756th TAS, 1976–79; 7th ACCS, 1979–80.

62-1836 (C/N 3799) 314th TCW, 1966. Became EC-130E, 1966; 7th ACCS, *c*1970–74; 16th TATS, 1975–76; 158th TAS, Georgia ANG, 1977; 7th ACCS, 1977–81.

62-1841 (C/N 3804) 516th TCW, 1964; 314th TAW, 1970; 374th TAW, 1973; caught fire and burnt out, Andersen AFB, Guam, 20-4-74.

62-1842 (C/N 3805) 464th TAW, 1968–70; 115th TAS, California ANG, 1974–81.

62-1843 (C/N 3806) 516th TCW, 1964; force landed, 20-12-65, but repaired; 1174th SS, 1971–72. Became C-130E-I; 1st SOS, 1977–81. Became MC-130E-Y, 1978.

62-1844 (C/N 3807) 314 TAW, 1968; 374th TAW, 1972–73; 756th TAS, 1977–80.

62-1845 (C/N 3808) 314th TAW, 1973; crashed, Sugar Loaf Mountain, Arkansas, 15-10-73.

62-1846 (C/N 3809) 158th TAS, Georgia ANG, 1974–81.

62-1852 (C/N 3816) 516th TCW, 1964; 374th TAW, 1973; 756th TAS, 1976–80.

62-1853 (C/N 3817) 516th TCW, 1964; 345th TAS, 1971; shot down, South Vietnam, 12-8-72.

62-1854 (C/N 3818) 516th TCW, 1964; 314th TAW, 1970–71; 21st TAS, 1971–72; written off at Kontum City, South Vietnam, 17-5-72.

62-1855 (C/N 3819) 314th TAW, 1970; 374th TAW, 1973; 21st TAS, 1975–80; 314th TAW, 1980–81.

62-1856 (C/N 3820) 464th TAW, 1969–70; 158th TAS, Georgia ANG, 1975–81.

62-1857 (C/N 3821) Wheels-up landing, Eglin AFB, 1965. Repaired and became EC-130E, 1967. 7th ACCS, 1971–80;

given air refuelling facility, 1977. Became EC-130H, 1978; took part in attempted rescue of US hostages, Tabas, Iran, 25-4-80.

62-1858 (C/N 3822) 464th TAW, 1968–70; 316th TAW, 1971–73; 303d TAS, 1975–81.

62-1859 (C/N 3823) 516th TCW, 1965; 21st TAS, 1971–81.

62-1860 (C/N 3824) 777th TAS, 1967–68; 464th TAW, 1968–71; 303d TAS, 1975–81.

62-1861 (C/N 3825) Shot down over South Vietnam, 25-6-68.

62-1862 (C/N 3826) 778th TAS, 1968; 464th TAW, 1968–70; 115th TAS, California ANG, 1974–81.

62-1863 (C/N 3827) 374th TAW, 1971. Became EC-130E, 1971; 7th ACCS, 1975–81.

62-1864 (C/N 3828) 464th TAW, 1968–71; 16th TATS, 1974–75; 463d TAW, 1975; 158th TAS, Georgia ANG, 1975–81.

62-1865 (C/N 3829) Destroyed in mortar attack on Dak To, South Vietnam, 15-11-67.

62-1866 (C/N 3830) 464th TAW, 1968–70; 314th TAW, 1975; 303d TAS, 1975–81.

LOCKHEED MODEL 382-8B C-130E HERCULES
(1963 USAF Appropriations for TAC) (C/Ns 3813, 3831 to 3847, 3861 to 3870, 3884 to 3887, 3890 to 3893, 3903, 3904, 3908 to 3912, 3927 to 3931, 3933 to 3938, 3947 to 3952, 3956 to 3958, 3966 to 3973, 3977 and 3978) 73 standard transports without SKE or forward loading door, USAF Nos *63-7764* to *63-7781*, *63-7795* to *63-7804*, *63-7818* to *63-7827*, *63-7838* to *63-7842*, *63-7857* to *63-7861*, *63-7863* to *63-7868*, *63-7876* to *63-7881*, *63-7885* to *63-7887*, *63-7895* to *63-7899*, *63-9810* to *63-9812*, *63-9816* and *63-9817*). Details as for 1962 USAF Appropriations. Completed in 1963–64.

63-7764 (C/N 3813) 516th TAW, 1968–70; 463d TAW, 1975–76; 144th TAS, Alaska ANG, 1977–81.

63-7765 (C/N 3831) 516th TAW, 1968–69; 7th ACCS, 388th TFW, Korat RTAFB, Thailand, 1971–72; 314th TAW, 1973; 374th TAW, 1975–76; 314th TAW, 1977–81.

63-7766 (C/N 3832) 464th TAW, 1967–69; 516th TAW, 1972–73; 17th TAS, 1975–78; undershot runway and crashed, Sparrevohm AFS, Alaska, 28-4-78.

63-7767 (C/N 3833) 516th TAW, 1970–74; 463d TAW, 1974–76; 36th TAS, 1977–82.

63-7768 (C/N 3834) 464th TAW, 1968–72; 317th TAW, 1975–76; 314th TAW, 1976–81.

63-7769 (C/N 3835) 516th TAW, 1968–74; 773d TAS, 1975; 314th TAW, 1976–78; 4950th TW, 1979; 314th TAW, 1979–81.

63-7770 (C/N 3836) 464th TAW, 1968–70; 516th TAW, 1973–74; 463d TAW, 1975–76; 144th TAS, Alaska ANG, 1977–81.

63-7771 (C/N 3837) 516th TAW, 1969–71; 314th TAW, 1975–82.

63-7772 (C/N 3838) Crashed and written off in South Vietnam, 13-3-67.

63-7773 (C/N 3839) 516th TAW, 1968–71; 36th TAS, 62d MAW, 1975–77; 193d ECS, Pennsylvania ANG, 1977–81. Became EC-130E(RR), 11-79.

63-7774 (C/N 3840) 516th TAW, 1970–73. Sold to Israel as *4X-FBF*, 10-73.

63-7775 (C/N 3841) 346th TAS, 516th TAW, 1968; 347th TAS, 1969; 374th TAW, 1970–71; shot down over South Vietnam, 18-4-72.

63-7776 (C/N 3842) 346th TAS, 516th TAW, 1969–73;

463d TAW, 1973; 32d TAS, 314th TAW, 1975; 17th TAS, 21st CW, 1976–78; 317th TAW, 1979–82.

63-7777 (C/N 3843) 344th TAS, 516th TCW/TAW, 1966–69; 347th TAS, 1970; 374th TAW, 1973; 345th TAS, 374th TAW, 1975–81.

63-7778 (C/N 3844) 516th TCW, 1963–71; 463d TAW, 1975–77; Sheppard TTC, 1977; 314th TAW, 1978–81.

63-7779 (C/N 3845) 516th TAW, 1968–69; 316th TAW, 1969; 516th TAW, 1969–70; 463d TAW, 1973; 17th TAS, 21st CW, 1975–81.

63-7780 (C/N 3846) 776th TCS (*The North Carolina*), c1965; 314th TCW, 1966; 776th TAS, 1968; damaged (and probably written off) in take-off accident, Taiwan, 2-1-69.

63-7781 (C/N 3847) 464th TAW, 1968–73; 317th TAW, 1975–76; 314th TAW, 1976–81.

63-7795 (C/N 3861) 464th TAW, 1968–73; 317th TAW, 1975–76; 314th TAW, 1976–81.

63-7796 (C/N 3862) 317th TAW, 1971–75; 314th TAW, 1975–81.

63-7797 (C/N 3863) 464th TAW, 1965; hit high tension cables, Alencon, France, 25-3-65, and crashed.

63-7798 (C/N 3864) 345th TAS, 314th TAW; shot down at An Loc, South Vietnam, 6-5-72.

63-7799 (C/N 3865) 464th TAW, 1967–70; 314th TAW, 1970; 463d TAW, 1975–76; 314th TAW, 1977–81.

63-7800 (C/N 3866) 777th TAS, 464th TAW, 1967–68; 464th TAW, 1968–70; 346th TAS, 516th TAW, 1973; 345th TAS, 314th TAW, 1975–81.

63-7801 (C/N 3867) 777th TAS, 464th TAW, 1967; written off following landing accident, Pope AFB, North Carolina, 22-6-67.

63-7802 (C/N 3868) 347th TAS, 516th TAW, 1968; 374th TAW, 1973; 345th TAS, 1974; destroyed in landing accident, Kadena AB, Okinawa, 9-74.

63-7803 (C/N 3869) 464th TAW (*Flying Pig*), 1968–70; 345th TAS, 1975–81.

63-7804 (C/N 3870) 516th TAW, 1967–68; 316th TAW, 1968; 464th TAW, 1969–73; 317th TAW, 1975–76; 314th TAW, 1976–77; 17th TAS, 1978–81.

63-7818 (C/N 3884) 464th TAW, 1967–73; 317th TAW, 1975–76; 314th TAW, 1976–79; 17th TAS, 1979–81.

63-7819 (C/N 3885) 776th TAS, 314th TAW, 1970; 345th TAS, 1975–81.

63-7820 (C/N 3886) 777th TAS, 1968; 464th TAW, 1968–70; 516th TAW, c1972; 463d TAW, 1975–76; 314th TAW, 1977–81.

63-7821 (C/N 3887) 316th TAW, 1968; 516th TAW, 1969–70; 463d TAW, 1975–76; 314th TAW, 1977–81.

63-7822 (C/N 3890) 346th TAS, 1968; 516th TAW, 1969–70; 463d TAW, 1975–76; 144th TAS, Alaska ANG, 1977–81.

63-7823 (C/N 3891) 464th TAW, 1968–73; 317th TAW, 1975–76; 314th TAW, 1976–79; 317th TAW, 1979–82.

63-7824 (C/N 3892) 516th TAW, 1968–69; 374th TAW, 1973–75; 345th TAS, 1976–77; 21st TAS, 1977; 345th TAS, 1979–81.

63-7825 (C/N 3893) 516th TAW, 1968; 374th TAW, 1973; 345th TAS, 1975–81.

63-7826 (C/N 3903) 346th TAS, 1968; 516th TAW, 1969–70; 463d TAW, 1975–76; 327th TAS, 1976–80.

63-7827 (C/N 3904) 316th TAW, 1967; 314th TAW, 1967; destroyed in mortar attack on Dak To, 15-11-67.

63-7838 (C/N 3908) 464th TAW, 1968–70; 316th TAW,

1973; 314th TAW, 1975–81.

63-7839 (C/N 3909) 464th TAW, 1968–69; 516th TAW, 1970; 316th TAW, 1975; 314th TAW, 1975–81.

63-7840 (C/N 3910) 347th TAS, 1969; 374th TAW, 1973; 345th TAS, 1975–81.

63-7841 (C/N 3911) 464th TAW, 1967–69; 316th TAW, 1973; 314th TAW, 1975–81.

63-7842 (C/N 3912) 516th TAW, 1968–73; 463d TAW, 1975–76; 36th TAS, 1977–81.

63-7857 (C/N 3927) 464th TAW, 1966–69; 316th TAW, 1971–74; 314th TAW, 1975–81.

63-7859 (C/N 3929) 346th TAS, 1968; 374th TAW, 1973; 345th TAS, 1975–77; 21st TAS, 1977–78; 345th TAS, 1979–81.

63-7860 (C/N 3930) 464th TAW, 1968–73; 316th TAW, 1974; 314th TAW, 1975–81.

63-7861 (C/N 3931) 31st TAS, 1967; 464th TAW, 1968–69; 316th TAW, 1973; 314th TAW, 1975–82.

63-7863 (C/N 3933) 516th TAW, 1969; 38th TAS, 313th TAW, 1971; 346th TAS, 516th TAW, 1973; 463d TAW, 1975–76; 144th TAS, Alaska ANG, 1978–81.

63-7864 (C/N 3934) Tests with SKE, 1964; 516th TAW, 1968; 47th TAS, 313th TAW, 1969; 516th TAW, 1972; 374th TAW, 1973; 345th TAS, 1975–80; 314th TAW, 1980–81.

63-7865 (C/N 3935) 516th TAW, 1966–70; 374th TAW, 1973; 345th TAS, 1975–81.

63-7866 (C/N 3936) 346th TAS, 1968; 313th TAW, 1970; 463d TAW, 1975; 21st TAS, 1975–81.

63-7867 (C/N 3937) 516th TAW, 1969–70; 463d TAW, 1976; 303d TAS, 1977; 327th TAS, 1977–80.

63-7868 (C/N 3938) 374th TAW, 1971–81.

63-7876 (C/N 3947) 464th TAW, 1968–74; 317th TAW, 1975–76; 314th TAW, 1976–81.

63-7877 (C/N 3948) 776th TCS, 1965–69; 374th TAW, 1973; 345th TAS, 1975–81.

63-7878 (C/N 3949) 777th TCS, 1964; written off, 9-66.

63-7879 (C/N 3950) 346th TAS, 1968; 347th TAS, 516th TAW, 1969; 21st TAS, 1971–81.

63-7880 (C/N 3951) 516th TAW, 1969–74; 463d TAW, 1976; 314th TAW, 1977–81.

63-7881 (C/N 3952) 776th TAS, 314th TAW, 1970; 374th TAW, 1973; 345th TAS, 1975–81.

63-7885 (C/N 3956) 464th TAW, 1968–73; Cambodian resupply operation, 1974 (*Thi Am,* Bird Air); 317th TAW, 1975–77; 37th TAS, 1977–81.

63-7886 (C/N 3957) Written off, 10-66.

63-7887 (C/N 3958) 438th MAW, 1968; 314th TAW, 1971–81.

63-7895 (C/N 3966) 314th TAW, 1970; 374th TAW, 1973; 345th TAS, 1975–81.

63-7896 (C/N 3967) 778th TAS, 1968; 464th TAW, 1969–73; 516th TAW, 1974; 317th TAW, 1975–76; 314th TAW, 1976–82.

63-7897 (C/N 3968) 314th TAW, 1969; 345th TAS, 1973; 7th ACCS, 388th TFW, 1974; 345th TAS, 1975–81.

63-7898 (C/N 3969) 464th TAW (*African Turbo-Sow*), 1968–73; 314th TAW, 1975–80.

63-7899 (C/N 3970) 464th TAW, 1968–73; 317th TAW, 1975–76; 314th TAW, 1976–77; 62d MAW, 1978; 317th TAW, 1978–82.

63-9810 (C/N 3971) 778th TAS, 1967; 464th TAW, 1968–73; 317th TAW, 1975–76; 314th TAW, 1976–79;

435th TAW, 1980; 317th TAW, 1980–82.

63-9811 (C/N 3972) 347th TAS, 1968; 374th TAW, 1973; 21st TAS, 1975–80; 314th TAW, 1981.

63-9812 (C/N 3973) 464th TAW, 1968–69; 47th TAS, 313th TAW, 1969; 464th TAW, 1971–73; 314th TAW, 1976–81.

63-9816 (C/N 3977) 778th TAS, 1968; 464th TAW, 1968–73; 317th TAW, 1975–76; 314th TAW, 1976–77; 193d SOS/ECS, Pennsylvania ANG, 1977–81. EC-130E(CL) from 1979.

63-9817 (C/N 3978) 50th TAS, 314th TAW, Ching Chuan Kang ROCAB, Taiwan, 1969; 464th TAW, 1975; 317th TAW, 1975–76; 314th TAW, 1976–77; 193d SOS/ECS, Pennsylvania ANG, 1977–81. EC-130E(RR) from 1979.

LOCKHEED MODEL 382-4B C-130E HERCULES
(1963 USAF Appropriations for MAC) (C/Ns 3848, 3850 to 3857, 3859, 3860, 3872 to 3877, 3879 to 3883, 3888, 3889, 3894 to 3902, 3905 to 3907, 3913 to 3926, 3932, 3939 to 3945, 3953 to 3955, 3959 to 3965 and 3974 to 3976.) 71 standard transports with SKE but no forward cargo door, USAF Nos *63-7782* to *63-7794, 63-7805* to *63-7817, 63-7828* to *63-7837, 63-7843* to *63-7856, 63-7862, 63-7869* to *63-7875, 63-7882* to *63-7884, 63-7888* to *63-7894* and *63-9813* to *63-9815*. Details as for 1962 Appropriations. Completed in 1963–64, and all transferred to TAC during 1964–67.

63-7782 (C/N 3848) 37th TAS, 1970; 36th TAS, 1974–81.

63-7783 (C/N 3850) 316th TAW, 1968; 36th TAS, 1969; 37th TAS, 1970; 36th TAS, 1975–77; 193d SOS/ECS, Pennsylvania ANG, 1977–81. Became EC-130E(CL) in 1979, and EC-130E(RR) in 1980.

63-7784 (C/N 3851) 438th MAW, 1967–68; 346th TAS, 1969; 316th TAW, 1970–73; 463d TAW, 1976; 36th TAS, 1976–81.

63-7785 (C/N 3852) Crashed 17-6-66 but repaired; 1174th SS, 1972. Became C-130E-I; 1st SOS, 1977–80. Became MC-130E-Y in 1978.

63-7786 (C/N 3853) 1501st ATW, 1964; 779th TAS, 1968; 776th TAS, 1968; 316th TAW, 1968–70; 374th TAW, 1972; 316th TAW, 1973; 314th TAW, 1975–77; 317th TAW, 1979–81.

63-7787 (C/N 3854) 316th TAW, 1969; 374th TAW, 1973; 314th TAW, 1977–78; crashed following fin stall, Barstow, California, 15-4-78.

63-7788 (C/N 3855) 438th MAW, 1967–68; 316th TAW, 1970–74; 36th TAS, 1975–81.

63-7789 (C/N 3856) 464th TAW, 1968; 36th TAS, 316th TAW, 1969. Crashed in English Channel off Alderney, 23-5-69, following theft from RAF Mildenhall, England.

63-7790 (C/N 3857) 47th TAS, 313th TAW, 1971; 314th TAW, 1975–81.

63-7791 (C/N 3859) 316th TAW, 1968; 7th ACCS, 388th TFW, Korat RTAFB, Thailand, 1971; 316th TAW, 1975; 314th TAW, 1976–82.

63-7792 (C/N 3860) 346th TAS, 516th TAW, 1968; 36th TAS, 316th TAW, 1975–81.

63-7793 (C/N 3872) 316th TAW, 1968; 313th TAW, 1969; 516th TAW, c1973; 463d TAW, 1975–76; 314th TAW, 1976–81.

63-7794 (C/N 3873) 464th TAW (*The African Queen*), 1968–75; 317th TAW, 1975–76; 314th TAW, 1976–81.

63-7805 (C/N 3874) 438th MAW, 1967; 516th TAW, 1970; 316th TAW, 1971–72; 463d TAW, 1975; 144th TAS, Alaska ANG, 1977–81.

63-7806 (C/N 3875) 438th MAW, 1967–68; 36th TAS, 316th TAW, 1969; 313th TAW, 1969–70; 516th TAW, 1974; 463d TAW, 1975; 17th TAS, 1976–78; Sheppard TTC, 1978–79; 314th TAW, 1979–81.

63-7807 (C/N 3876) 316th TAW, 1967–74; 316th TAW, 1975; 37th TAS, 1976; 317th TAW, 1977–82.

63-7808 (C/N 3877) 316th TAW, 1967–70; 516th TAW, c1973; 463d TAW, 1975–76; 314th TAW, 1977–81.

63-7809 (C/N 3879) 316th TAW, 1967–74; 37th TAS, 1976; 317th TAW, 1977–82.

63-7810 (C/N 3880) 778th TAS, 1968; 313th TAW, c1970; 346th TAS, 516th TAW, 1973. Sold to Israel, 10-73, as *4X-FBG*.

63-7811 (C/N 3881) 346th TAS, 516th TAW, 1967–68; 345th TAS, 314th TAW, 1970–81.

63-7812 (C/N 3882) 516th TAW, 1969; 374th TAW, 1973; 314th TAW, 1975–81.

63-7813 (C/N 3883) 516th TAW, 1970–71; 316th TAW, 1975; 37th TAS, 1976; 317th TAW, 1979–82.

63-7814 (C/N 3888) 316th TAW, 1968–73; 36th TAS, 62d MAW, 1976–81.

63-7815 (C/N 3889) 316th TAW, 1968–69; 313th TAW, 1970; 346th TAS, 516th TAW, 1973; 463d TAW, 1975–77; damaged on ground by fire in cockpit, Dyess AFB, 1977, but repaired. 193d SOS/ECS, Pennsylvania ANG, 1977–80; became EC-130E(CL), 1979.

63-7816 (C/N 3894) 47th TAS, 313th TAW, 1968; 516th TAW, 1969–70; 314th TAW, 1975–77; 193d SOS/ECS, Pennsylvania ANG, 1977–81; became EC-130E(CL), 1979.

63-7817 (C/N 3895) 438th MAW, 1967–68; 516th TAW, 1969–74; 463d TAW, 1975–76; 144th TAS, Alaska ANG, 1977–81.

63-7828 (C/N 3896) 316th TAW, 1969; 313th TAW, 1970–71; 346th TAS, 516th TAW, 1973; 463d TAW, 1975–77; 193d SOS/ECS, Pennsylvania ANG, 1977–81; became EC-130E(CL), 1979.

63-7829 (C/N 3897) 438th MAW, 1968; 516th TAW, 1969–70; 313th TAW, 1970; 516th TAW, 1974; 463d TAW, 1975; 17th TAS, 1975–81.

63-7830 (C/N 3898) 438th MAW, 1967–68; 516th TAW, 1969–70; 316th TAW, 1971; 516th TAW, 1974; 463d TAW, 1975; 17th TAS, 1975–81.

63-7831 (C/N 3899) 438th MAW, 1968; 516th TAW, 1969–70; 463d TAW, 1974; 32d TAS, 314th TAW, 1976; 17th TAS, 1976–81.

63-7832 (C/N 3900) 438th MAW, 1967–68; 516th TAW, 1969–70; 463d TAW, 1975–76; 756th TAS, 1976; 327th TAS, 1977–80.

63-7833 (C/N 3901) 438th MAW, 1967–68; 463d TAW, 1975–76; 327th TAS, 1976–80.

63-7834 (C/N 3902) 438th MAW, 1967–68; 516th TAW, 1969–70; 438th MAW, 1971; 463d TAW, 1975–76; 327th TAS, 1977–80.

63-7835 (C/N 3905) 464th TAW, 1968–73 (*Marrakech Express*); 317th TAW, 1975–76; 314th TAW, 1976; 327th TAS, 1976; 314th TAW, 1977–81.

63-7836 (C/N 3906) 778th TAS, 1967; 464 TAW, 1968–73; 317th TAW (*The Desert Rat*), 1973; 314th TAW, 1975–81.

63-7837 (C/N 3907) 438th MAW, 1968; 516th TAW, 1969–72; 17th TAS, 1976–81.

63-7843 (C/N 3913) 438th MAW, 1968; 516th TAW, 1969–73. Sold to Israel, 10-73, as *4X-FBH*.

63-7844 (C/N 3914) 438th MAW, 1967–68; 516th TAW, 1969–70. Sold to Israel, 10-73, as *4X-FBI*.

63-7845 (C/N 3915) 316th TAW, 1968–75; 37th TAS, 1975–76; 317th TAW, 1977–82.

63-7846 (C/N 3916) 438th MAW, 1968; 36th TAS, 316th TAW, 1969; 463d TAW, 1973, 76; 17th TAS, 1978–81.

63-7847 (C/N 3917) 316th TAW, 1969; 374th TAW, c1971; 316th TAW, 1973; 37th TAS, 1975–76; 317th TAW, 1977–82.

63-7848 (C/N 3918) 438th MAW, 1968; 516th TAW, 1969–72; 463d TAW, 1975–76; 756th TAS, 1976; 327th TAS, 1977; 756th TAS, 1978; 327th TAS, 1979–81.

63-7849 (C/N 3919) 316th TAW, 1968–75; 37th TAS, 1976; 317th TAW, 1977–82.

63-7850 (C/N 3920) 316th TCW, 1967; 314th TAW, 1971–81.

63-7851 (C/N 3921) 316th TAW, 1968–69; 313th TAW, 1969; 17th TAS, 1976–81.

63-7852 (C/N 3922) 346th TAS, 1968; 516th TAW, 1971; 463d TAW, 1975–76; 144th TAS, Alaska ANG, 1977; 17th TAS, 1978–79; 144th TAS, 1979–81.

63-7853 (C/N 3923) 316th TAW, 1968–69; 313th TAW, 1969–70; 516th TAW, 1974; 463d TAW, 1975–76; 327th TAS, 1976–80.

63-7875 (C/N 3945) 438th MAW, 1968; crashed and written off, South Vietnam, 15-5-68.

63-7882 (C/N 3953) 316th TAW, 1970; 314th TAW, 1975–80; 158th TAS, Georgia ANG, 1981.

63-7883 (C/N 3954) 438th MAW, 1967–68; 516th TAW, 1969–72; 463d TAW, 1975–76; 327th TAS, 1976–80.

63-7884 (C/N 3955) 346th TAS, 1968; 516th TAW, 1969–72; 463d TAW, 1976–77; 317th TAW, 1977; 62d MAW, 1978; 317th TAW, 1979–82.

63-7888 (C/N 3959) 438th MAW, 1968; 316th TAW, 1969–74; 314th TAW, 1975–80.

63-7889 (C/N 3960) 348th TAS, 516th TAW, 1969; 314th TAW, 1975–81.

63-7890 (C/N 3961) 438th MAW, 1968; 313th TAW, 1969; 316th TAW, 1972–74; 37th TAS, 1976; 317th TAW, 1977–78; 62d MAW, 1978; 317th TAW, 1978–82.

63-7891 (C/N 3962) 438th MAW, 1968; 316th TAW, 1969–70; 314th TAW, 1975; 36th TAS, 1976–81.

63-7892 (C/N 3963) 438th MAW, 1967–68; 316th TAW, 1969–70; 314th TAW, 1975–80; 327th TAS, 1981.

63-7893 (C/N 3964) 438th MAW, 1967; 316th TAW, 1969–70; 36th TAS, 1976–81.

63-7894 (C/N 3965) 516th TAW, 1969–70; 463d TAW, 1975–76; 314th TAW, 1977–82.

63-9813 (C/N 3974) 438th MAW, 1968; AFSC, Eglin AFB, c1969; 313th TAW, 1969–70; 316th TAW, 1970; 1174th SS, 1970–73; 1st SOW, 1973; 316th TAW, 1973; 314th TAW, 1975–79; 756th TAS, 1981.

63-9814 (C/N 3975) 438th MAW, 1968; 316th TAW, 1969; 313th TAW, 1969–70; 316th TAW, 1973; 37th TAS, 1975; 314th TAW, 1976–81.

63-9815 (C/N 3976) 438th MAW, 1967–68; 316th TAW, 1969; 313th TAW, 1969–70; AFSC, Duke Field, 1970; 1174th SS, 1971–73; 1st SOW, 1973; 1115th MAS, Hurlburt Field, 1973; 316th TAW, 1973–74; 314th TAW, 1975–81.

LOCKHEED MODEL 382-4B C-130G HERCULES (C/Ns 3849, 3858, 3871, and 3878) Four aircraft, US Navy Nos *151888* to *151891*, ordered for the US Navy and completed in 1963–64; all converted to EC-130G Navy communications aircraft, c1966.

151888 (C/N 3849) Navy Squadron VR-1, NAS Norfolk, Virginia, 1965–67. Became EC-130G; VQ-4, NAS Patuxent River, Maryland, 1968–81.

151889 (C/N 3858) VR-1, NAS Norfolk, Virginia, 1965–66. Became EC-130G. VQ-4, NAS Patuxent River, Maryland, 1969–81.

151890 (C/N 3871) VW-1. NAS Agana, Guam, c1966. Became EC-130G. VQ-4, NAS Patuxent River, Maryland, 1969–72; written off, Patuxent River, 1-72.

151891 (C/N 3878) VW-1, NAS Agana, Guam, c1966. Became EC-130G. VQ-4, NAS Patuxent River, Maryland, 1969–76. Anti-magnetic calibration trials, Kirtland AFB, 1977; NATC, Patuxent River, 1978–80.

LOCKHEED MODEL 382-4B C-130E HERCULES (1964) USAF Appropriations for MAC)

(C/Ns 3985 to 3987, 4047 to 4049, 4079, 4085, 4087 and 4090) Ten standard transports with SKE but no forward cargo door, USAF Nos *64-0501* to *64-0503*, *64-0552* to *64-0554* and *64-0569* to *64-0572*. Details as for 1962 Appropriations. Completed in 1964, and all transferred to TAC during 1964–68.

64-0501 (C/N 3985) 1608th ATW, 1965; 464th TAW, 1969–73; 317th TAW, 1976–82.

64-0502 (C/N 3986) 464th TAW, 1968–73; 317th TAW, 1976–80; 435th TAW, 1980–81.

64-0503 (C/N 3987) 62d TAS, 1967–68; 374th TAW, 1973; 21st TAS, 1976–81.

64-0552 (C/N 4047) Became WC-130E; 55th WRS, 1972; 53d WRS, 1974; 54th WRS, 1976–81.

64-0553 (C/N 4048) 313th TAW c1970. Became WC-130E; 53d WRS, 1971; 55th WRS, 1975; 53d WRS, 1977–80.

64-0554 (C/N 4049) 313th TAW, c1970. Became WC-130E; 53d WRS, c1971; 54th WRS, 1972; 55th WRS, 1973–75; 54th WRS, 1976–77; 53d WRS, 1978–81.

64-0569 (C/N 4079) 61st TAS, 1968; 314th TAW, 1975–81.

64-0570 (C/N 4085) 62d TAS, 64th TAW, 1968; 313th TAW, 1969; 314th TAW, 1976; 62d MAW, c1978; 317th TAW (*Burt*), 1978–82.

64-0571 (C/N 4087) 779th TAS, 1967; 1st SOS, 1967–70; 318th SOS, 1971–72; 7th SOS, 1973; ADTC, 1973. Became NC-130E test aircraft with AEP pods under outer wings; 4900th TS, 1974. Became MC-130E-S, 1975; 4950th TW, ASD, 1977–80; 8th SOS, 1st SOW, Hurlburt Field, Florida, 1982. Scheduled to become MC-130E-Y, 1982–83.

64-0572 (C/N 4090) 316th TAW, 1967; 779th TAS, 464th TAW, 1968; 7th ACCS, 1969; 7th SOS, 1972; 1174th SS, 1973; to State Dept, Andrews AFB, for Embassy Supply Flight, 1973. Became NC-130E test aircraft, 1973–74; 6512th TS, 1974–76. Became C-130E-I; 8th SOS, 1st SOW, 1977–81; became MC-130E-C, 1978, and took part in attempted rescue of US hostages, Tabas, Iran, 25-4-80.

LOCKHEED MODEL 382-8B C-130E HERCULES (1964 USAF Appropriations for TAC)

(C/Ns 3979 to 3984, 3988 to 4010, 4013, 4014, 4017 to 4019, 4021 to 4025, 4027 to 4035, 4040, 4043 to 4046, 4048, 4049, 4056 to 4059, 4062 to 4065, 4069, 4071, 4074, 4077, 4080, 4083, 4086 and 4105) 70 standard transports, USAF Nos *64-0495* to *64-0500*, *64-0504* to *64-0545*, *64-0547* to *64-0551*, *64-0555* to *64-0568*, *64-17680*, *64-17681* and *64-18240* (not respectively). Details as for 1962 Appropriations. Completed in 1964–65.

64-0495 (C/N 3979) 464th TAW, 1968–74; 317th TAW, 1975–77; 62d MAW, 1978; 317th TAW, 1978–82.

64-0496 (C/N 3980) 464th TAW, 1967–74; Cambodia Resupply Operation (*Thi Am*, Bird Air), 1974; 317th TAW, 1975–77; 62d MAW, 1978; 317th TAW, 1978–82.

64-0497 (C/N 3981) 776th TAS, 314th TAW, 1969; 21st TAS, 1971–81.

64-0498 (C/N 3982) 778th TAS, 1967–68; 464th TAW, 1968–73; 317th TAW, 1975–82.

64-0499 (C/N 3983) 464th TAW, 1971–73; Cambodia Resupply Operation, (*Thi Am*, Bird Air), 1974; 317th TAW, 1975–77; 62d MAW, 1978; 317th TAW, 1978–82.

64-0500 (C/N 3984) 314th TAW, 1968–70; 374th TAW, 1973; 21st TAS, 1976; 314th TAW, 1977; 17th TAS, 1978–81.

64-0504 (C/N 3988) 62d TAS, 1967–68; 47th TAS, 1969; 314th TAW, 1973–75; 36th TAS, 1976–77; damaged by fire, McChord AFB, 13-3-77, but repaired; 317th TAW, 1978–82; tests with two-grey camouflage, 1978–80.

64-0505 (C/N 3989) 314th TAW, 1968–72; ditched in sea off Taiwan, 12-72.

64-0506 (C/N 3990) Removed from USAF inventory, 2-70; disposal unknown.

64-0507 (C/N 3991) Removed from USAF inventory, 2-70; disposal unknown.

64-0508 (C/N 3992) 314th TAW, 1969; 313th TAW, c1970. Became C-130E-I; 318th SOS, 1971–72; shot down over South Vietnam, 25-4-72.

64-0509 (C/N 3993) 64th TCW, 1966; 61st TCS, 1967–68; 64th TAW, 1969; 313th TAW, 1970–72. Sold to Israel, 10-73, as *4X-FBO*.

64-0510 (C/N 3994) 313th TAW, 1969–73; 314th TAW, 1974; 36th TAS, 1975–81.

64-0511 (C/N 3995) Shot down during Operation Carolina Moon against Thanh Hoa bridge over Song Ma river, South Vietnam, 31-5-66.

64-0512 (C/N 3996) 313th TAW, 1968–72; 314th TAW, 1974–75; 36th TAS, 1976–81.

64-0513 (C/N 3997) 313th TAW, 1968–72; 314th TAW, 1974–75; 36th TAS, 1976–81.

64-0514 (C/N 3998) 314th TAW, c1974–75; 21st TAS, 1976–81.

64-0515 (C/N 3999) 314th TAW, c1970; 21st TAS, 1971–81.

64-0516 (C/N 4000) 61st TAS, 1968; 516th TAW, 1970; 313th TAW, 1972; 64th TAW, 1973. Sold to Israel, 10-73, as *4X-FBP*.

64-0517 (C/N 4001) 4313th TCW, 1966; 62d TAS, 1967–69; 464th TAW, 1971–73; 317th TAW, 1976–82.

64-0518 (C/N 4002) 62d TAS, 1967–69; 516th TAW, 1971; 21st TAS, 1976; 345th TAS, 1977; 21st TAS, 1979–81.

64-0519 (C/N 4003) 62d TAS, 1967–69; 313th TAW, 1970–71; 314th TAW, 1973–75; 36th TAS, 1976–81.

64-0520 (C/N 4004) 314th TAW, c1970; 374th TAW, 1973; 21st TAS, 1976–81.

64-0521 (C/N 4005) 314th TAW, 1967; 61st TAS, 1968; 313th TAW, 1970–73; 314th TAW, 1975; 36th TAS, 1976–81.

64-0522 (C/N 4006) Shot down during take-off at Song Ba, Vietnam, 29-2-68.

64-0523 (C/N 4007) 374th TAW, 1971. Became C-130E-I; 7th SOS, 1973–75; 8th SOS, 1976–77. Became MC-130E-C, 1978; 7th SOS, 1979–82.

64-0524 (C/N 4008) 61st TAS, 1968; 313th TAW, 1970; 314th TAW, 1975; 36th TAS, 1976–81.

64-0525 (C/N 4009) 61st TAS, 1968–69; 464th TAW, 1971–73; 317th TAW, 1976–82.

64-0526 (C/N 4010) 61st TAS, 1968; 313th TAW, *c*1971; 314th TAW, 1975–81.

64-0527 (C(N 4013) 62d TAS, 1967–69; 464th TAW, 1969–74; 317th TAW, 1975–77; 435th TAW, 1978–81.

64-0528 (C/N 4014) 63d TAS; 62d TAS, 1969; 50th TAS, 314th TAW, 1970. Sold to Israel, 10-73, as *4X-FBQ;* reregistered as *4X-FBD*, 1975.

64-0529 (C/N 4017) 61st TAS, 1968; 516th TAW, 1969–71; 464th TAW, 1971–74; 516th TAW, 1974; 317th TAW, 1975–82.

64-0530 (C/N 4018) 63d TAS, 1968; 62d TAS, 1969; 47th TAS, 1969–72; 314th TAW, 1975–81.

64-0531 (C/N 4019) 314th TAW, 1967; 61st TAS, 1968; 516th TAW, 1969–70; 464th TAW, 1971–74; 317th TAW, 1975–82.

64-0532 (C/N 4021) 62d TAS, 1967; 313th TAW, 1970–71; 314th TAW, 1975–77; crashed into mountain in Arkansas in bad weather, 8-9-78.

64-0533 (C/N 4022) 62d TAS, 1968; 464th TAW, 1970; 313th TAW, 1970; 314th TAW, 1975–81.

64-0534 (C/N 4023) 314th TAW, 1969–72; 374th TAW, 1973; 21st TAS, 1976–81.

64-0535 (C/N 4024) 463d TCW, 1966; 62d TCS, 1967; 64th TAW, 1968; 313th TAW, 1969–72; 314th TAW, 1975–81.

64-0536 (C/N 4025) 776th TAS, 314th TAW, Ching Chuan Kang ROCAB, Taiwan; crashed in Cha Tien Shan mountains after take-off from Taipeh, Taiwan, 2-10-70.

64-0537 (C/N 4027) 61st TAS, 1968; 777th TAS, 1968; 516th TAW, 1969–70; 464th TAW, 1971–73; 317th TAW, 1975–76; 21st TAS, 1978; 317th TAW, 1979–82.

64-0538 (C/N 4028) 61st TAS, 1968–69; 313th TAW, *c*1970; 314th TAW, 1975–82.

64-0539 (C/N 4029) 61st TAS, 1968; 313th TAW, 1970; 314th TAW, 1975–77; 62d MAW, 1978; 317th TAW, 1978–82.

64-0540 (C/N 4030) 61st TAS, 1967–68; 464th TAW, 1969–73; 317th TAW, 1976–77; 435th TAW, 1978–80; 317th TAW, 1980–82.

64-0541 (C/N 4031) 62d TAS, 1967–69; 313th TAW, 1970–71; 314th TAW, 1975; 62d MAW, 1978; 317th TAW, 1978–82.

64-0542 (C/N 4032) 62d TAS, 1967–68; 64th TAW, 1968; 464th TAW, 1969–70; 313th TAW, 1970–72; 314th TAW, 1975–78; 62d MAW, 1978; 317th TAW, 1978–82.

64-0543 (C/N 4033) 314th TAW, 1970; 313th TAW, 1971–72; 314th TAW, 1975; 17th TAS, 1977; 314th TAW, 1979–82. Exploded in air, 64 miles NE Little Rock AFB, 13-5-82.

64-0544 (C/N 4034) 62d TAS, 1967; 314th TAW, 1970; 374th TAW, 1973, 21st TAS, 1976–81.

64-0545 (C/N 4035) Written off, 3-69.

64-0547 (C/N 4040) Became C-130E-I; 15th SOS; shot down over North Vietnam and crashed in Laos, 9-12-67.

64-0548 (C/N 4043) 62d TAS, 1967; 50th TAS, 314th TAW; crashed undershooting runway at Khe Sanh, 15-10-67.

64-0549 (C/N 4044) 62d TAS, 1967; 64th TAW, 1968–69; 313th TAW, 1970; 314th TAW, 1975–82.

64-0550 (C/N 4045) 62d TAS, 1967; 64th TAW, 1968–69; 464th TAW, 1969–73; 317th TAW, 1975–77; 37th TAS, 1977–78; damaged in landing accident, Naples, 30-5-78, but repaired; AFSC, 1979; 317th TAW, 1979–81.

64-0551 (C/N 4046) Became C-130E-I; 1st SOS, 1967; 15th SOS, 1967; 7th ACCS, 1968–69; 7th SOS (*Wallard Waynell*)

1973–79. Became MC-130E-C, 1978; 8th SOS, 1979–80; 7th SOS, 1981; 8th SOS, 1981–82.

64-0555 (C/N 4056) 314th TAW, *c*1967. Became C-130E-I; 1st SOS, 1967; 15th SOS, 1967; 7th SOS, 1972–82. Became MC-130E-C, 1978.

64-0556 (C/N 4057) 314th TAW (*The Iron Butterfly*), 1969–71; 374th TAW, 1973; 21st TAS, 1976–81.

64-0557 (C/N 4058) 314th TAW, 1971–72; 374th TAW, 1973; 21st TAS, 1976–81; 314th TAW, 1981–82.

64-0558 (C/N 4059) 779th TCS, 1965–67. Became C-130E-I, 1967; 1st SOS, 1967–69; 318th SOS, 1971–72; collided with Convair F-102A near Myrtle Beach, South Carolina, 5-12-72.

64-0559 (C/N 4062) Became C-130E-I, 1967; 7th ACCS, 1968; 7th SOS, 1968–71; 318th SOS, 1973–74; 8th SOS, 1974–77; 7th SOS, 1977–79. Became MC-130E-C, 1978; 8th SOS, 1979–81.

64-0560 (C/N 4063) 313th TAW, 1969–71; 314th TAW, *c*1972–81.

64-0561 (C/N 4065) 779th TAS, 1967. Became C-130E-I, 1967; 15th SOS, 1967; 1st SOS, 1967; 7th ACCS, 1969; 7th SOS, 1969; 15th SOS, 1971; 7th SOS, 1972–74; 318th SOS, 1975; 7th SOS, 1976–81. Became MC-130E-C, 1978.

64-0562 (C/N 4068) 779th TAS, 1967. Became C-130E-I, 1967; 15th SOS, 1967; 1st SOS, 1967–69; 318th SOS, 1972–73; 7th SOS, 1974; 8th SOS, 1977–81. Became MC-130E-C, 1978.

64-0563 (C/N 4071) Became C-130E-I, 1967; 1st SOS, 1967; 15th SOS, 1967; destroyed in mortar attack on Nha Trang, South Vietnam, 25-11-67.

64-0564 (C/N 4074) Became C-130E-I, 1967; 1174th SS, 1972; 1st SOS, 1977–81. Became MC-130E-Y; crashed into sea off the Philippines, 26-2-81.

64-0565 (C/N 4077) Became C-130E-I, 1967; 1174th SS, 1972–73; 1st SOS, 1977–80. Became MC-130E-Y; took part in attempted rescue of US hostages, Tabas, Iran, and sustained damage on take-off, 25-4-80.

64-0566 (C/N 4080) 779th TAS, 1967. Became C-130E-I, 1967; 15th SOS, 1967; 1st SOS, 1967–71; 7th SOS, 1972; 1st SOS, 1973; 318th SOS, 1973; 8th SOS, 1974–79. Became MC-130E-C, 1978; 7th SOS, 1979–82.

64-0567 (C/N 4083) Became C-130E-I; 318th SOS, 1973; 8th SOS, 1974–77; 7th SOS, 1977–78. Became MC-130E-C, 1978; 8th SOS, 1978–81.

64-0568 (C/N 4086) Became C-130E-I, 1967; 15th SOS, 1967; 1st SOS, 1969; 318th SOS, 1971–73; 1st SOS, 1973–74; AFSWC, 1974; 8th SOS, 1974–81. Became MC-130E-C, 1978.

64-17680 (C/N 4064) 314th TAW, 1970; 374th TAW, 1973. 21st TAS, 1976; 314th TAW, 1977; 17th TAS, 1977; 314th TAW, 1978–81.

64-17681 (C/N 4069) 62d TAS, 1967; 464th TAW, 1969–74; Cambodia Resupply Operation, 1974 (*Thi Am*, Bird Air); 317th TAW, 1975–77; 37th TAS, (*Sonja*), 1977–81.

64-18240 (C/N 4105) Replacement for *64-0546* (C/N 4039), diverted from USAF order to Sweden. 464th TAW, 1968–73; Cambodia Resupply Operation (*Thi Am*, Bird Air), 1974; 317th TAW, 1975; 62d MAW, 1978; 435th TAW, 1979–81.

LOCKHEED MODEL 382-13B C-130E HERCULES (for Turkey) (C/Ns 4011, 4012, 4015, 4016 and 4100; offset under Mutual Assistance Programme from USAF blocks

USAF Nos *63-13186* to *63-13189*, and *64-17949*, THK Nos *ETI-186* to *ETI-189*, and *ETI-949*) Five standard transports for *Turk Hava Kuvvetleri*. Completed and delivered in 1964–65.

63-13186, *ETI-186* (C/N 4011) MAP. *221 Filo, Hava Nakil Kuvveti*, Erkilet/Kayseri.

63-13187, *ETI-187* (C/N 4012) MAP. *221 Filo, Hava Nakil Kuvveti*, Erkilet/Kayseri.

63-13188, *ETI-188* (C/N 4015) MAP. *221 Filo, Hava Nakil Kuvveti*, Erkilet/Kayseri.

63-13189, *ETI-189* (C/N 4016) MAP. *221 Filo, Hava Nakil Kuvveti*, Erkilet/Kayseri.

64-17949, *ETI-949* (C/N 4100) MAP. *131 Filo, Birinci Taktik Hava Kuvveti*, Konya, 3rd Jet Air Base; written off, 10-68.

LOCKHEED MODEL 382-15B C-130E (CC-130E) HERCULES (for Canada) (C/Ns 4020, 4026, 4041, 4042, 4050, 4060, 4061, 4066, 4067, 4070, 4075, 4095, 4096, 4122, 4124, 4191 to 4194) 20 aircraft, USAF Nos *64-17624* to *64-17639*, and *65-12766* to *65-12769* (RCAF Nos *10305* to *10324*, re-registered as *130305* to *130324*). Standard transports for RCAF. Completed and delivered in 1965–67.

10305, *64-17624* (C/N 4020) No 436 Sqn, RCAF, Edmonton, 1969; Air Navigation School, Winnipeg, 1975. Re-registered *130305*.

10306, *64-17625* (C/N 4026) No 436 Sqn, RCAF, Edmonton, 1968; re-registered *130306*, and returned to No 436 Sqn, 1981.

10307, *64-17626* (C/N 4041) No 436 Sqn, RCAF, Edmonton, 1968; re-registered *130307*.

10308, *64-17627* (C/N 4042) No 436 Sqn, RCAF, Edmonton, 1969; Air Navigation School, Winnipeg, 1975; re-registered *130308*, and returned to No 436 Sqn.

10309, *64-17628* (C/N 4050) Written off, Trenton, Ontario, 28-4-67.

10310, *64-17629* (C/N 4051) No 436 Sqn, RCAF, Edmonton, 1968; Air Navigation School, Winnipeg, 1975; re-registered *130310*, and returned to No 436 Sqn.

10311, *64-17630* (C/N 4060) No 436 Sqn, RCAF, Edmonton, 1968; re-registered *130311*.

10312, *64-17631* (C/N 4061) No 436 Sqn, RCAF, Edmonton, 1968–74; crashed west of Chibougamau, Quebec, during low level search/rescue flight, 15-10-80.

10313, *64-17632* (C/N 4066) No 436 Sqn, RCAF, Edmonton, 1968; re-registered *120313*.

10314, *64-17633* (C/N 4067) No 436 Sqn, RCAF, Edmonton, 1968; re-registered *130314*.

10315, *64-17634* (C/N 4070) No 436 Sqn, RCAF, Edmonton, 1968; re-registered *130315*.

10316, *64-17635* (C/N 4075) No 436 Sqn, RCAF, Edmonton, 1968; re-registered *130316*.

10317, *64-17636* (C/N 4122) No 436 Sqn, RCAF, Edmonton, 1968; Air Navigation School, Winnipeg, 1975–76; re-registered *130317*.

10318, *64-17637* (C/N 4124) No 436 Sqn, RCAF, Edmonton, 1969; re-registered *13018*.

10319, *64-17638* (C/N 4095) No 436 Sqn, RCAF, Edmonton, 1969; re-registered *130319*.

10320, *64-17639* (C/N 4096) No 436 Sqn, RCAF, Edmonton, 1969; re-registered *130320*.

10321, *65-12766* (C/N 4191) No 436 Sqn, RCAF, Edmonton, 1969; re-registered *130321*.

10322, *65-12767* (C/N 4192) No 436 Sqn, RCAF, Edmonton,

1969; re-registered *13023*.

10323, *65-12768* (C/N 4193) No 436 Sqn, RCAF, Edmonton, 1969; re-registered *130323*.

10324, *65-12769* (C/N 4194) No 436 Sqn, RCAF, Edmonton, 1969; re-registered *130324*.

LOCKHEED MODEL 382-14B C-130E HERCULES (for New Zealand) (C/Ns 4052 to 4054) Three aircraft, USAF Nos *64-15094* to *64-15096* (RNZAF Nos *NZ7001* to *NZ7003*). Standard transports for the Royal New Zealand Air Force; completed and delivered in 1964–65.

NZ7001, *64-15094* (C/N 4052) First flown 19-11-64; delivered 24-3-65; No 40 Sqn, RNZAF, Whenuapai, Auckland.

NZ7002, *64-15095* (C/N 4053) No 40 Sqn, RNZAF, Whenuapai, Auckland.

NZ7003, *64-15096* (C/N 4054) No 40 Sqn, RNZAF, Whenuapai, Auckland.

LOCKHEED MODEL 382-15B C-130E HERCULES (for Saudi Arabia) (C/Ns 4076, 4078, 4128 and 4136, RSAF Nos *451* to *454*) Four aircraft, standard transports for the Royal Saudi Air Force. Delivered 1965–66?

451 (C/N 4076) Civil registered *N9258R*, in 1965; No 4 Sqn, RSAF, Jedda.

452 (C/N 4078) No 4 Sqn, RSAF, Jedda.

453 (C/N 4128) No 4 Sqn, RSAF, Jedda; crashed on take-off, Medina, Saudi Arabia, 14-9-80; wrong engine feathered following engine fire.

454 (C/N 4136) No 4 Sqn, RSAF, Jedda; crashed at Le Bourget, France, 1-1-69.

LOCKHEED MODEL 382-16B C-130E HERCULES (for Brazil) (C/Ns 4091 to 4093, 4113 and 4114, FAB Nos *2450* to *2454*) Five aircraft, standard transports for *Forca Aerea Brasileira*. Delivered 1965–66?

2450 (C/N 4091) *1° Esquadrao, 1° Grupo*, Galeao, Rio de Janeiro; written off, Recife, 21-12-69.

2451 (C/N 4092) *1° Esquadrao, 1° Grupo*, Galeao, Rio de Janeiro.

2452 (C/N 4093) *1° Esquadrao, 1° Grupo*, Galeao, Rio de Janeiro; written off, 10-66.

2453 (C/N 4113) *1° Esquadrao, 1° Grupo*, Galeao, Rio de Janeiro.

2454 (C/N 4114) *1° Esquadrao, 1° Grupo*, Galeao, Rio de Janeiro.

LOCKHEED MODEL 382C-1D C-130E HERCULES (for Iran) (C/Ns 4115, 4117 to 4119, 4148, 4149, 4153 and 4154) Eight aircraft, BuAer Nos *65-10686* to *65-10689* and *66-4310* to *66-4313* (IIAF Nos *5-105* to *5-112*), standard transports for the Imperial Iranian Air Force. Delivered 1965–66?

5-105, *65-10686* (C/N 4115) No 5 Air Transport Sqn (ATS), IIAF, Mehrabad; re-registered as *5-101*, 1973; re-registered *5-8501*, 1976.

5-106, *65-10687* (C/N 4117) No 5 ATS, IIAF, Mehrabad; re-registered as *5-102*, 1973. Sold to Pakistan, *c*1975, as *10687*; collided with C-130B (C/N 3698) on ground and written off, 3-79.

5-107, *65-10688* (C/N 4118) Struck by lightning and written off, 18-4-67.

5-108, *65-10689* (C/N 4119) No 5 ATS, IIAF, Mehrabad; re-registered as *5-103*, 1973. Sold to Pakistan, *c*1975, as *10689*.

5-109, *66-4310* (C/N 4148) No 5 ATS, IIAF, Mehrabad; re-registered as *5-104*, 1973. Sold to Pakistan, *c*1975, as *64310*; No 6 Sqn, PAF, Chaklala, 1975; aircraft 'J'.

5-110, *66-4311* (C/N 4149) No 5 ATS, IIAF, Mehrabad; re-registered as *5-105*, 1973; re-registered *5-8502*, 1976.

5-111, *66-4312* (C/N 4153) No 5 ATS, IIAF, Mehrabad; re-registered as 5-106, 1973. Sold to Pakistan, c1975, as *64312*; No 6 Sqn, PAF, Chaklala, 1975–80; aircraft 'L'.

5-112, *66-4313* (C/N 4154) No 5 ATS, IIAF, Mehrabad; written off, 4-69.

LOCKHEED MODEL 382-4B EC-130E HERCULES
(C/N 4158) One aircraft, USAF No *66-4299* (US Coast Guard No *CG1414*). LORAN A & C calibration aircraft for US Coast Guard.

66-4299, *CG1414* (C/N 4158) Delivered 23-8-66; based at Elizabeth City, North Carolina, 1976; St Petersburg (Clearwater), Florida, 1979–81.

LOCKHEED MODEL 382C-2D C-130E HERCULES (for Australia) (C/Ns 4159, 4160, 4167, 4168, 4171, 4172, 4177, 4178, 4180, 4181, 4189 and 4190) 12 aircraft, USAF Nos *65-12896* to *65-12907* (RAAF Nos *A97-159*, *A97-160*, *A97-167*, *A97-168*, *A97-171*, *A97-172*, *A97-177*, *A97-178*, *A97-180*, *A97-181*, *A97-189* and *A97-190*), standard transports for the Royal Australian Air Force; delivered 1966–67.

A97-159, *65-12896* (C/N 4159) No 37 Sqn, RAAF, Richmond, NSW.

A97-160, *65-12897* (C/N 4160) No 37 Sqn, RAAF, Richmond, NSW.

A97-167, *65-12898* (C/N 4167) No 37 Sqn, RAAF, Richmond, NSW.

A97-168, *65-12899* (C/N 4168) No 37 Sqn, RAAF, Richmond, NSW.

A97-171, *65-12900* (C/N 4171) No 37 Sqn, RAAF, Richmond, NSW.

A97-172, *65-12901* (C/N 4172) No 37 Sqn, RAAF, Richmond, NSW.

A97-177, *65-12902* (C/N 4177) No 37 Sqn, RAAF, Richmond, NSW.

A97-178, *65-12903* (C/N 4178) No 37 Sqn, RAAF, Richmond, NSW; operated Red Cross relief flights to Kampuchea, 1980.

A97-180, *65-12904* (C/N 4180) No 37 Sqn, RAAF, Richmond, NSW; operated Red Cross relief flights to Kampuchea, 1980.

A97-181, *65-12905* (C/N 4181) No 37 Sqn, RAAF, Richmond, NSW.

A97-189, *65-12906* (C/N 4189) No 37 Sqn, RAAF, Richmond, NSW.

A97-190, *65-12907* (C/N 4190) No 37 Sqn, RAAF, Richmond, NSW.

LOCKHEED MODEL 382-8B C-130E HERCULES (for Sweden) (C/N 4039) One aircraft diverted from 1964 USAF Appropriations (USAF No *64-0546*) and leased by Lockheed to Sweden, 9-65, as *84001*.

84001, *64-0546* (C/N 4039) *Flygflottilj 7, Flygvapnet*, Satenäs. Civil registered as *SE-XBT* for Swedish Red Cross, 1968. Became C-130H, 1982.

LOCKHEED MODEL 382-12B HC-130H HERCULES
(C/Ns 4036 to 4038, 4055, 4072, 4073, 4081, 4082, 4088, 4089, 4094, 4097 to 4099, 4102 to 4104, 4106 to 4108, 4110 to 4112, 4116, 4120, 4121, 4123, 4125 to 4127, 4130 to 4133, 4135, 4138 to 4142, 4150 and 4151) 43 aircraft, USAF Nos *64-14852* to *64-14866*, *65-0962* to *65-0987*, *65-0989* and *65-0990*). Rescue and recovery aircraft equipped as tankers fitted with Fulton recovery gear for the USAF's Aerospace Rescue and Recovery Service (ARRS). Delivered 1965–66 (were the first C-130H aircraft to be completed).

64-14852 (C/N 4036) First flown, 30-11-64. 57th ARRS, 1967; 305th ARRS, 403d RWRW, Selfridge ANGB, Michigan, 1977–78; 301st ARRS, 403d RWRW, Homestead AFB, Florida, 1979–81.

64-14853 (C/N 4037) Delivered 28-2-65 to AFFTC; 305th ARRS, 403d RWRW, Selfridge ANGB, Michigan, 1976–81.

64-14854 (C/N 4038) Became NC-130H test aircraft. 6593d TS, 6594th TG, Space Division of AFSC, Los Angeles AFS, California, 1977–80.

64-14855 (C/N 4055) 57th ARRS, 1967; 48th ARRS, 1969; 303d ARRS, 403d RWRW, March AFB, California, 1976–80.

64-14856 (C/N 4072) 305th ARRS, 403d RWRW, Selfridge ANGB, Michigan, 1975 and 1979; 303d ARRS, 403d RWRW, March AFB, California, 1977–79 and 1980.

64-14857 (C/N 4073) Became NC-130H test aircraft for USAF; 6593d TS, 6594th TG, Space Division of AFSC, Los Angeles AFS, California, 1977–81.

64-14858 (C/N 4081) Became JC-130H test aircraft for USAF; 6593d TS, 6594th TG, Space Division of AFSC, Los Angeles AFS, California, 1976–81.

64-14859 (C/N 4082) 76th ARRS, 1971; 305th ARRS, 403d RWRW, Selfridge ANGB, Michigan, 1972–79; damaged when drop tank exploded, Warner Robins AFB, Georgia, 13-7-79.

64-14860 (C/N 4084) 303d ARRS, 403d RWRW, March AFB, California, 1977–80.

64-14861 (C/N 4088) 57th ARRS, 1970. Became WC-130H, c1974; 54th WRS, 41st RWRW, Anderson AFB, Guam, 1975–81.

64-14862 (C/N 4089) 303d and 305th ARRS, 403d RWRW, Selfridge ANGB, Michigan, 1975–80.

64-14863 (C/N 4094) 305th ARRS, 403d RWRW, Selfridge ANGB, Michigan, 1977–79 and 1981; 301st ARRS, 403d RWRW, Homestead AFB, Florida, 1980.

64-14864 (C/N 4097) 57th ARRS, 1971–74; 303d ARRS, 403d RWRW, Selfridge ANGB, Michigan, 1977–80.

64-14865 (C/N 4098) 303d ARRS, 403d RWRW, Selfridge ANGB, Michigan, 1977–81.

64-14866 (C/N 4099) 57th ARRS, 1970. Became WC-130H, c1974; 53d WRS, 41st RWRW, Keesler AFB, Mississippi, 1976; 815th WRS, 920th WRG, 403d RWRW, Keesler AFB, 1977–80.

65-0962 (C/N 4102) 67th ARRS, 39th ARRW, RAF Woodbridge, England, 1969–80; Wright Patterson AFB, Ohio, 1981.

65-0963 (C/N 4103) 36th ARRS, 1968–71. Became WC-130H; 54th WRS, 41st RWRW, Anderson AFB, Guam, 1976–77; 53d WRS, 41st RWRW, Keesler AFB, Mississippi, 1978–81.

65-0964 (C/N 4104) 67th ARRS, 39th ARRW, RAF Woodbridge, England, 1969–74. Became WC-130H, c1974–75; 53d WRS, 1975; 815th WRS, 1977–81.

65-0965 (C/N 4106) 36th ARRS, 1970. Became WC-130H, c1974; 53d WRS; missing on flight 650 miles north of Clark AB, Philippines, 13-10-74.

65-0966 (C/N 4107) 41st ARRS, 1968; 76th ARRS, c1971. Became WC-130H, c1974; 55th WRS, 1975; 53d WRS, 1976–77 and 1978–80; 54th WRS, 1977.

65-0967 (C/N 4108) 76th ARRS, 1968; 36th ARRS, 1970. Became WC-130H, c1974; 53d WRS, 1975; 815th WRS, 1977–80.

65-0968 (C/N 4100) Became WC-130H; 55th WRS, 1975; 53d WRS, 1977–81.

65-0969 (C/N 4111) 76th ARRS, 1968; 36th ARRS, 1968; 48th ARRS, 1968; 31st ARRS, 1968. Became WC-130H, c1974; 53d WRS, 1975; 815th WRS, 1977–80.

65-0970 (C/N 4112) 67th ARRS, 39th ARRW, RAF Woodbridge, England, 1969–71; 57th ARRS, 1971; 303d ARRS, 403d RWRW, March AFB, California, 1976–80.

65-0971 (C/N 4116) 35th ARRS, 1969; 36th ARRS, 1970–71. Became DC-130H drone and RPV launch aircraft; 6514th TS (Drone and Remotely Piloted Vehicle Test Squadron), AFFTC, Hill AFB, Utah, 1977–80.

65-0972 (C/N 4120) 57th ARRS. Became WC-130H; 815th WRS, 1977–81.

65-0973 (C/N 4121) 41st ARRS, 1551st FTS, 1550th ATTW, Kirtland, AFB, New Mexico, 1977–80.

65-0974 (C/N 4123) 79th ARRS, 1968–70; 36th ARRS, 1970; 54th ARRS, 1974; 102d ARRS, 106th ARRG, Suffolk County Airport, New York ANG, 1977–81.

65-0975 (C/N 4125) 67th ARRS, 39th ARRW, RAF Woodbridge, England, 1969–76; 41st ARRS, 1977; 1551st FTS, 1550th ATTW, Kirtland AFB, New Mexico, 1979–80.

65-0976 (C/N 4126) 67th ARRS, 39th ARRW, Woodbridge, England, c1969–74. Became WC-130H; 53d WRS, 1976; 54th WRS, 1977–81.

65-0977 (C/N 4127) 67th ARRS, 39th ARRW, RAF Woodbridge, England, 1969. Became WC-130H; 55th WRS, 1975; 53d WRS, 1976; 815th WRS, 1977–80.

65-0978 (C/N 4130) 71st ARRS, 1974; 102d ARRS, 106th ARRG, Suffolk County Airport, New York ANG, 1976–81.

65-0979 (C/N 4131) 54th ARRS, 1972. Became DC-130H drone and RPV launch aircraft. 6514th TS (Drone and Remotely Piloted Vehicle Test Squadron), AFFTC, Hill AFB, Utah, 1977–80.

65-0980 (C/N 4132) 41st ARRS. Became WC-130H; 53d WRS, 1976; 815th WRS, 1977–80.

65-0981 (C/N 4133) 76th ARRS; 303d ARRS, 1976; 129th ARRS, 129th ARRG, Moffett Field NAS, California ANG, 1975–81.

65-0982 (C/N 4135) 305th ARRS, 1976–78; 67th ARRS, 1978; 305th ARRS, 1978–80.

65-0983 (C/N 4138) 41st ARRS, 1967; 303d ARRS, 1976; 129th ARRS, Moffett Field NAS, California ANG, 1976–81.

65-0984 (C/N 4139) 57th ARRS, 1969; 76th ARRS, 1973. Became WC-130H; 54th WRS, 1976–81.

65-0985 (C/N 4140) 57th ARRS, 1969; 36th ARRS, 1970; 79th ARRS, 1970–71. Became WC-130H, c1975; 53d WRS, 1977–80.

65-0986 (C/N 4141) 55th ARRS, 1978–79; 71st ARRS, 1979–81.

65-0987 (C/N 4142) 48th ARRS, 1968; 1551st FTS, 1550th ATTW, 1977–78; 33d ARRS, 41st RWRW, Kadena AB, Okinawa, 1979–81.

65-0989 (C/N 4150) 36th ARRS; 41st ARRS, 41st RWRW, McClellan AFB, California, 1977–80.

65-0990 (C/N 4151) Ditched in sea off Taiwan, 4-2-69.

LOCKHEED MODEL 382 L-100 HERCULES (C/N 3946) Prototype civil aircraft, registered *N1130E* by Lockheed-Georgia Company. Four 4,050 eshp Allison 501-D22 turboprops. First flown 20-4-64; FAA Certification 16-2-65.
N1130E (C/N 3946) Lockheed demonstration aircraft, 1964. Leased to Alaska Airlines, 1965. Became Model 382E proto-

type (with 2.5 m fuselage stretch), and first flown as such, 19-4-68. Leased to Delta Airlines, 10-68; operated by Flying 'W' Airways, with registration *N50FW*, 3-69; leased to Airlift International Inc, 5-69; to Pepsico Airlease Corp, 7-71; to Philippines Government, 4-73, as *PI-97*. Sold to Philippines Aerospace Development Corp, as *RP-C97*, 10-78; operated by 222d Heavy Airlift Sqn, Philippines Air Force, Mactan AB; into storage at Manila, 1981.

LOCKHEED MODEL 382B-1C L-100 HERCULES (C/Ns 4101 and 4109) Two civil aircraft, registered *N9260R* and *N9261R*, for leasing by Lockheed-Georgia Company.
N9260R (C/N 4101) ff 17-9-65. Leased by Lockheed to Continental Air Services, 11-65. Sold to the Government of the Republic of Zambia as *9J-RCV*, 8-66; leased to Zambian Air Cargoes, 8-66. Sold to National Aircraft Leasing as *N920NA*, 3-69; leased to Alaska Airlines, 4-69; leased to Saturn Airways Inc as *N24ST*, 6-72. Became L-100-30, 11-72, with 4.6 m fuselage stretch and Allison 501-D22A engines; leased to TIA (ex-Saturn), 12-76; damaged by explosion in wing, 24-5-77, but repaired; damaged in landing accident, Wichita, 1978, but repaired. Sold to TIA, 4-79 (thence TransAmerica, 10-79).
N9261R (C/N 4109) Leased by Lockheed to Continental Air Services, 11-65. Sold to the Government of the Republic of Zambia, 8-66; leased to Zambian Air Cargoes as *9J-RCY*, 8-66; damaged at Dar es Salaam, 1-6-67, but repaired; destroyed in ground collision with L-100 Hercules (C/N 4137) at Ndola, 11-4-68.

LOCKHEED MODEL 382B-2C L-100 HERCULES (for Zambia) (C/Ns 4129 and 4137) Two civil aircraft, registered *9J-RBW* and *9J-RBX*, for commercial sale by Lockheed-Georgia Company.
9J-RBW (C/N 4129) Zambian Air Cargoes (*Alexander*), 4-66. Sold to Maple Leaf Leasing, 1969; leased to Pacific Western Airlines, 3-69; damaged at Eureka, NWT, 8-69. Rebuilt as Model 382F-2C with 2.5 m fuselage stretch; leased to Alaska International Air, 12-69, as *N109AK*. Sold to Pacific Western Airlines, 1977, as *CF-PWN* (later *C-FPWN*).
9J-RBX (C/N 4137) Zambian Air Cargoes (*Ajax*), 4-66. Destroyed in ground collision with L-100 Hercules (C/N 4109), Ndola, 11-4-68.

LOCKHEED MODEL 382B-3C L-100 HERCULES (C/N 4134) One civil aircraft registered *N9263R*, for leasing by Lockheed-Georgia Company.
N9263R (C/N 4134) Leased to Pacific Western Airlines, 2-66; leased to Alaska Airlines, 3-66. Sold to Alaska Airlines, 4-66. Sold to Saturn Airways Inc, 7-71, as *N16ST*. Became Model 382G-3C (L-100-30) with 4.6 m fuselage stretch and -D22A engines. Leased to TIA, 12-76 (thence TransAmerica, 10-79).

LOCKHEED MODEL 382B-4C L-100 HERCULES (for Pakistan) (C/Ns 4144 and 4145) Two civil aircraft, registered *AP-AUT* and *AP-AUU*, for commercial sale by Lockheed-Georgia Company.
AP-AUT (C/N 4144) Sold to Pakistan Government for Pakistan International Airlines, 10-66; also flown by Pakistan Air Force as *64144*; No 6 Sqn, PAF, Chaklala; aircraft 'T'.
AP-AUU (C/N 4145) Sold to Pakistan Government for Pakistan International Airlines, 10-66; also flown by Pakistan Air Force as *64145*; No 6 Sqn, PAF, Chaklala; aircraft 'U';

crashed near Chaklala, 4-68.

LOCKHEED MODEL 382B-5C L-100 HERCULES

(C/N 4146) One civil aircraft, registered *N9267R*, for commercial sale by Lockheed-Georgia Company.

N9267R (C/N 4146) International Aerodyne. Leased by Bank of America to Alaska Airlines (*City of Anchorage*), 6-66; leased to *Aerea-Aerovias Ecuatorianas*, 4-68; destroyed by fire after propeller struck obstruction during taxying at Macuma, Ecuador, 16-5-68.

LOCKHEED MODEL 382B-6C L-100 HERCULES

(C/Ns 4147, 4170 and 4176) Three civil aircraft, registered *N9268R*, *N9258R* and *N9259R*, sold by Lockheed to Delta Airlines.

N9268R (C/N 4147) Delta Airlines, 8-66. Became Model 382E-6C L-100-10, 12-68. Sold to Air Finance, *c*1970. Sold to Saturn Airways Inc, 9-73, as *N19ST*. Became Model 382G-6C, 3-74. Was the first Hercules to achieve 30,000 flying hours, 2-77. Sold to TIA, 12-76 (thence TransAmerica, 10-79).

N9258R (C/N 4170) Delta Airlines, 9-66. Became Model 382E-6C L-100-20, 12-68. Sold to Air Finance, *c*1970. Sold to Pacific Western Airlines, 11-73, as *CF-PWK* (later *FPWK*); leased to Northwest Territorial Airways. Caught fire on ground off-loading fuel, Northwest Territories, 11-4-82.

N9259R (C/N 4176) Delta Airlines, 10-66. Became Model 382E-6C L-100-20, 12-68. Sold to Air Finance, 9-73; leased to Alaska International Air, 7-75, as *N105AK*. Sold to *Consorcio Technice de Aeronautica*, Luanda, Angola, 9-77, as *D2-FAF*. TAAG-Angola Airlines, 4-79. Written off after landing accident, Sao Thome, 15-5-79.

LOCKHEED MODEL 382-12B HC-130P HERCULES

(C/Ns 4143, 4152, 4155 to 4157, 4161 to 4166, 4173 to 4175, 4179 and 4183 to 4187) 20 rescue and recovery aircraft, USAF Nos *65-0988*, *65-0991* to *65-0994*, and *66-0211* to *66-0225*, for the USAF's Aerospace Rescue and Recovery Service (ARRS). Delivered 1966-70.

65-0988 (C/N 4143) Aeronautical Systems Division, AFSC, for helicopter refuelling trials. 102d ARRS, 106th ARRG, Suffolk County Airport, New York ANG, 1977-80.

65-0991 (C/N 4152) 41st ARRS, 41st RWRW, McClellan AFB, California, 1977-80.

65-0992 (C/N 4155) 6593d TS, 6594th TG, AFSC, Los Angeles AFS, California, 1977-81.

65-0993 (C/N 4156) 71st ARRS, 1976-77; 41st ARRS, 1978-80.

65-0994 (C/N 4157) 33d ARRS, 41st RWRW, Kadena AFB, Okinawa, 1976-80.

66-0211 (C/N 4161) 1551st FTS, 1550th ATTW, Kirtland AFB, New Mexico, 1977-80.

66-0212 (C/N 4162) 1551st FTS, 1550th ATTW, Kirtland AFB, New Mexico, 1977-80.

66-0213 (C/N 4163) 1551st FTS, 1550th ATTW, Kirtland AFB, New Mexico, 1977-80.

66-0214 (C/N 4164) 39th ARRS, 7-68; damaged by satchel charge at Tuy Hoa, 29-7-68, and written off.

66-0215 (C/N 4165) 31st ARRS, 1971; 56th ARRS, 1974; 55th ARRS, 1977-80.

66-0216 (C/N 4166) 33d ARRS, 1976; 21st TAS, 1977; 33d ARRS, 1979-80.

66-0217 (C/N 4173) 41st ARRS, 1974; 55th ARRS, 1976-81.

66-0218 (C/N 4174) 39th ARRS, 1968; damaged by satchel charge at Tuy Hoa, 29-7-68, and written off.

66-0219 (C/N 4175) 56th ARRS, 1974; 41st ARRS, 1977-79.

66-0220 (C/N 4179) 39th ARRS, 1972; 56th ARRS, 1974-75; 67th ARRS, 1977-81.

66-0221 (C/N 4183) 67th ARRS, 39th ARRW, RAF Woodbridge, England, 1969; 55th ARRS, 39th ARRW, Eglin AFB, Florida, 1972; 129th ARRS, 129th ARRG, California ANG, 1977-81.

66-0222 (C/N 4184) 35th ARRS, 1969; 36th ARRS, 1970; 102d ARRS, 106th ARRG, Suffolk County Airport, New York ANG, 1976-80.

66-0223 (C/N 4185) 1550th ATTW, 1973; 6593d TS, Los Angeles AFS, 1977-80.

66-0224 (C/N 4186) 1550th ATTW, 1973; 303d ARRS, 1976; 129th ARRS, 1977-80.

66-0225 (C/N 4187) 1550th ATTW, 1972; 67th ARRS, 1973; 6593d TS, 1977-81.

LOCKHEED MODEL 382-19B C-130K HERCULES C MARK 1 (for Great Britain)

(C/Ns 4169, 4182, 4188, 4195, 4196, 4198 to 4201, 4203 to 4207, 4210 to 4214, 4216 to 4220, 4223, 4224, 4226 to 4228, 4230 to 4233, 4235 to 4238, 4240 to 4247, 4251 to 4254, 4256 to 4259, 4261 to 4264, 4266 to 4268 and 4270 to 4275) 66 aircraft, USAF Nos *65-13021* to *65-13044*, *66-8550* to *66-8573* and *66-13533* to *66-13550* (RAF Nos *XV176* to *XV223* and *XV290* to *XV307*), ordered by HM Government in 1965 and delivered in 1966-68 to the UK. Basic specification as for C-130H standard transport. Prime Contractor and technical support centre for maintenance, engineering and conversions, Marshall of Cambridge (Engineering) Ltd, England. Continuing conversion programme to C Mark 3 (4.6 m fuselage stretch).

XV176, *65-13021* (C/N 4169) ff 19-10-66; delivered 5-5-67 to Marshall; No 242 OCU, 7-67; Lyneham Wing, 1971. Became C Mk 3, 1981 (mod by Marshall).

XV177, *65-13022* (C/N 4182) Delivered 16-12-66 to Marshall; A&AEE, Boscombe Down, 2-67; No 242 OCU, RAF, 1969; Lyneham Wing, 1971-82.

XV178, *65-13023* (C/N 4188) Delivered 21-1-67 to Marshall; A&AEE, Boscombe Down, 1967-75; Lyneham Wing, 1980-81. Given air refuelling facility, 5-82; established Hercules endurance record of 28 hr 4 min, (flown by No 70 Sqn crew) on 18-6-82 during flight between Ascension Island and Falkland Islands.

XV179, *65-13024* (C/N 4195) Delivered 22-3-67 to Marshall; No 242 OCU, RAF, 1967-69; Fairford Wing, 1970; Lyneham Wing, 1971-82; first aircraft to be equipped with Omega navaid (Mod 5309); second aircraft to become C Mk 1(K) tanker (Mod 5310) and equipped for air refuelling (Mod 5308).

XV180, *65-13025* (C/N 4196) Delivered 3-3-67 to Marshall; No 242 OCU, RAF, 5-67; Fairford Wing, 1969; crashed at Fairford, 24-3-69.

XV181, *65-13026* (C/N 4198) Delivered 25-5-67 to Marshall; No 36 Sqn, RAF, 6-67; Lyneham Wing; No 242 OCU, 1975; damaged in landing accident at Thorney Island, 4-6-75, but repaired, 1978; Lyneham Wing, 1980-82.

XV182, *65-13027* (C/N 4199) Delivered 1-4-67 to Marshall; No 242 OCU, RAF, 1967; No 30/47 Sqns, Fairford, 1969; No 70 Sqn (*Hector*), 1970; Lyneham Wing, 1975-82.

XV183, *65-13028* (C/N 4200) Delivered 24-3-67 to Marshall; No 242 OCU, RAF, 1967; No 30/47 Sqns, Fairford, 1969; No 70 Sqn, 1970; Lyneham Wing, 1974. Became C Mk 3, 1981 (mod by Marshall).

XV184, *65-13029* (C/N 4201) Delivered 25-3-67 to Marshall; No 242 OCU, RAF, 1967; Lyneham Wing, 1975–81. Became C Mk 3, 1982 (mod by Marshall).

XV185, *65-13030* (C/N 4203) Delivered 7-4-67 to Marshall; No 242 OCU, RAF, 1967; Lyneham Wing, 1975–82.

XV186, *65-13031* (C/N 4204) Delivered 19-4-67 to Marshall; No 242 OCU, RAF, 1967; No 70 Sqn, 1970–71; No 242 OCU, c1972; Lyneham Wing, 1975–82.

XV187, *65-13032* (C/N 4205) Delivered 20-4-67 to Marshall; No 242 OCU, RAF, 1967; Lyneham Wing, 1972; No 70 Sqn, 1974; Lyneham Wing, 1975–82.

XV188, *65-13033* (C/N 4206) Delivered 24-4-67 to Marshall; No 242 OCU, RAF, 1967; Lyneham Wing, 1972–81. Became C Mk 3, 1982 (mod by Marshall).

XV189, *65-13034* (C/N 4207) Delivered 28-4-67 to Marshall; No 242 OCU, RAF, 1967; No 70 Sqn, 1974; Lyneham Wing, 1975–81.

XV190, *65-13035* (C/N 4210) Delivered 11-5-67 to Marshall; No 36 Sqn, RAF, 1967–75; Lyneham Wing, 1981.

XV191, *65-13036* (C/N 4211) Delivered 25-5-67 to Marshall; No 36 Sqn, RAF, 1967; A&AEE, Boscombe Down; Lyneham Wing, 1975–82.

XV192, *65-13037* (C/N 4212) Delivered 15-5-67 to Marshall; No 36 Sqn, RAF, 1967; No 70 Sqn (*Horatius*) 1970; Lyneham Wing, 1974–81; wing damaged by fire, but repaired, 1981. Became fourth C Mk 1(K) tanker, 1982 (mod by Marshall).

XV193, *65-13038* (C/N 4213) Delivered 26-5-67 to Marshall; No 36 Sqn, RAF, 1967; No 48 Sqn, 1970; Lyneham Wing, 1971; No 242 OCU; Lyneham Wing, 1981–82.

XV194, *65-13039* (C/N 4214) Delivered 9-6-67 to Marshall; No 36 Sqn, RAF, 1967; No 48 Sqn, 1970; Lyneham Wing, 1971; crashed at Tromso, Norway, 12-9-72; written off for spares.

XV195, *65-13040* (C/N 4216) Delivered 10-6-67 to Marshall; No 36 Sqn, RAF, 1967; No 70 Sqn, 1970; Lyneham Wing, 1975–82. Refuelling probe.

XV196, *65-13041* (C/N 4217) Delivered 23-6-67 to Marshall; No 36 Sqn, RAF, 1967; No 48 Sqn, 1970; Lyneham Wing, 1971–81.

XV197, *65-13042* (C/N 4218) Delivered 6-7-67 to Marshall; No 36 Sqn, RAF, 1967; No 242 OCU; Lyneham Wing, 1975. Became C Mk 3, 1980 (mod by Marshall).

XV198, *65-13043* (C/N 4219) Delivered 7-7-67 to Marshall; No 48 Sqn, RAF, 1967–70; Fairford Wing, 1971; Lyneham Wing, 1971; crashed at Colerne, Wiltshire, during practice landing, 10-9-73, and written off.

XV199, *65-13044* (C/N 4220) Delivered 7-67 to Marshall; No 242 OCU, RAF, 1967; No 48 Sqn, c1968; Lyneham Wing, 1975–82.

XV200, *66-8550* (C/N 4223) Delivered 29-7-67 to Marshall; No 48 Sqn, RAF, 1967–70; Lyneham Wing, 1971–82. Was first RAF Hercules to be modified for air refuelling, 4-82 (mod 5308 by Marshall).

XV201, *66-8551* (C/N 4224) Delivered 11-8-67 to Marshall; No 48 Sqn, RAF, 1967; No 30/47 Sqns, 1970; Lyneham Wing, 1974; No 242 OCU, 1975; Lyneham Wing, 1975–82. Became second C Mk 1(K) tanker, 1982 (mod by Marshall); detached to Stanley, Falkland Islands, 10-82.

XV202, *66-8552* (C/N 4226) Delivered 17-8-67 to Marshall; No 48 Sqn, RAF, 1967; Lyneham Wing, 1971–74; No 242 OCU, 1975. Became C Mk 3, 1981 (mod by Marshall).

XV203, *66-8553* (C/N 4227) Delivered 25-8-67 to Marshall; No 48 Sqn, RAF, 1969; Lyneham Wing, 1971–82. Became C Mk 3, 1980 (mod by Marshall).

XV204, *66-8554* (C/N 4228) Delivered 1-9-67 to Marshall; No 48 Sqn, RAF, 1969; Lyneham Wing, 1970–80; A&AEE, Boscombe Down, RWR TI, 1980–81. Became third C Mk 1(K) tanker, 7-82 (mod by Marshall).

XV205, *66-8555* (C/N 4230) Delivered 9-9-67 to Marshall; No 48 Sqn, RAF, 1968; Lyneham Wing, 1970–82.

XV206, *66-8556* (C/N 4231) Delivered 9-9-67 to Marshall; No 48 Sqn, RAF, 1968; Lyneham Wing, 1971–80.

XV207, *66-8557* (C/N 4232) Delivered 22-9-67 to Marshall; No 48 Sqn, RAF, 1968; A&AEE, Boscombe Down, Lyneham Wing, 1975. Became C Mk 3, 1981 (mod by Marshall).

XV208, *66-8558* (C/N 4233) Delivered 28-9-67 to Marshall; No 48 Sqn, RAF, 1968–70. Became W Mk 2 for weather research (mod by Marshall, first flown 31-3-73); flown by the RAE, Farnborough.

XV209, *66-8559* (C/N 4235) Delivered 7-10-67 to Marshall; No 48 Sqn, RAF, 1968; damaged at Dhekhelia, Cyprus, 1973, but repaired; Lyneham Wing, 1970–75.

XV210, *66-8560* (C/N 4236) Delivered 14-10-67 to Marshall. No 24 Sqn, RAF, 1968; Lyneham Wing, 1974–81.

XV211, *66-8561* (C/N 4237) Delivered 20-10-67 to Marshall; No 24 Sqn, RAF, 1968; No 70 Sqn (*Homer*), 1970; No 242 OCU; Lyneham Wing, 1975–81.

XV212, *66-8562* (C/N 4238) Delivered 27-10-67 to Marshall; No 24 Sqn, RAF, 1968; No 70 Sqn, 1970; Lyneham Wing, c1974–81. Became C Mk 3, 1982 (mod by Marshall).

XV213, *66-8563* (C/N 4240) Delivered 2-11-67 to Marshall; No 24 Sqn, RAF, 1968; No 48 Sqn, 1970; Lyneham Wing, 1971–81.

XV214, *66-8564* (C/N 4241) Delivered 11-67 to Marshall; No 24 Sqn, RAF, 1968; Lyneham Wing, 1975–82.

XV215, *66-8565* (C/N 4242) Delivered 11-11-67 to Marshall; No 24 Sqn, RAF, 1968; Lyneham Wing, 1975–82.

XV216, *66-8566* (C/N 4243) Delivered 22-11-67 to Marshall; No 36 Sqn, RAF, 1968; No 242 OCU, 1969; Lyneham Wing, 1970; crashed during take-off at Melovia, Italy, 9-11-71, and written off.

XV217, *66-8567* (C/N 4244) Delivered 30-11-67 to Marshall; No 24 Sqn, RAF, 1968; Lyneham Wing, 1975–81.

XV218, *66-8568* (C/N 4245) Delivered 2-12-67 to Marshall; No 47 Sqn, RAF, 1968; No 242 OCU, 1970; Lyneham Wing, 1971; No 70 Sqn, Lyneham Wing, 1975–82.

XV219, *66-8569* (C/N 4246) Delivered 9-12-67 to Marshall; No 30/47 Sqns, 1969; Lyneham Wing, 1971–82. Became C Mk 3, 1981 (mod by Marshall).

XV220, *66-8570* (C/N 4247) Delivered 22-12-67 to Marshall; No 24 Sqn, RAF, 1968; No 242 OCU, 1975; Lyneham Wing. Became C Mk 3, 1981 (mod by Marshall).

XV221, *66-8571* (C/N 4251) Delivered 1-68 to Marshall; No 30/47 Sqns, RAF, 1969; Lyneham Wing, 1971–81. Became C Mk 3, 1982 (mod by Marshall).

XV222, *66-8572* (C/N 4252) Delivered 13-1-68 to Marshall; No 47 Sqn, RAF, 1969; Lyneham Wing, 1971–75.

XV223, *66-8573* (C/N 4353) Delivered 19-1-68 to Marshall; No 47 Sqn, RAF, 1969; Lyneham Wing, 1971; No 242 OCU; Lyneham Wing, 1974–75. Became prototype C Mk 3, 1979 (mod by Lockheed-Georgia); A&AEE, Boscombe Down, 1980.

XV290, *66-13533* (C/N 4254) Delivered 25-1-68 to Marshall; No 47 Sqn, RAF, 1969; Lyneham Wing, 1971; No 70 Sqn, c1973; Lyneham Wing, 1975–81. Became C Mk 3, 1981 (mod by Marshall).

XV291, *66-13534* (C/N 4256) Delivered 1-2-68 to Marshall; No 30/47 Sqns, RAF, 1970; Lyneham Wing, 1971–82.

XV292, *66-13535* (C/N 4257) Delivered 8-2-68 to Marshall; No 47 Sqn, RAF, 1968; No 48 Sqn, 1970; Lyneham Wing, 1971–80.

XV293, *66-13536* (C/N 4258) Delivered 22-2-68 to Marshall; No 30/47 Sqns, RAF, 1969; Lyneham Wing, 1969; No 70 Sqn, 1971; Lyneham Wing, 1975.

XV294, *66-13537* (C/N 4259) Delivered 29-2-68 to Marshall; No 30/47 Sqns, 1969; Lyneham Wing, 1972; No 70 Sqn (*Hephaestos*); Lyneham Wing, 1975–80. Became C Mk 3, 1980 (mod by Marshall).

XV295, *66-13538* (C/N 4261) Delivered 8-3-68 to Marshall; No 30/47 Sqns, RAF, 1969; No 242 OCU, 1970; Lyneham Wing, 1971–74.

XV296, *66-13539* (C/N 4262) Delivered 3-68 to Marshall; No 30 Sqn, RAF, 1969; Lyneham Wing, 1971; No 242 OCU; Lyneham Wing, 1975–81. Became the first C Mk 1(K) tanker, 6-82 (Mod 5310 by Marshall).

XV297, *66-13540* (C/N 4263) Delivered 22-3-68 to Marshall; No 30 Sqn, RAF, 1969; No 40 Sqn, 1970; No 242 OCU; Lyneham Wing, 1974–81.

XV298, *66-13541* (C/N 4264) Delivered 28-3-68 to Marshall; No 30/47 Sqns, RAF, 1969; Lyneham Wing, 1971–82.

XV299, *66-13542* (C/N 4266) Delivered 25-4-68 to Marshall; No 30 Sqn, RAF, 1969; Lyneham Wing, 1969; No 70 Sqn (*Homer*), c1971; Lyneham Wing, 1975–82.

XV300, *66-13543* (C/N 4267) Delivered 4-4-68 to Marshall; No 30 Sqn, RAF, 1969; Lyneham Wing, 1971–82.

XV301, *66-13544* (C/N 4268) Delivered 27-3-68 to Marshall; No 30/47 Sqns, RAF, 1969–70; Lyneham Wing, 1971; No 70 Sqn, 1975; Lyneham Wing, 1981. Became C Mk 3, 1982 (mod by Marshall).

XV302, *66-13545* (C/N 4270) Delivered 11-4-68 to Marshall; No 30/47 Sqns, RAF, 1969–70; Lyneham Wing, 1971–81.

XV303, *66-13546* (C/N 4271) Delivered 5-5-68 to Marshall; No 30/47 Sqns, RAF, 1969–70; Lyneham Wing, 1971; No 70 Sqn, 1975; Lyneham Wing, 1975–81.

XV304, *66-13547* (C/N 4272) Delivered 5-68 to Marshall; No 30/47 Sqns, RAF, 1969; Lyneham Wing, 1971–82.

XV305, *66-13548* (C/N 4273) Delivered 5-68 to Marshall; No 30/47 Sqns, RAF, 1969; Lyneham Wing, 1971; No 70 Sqn (*Hyperion*), 1973; Lyneham Wing, 1975–81; Became C Mk 3, 1981 (mod by Marshall).

XV306, *66-13549* (C/N 4274) Delivered 1-5-68 to Marshall; No 30/47 Sqns, RAF, 1969–70; Lyneham Wing, 1974–81.

XV307, *65-13550* (C/N 4275) Delivered 31-5-68 to Marshall; No 242 OCU, RAF, Lyneham Wing, 1972–82.

LOCKHEED MODEL 382C-3D C-130E HERCULES (for Saudi Arabia) (C/N 4215) One standard transport (RSAF No *455*) for the Royal Saudi Air Force. Delivered in 1967.

455 (C/N 4215) No 4 Sqn, RSAF, Jeddah, 1968–80.

LOCKHEED MODEL 382C-4D EC-130Q HERCULES (C/Ns 4239, 4249, 4269 and 4277 to 4281) Eight communications aircraft, US Navy Nos *156170* to *156177*, for the US Navy. Four 4,150 eshp Allison T56A-15 turboprops; equipped with ramp antenna guides. Delivered in 1967–68. Employed for communication with nuclear submarines.

156170 (C/N 4239) US Navy Sqn VQ-4, NAS Patuxent

River, Maryland, 1969–80.

156171 (C/N 4249) VQ-3, NAS Agana, Guam, 1976–79.

156172 (C/N 4269) VQ-3, NAS Agana, Guam, 1968; VQ-4, NAS Patuxent River, 1974–79; VQ-3, 1979.

156173 (C/N 4277) VQ-4, NAS Patuxent River, Maryland, 1969–79.

156174 (C/N 4278) VQ-4, NAS Patuxent River, Maryland, 1969–75.

156175 (C/N 4279) VQ-4, NAS Patuxent River, Maryland, 1969–76.

156176 (C/N 4280) VQ-4, NAS Patuxent River, Maryland, 1969–75.

156177 (C/N 4281) VQ-3, NAS Agana, Guam, 1969; VQ-4, NAS Patuxent River, Maryland, 1981.

LOCKHEED MODEL 382C-5D C-130E HERCULES (for Brazil) (C/N 4202, FAB No *2455*) One standard transport for the *Forca Aerea Brasileira*. Delivered in 1967.

2455 (C/N 4202) *1° Esquadrao, 1° Grupo*, FAB, Galeao, Rio de Janeiro, 1969.

LOCKHEED MODEL 382-12B HC-130H HERCULES (C/Ns 4255, 4260 and 4265) Three search and rescue aircraft, USAF Nos *67-7183* to *67-7185* (US Coast Guard Nos *CG1452* to *CG1454*), for US Coast Guard. Delivered in 1968.

67-7183, *CG1452* (C/N 4255) Based at San Francisco, California, 1975–78; Sacramento, California (McClellan AFB), 1978.

67-7184, *CG1453* (C/N 4260) San Francisco, California, 1975–77; Sacramento, California, (McClellan AFB), 1978. Was the 1,000th Hercules built.

67-7185, *CG1454* (C/N 4265) Kodiak, Alaska, 1970; San Francisco, California, 1974–78; Sacramento, California (McClellan AFB), 1978.

LOCKHEED MODEL 382C-6D C-130E HERCULES (for Iran) (C/Ns 4276 and 4282 to 4284) Four standard transports, USAF Nos *67-14726* to *67-14729* (IIAF Nos *5-113* to *5-116*), offset under Mutual Assistance Programme (MAP) from USAF blocks for the Imperial Iranian Air Force. Delivered in 1968.

5-113, *67-14726* (C/N 4276) MAP. No 5 Air Transport Sqn (ATS), Mehrabad and Shiraz, 1970; re-registered *5-107*, 1973; re-registered *5-8503*, 1976.

5-114, *67-14727* (C/N 4282) MAP. No 5 ATS, Mehrabad and Shiraz, 1970; re-registered *5-108*, 1973. Sold to Pakistan, 1975, as *14727*; No 6 Sqn, PAF, Chaklala; aircraft 'S'.

5-115, *67-14728* (C/N 4283) MAP. No 5 ATS, IIAF, Mehrabad and Shiraz, 1970; re-registered *5-109*, 1973; re-registered *5-8504*, 1976.

5-116, *67-14729* (C/N 4284) MAP. No 5 ATS, IIAF, Mehrabad and Shiraz, 1970; re-registered *5-110*, 1973; re-registered *5-8505*, 1976.

LOCKHEED MODEL 382C-7D C-130E HERCULES (for Canada) (C/Ns 4285, 4286, 4288 and 4289) Four standard transports, RCAF Nos *10325* to *10328*, for the Royal Canadian Air Force. Delivered 1968.

10325 (C/N 4285) No 436 Sqn, RCAF, Edmonton and Trenton, 1970; re-registered *130325* with CAF.

10326 (C/N 4286) No 436 Sqn, RCAF, Edmonton and Trenton, 1970; re-registered *130326* with CAF.

10327 (C/N 4288) No 436 Sqn, RCAF, Edmonton and Trenton, 1970; re-registered *130327* with CAF.

10328 (C/N 4289) No 436 Sqn, RCAF, Edmonton and Trenton, 1970; re-registered *130328* with CAF.

LOCKHEED MODEL 382C-8D C-130E HERCULES

(for Brazil) (C/Ns 4287, 4290 to 4293) Five standard transports, FAB Nos *2456* to *2460*, for the *Forca Aerea Brasileira*. Delivered in 1968.

2456 (C/N 4287) *1° Esquadrao, 1° Grupo*, FAB, Galeao, Rio de Janeiro, 1970.

2457 (C/N 4290) *1° Esquadrao, 1° Grupo*, FAB, Galeao, Rio de Janeiro, 1970–80; damaged in landing accident, Salvador, 25-6-79, but repaired.

2458 (C/N 4291) Sold with civil registration *N7983R* as search/rescue/reconnaissance aircraft with paratroop doors interchangeable with transparent panels; served as *2458* with *1° Esquadrao, 6° Grupo*, FAB, Recife, c1970.

2459 (C/N 4292) SAR/R aircraft as C/N 4291; *1° Esquadrao, 6° Grupo*, FAB, Recife.

2460 (C/N 4293) SAR/R aircraft as C/N 4291; *1° Esquadrao, 6° Grupo*, FAB, Recife.

LOCKHEED MODEL 382C-9D LC-130R HERCULES (C/N 4305) One ski-equipped transport, US Navy No *155917*, for the US Navy; specification otherwise as for C-130H. Delivered 11-68.

155917 (C/N 4305) US Navy Sqn VX-6, NAS Point Mugu, California, 1969; Operation Deep Freeze, Antarctica; crashed during landing at Amundsen-Scott South Pole Station, 28-1-73, and written off.

LOCKHEED MODEL 382C-10D C-130E HERCULES (for Iran) (C/Ns 4294 to 4298) Five standard transports, USAF Nos *69-7706* to *69-7710* (IIAF Nos *5-117* to *5-121*) for the Imperial Iranian Air Force, offset under Mutual Assistance Programme from USAF Blocks. Delivered in 1968.

5-117, *69-7706* (C/N 4294) MAP. No 5 ATS, IIAF, Mehrabad and Shiraz, 1970; re-registered *5-111*, 1973; re-registered *5-8506*, 1976.

5-118, *69-7707* (C/N 4295) MAP. No 5 ATS, IIAF, Mehrabad and Shiraz, 1970; re-registered *5-112*, 1973; re-registered *5-8507*, 1976.

5-119, *69-7708* (C/N 4296) MAP. No 5 ATS, IIAF, Mehrabad and Shiraz, 1970; re-registered *5-113*, 1973; re-registered *5-8508*, 1976.

5-120, *69-7709* (C/N 4297) MAP. No 5 ATS, IIAF, Mehrabad and Shiraz, 1970; re-registered *5-114*, 1973; re-registered *5-8509*, 1976.

5-121, *69-7710* (C/N 4298) MAP. No 5 ATS, IIAF, Mehrabad and Shiraz, 1970; re-registered *5-115*, 1973; re-registered *5-8510*, 1976.

LOCKHEED MODEL 382B-7C L-100 HERCULES (C/N 4208) One civil aircraft, registered *N9227R*, for commercial sale by Lockheed-Georgia Company.

N9227R (C/N 4208) Sold to Alaska Airlines (*City of Juneau*) and delivered 27-3-67. Sold to National Aircraft Leasing, 1970. Sold to Alaska International Air, 11-72. Sold to Saturn Airways Inc, registered *N18ST*, 1-73. Became Model 382G-7C, 2-73; TIA, 1976 (thence TransAmerica, 1979).

LOCKHEED MODEL 382B-8C L-100 HERCULES (for Canada) (C/N 4197) One civil aircraft, registered *N9269R*, for commercial sale by Lockheed-Georgia Company. Delivered 5-67.

N9269R (C/N 4197) Sold to Pacific Western Airlines as *CF-PWO*, 5-67; leased to Trans-Mediterranean Airways, 7-67 to 9-67, then returned to PWA. Crashed at Ciro Alegerie, Peru, 16-7-69.

LOCKHEED MODEL 382B-9C L-100-10 HERCULES (for Zambia) (C/N 4209) One civil aircraft, registered *9J-REZ*, for commercial sale by Lockheed-Georgia Company.

Delivered 4-67.

9J-REZ (C/N 4209) Sold to the Government of the Republic of Zambia, 1967. Leased to Zambian Air Cargoes, 4-67. Sold to National Aircraft Leasing, 1969, as *N921NA*; leased to Interior Airways Inc, 1969–72; leased to Alaska International Air, 7-72; severely damaged on ice island 700 miles north of Point Barrow, 28-2-72, but repaired. Sold to Alaska International Air, 2-73; destroyed by explosion in cargo at Galbraith Lake, 30-8-74.

LOCKHEED MODEL 382B-10C L-100 HERCULES (C/Ns 4221, 4222, 4225 and 4229) Four civil aircraft, registered *N9248R*, *N9245R*, *N759AL* and *N760AL*, sold by Lockheed-Georgia Company to Airlift International Inc. Delivered 1967.

N9248R (C/N 4221) Sold to Airlift International Inc (AII), 7-67; leased to Alaska Airlines, 1968–69. Became Model 382E-10C L-100-20 with 2.5 m fuselage stretch, 10-69. Sold to Saturn Airways Inc, 9-10-70; crashed 11-10-70 at McGuire AFB and written off.

N9254R (C/N 4222) Sold to AII, 7-67. Became Model 383E-10C L-100-20 with 2.5 m fuselage stretch, 7-69; sold to Saturn Airways Inc, 10-70, as *N13ST*. Became Model 382G-10C L-100-30 with 4.6 m fuselage stretch, 1972. Leased to Alaska International Air (AIA), 10-72, as *N103AK*. Sold to AIA, 1973. Sold to *Consorcio Technice de Aeronautica*, Luanda, Angola, 11-77, as *D2-FAG*, thence *TAAG-Linhas Aereas de Angola*, 4-79, as *D2-THB*.

N759AL (C/N 4225) Sold to AII, 9-67. Became Model 382E-10C L-100-20 with 2.5 m fuselage stretch, 8-69. Sold to Saturn Airways Inc (*Bozo*), 10-70. Became Model 382G-10C L-100-30 with 4.6 m fuselage stretch, 7-72. Crashed after wing failure in severe turbulence, Springfield, Illinois, 23-5-74.

N760AL (C/N 4229) Sold to AII, 10-67. Leased to Interior Airways Inc, 1968; crashed, Prudhoe Bay, 24-12-68, and written off.

LOCKHEED MODEL 382B-14C L-100 HERCULES (C/Ns 4234, 4248 and 4250) Three civil aircraft, registered *N7999S*, *N9262R* and *N9266R*, for leasing by the Lockheed Aircraft Corporation. Completed in 1967.

N7999S (C/N 4234) Leased to Interior Airways Inc (IAI), 4-69; leased to Delta Airlines, 1970. Sold to National Aircraft Leasing; leased to Alaska International Air (AIA), 7-72, as *N102AK*; crashed when wing separated while landing at Old Man 'n Camp, Alaska, 27-10-74.

N9262R (C/N 4248) Sold to National Aircraft Leasing, 1967; leased to IAI, 11-69; leased to AIA, 7-72, as *N101AK*. Became Model 382G-14C L-100-30 with 4.6 m fuselage stretch; sold to AIA, 12-77.

N9266R (C/N 4250) Sold to National Aircraft Leasing, 1967; leased to IAI, 12-68. Became Model 382F-14C L-100-20 with 2.5 m fuselage stretch, 8-70; leased to Saturn Airways Inc, 1-71, as *N22ST*; leased to Southern Air Transport (SAT), 9-72; leased to AIA, 10-75, as *N9266R*; leased to SAT, 4-77. Sold to SAT, 1-82; leased to Air Algerie for six months in 1982; returned to SAT, 10-82.

LOCKHEED MODEL 382C-11D C-130E HERCULES (for Saudi Arabia) (C/Ns 4304, 4306, 4307 and 4311) Four standard transport, RSAF Nos *1606* to *1609*, for the Royal Saudi Air Force. Delivered late in 1968.

1606 (C/N 4304) Delivered 11-68. No 16 Sqn, RSAF, Jeddah, 1970–81.

1607 (C/N 4306) Delivered 11-68. No 16 Sqn, RSAF,

Jeddah, 1970–81.

1608 (C/N 4307) Delivered 11-68. No 16 Sqn, RSAF, Jeddah, 1970–81.

1609 (C/N 4311) Delivered 12-68. No 16 Sqn, RSAF, Jeddah, 1970–81.

LOCKHEED MODEL 382C-12D C-130E HERCULES

(for Argentina) (C/Ns 4308 to 4310) Three standard transports, FAA Nos *TC-61* to *TC-63*, for the *Fuerza Aerea Argentina*. Delivered late in 1968.

TC-61 (C/N 4308) Delivered 11-68. *1 Escuadron de Transporte, 1 Brigada Aerea*, El Palomar, Buenos Aires, 1974; *2 Grupe de Transporte, 1 Brigada Aerea*, El Palomar, 1979.

TC-62 (C/N 4309) Delivered 11-68. Destroyed by bomb during take-off at Tucuman, 28-8-75.

TC-63 (C/N 4310) Delivered 12-68. *1 Brigada Aerea*, El Palomar, 1979–82; shot down by British Sea Harrier during Falkland Islands campaign, 1-6-82; crew killed.

LOCKHEED MODEL 382C-13D C-130E HERCULES

(for New Zealand) (C/Ns 4312 and 4313) Two standard transports, USAF Nos *68-8218* and *68-8219* (RNZAF Nos *NZ7004* and *NZ7005*), for the Royal New Zealand Air Force. Delivered 12-68.

NZ7004, *68-8218* (C/N 4312) No 40 Sqn, RNZAF, Whenuapai, 1970–80.

NZ7005, *68-8219* (C/N 4313) No 40 Sqn, RNZAF, Whenuapai, 1970–80.

LOCKHEED MODEL 382C-14D C-130E HERCULES

(for Norway) (C/Ns 4334 to 4339) Six standard transports, USAF Nos *68-10952* to *68-10957* (RNoAF Nos *UN-952* to *UN957*), for the Royal Norwegian Air Force (*Flyvapnet*). Delivered in 1969.

UN-952, *69-10952* (C/N 4334) No 335 Sqn (*Odin*), Gardermoen, 1970–80. Also registered *LN-SUW*.

UN-953, *68-10953* (C/N 4335) No 335 Sqn (*Tor*), Gardermoen, 1970–80. Also registered *LN-SUR*.

UN-954, *68-10954* (C/N 4336) No 335 Sqn (*Balder*), Gardermoen, 1970–80.

UN-955, *68-10955* (C/N 4337) No 335 Sqn (*Fröy*), Gardermoen, 1970–80.

UN-956, *68-10956* (C/N 4338) No 335 Sqn, (*Ty*), Gardermoen, 1970–80.

UN-957, *68-10957* (C/N 4339) No 335 Sqn (*Brage*), Gardermoen, 1970–80.

LOCKHEED MODEL 382C-15D C-130E HERCULES

(1968 USAF Appropriations for TAC) (C/Ns 4314 to 4331) 18 standard transports, USAF Nos *68-10934* to *68-10951*. General specification as for 1962 Appropriations. Completed in 1969 and delivered to TAC between 1-69 and 6-69.

68-10934 (C/N 4314) 64th TAW, 1969–70; 314th TAW, 1973–76; 317th TAW, 1976–82.

68-10935 (C/N 4315) 64th TAW, 1969–70; 314th TAW, 1973; 464th TAW, 1974; 314th TAW, 1975; 317th TAW, 1975–76; 435th TAW, 1977–81.

68-10936 (C/N 4316) 64th TAW, 1969–70; 314th TAW, 1974–76; 317th TAW, 1976; crashed 35 miles from Charleston, South Carolina, following lightning strike, 30-11-78.

68-10937 (C/N 4317) 64th TAW, 1969–70; 314th TAW, 1975–76; 317th TAW, 1976–83.

68-10938 (C/N 4318) 64th TAW, 1969–70; 314th TAW, 1973–76; 317th TAW, 1976; 435th TAW, 1978–82.

68-10939 (C/N 4319) 64th TAW, 1969–70; 314th TAW,

1973–76; 317th TAW, 1976–77; 37th TAS, 1977–78; 317th TAW, 1979–82.

68-10940 (C/N 4320) 64th TAW, 1969–70; 314th TAW, 1973–76; 317th TAW, 1976–78; 62d MAW, 1978; 317th TAW, 1979–82.

68-10941 (C/N 4321) 64th TAW, 1969–70; 314th TAW, 1973–76; 317th TAW, 1976–77; 62d MAW, 1978; 317th TAW, 1979–82.

68-10942 (C/N 4322) 64th TAW, 1969–70; 314th TAW, 1973; 317th TAW, 1979–82.

68-10943 (C/N 4323) 64th TAW, 1969–70; 314th TAW, 1973–76; 317th TAW, 1976–77; 37th TAS, 1977–81.

68-10944 (C/N 4324) 64th TAW, 1969–70; 314th TAW, 1973–76; 317th TAW, 1976–77; 37th TAS, 1977–81.

68-10945 (C/N 4325) 64th TAW, 1969–70; 314th TAW, 1973–76; 317th TAW, 1976–82.

68-10946 (C/N 4326) 64th TAW, 1969–70; 314th TAW, 1973–76; 317th TAW, 1976–78; 62d MAW, 1978–79; 317th TAW, 1979–82.

68-10947 (C/N 4327) 64th TAW, 1969–70; 314th TAW, 1973–76; 317th TAW, 1976–77; 37th TAS, 1977–81.

68-10948 (C/N 4328) 64th TAW, 1969–70; 314th TAW, 1973–81.

68-10949 (C/N 4329) 64th TAW, 1969–70; 314th TAW, 1974–81.

68-10950 (C/N 4330) 64th TAW, 1969–70; 314th TAW, 1975–81.

68-10951 (C/N 4331) 64th TAW, 1969–70; 314th TAW, 1975–78; crashed on landing approach at Fort Campbell Army Air Field following engine control failure, 10-12-78.

LOCKHEED MODEL 382C-15D C-130E HERCULES

(for Sweden) (C/N 4332) One standard transport diverted from USAF Appropriations (*68-10951*) and sold to Sweden, 5-69 as *84002*.

84002, *68-10951* (C/N 4332) *Flygflottilj 7, Flygvapnet*, Satenäs, 1970–81; became C-130H, 1982.

LOCKHEED MODEL 382C-15D C-130E HERCULES

(1969 USAF Appropriations for TAC) (C/Ns 4340 to 4349, 4351 to 4354, 4356, 4357, 4359 and 4360) 18 standard transports, USAF Nos *69-6566* to *69-6583*. General specification as for 1962 Appropriations. Completed in 1969.

69-6566 (C/N 4340) 64th TAW, 1969–70; 314th TAW, 1973; 464th TAW, 1973–74; 314th TAW, 1975–76; 317th TAW, 1976–77; 37th TAS, 1977–81.

69-6567 (C/N 4341) 64th TAW, 1969–70. Became AC-130E, 1970; 415th SOTS, 1971–72. Became AC-130H, 1973; 16th SOS, 1973; 415th SOTS, 1974–77; 16th SOS, 1978–81.

69-6568 (C/N 4342) 64th TAW, 1969–70. Became AC-130E, 1970; 415th SOTS, 1972. Became AC-130H, 1973; 415th SOTS, 1974–77; 16th SOS, 1978–84.

69-6569 (C/N 4343) 64th TAW, 1969–70. Became AC-130E, 1970; 16th SOS, 8th TFW, Ubon RTAFB, Thailand, 1972–73. Became AC-130H, 1973; 415th SOTS, 1977; 16th SOS, 1977–84.

69-6570 (C/N 4344) 64th TAW, 1969–70. Became AC-130E, 1970; 16th SOS, 8th TFW, 1972. Became AC-130H, 1973; 415th SOTS, 1975–77; 16th SOS, 1978–84.

69-6571 (C/N 4345) 64th TAW, 1969–70. Became AC-130E, 1970; 16th SOS, 8th TFW, 1971–72; shot down near An Loc, 30-3-72.

69-6572 (C/N 4346) 64th TAW, 1970. Became AC-130E, 1970; 16th SOS, 8th TFW, 1972. Became AC-130H, 1973; 415th SOTS, 1976–77; 16th SOS, 1978–84.

69-6573 (C/N 4347) 64th TAW, 1970. Became AC-130E, 1970; 16th SOS, 8th TFW, 1972. Became AC-130H, 1973; 16th SOS, 1975; 415th SOTS, 1977; 16th SOS, 1978–84.

69-6574 (C/N 4348) 64th TAW, 1970. Became AC-130E, 1970; 16th SOS, 8th TFW, 1972–73. Became AC-130H, 1973; 415th SOTS, 1977; 16th SOS, 1978–84.

69-6575 (C/N 4349) 64th TAW, 1969–70. Became AC-130E, 1970; 16th SOS, 8th TFW, 1973. Became AC-130H, 1973; 415th SOTS, 1975–77; 16th SOS, 1978–84.

69-6576 (C/N 4351) 64th TAW, 1970. Became AC-130E, 1970; 16th SOS, 8th TFW, 1973. Became AC-130H, 1973; 415th SOTS, 1975–77; 16th SOS, 1978–84.

69-6577 (C/N 4352) 64th TAW, 1970. Became AC-130E, 1970; 16th SOS, 8th TFW, 1973. Became AC-130H, 1973; AFSC, 1974; 4950th TW, 1975–77; 16th SOS, 1978–84.

69-6578 (C/N 4353) 64th TAW, 1970–71; crashed following fin stall, Little Rock AFB, Arkansas, 12-11-71, and written off.

69-6579 (C/N 4354) 61st TAS, 64th TAW, 1970; 314th TAW, 1975–81.

69-6580 (C/N 4356) 61st TAS, 64th TAW, 1970; 314th TAW, 1975–81.

69-6581 (C/N 4357) 61st TAS, 64th TAW, 1970; 314th TAW, 1975–76; 317th TAW, 1976–77; 37th TAS, 435th TAW, 1977–81; crashed following fin stall on take-off at Ramstein AB, Germany, 14-1-81, and written off.

69-6582 (C/N 4359) 61st TAS, 64th TAW, 1970; 314th TAW, 1973–76; 317th TAW, 1976; 37th TAS, 435th TAW, 1977–82.

69-6583 (C/N 4360) 314th TAW, 1973–76; 317th TAW, 1976–77; 37th TAS, 1977–82.

LOCKHEED MODEL 382-20B HC-130N HERCULES

(C/Ns 4363, 4367, 4368, 4370 to 4372 and 4374 to 4382) 15 search and rescue aircraft, USAF Nos *69-5819* to *69-5833*. As HC-130H but without Fulton recovery gear. Delivered to USAF's Aerospace Rescue and Recovery Service in 1970.

69-5819 (C/N 4363) 55th ARRS, 39th ARRW, Eglin AFB, Florida, 1977–81.

69-5820 (C/N 4367) 67th ARRS, 39th ARRW, RAF Woodbridge, England, 1974–81.

69-5821 (C/N 4368) 36th ARRS, 1970–71; 46th ARRS; 33d ARRS, 1976–80.

69-5822 (C/N 4370) 36th ARRS, 1970–72; 67th ARRS, *c*1974; 33d ARRS, 1976; 67th ARRS, 1976; 33d ARRS, 1977–81.

69-5823 (C/N 4371) 67th ARRS, 1970; 33d ARRS; 46th ARRS; 67th ARRS, 39th ARRW, 1975–80.

69-5824 (C/N 4372) 71st ARRS, 1975–79; 301st ARRS, 403d RWRW, USAFRES, Homestead AFB, Florida, 1979–80.

69-5825 (C/N 4374), 41st ARRS, 41st RWRW, 1977; 71st ARRS, 1977–81.

69-5826 (C/N 4375) 67th ARRS, 1970–77; 55th ARRS, 1977–78; 67th ARRS, 1979–82.

69-5827 (C/N 4376) 67th ARRS, 39th ARRW, RAF Woodbridge, England, 1977–82.

69-5828 (C/N 4377) 55th ARRS, 39th ARRW, Eglin AFB, Florida, 1977–80.

69-5829 (C/N 4378) 55th ARRS; 305th ARRS, 403d RWRW, 1976–80.

69-5830 (C/N 4379) 36th ARRS, 1971; 33d ARRS, 1976–77; 301st ARRS, 1979–81.

69-5831 (C/N 4380) 71st ARRS, 1976–81.

69-5832 (C/N 4381) 41st ARRS, 41st RWRW, McClellan AFB, California, 1976–80.

69-5833 (C/N 4382) 55th ARRS, 1972; 1550th ATTW, 1975; 305th ARRS, 1976–80.

LOCKHEED MODEL 382E-11C L-100-20 HERCULES

(C/Ns 4299 and 4301) Two civil aircraft, registered *N9232R* and *N9751S*, for commercial sale by Lockheed in 1968; 2.5 m fuselage stretch.

N9232R (C/N 4299) Sold to Southern Air Transport (SAT), 12-68. Became Model 382G-11C L-100-30 with 4.6 m fuselage stretch, 1-74; leased to AIA, 3-74. Undercarriage collapsed during heavy landing at Otavalo, Ecuador, but repaired and returned to SAT, 1976; leased to Air Algerie, 1980; leased to Cassair, 7-81; leased to Cargolux, 7-81.

N9751S (C/N 4301) Sold to Air America (AA), 10-68; leased to SAT, 11-68; sold to SAT, 7-70; sold back to AA, 7-71. Became Model 382G-11C L-100-30 with 4.6 m fuselage stretch, 9-71. Sold to Saturn Airways Inc, 1-74, as *N23ST*; to TIA, 12-76; undercarriage collapsed while landing at Dover AFB, 10-8-78, but repaired; to TransAmerica, 10-79.

LOCKHEED MODEL 382E-13C L-100-20 HERCULES

(C/N 4300) One civil aircraft, registered *N9265R*, for commercial sale by Lockheed-Georgia Company in 1968. 2.5 m fuselage stretch.

N9265R (C/N 4300) Sold to First National Bank of Chicago; delivered 10-68; leased to Interior Airways Inc, 10-68; leased to AIA, 7-72, as *N104AK*. Sold to AIA, 11-75. Became Model 382G-13C L-100-30 with 4.6 m fuselage stretch.

LOCKHEED MODEL 382E-15C L-100-20 HERCULES

(C/Ns 4302 and 4303) Two civil aircraft, registered *N7952S* and *N9237R*, for commercial sale by Lockheed to Flying W Airways (FWS) in 1968. 2.5 m fuselage stretch.

N7952S (C/N 4302) Delivery taken up by the Girard Trust, 11-68, and leased to FWA, 4-69; to Red Dodge Aviation (RDA), 12-69, as *N30FW*. Sold to Southern Air Transport, 2-73. Sold to Government of the Philippines as *PI-99*, and leased to Philippines Air Force, thence to Philippine Aerospace Development Corporation (PADC) as *RP-C99*. Sold to United African Airlines, 1982–83, as *5J-DJR*.

N9237R (C/N 4303) Delivery taken up by the Girard Trust, 11-68, and leased to FWA, 4-69; to RDA, 10-69, as *N40FW*. Sold to Government of the Philippines as *PI-98*, 4-73, and leased to PADC as *RP-C98*, 7-73. Sold to James Bay Energy Corp of Canada as *CF-DSX*, 9-73; leased to Quebecair, 9-73. Sold to Echo Bay Mines, (*Smokey Heel*), 1980–82.

LOCKHEED MODEL 382E-16C L-100-20 HERCULES

(for Kuwait) (C/Ns 4350 and 4412) Two civil aircraft, registered *KAF317* and *KAF318*, for commercial sale to the Government of Kuwait. 2.5 m fuselage stretch.

KAF317 (C/N 4350) Delivered, 12-69, with civil registration *N7954S*; entered service with Kuwait Air Force, 12-70, as *KAF317*; crashed following lightning strike near Montelimar, France, 5-9-80.

KAF318 (C/N 4412) Delivered, 4-71, and entered service with Kuwait Air Force as *KAF318*, 1971–81.

LOCKHEED MODEL 382E-18C L-100-20 HERCULES

(C/N 4361) One civil aircraft, registered *N7982S*, for commercial sale by Lockheed-Georgia Company in 1969; 2.5 m fuselage stretch.

N7982S (C/N 4361) Sold to Pacific Western Airlines, 12-69, as *CF-PWX*; crashed at Eastville, near Kisangani, Zaïre, 21-11-76, and written off.

LOCKHEED MODEL 382E-19C L-100-20 HERCULES
(C/N 4355) One civil aircraft, registered *N7960S*, for commercial sale by Lockheed-Georgia Company in 1969; 2.5 m fuselage stretch.

N7960S (C/N 4355) Sold to National Aircraft Leasing/Maple Leaf Leasing, 11-69; leased to Pacific Western Airlines (PWA), 11-69, as *CF-PWR*. Sold to PWA, 1-77. Sold to Cargolux as *LX-GCV*, 12-80. Sold to United African Airlines, 1-81, as *5A-DHJ*; re-registered *5A-DHI*, 6-81.

LOCKHEED MODEL 382E-20C L-100-20 HERCULES
(C/N 4362) One civil aircraft, registered *N7984S*, for commercial sale in 11-69. 2.5 m fuselage stretch.

N7984S (C/N 4362) Southern Air Transport, 1969-82.

LOCKHEED MODEL 382E-21C L-100-20 HERCULES
(C/N 4333), One civil aircraft, registered *N7957S*, for leasing by the Lockheed Aircraft Corporation in 1969. 2.5 m fuselage stretch.

N7957S (C/N 4333) Leased to the US Navy for trials, 5-69; leased to Saturn Airways Inc (*Wimpy*), 5-70; sold to Saturn, 10-72, as *N17ST*. Became Model 382G-21C L-100-30 with 4.6 m fuselage stretch; TIA, 12-76, thence TransAmerica, 10-79; operated for Red Cross in Far East, 12-79.

LOCKHEED MODEL 382C-17D C-130E HERCULES
(for Iran) (C/Ns 4365, 4386, 4387, 4389, 4390, 4392 to 4394, 4398, 4399 and 4402) 11 standard military transports, USAF Nos *71-0213* to *71-0223* (IIAF Nos *5-122* to *5-132*), for the Imperial Iranian Air Force, offset from USAF Blocks. Delivered 1970-71.

5-122, 71-0213 (C/N 4365) No 5 Air Transport Squadron (ATS), IIAF, Mehrabad and Shiraz, 1971; re-registered *5-116*, 1973; re-registered *5-8511*, 1976.

5-123, 71-0214 (C/N 4386) No 5 ATS, IIAF, Mehrabad and Shiraz, 1971; re-registered *5-117*, 1973; re-registered *5-8512*, 1976.

5-124, 71-0215 (C/N 4387) No 5 ATS, IIAF, Mehrabad and Shiraz, 1971; re-registered *5-118*, 1973; re-registered *5-8513*, 1976.

5-125, 71-0216 (C/N 4389) No 5 ATS, IIAF, Mehrabad and Shiraz, 1971; re-registered *5-119*, 1973; re-registered *5-8514*, 1976.

5-126, 71-0217 (C/N 4390) Registered by Lockheed as *N7927S* before delivery as *5-126*; No 5 ATS, IIAF, Mehrabad and Shiraz, 1971; re-registered *5-120*, 1973; re-registered *5-8515*, 1976.

5-127, 71-0218 (C/N 4392) No 5 ATS, IIAF, Mehrabad and Shiraz, 1971; re-registered *5-121*, 1973; re-registered *5-8516*, 1976.

5-128, 71-0219 (C/N 4393) No 5 ATS, IIAF, Mehrabad and Shiraz, 1971; re-registered *5-122*; written off, 2-74.

5-129, 71-0220 (C/N 4394) No 5 ATS, IIAF, Mehrabad and Shiraz, 1971; re-registered *5-123*, 1973; re-registered *5-8517*, 1976.

5-130, 71-0221 (C/N 4398) No 5 ATS, IIAF, Mehrabad and Shiraz, 1971; re-registered *5-124*, 1973; re-registered *5-8518*, 1976.

5-131, 71-0222 (C/N 4399) No 5 ATS, IIAF, Mehrabad and Shiraz, 1971; re-registered *5-125*, 1973; re-registered *5-8519*, 1976.

5-132, 71-0223 (C/N 4402) No 5 ATS, IIAF, Mehrabad and Shiraz, 1971; re-registered *5-126*, 1973; re-registered *5-8520*,

1976. Believed crashed and written off, Shiraz, 19-6-79.

LOCKHEED MODEL 382C-18D C-130H HERCULES
(for Libya) (C/Ns 4366, 4369, 4373, 4395, 4400, 4401, 4403 and 4405) Eight standard military transports, LARAF Nos *111* to *118*, for *Al Quwwat Aljawwiya Al Libiyya* (Libyan Arab Republic Air Force). Four 4,510 eshp Allison T56A-15 turboprops. First C-130H Hercules for export. Delivery delayed until 1971 by temporary arms embargo on sales to Libya.

111 (C/N 4366) Based at Okba ben Nafi, 1975.

112 (C/N 4369) Based at Okba ben Nafi, 1975.

113 (C/N 4373) Based at Okba ben Nafi, 1975.

114 (C/N 4395) Based at Okba ben Nafi, 1975-79.

115 (C/N 4400) Based at Okba ben Nafi, 1975-79.

116 (C/N 4401) Based at Okba ben Nafi, 1975; caught fire and burned out, Entebbe, Uganda, 8-4-79.

117 (C/N 4403) Based at Okba ben Nafi, 1975-79.

118 (C/N 4405) Based at Okba ben Nafi, 1975-79.

LOCKHEED MODEL 382C-19D C-130E HERCULES
(for Saudi Arabia) (C/Ns 4396 and 4397) Two standard military transports, RSAF Nos *1610* and *1611*, for the Royal Saudi Air Force. Delivered in 1970.

1610 (C/N 4396) No 16 Sqn, RSAF, Jeddah, 1971; used for KC-130H training.

1611 (C/N 4397) No 16 Sqn, RSAF, Jeddah, 1971; used for KC-130H training.

LOCKHEED MODEL 382C-20D C-130H HERCULES
(for Venezuela) (C/N 4406 to 4409) Four standard military transports, FAV Nos *3556*, *4951*, *7772* and *9508*, for *Fuerza Aérea Venezolana* (Venezuelan Air Force). Delivered in 1971.

3556 (C/N 4406) Esc/1, *Grupo de Transporte*, Caracas; crashed on take-off, Caracas, 4-11-80.

4951 (C/N 4407) Esc/1, *Grupo de Transporte*, Caracas (*24 de Junio*), 1972-81.

7772 (C/N 4408) Esc/1, *Grupo de Transporte*, Caracas; crashed on landing approach at Lajes, Azores, in poor weather, 27-8-76.

9508 (C/N 4409) Esc/1, *Grupo de Transporte*, Caracas, 1972-80.

LOCKHEED MODEL 382C-21D C-130H HERCULES
(for Zaïre) (C/Ns 4411, 4416 and 4422) Three standard military transports, USAF Nos *71-1067* to *71-1069*, registered *9T-TCA*, *9T-TCB* and *9T-TCD*, for the *Force Aérienne Zaïroise* (FAZ, Zaïre Air Force). Delivered in 1971.

9T-TCA, *71-1067* (C/N 4411) 19 Wing, *1ere Groupement Aérien*, Kinshasa, 1971-79.

9T-TCB, *71-1068* (C/N 4416) 19 Wing, *1ere Groupement Aérien*, Kinshasa, 1971-79.

9T-TCD, *71-1069* (C/N 4417) 19 Wing, *1ere Groupement Aérien*, Kinshasa, 1971-74; crashed, Kisangani, 18-8-74.

LOCKHEED MODEL 382C-15D C-130E HERCULES
(1970 USAF Appropriations for TAC) (C/Ns 4404, 4410, 4413 to 4415, 4417 to 4421, 4423 to 4425, 4428, 4429, 4434 and 4435) 18 standard transports, USAF Nos *70-1259* to *70-1276*. General specification as for 1962 Appropriations. Delivered to TAC in 1971.

70-1259 (C/N 4404) 464th TAW, 1971-73; 314th TAW, 1974; 317th TAW (*Aerospace Chicken*), 1975-83.

70-1260 (C/N 4410) 464th TAW, 1971-73; 314th TAW, 1974; 317th TAW, 1975-76; 37th TAS, 1977-81.

70-1261 (C/N 4413) 64th TAW, 1971; 464th TAW, 1971-73; 317th TAW, 1975-82.

70-1262 (C/N 4414) 777th TAS, 464th TAW, 1971-73;

317th TAW, 1975–82.

70-1263 (C/N 4415) 777th TAS, 464th TAW, 1971–73; 317th TAW, 1975–82.

70-1264 (C/N 4417) 777th TAS, 1971–73; 317th TAW, 1975–77; 37th TAS, 1977–82.

70-1265 (C/N 4418) 777th TAS, 464th TAW, 1971–73; 317th TAW, 1975–76; 435th TAW, 1978; 317th TAW, 1978–82.

70-1266 (C/N 4419) 777th TAS, 464th TAW, 1971–73; 317th TAW (*California Moonhunter*), 1975–82.

70-1267 (C/N 4420) 777th TAS, 464th TAW, 1971–73; 317th TAW, 1975–82.

70-1268 (C/N 4421) 777th TAS, 464th TAW, 1971–73; 317th TAW, 1975–82.

70-1269 (C/N 4423) 777th TAS, 464th TAW, 1971–74; 317th TAW, 1975–82.

70-1270 (C/N 4424) 464th TAW, 1971–73; 317th TAW, U-Tapao RTAFB, Thailand, 1973; 464th TAW, 1973–75; 317th TAW, 1975–82.

70-1271 (C/N 4425) 464th TAW, 1971–73; 317th TAW (U-Tapao RTAFB, Thailand, 1973) 1973–77; 37th TAS, 1977–82.

70-1272 (C/N 4426) 464th TAW, 1971–73; 317th TAW (U-Tapao RTAFB, Thailand, 1973), 1973–82; damaged when undercarriage door detached in flight, 2-80, but repaired.

70-1273 (C/N 4428) 464th TAW, 1971–73; 317th TAW, 1976–82.

70-1274 (C/N 4429) 464th TAW, 1971–73; 317th TAW (*Playboy Bunny*, later named *Easter Bunny*; was first aircraft to Hanoi after truce, 27-1-73), 1973–76; 37th TAS, 1977–81.

70-1275 (C/N 4434) 777th TAS, 464th TAW, 1971–73; 317th TAW, 1975–82.

70-1276 (C/N 4435) 777th TAS, 464th TAW, 1971–73; 317th TAW, 1975–82.

LOCKHEED MODEL 382C-15D C-130E HERCULES (for Turkey) (C/Ns 4427, 4514 and 4524) Three standard military transports, USAF Nos *70-1947*, *71-1468* and *73-0991* (TAF Nos *ETI-947*, *ETI-468* and *ETI-991*), for *Turk Hava Kuvvetleri* (Turkish Air Force) offset under Mutual Assistance Programme.

ETI-947, *70-1947* (C/N 4427) MAP. Delivered 1971. No 221 *Filo*, *Hava Nakil Kuvveti* (HNK), TAF, Erliket, 1972–81.

ETI-468, *71-1468* (C/N 4514) MAP. Delivered 11-73. No 221 *Filo*, HNK, TAF, Erliket, 1974–81.

ETI-991, *73-0991* (C/N 4524) MAP. Delivered 2-74. No 221 *Filo*, HNK, TAF, Erliket, 1974–82.

LOCKHEED MODEL 382C-17D C-130H HERCULES (for Iran) (C/Ns 4432, 4433, 4438 to 4440, 4442, 4444, 4445, 4448, 4454, 4456 to 4459, 4462, 4463, 4465, 4466, 4468, 4469, 4471, 4474, 4480 and 4484 to 4490) 30 standard military transports, IIAF Nos *5-133* to *5-162*, for the Imperial Iranian Air Force. Delivered between 17-11-71 and 1-73.

5-133 (C/N 4432) No 5 Air Transport Squadron (ATS), IIAF, Shiraz; re-registered *5-127*, 1973, and *5-8521*, 1976.

5-134 (C/N 4433) No 5 ATS, IIAF, Shiraz; No 7 Transport Wing, Tadayou, Shiraz, 1973–79; re-registered *5-128*, 1973, and *5-8522*, 1976.

5-135 (C/N 4438) No 5 ATS, Shiraz, 1973–79; re-registered *5-129*, 1973, and *5-8523*, 1976.

5-136 (C/N 4439) No 7 Transport Wing, Tadayou, Shiraz, 1972–79; re-registered *5-130*, 1973, and *5-8524*, 1976.

5-137 (C/N 4440) No 5 ATS, Shiraz, 1972–79; re-registered

5-131, 1973, and *5-8525*, 1976.

5-138 (C/N 4442) No 5 ATS, Shiraz, 1972–79; re-registered *5-132*, 1973, and *5-8526*, 1976.

5-139 (C/N 4444) No 5 ATS, Shiraz, 1972–79; re-registered *5-133*, 1973, and *5-8527*, 1976.

5-140 (C/N 4445) No 5 ATS, Shiraz, 1972–78; re-registered *5-134*, 1973, and *5-8528*, 1976.

5-141 (C/N 4448) No 5 ATS, Shiraz, 1972–78; re-registered *5-135*, 1973, and *5-8529*, 1976.

5-142 (C/N 4454) No 5 ATS, Shiraz, 1972–78; re-registered *5-136*, 1973, and *5-8530*, 1976.

5-143 (C/N 4456) No 5 ATS, Shiraz, 1972–79; re-registered *5-137*, 1973, and *5-8531*, 1976.

5-144 (C/N 4457) No 5 ATS, Shiraz, 1972–78; re-registered *5-138*, 1973, and *5-8532*, 1976; crashed during three-engine overshoot, Doshan Teppeh, 19-9-78, and written off.

5-145 (C/N 4458) No 5 ATS, Shiraz, 1972–79; re-registered *5-139*, 1973, and *5-8533*, 1976.

5-146 (C/N 4459) No 5 ATS, Shiraz, 1972–78; re-registered *5-140*, 1973, and *5-8534*, 1976.

5-147 (C/N 4462) No 5 ATS, Shiraz, 1972–79; re-registered *5-141*, 1973, and *5-8535*, 1976.

5-148 (C/N 4463) No 5 ATS, Shiraz, 1972–76; re-registered *5-142*, 1973, and *5-8536*, 1976; written off, 12-76.

5-149 (C/N 4465) No 5 ATS, Shiraz, 1972–78; re-registered *5-143*, 1973, and *5-8537*, 1976.

5-150 (C/N 4466) No 5 ATS, Shiraz, 1972–78; re-registered *5-144*, 1973, and *5-8538*, 1976.

5-151 (C/N 4468) No 5 ATS, Shiraz, 1972–79; re-registered *5-145*, 1973, and *5-8539*, 1976.

5-152 (C/N 4469) No 7 Transport Wing, Tadayou, Shiraz, 1973–79; re-registered *5-146*, 1973, and *5-8540*, 1976.

5-153 (C/N 4471) No 5 ATS, Shiraz, 1972–79; re-registered *5-147*, 1973, and *5-8541*, 1976.

5-154 (C/N 4474) No 7 Transport Wing, Tadayou, Shiraz, 1973–79; re-registered *5-148*, 1973, and *5-8542*, 1976.

5-155 (C/N 4480) No 5 ATS, Shiraz, 1972–79; re-registered *5-149*, 1973, and *5-8543*, 1976.

5-156 (C/N 4484) No 5 ATS, Shiraz, 1972–80; re-registered *5-150*, 1973, and *5-8544*, 1976.

5-157 (C/N 4485) No 5 ATS, Shiraz, 1972–79; re-registered *5-151*, 1973, and *5-8545*, 1976.

5-158 (C/N 4486) No 7 Transport Wing, Tadayou, Shiraz, 1973–79; re-registered *5-152*, 1973, and *5-8546*, 1976.

5-159 (C/N 4487) No 7 Transport Wing, Tadayou, Shiraz, 1973–79; re-registered *5-153*, 1973, and *5-8547*, 1976.

5-160 (C/N 4488) No 7 Transport Wing, Tadayou, Shiraz, 1973–79; re-registered *5-154*, 1973, and *5-8548*, 1976.

5-161 (C/N 4489) No 7 Transport Wing, Tadayou, Shiraz, 1973–79; re-registered *5-155*, 1973, and *5-8549*, 1976.

5-162 (C/N 4490) No 7 Transport Wing, Tadayou, Shiraz, 1973–79; re-registered *5-156*, 1973, and *5-8550*, 1976.

LOCKHEED MODEL 382C-22D C-130H HERCULES (for Italy) (C/Ns 4441, 4443, 4446, 4447, 4449, 4451, 4452, 4491 to 4495, 4497 and 4498) 14 standard military transports, AM Nos *MM61988* to *MM62001*, for *Aeronautica Militare* (Italian Air Force). Delivered in 1972–73.

MM61988 (C/N 4441) Delivered 26-3-72. *46ª Aerobrigata Trasporti Medi*, Pisa-San Giusto, '46-02', 1973–80.

MM61989 (C/N 4443) Delivered 27-3-72. *46ª Aerobrigata*, Pisa-San Giusto, '46-03', 1973–80.

MM61990 (C/N 4446) Delivered 30-3-72. *50º Gruppo*, *46ª Aerobrigata*, Pisa-San Giusto, '46-04', 1973–80.

MM61991 (C/N 4447) Delivered 14-4-72. *46ª Aerobrigata*, Pisa-San Giusto, '46-05', 1973–80.

MM61992 (C/N 4449) *46ª Aerobrigata*, Pisa-San Giusto, '46-06', 1973–80.

MM61993 (C/N 4451) *46ª Aerobrigata*, Pisa-San Giusto, '46-07', 1973–80.

MM61994 (C/N 4452) *50° Gruppo*, *46ª Aerobrigata*, Pisa-San Giusto, '46-08', 1973–79; *48° Gruppo*, 1980.

MM61995 (C/N 4491) *46ª Aerobrigata*, Pisa-San Giusto, '46-09', 1973–76; cannibalised for spares, 1976, but restored to flying condition with parts from C-130H, C/N 4497, 1980.

MM61996 (C/N 4492) *46ª Aerobrigata*, Pisa-San Giusto, '46-10', 1973–77; crashed into Monte Serra, near Pisa, 3-3-77, and destroyed.

MM61997 (C/N 4493) *46ª Aerobrigata*, Pisa-San Giusto, '46-11' (*Portobello*), 1973–79; wing damaged at Caselle, 30-8-79, but repaired.

MM61998 (C/N 4494) *46ª Aerobrigata*, Pisa-San Giusto, '46-12', 1973–80.

MM61999 (C/N 4495) *46ª Aerobrigata*, Pisa-San Giusto, '46-13', 1973–80.

MM62000 (C/N 4497) *46ª Aerobrigata*, Pisa-San Giusto, '46-14', 1973–79; severely damaged when aircraft over-ran chocks during engine run, Milan-Malpensa, 23-1-79; written off and used for spares to restore C-130H, C/N 4491, 1980.

MM62001 (C/N 4498) *50° Gruppo*, *46ª Aerobrigata*, Pisa-San Giusto, '46-15', 1973–82.

LOCKHEED MODEL 382C-23D C-130H HERCULES (for Argentina) (C/Ns 4436, 4437 and 4464) Three standard military transports, FAA Nos *TC-64* to *TC-66*, for *Fuerza Aerea Argentina* (Argentine Air Force). Delivered in 1972.

TC-64 (C/N 4436) *1 Esc de Transporte, I Brigada Aerea*, El Palomar, 1973–82.

TC-65 (C/N 4437) *1 Esc de Transporte, I Brigada Aerea*, El Palomar, 1973–82.

TC-66 (C/N 4464) *1 Esc de Transporte, I Brigada Aerea*, El Palomar, 1973–82.

LOCKHEED MODEL 382C-24D C-130H HERCULES (for Israel) (C/Ns 4430 and 4431) Two standard military transports, USAF Nos *71-1374* and *71-1375* (IDFAF Nos *4X-JUA* and *4X-JUB*), for the Israel Defence Force/Air Force.

4X-JUA, 71-1374 (C/N 4430) Delivered 10-71; carried IDFAF No '02', later '102'. Also re-registered *4X-FBA*, c1976.

4X-JUB, 71-1375 (C/N 4431) Delivered 11-71; carried IDFAF No '06', later '106'. To Israeli Air Industries as *4X-EBA*, 1-78; again re-registered *4X-FBB*, c4-78.

LOCKHEED MODEL 382D-25C C-130H HERCULES (for Belgium) (C/Ns 4455, 4460, 4461, 4467, 4470, 4473, 4476, 4478, 4479 and 4481 to 4483) 12 standard military transports, USAF Nos *71-1797* to *71-1808* (BAF Nos *CH-01* to *CH-12*), for the *Force Aérienne Belge* (Belgian Air Force). Delivered 1972–73.

CH-01, 71-1797 (C/N 4455) Delivered 12-6-72; No 20 Sqn, 15 Wing, BAF, Melsbroek, 1972–81.

CH-02, 71-1798 (C/N 4460) Delivered 26-7-72; No 20 Sqn, 15 Wing, BAF, Melsbroek, 1972–81.

CH-03, 71-1799 (C/N 4461) Delivered 8-8-72; No 20 Sqn, 15 Wing, BAF, Melsbroek, 1972–81.

CH-04, 71-1800 (C/N 4467) Delivered 6-9-72; No 20 Sqn, 15 Wing, BAF, Melsbroek, 1973–81.

CH-05, 71-1801 (C/N 4470) Delivered 3-11-72; No 20 Sqn, 15 Wing, BAF, Melsbroek, 1973–81.

CH-06, 71-1802 (C/N 4473) Delivered 1-12-72; No 20 Sqn, 15 Wing, BAF, Melsbroek, 1973–81.

CH-07, 71-1803 (C/N 4476) Delivered 15-1-73; No 20 Sqn, 15 Wing, BAF, Melsbroek, 1973–81.

CH-08, 71-1804 (C/N 4478) Delivered 30-1-73; No 20 Sqn, 15 Wing, BAF, Melsbroek, 1973–81.

CH-09, 71-1805 (C/N 4479) Delivered 1-2-73; No 20 Sqn, 15 Wing, BAF, Melsbroek, 1973–81.

CH-10, 71-1806 (C/N 4481) Delivered 26-2-73; No 20 Sqn, 15 Wing, BAF, Melsbroek, 1973–81.

CH-11, 71-1807 (C/N 4482) Delivered 6-3-73; No 20 Sqn, 15 Wing, BAF, Melsbroek, 1973–81.

CH-12, 71-1808 (C/N 4483) Delivered 16-6-73; No 20 Sqn, 15 Wing, BAF, Melsbroek, 1973–81.

LOCKHEED MODEL 382E-22C L-100-20 HERCULES (C/Ns 4383 and 4384) Two civil aircraft, registered *N10ST* and *N11ST*, for commercial sale to Saturn Airways Inc in 1970. 2.5 m fuselage stretch.

N10ST (C/N 4383) Delivered 6-70 to Saturn (*Rudolph*). Became Model L-100-30, 2-71, with 4.6-m fuselage stretch. Leased to AIA. To TIA, 12-76, thence TransAmerica, 1979.

N11ST (C/N 4384) Delivered 7-70 to Saturn (*W.C. Fields*). Became model L-100-30, 4.6 m fuselage stretch. Leased to AIA. To TIA, 12-76, thence TransAmerica, 1979.

LOCKHEED MODEL 382G-23C L-100-30 HERCULES (C/Ns 4388 and 4391) Two civil aircraft, registered *N7988S* and *N15ST*, for commercial sale to Saturn Airways. *N7988S* was the first -30 Hercules (with 4.6 m fuselage stretch) to be completed from new on assembly line.

N7988S (C/N 4388) First flown 18-4-70; delivered to Saturn, 12-70, as *N12ST* (*Schnozz*). To TIA, 12-76, thence TransAmerica, 1979.

N15ST (C/N 4391) Delivered to Saturn (*Barney G*), 6-71. To TIA, 12-76; leased to Saudia, 3-78; TransAmerica, 1979.

LOCKHEED MODEL 382E-25C L-100-20 HERCULES (for South Africa) (C/N 4385) One civil aircraft, registered *ZS-GSK*, for commercial sale to Safair Freighters of South Africa. 2.5 m fuselage stretch.

ZS-GSK (C/N 4385) Delivered to Safair, 8-70. Sold to Safmarine (*Boland*), 8-70, and re-leased to Safair, 8-70. Sold to Safair, 2-82.

LOCKHEED MODEL 382E-26C L-100-20 HERCULES (C/Ns 4358 and 4364) Two civil aircraft, registered *N7985S* and *N7986S*, for commercial sale to Flying 'W' Airways by Lockheed-Georgia Company. 2.5-m fuselage stretch.

N7985S (C/N 4385) Sold to Flying 'W' Airways (FWA), 7-70, as *N60FW*. Resold back to Lockheed-Georgia, 9-70. Sold to *Fuerza Aerea Peruana* (FAP), 10-70, with military registration *394*. Leased to SATCO, 10-70, with civil registration *OB-R-1188*, 10-70.

N7986S (C/N 4364) Sold to FWA, 7-70, as *N70FW*. Resold back to Lockheed-Georgia, 9-70. Sold to FAP, 10-70, with military registration *395*. Leased to SATCO, 10-70, with civil registration *OB-R-1004*, 10-70. Crashed when engine shut down during take-off, 19-2-78, at Tarapota and written off.

LOCKHEED MODEL 382E-27C L-100-20 HERCULES (for Peru) (C/N 4450) One civil aircraft, FAP No *396*, for the *Fuerza Aerea Peruana* (Peruvian Air Force) in 1972. 2.5 m fuselage stretch.

396 (C/N 4450) Delivered to FAP, 4-72; leased to SATCO,

4-72, with civil registration *OB-R-956*, 4-72. Damaged during take-off at Iquitos, 2-6-73, but repaired. Crashed during emergency landing near San Juan, Peru, 24-4-81, and believed written off.

LOCKHEED MODEL 382G-28C L-100-30 HERCULES (for South Africa) (C/Ns 4472, 4475 and 4477) Three civil aircraft, registered *ZS-RSB, ZS-RSC* and *ZS-RSD*, for commercial sale to Safair. 4.6 m fuselage stretch.

ZS-RSB(C/N 4472) Delivered to Safair, 12-72; leased to South African Airways (SAA), 9-74; leased to AIA, 11-74, as *N107AK*. Sold to AIA, 1976; damaged by fire in wheel bay, Sondrestrom, 23-2-76, but repaired.

ZS-RSC (C/N 4475) Delivered to Safair, 12-72; leased to SAA, 9-74. Returned to Safair, 1976.

ZS-RSD (C/N 4477) Delivered to Safair, 12-72; leased to AIA, 11-74. Sold to AIA, 4-76, as *N106AK*.

LOCKHEED MODEL 382E-29C L-100-20 HERCULES (for Philippines) (C/N 4512) One civil aircraft, registered *N7967S*, for commercial sale to the Government of the Philippines. 2.5 m fuselage stretch.

N7967S (C/N 4512) Delivered to the Government of the Philippines, 10-73; leased to Philippine Aero Transport, 1974. Sold to Philippine Aerospace Development Corporation as *RP-C100*.

LOCKHEED MODEL 382C-26D LC-130R HERCULES (C/Ns 4508, 4516 and 4522) Three ski-equipped transports, USAF Nos *73-0839* to *73-0841*, US Navy Nos *159129* to *159131*, for the US Navy. Delivered in 1973-74.

159129, 73-0839 (C/N 4508) Flown by Navy Squadron VXE-6 for National Science Foundation (NSF), Christchurch, New Zealand ('JD-129' from parent unit, VX-6, Point Mugu, California) for Operation Deep Freeze, 1975-76. Suffered damage when nose ski failed during take-off from Dome Charlie, 15-1-75, with crew from LC-130F (C/N 3564, *qv*); repaired on site, 14-1-76.

159130, 73-0840 (C/N 4516) Flown by VXE-6 for NSF, Christchurch, New Zealand, for Operation Deep Freeze, 1975-82.

159131, 73-0841 (C/N 4522) Flown by VXE-6 for NSF, Christchurch, New Zealand, for Operation Deep Freeze, 1975-82.

LOCKHEED MODEL 382C-27D HC-130H HERCULES (C/Ns 4501, 4507, 4513, 4528 and 4529) Five search and rescue aircraft, USAF Nos *72-1300* to *72-1302, 73-0844* and *73-0845* (US Coast Guard Nos *CG1500* to *CG1504*), for the US Coast Guard. Delivered in 1973-74.

72-1300, CG1500 (C/N 4501) Based at Kodiak, Alaska, 1978-79.

72-1301, CG1501 (C/N 4507) Based at Kodiak, Alaska, 1974-78.

72-1302, CG1502 (C/N 4513) Based at Kodiak, Alaska, 1974; Sacramento (McClellan AFB), California, 1979.

73-0844, CG1503 (C/N 4528) Based at San Francisco; Sacramento (McClellan AFB), California, 1978.

73-0845, CG1504 (C/N 4529) Based at San Francisco, California, 1975-78; Kodiak, Alaska, 1978; Sacramento (McClellan AFB), California, 1978-79; Elizabeth City, North Carolina, 1979-80.

LOCKHEED MODEL 382C-28D C-130H HERCULES (for Chile) (C/Ns 4453 and 4496) Two standard military transports, FAC Nos *995* and *996*, for the *Fuerza Aérea de Chile* (Chilean Air Force). Delivered in 1972-73.

995 (C/N 4453) No 40 Sqn, *Grupo 10*, FAC, Los Cerrillos, 1973-80.

996 (C/N 4496) No 40 Sqn, *Grupo 10*, FAC Los Cerrillos, 1974-80.

LOCKHEED MODEL 382C-15D C-130E HERCULES (1972 USAF Appropriations for TAC) (C/Ns 4499, 4500, 4502, 4504 to 4506, 4509, 4510, 4517, 4519, 4521 and 4527), 12 standard military transports, USAF Nos *72-1288* to *72-1299*, general specification as for 1962 Appropriations. Delivery between 7-73 and 3-74.

72-1288 (C/N 4499) 314th TAW, 1974-76; 21st TAS, 1976-81.

72-1289 (C/N 4500) 314th TAW, 1974-76; 345th TAS, 1977-81.

72-1290 (C/N 4502) 314th TAW, 1974-76; 21st TAS, 1976-81.

72-1291 (C/N 4504) 314th TAW, 1974-77; 17th TAS, 1977; 314th TAW, 1978-81.

72-1292 (C/N 4505) 314th TAW, 1974-81.

72-1293 (C/N 4506) 314th TAW, 1974-81.

72-1294 (C/N 4509) 314th TAW, 1974-81.

72-1295 (C/N 4510) 314th TAW, 1974-81.

72-1296 (C/N 4517) 314th TAW, 1974-81.

72-1297 (C/N 4519) 314th TAW, 1974-75; destroyed by rocket, Tan Son Nhut, South Vietnam, 28-4-75.

72-1298 (CN 4521) 314th TAW, 1974-81.

72-1299 (C/N 4527) 314th TAW, 1974-76; 345th TAS, 1976-81. Was the last C-130E delivered new to the USAF.

LOCKHEED MODEL 382C-29D KC-130H HERCULES (for Saudi Arabia) (C/Ns 4503, 4511, 4532 and 4539) Four air refuelling tankers, RSAF Nos *456* to *459*, for the Royal Saudi Air Force; specification similar to KC-130R. Delivery between 11-73 and 5-74.

456 (C/N 4503) Civil registered by Lockheed as *N7992S* before delivery; No 4 Sqn, RSAF, Jeddah, 1974; damaged in wheels-up landing, Jeddah, 26-11-78.

457 (C/N 4511) No 4 Sqn, RSAF, Jeddah, 1974-80.

458 (C/N 4532) No 4 Sqn, RSAF, Jeddah, 1974-80.

459 (C/N 4539) No 4 Sqn, RSAF, Jeddah, 1974-81.

LOCKHEED MODEL 382C-30D C-130H HERCULES (for Libya) (C/Ns 4515, 4518, 4523, 4525, 4536, 4538, 4540 and 4541) Eight standard military transports, LARAF Nos *119* to *126*, for *Al Quwwat Al jawwiya Al Libiyya* (Libyan Arab Republic Air Force). All aircraft completed between 11-73 and 10-74 but withheld in USA pending issue of export licence and removal of arms embargo on trade with Libya.

LOCKHEED MODEL 382C-31D C-130H (T-10) HERCULES (for Spain) (C/Ns 4520, 4526, 4531 and 4534) Four standard military transports, SpAF Nos *T10-1* to *T10-4*, for *Ejército del Aire* (EdA, Spanish Air Force). Delivered between 12-73 and 4-74.

T10-1 (C/N 4520) *Escuadron 301, Mando Aviacion Tactica* (MAT), EdA, Valenzuela-Zaragoza ('301-01'), 1974-78; *Escuadron 311*, MAT, EdA, Torrejon ('311-01'), 1978-80; crashed into mountain in Gran Canaria, 28-5-80.

T10-2 (C/N 4526) *Escuadron 301*, MAT, EdA, Valenzuela-Zaragoza ('301-02'), 1974-78; *Escuadron 311*, MAT, EdA, Torrejon ('311-02'), 1978-81.

T10-3 (C/N 4531) *Escuadron 301*, MAT, EdA, Valenzuela-Zaragoza ('301-03'), 1974-78; *Escuadron 311*, MAT, EdA, Torrejon ('311-03'), 1978-81.

T10-4 (C/N 4534) *Escuadron 301*, MAT, EdA, Valenzuela-

Zaragoza ('301-04'), 1974–78; *Escuadron 311*, MAT, EdA, Torrejon ('311-04'), 1978–81.

LOCKHEED MODEL 382C-32D EC-130Q HERCULES (C/Ns 4595 and 4601) Two communications aircraft, US Navy Nos *159469* and *159348*, for the US Navy. Equipped with ramp antenna guides. Delivered in 7-75 and employed for communication with nuclear submarines.

159348 (C/N 4601) US Navy Squadron VQ-4, NAS Patuxent River, Maryland ('HL-48'), 1976–81.

159469 (C/N 4595) VQ-4, NAS Patuxent River, Maryland ('HL-69'), 1976–81.

LOCKHEED MODEL 382C-33D C-130H HERCULES (1973 USAF Appropriations for TAC) (C/Ns 4542 to 4550, 4554, 4557, 4563, 4564, 4571 and 4573) 15 standard military transports, USAF Nos *73-1580* to *73-1588*, *73-1590*, *73-1592*, *73-1594*, *73-1595*, *73-1597* and *73-1598*. Four Allison T56A-15 turboprops. Delivery between 6-74 and 2-75.

73-1580 (C/N 4542) 314th TAW, Little Rock AFB, Arkansas, 1975–81.

73-1581 (C/N 4543) 314th TAW, 1975–80; 21st TAS, 374th TAW, 1982.

73-1582 (C/N 4544) 314th TAW, 1975–81.

73-1583 (C/N 4545) 314th TAW, 1975–81; 21st TAS, 374th TAW, 1982.

73-1584 (C/N 4546) 314th TAW, 1975–81; 21st TAS, 374th TAW, 1982.

73-1585 (C/N 4547) 314th TAW, 1975–81.

73-1586 (C/N 4548) 314th TAW, 1975–80; 21st TAS, 374th TAW, 1982.

73-1587 (C/N 4549) 314th TAW, 1975–80; 21st TAS, 374th TAW, 1982. To EC-130H.

73-1588 (C/N 4550) 314th TAW, 1975–80; 21st TAS, 374th TAW, 1982.

73-1590 (C/N 4554) 314th TAW, 1975–81.

73-1592 (C/N 4557) Tests with wing reinforced by boron-epoxy composite, 1975; 314th TAW, Little Rock AFB, Arkansas, 1975–80.

73-1594 (C/N 4563) 314th TAW, 1975–81.

73-1595 (C/N 4564) 314th TAW, 1975–81.

73-1597 (C/N 4571) 314th TAW, 1975–80; 21st TAS, 374th TAW, 1981–82. (Was the 1,300th Hercules completed.)

73-1598 (C/N 4573) 314th TAW, 1975–80; 21st TAS, 374th TAW, 1981.

LOCKHEED MODEL 382C-33D C-130H (CC-130H) HERCULES (for Canada) (C/Ns 4553, 4555, 4559, 4568 and 4574) Five standard military transports, USAF Nos *73-1589*, *73-1591*, *73-1593*, *73-1596* and *73-1599* (CAF Nos *130329* to *130333*), for Canadian Armed Forces (CAF). Delivered between 10-74 and 2-75.

130329, *73-1589* (C/N 4553) No 435/436 Sqn, CAF, Edmonton, 1975–81. Crashed during LAPES run-in, CFB Namao, Edmonton, 16-11-82.

130330, *73-1591* (C/N 4555) No 435/436 Sqn, CAF, Edmonton, 1975–81.

130331, *73-1593* (C/N 4559) No 435/436 Sqn, CAF, Edmonton, 1975–81.

130332, *73-1596* (C/N 4568) No 435/436 Sqn, CAF, Edmonton, 1975–81.

130333, *73-1599* (C/N 4574) No 435/436 Sqn, CAF, Edmonton, 1975–81.

LOCKHEED MODEL 382C-34D C-130H HERCULES (for Israel) (C/Ns 4530 and 4533) Two standard military transports, USAF Nos *73-1600* and *73-1601* (registered *4X-FBC* and *4X-FBD*) for the Israel Defence Force/Air Force. Delivered 5-74.

4X-FBC, *73-1600* (C/N 4530) Carried IDFAF Nos '009' and '109'.

4X-FBD, *73-1601* (C/N 4533) Carried IDFAF No '011'; crashed at Jebel Halal, Sinai, 25-11-75.

LOCKHEED MODEL 382C-35D C-130H HERCULES (for Morocco) (C/Ns 4535, 4537, 4551, 4575, 4581 and 4583) Six standard military transports, re-registered *CN-AOA* to *CN-AOF*, for *Al Quwwat Aljawwiya Almalakiya Marakishiya* (Royal Maroc Air Force). Delivered between 5-74 and 3-75.

CN-AOA, (C/N 4535) Delivered 5-74; aircraft 'A', based at Kenitra.

CN-AOB, (C/N 4537) Delivered 5-74; aircraft 'B', based at Kenitra; written off, 12-76.

CN-AOC, (C/N 4551) Delivered 12-74; aircraft 'C', based at Kenitra.

CN-AOD, (C/N 4575) Delivered 2-75; aircraft 'D', based at Kenitra.

CN-AOE, (C/N 4581) Delivered 3-75; aircraft 'E', based at Kenitra; damaged in landing accident, 5-12-79.

CN-AOF (C/N 4583) Delivered 3-75; aircraft 'F', based at Kenitra.

LOCKHEED MODEL 382C-36D C-130H HERCULES (for Zaïre) (C/Ns 4569, 4588 and 4589) Three standard military transports, registered *9T-TCE*, *9T-TCF* and *9T-TCG*, for the *Force Aérienne Zaïroise* (FAZ, Zaïre Air Force). Delivered in 1975.

9T-TCE (C/N 4569) Delivered 1-75; 19 Wing, *1ere Groupement Aérien*, FAZ, Kinshasa, 1975–79; crashed on take-off, Kindu, 14-9-80.

9T-TCF (C/N 4588) Delivered 5-75; 19 Wing, *1ere Groupement Aérien*, FAZ Kinshasa, 1975–80.

9T-TCG (C/N 4589) Delivered 4-75; registered as *9T-TCC*. 19 Wing, *1ereGroupement Aérien*, FAZ, Kinshasa, 1975–80.

LOCKHEED MODEL 382C-37D C-130H HERCULES (for Iran) (C/Ns 4591 and 4594) Two standard military transports, IIAF Nos *5-157* and *5-158*, for the Imperial Iranian Air Force. Both delivered in 5-75.

5-157 (C/N 4591) No 5 ATS, IIAF, Shiraz; re-registered *5-8551*, 1976.

5-158 (C/N 4594) No 5 ATS, IIAF, Shiraz; re-registered *5-8552*, 1976.

LOCKHEED MODEL 382C-38D C-130H HERCULES (for Denmark) (C/Ns 4572, 4587 and 4599) Three standard military transports, USAF Nos *73-1678* to *73-1680* (RDAF Nos *B-678* to *B-680*). Delivered between 4-75 and 7-75.

B-678, *73-1678* (C/N 4572) *Eskadrille 721*, RDAF, Vaerlose, 1975–82.

B-679, *73-1679* (C/N 4587) *Eskadrille 721*, RDAF, Vaerlose, 1975–82.

B-680, *73-1680* (C/N 4599) *Eskadrille 721*, RDAF, Vaerlose, 1975–82.

LOCKHEED MODEL 382C-39D C-130H HERCULES (for Saudi Arabia) (C/Ns 4552, 4560, 4566 and 4567) Four standard military transports, RSAF Nos *1612*, *1614*, *460* and *461* respectively, for the Royal Saudi Air Force. Delivered between 9-74 and 12-74.

1612 (C/N 4552) Delivered 9-74; No 16 Sqn, RSAF, Jeddah, 1975–80.

1614 (C/N 4560) Delivered 12-74; No 16 Sqn, RSAF, Jeddah, 1975–80.

460 (C/N 4566) Delivered 12-74; No 4 Sqn, RSAF, Jeddah, 1975–80.

461 (C/N 4567) Delivered 12-74; No 4 Sqn, RSAF, Jeddah, 1975–80.

LOCKHEED MODEL 382C-40D C-130H HERCULES (for Abu Dhabi) (C/Ns 4580 and 4584) Two standard military transports, ADAF Nos *1211* and *1212*, for the Abu Dhabi Air Force (United Emirates Air Force); delivered 3-75 and 4-75.

1211 (C/N 4580) UEAF, Abu Dhabi, 1975–8∠.

1212 (C/N 4584) UEAF, Abu Dhabi, 1975–82.

LOCKHEED MODEL 382C-41D C-130H HERCULES (First 1974 USAF Appropriation for MAC) (C/Ns 4579, 4585, 4592, 4596 to 4598, 4603, 4604, 4611, 4613, 4616, 4617, 4620, 4621, 4623, 4627, 4631, 4640, 4643, 4645, 4646, 4651, 4654, 4657, 4658, 4663, 4666, 4669, 4670, 4675, 4681, 4682, 4687, 4688 and 4693) 36 standard military transports USAF Nos *74-1658* to *74-1693*. Allison T56A-15 turboprops; not fitted to accommodate ATO installation. Delivered between 3-75 and 10-76.

74-1658 (C/N 4579) Delivered 3-75. 463d TAW, Dyess AFB, Texas, 1975–82.

74-1659 (C/N 4585) Delivered 4-75. 463d TAW, Dyess AFB, Texas, 1975–82.

74-1660 (C/N 4592) Delivered 5-75. 463d TAW, Dyess AFB, Texas, 1975–82.

74-1661 (C/N 4596) Delivered 6-75. 463d TAW, Dyess AFB, Texas; loaned to Naval Surface Weapons Center, Silver Springs, Maryland, for tests with Cargo Aircraft Minelaying System (CAML), 1980–81.

74-1662 (C/N 4597) Delivered 6-75. 463d TAW, Dyess AFB, Texas, 1975–81.

74-1663 (C/N 4598) Delivered 6-75. 463d TAW, Dyess AFB, Texas, 1975–81.

74-1664 (C/N 4603) Delivered 7-75. 463d TAW, Dyess AFB, Texas, 1975–81.

74-1665 (C/N 4604) Delivered 7-75. 463d TAW, Dyess AFB, Texas, 1975–81.

74-1666 (C/N 4611) Delivered 8-75. 463d TAW, Dyess AFB, Texas, 1975–81.

74-1667 (C/N 4613) Delivered 8-75. 463d TAW, Dyess AFB, Texas, 1975–81.

74-1668 (C/N 4616) Delivered 9-75. 463d TAW, Dyess AFB, Texas, 1975–81.

74-1669 (C/N 4617) Delivered 9-75. 463d TAW, Dyess AFB, Texas, 1975–81.

74-1670 (C/N 4620) Delivered 9-75. 463d TAW, Dyess AFB, Texas, 1975–81.

74-1671 (C/N 4621) Delivered 9-75. 463d TAW, Dyess AFB, Texas, 1975–81.

74-1672 (C/N 4623) Delivered 10-75. 463d TAW, Dyess AFB, Texas, 1976–81; crashed on night landing at desert strip near Indian Springs AB, Nevada, 21-9-81.

74-1673 (C/N 4627) Delivered 10-75. 463d TAW, Dyess AFB, Texas, 1976–81.

74-1674 (C/N 4631) Delivered 11-75. 463d TAW, Dyess AFB, Texas, 1976–81.

74-1675 (C/N 4640) Delivered 12-75. 463d TAW, Dyess AFB, Texas, 1976–81.

74-1676 (C/N 4641) Delivered 1-76. 463d TAW, Dyess AFB, Texas, 1976–81.

74-1677 (C/N 4643) Delivered 1-76. 314th TAW, Little

Rock AFB, Arkansas, 1976; 463d TAW, Dyess AFB, Texas, 1977–82.

74-1678 (C/N 4645) Delivered 2-76. 463d TAW, Dyess AFB, Texas, 1977–81. Caught fire in the air, NE Turkey, 13-4-82.

74-1679 (C/N 4646) Delivered 2-76. 463d TAW, Dyess AFB, Texas, 1977–81.

74-1680 (C/N 4651) Delivered 3-76. 463d TAW, Dyess AFB, Texas, 1977–81.

74-1681 (C/N 4654) Delivered 3-76. 463d TAW, Dyess AFB, Texas, 1977–82.

74-1682 (C/N 4657) Delivered 4-76. 463d TAW, Dyess AFB, Texas, 1977–81.

74-1683 (C/N 4658) Delivered 4-76. 463d TAW, Dyess AFB, Texas, 1977–80. Was specially modified for operation to attempt rescue of US hostages in Iran, 1980; given air re-fuelling and short landing facility with two downwards-directed rockets. Crashed, 10-80, during landing demonstration when rocket programme computer malfunctioned and fired the rockets early; aircraft written off.

74-1684 (C/N 4663) Delivered 5-76. 463d TAW, Dyess AFB, Texas, 1977–81.

74-1685 (C/N 4666) Delivered 5-76. 463d TAW, Dyess AFB, Texas, 1977–82.

74-1686 (C/N 4669) Delivered 6-76. 463d TAW, Dyess AFB, Texas, 1976–81. Aircraft modified in similar manner to *74-1683* (C/N 4658), 1980.

74-1687 (C/N 4670) Delivered 6-76. 463d TAW, Dyess AFB, Texas, 1977–81.

74-1688 (C/N 4675) Delivered 6-76. 463d TAW, Dyess AFB, Texas, 1976–82.

74-1689 (C/N 4581) Delivered 8-76. 463d TAW, Dyess AFB, Texas, 1977–81.

74-1690 (C/N 4682) Delivered 8-76. 463d TAW, Dyess AFB, Texas, 1977–81; damaged in wheels-up landing at Lajes, Azores, early 1981, but repaired; again damaged in wheels-up landing at Cold Lake, Canada, 26-9-81.

74-1691 (C/N 4687) Delivered 9-76. 463d TAW, Dyess AFB, Texas, 1977–81.

74-1692 (C/N 4688) Delivered 9-76. 463d TAW, Dyess AFB, Texas, 1977–81.

74-1693 (C/N 4693) Delivered 10-76. 463d TAW, Dyess AFB, Texas, 1977–81.

LOCKHEED MODEL 382C-41D C-130H HERCULES (Second 1974 USAF Appropriation for MAC) (C/Ns 4644, 4647, 4655, 4659, 4667, 4671, 4678, 4694, 4699, 4700, 4703 and 4705) 12 standard military transports, USAF Nos *74-2061* to *74-2072*, general specification as for First 1974 Appropriation. Delivered between 1-76 and 12-76.

74-2061 (C/N 4644) Delivered 1-76. 463d TAW, Dyess AFB, Texas, 1977–81.

74-2062 (C/N 4647) Delivered 2-76. 463d TAW, Dyess AFB, Texas, 1977–81.

74-2063 (C/N 4655) Delivered 3-76. 463d TAW, Dyess AFB, Texas, 1977–81.

74-2064 (C/N 4659) Delivered 4-76. 463d TAW, Dyess AFB, Texas, 1977–80; crashed following fuel tank explosion on landing approach, Incirlik, Turkey, 14-3-80.

74-2065 (C/N 4667) Delivered 5-76. 314th TAW, Little Rock AFB, Arkansas, 1976; 463d TAW, Dyess AFB, Texas, 1976–81. Aircraft modified in similar manner to *74-1683* (C/N 4658), but stripped of equipment, 1981.

74-2066 (C/N 4671) Delivered 6-76. 463d TAW, Dyess

AFB, Texas, 1977–80; 21st TAS, 374th TAW, Clark AB, Philippines, 1981.

74-2067 (C/N 4678) Delivered 7-76. 463d TAW, Dyess AFB, Texas, 1977–81; 21st TAS, 374th TAW, Clark AB, Philippines, 1981.

74-2068 (C/N 4694) Delivered 10-76. 463d TAW, Dyess AFB, Texas, 1977–81.

74-2069 (C/N 4699) Delivered 11-76. 463d TAW, Dyess AFB, Texas, 1977–81.

74-2070 (C/N 4700) Delivered 12-76. 463d TAW, Dyess AFB, Texas, 1977–81.

74-2071 (C/N 4703) Delivered 11-76. 463d TAW, Dyess AFB, Texas, 1977–81.

74-2072 (C/N 4705) Delivered 12-76. 463d TAW, Dyess AFB, Texas, 1977–81.

LOCKHEED MODEL 382C-41D C-130H HERCULES (Third 1974 USAF Appropriation for MAC) (C/Ns 4711, 4718, 4722, 4730 and 4735) Five standard military transports, USAF Nos *74-2130* to *74-2134,* purchased to replace five aircraft diverted to Canada from 1973 Appropriations (C/Ns 4553, 4555, 4559, 4568 and 4574). General specification as for First 1974 Appropriation. Delivered between 1-77 and 5-77.

74-2130 (C/N 4711) Delivered 1-77. 463d TAW, Dyess AFB, Texas, 1977–81.

74-2131 (C/N 4718) Delivered 1-77. 463d TAW, Dyess AFB, Texas, 1977–81.

74-2132 (C/N 4722) Delivered 3-77. 463d TAW, Dyess AFB, Texas, 1977–81.

74-2133 (C/N 4730) Delivered 4-77. 463d TAW, Dyess AFB, Texas, 1977–81.

74-2134 (C/N 4735) Delivered 5-77. 463d TAW, Dyess AFB, Texas, 1977–81.

LOCKHEED MODEL 382C-42D C-130H HERCULES (for Venezuela) (C/Ns 4556 and 4577) Two standard military transports, FAV Nos *4224* and *5302,* for *Fuerza Aerea Venezolana* (FAV, Venezuela Air Force). Delivered in 1975.

4224 (C/N 4556) Delivered 2-75. Esc/1, *Grupo de transporte,* FAV, Caracas, 1976–81.

5302 (C/N 4577) Delivered 4-75. Esc/1, *Grupo de transporte,* FAV, Caracas, 1976–81.

LOCKHEED MODEL 382C-43D KC-130R HERCULES (C/Ns 4615, 4626, 4629, 4635, 4677, 4683, 4689 and 4696) Eight tankers, USAF Nos *74-1654* to *74-1657* and *75-0550* to *75-0553,* US Navy Nos *160013* to *160020),* for the US Marine Corps. Delivered in 1975–76.

160013, 74-1654 (C/N 4615) Delivered 9-75. Marine Corps Refuelling Squadron VMGR-352, MCAS El Toro, California, 1975–80.

160014, 74-1655 (C/N 4626) Delivered 10-75. VMGR-352, MCAS El Toro, 1975–80.

160015, 74-1656 (C/N 4629) Delivered 10-75. VMGR-352, MCAS El Toro, 1975–80.

160016, 74-1657 (C/N 4635) Delivered 11-75. VMGR-352, MCAS El Toro, 1975–80.

160017, 75-0550 (C/N 4677) Delivered 7-76. VMGR-352, MCAS El Toro, 1976–81.

160018, 75-0551 (C/N 4683) Delivered 8-76. VMGR-352, MCAS El Toro, 1977.

160019, 75-0552 (C/N 4689) Delivered 9-76. VMGR-352, MCAS El Toro, 1977.

160020, 75-0553 (C/N 4696) Delivered 10-76. VMGR-352, MCAS El Toro, 1977–80.

LOCKHEED MODEL 382G-30C L-100-30 HERCULES (for Gabon) (C/N 4582) One civil aircraft, registered *TR-KKA,* purchased by the Government of Gabon. 4.6 m fuselage stretch.

TR-KKA (C/N 4582) Delivered 4-75. Based at Libreville and employed in construction of Trans-Gabon Railway, 1975–80.

LOCKHEED MODEL 382G-31C L-100-30 HERCULES (for South Africa) (C/Ns 4558, 4562, 4565, 4590, 4600 and 4606) Six civil aircraft, registered *ZS-RSE* to *ZS-RSJ,* for commercial sale to Safair Freighters, South Africa; 4.6 m fuselage stretch.

ZS-RSE (C/N 4558) Delivered to Safair, 11-74; leased to Southern Air Transport, 1981.

ZS-RSF (C/N 4562) Delivered to Safair, 11-74; leased to Northwest Territorial Airways (NWT), 1978, as *C-FNWF.*

ZS-RSG (C/N 4565) Delivered to Safair, 12-74.

ZS-RSH (C/N 4590) Delivered to Safair, 5-75.

ZS-RSI (C/N 4600) Delivered to Safair, 6-75; leased to NWT, 1979, as *C-FNWY;* returned to Safair, 1980, as *ZS-RSI;* leased to SF Air, 1981, as *F-WDAQ,* and later as *F-GDAQ.*

ZS-RSJ (C/N 4606) Delivered to Safair, 7-75.

LOCKHEED MODEL 382G-32C L-100-30 HERCULES (C/Ns 4561 and 4586) Two civil aircraft, registered *N20ST* and *N21ST,* for commercial sale to Saturn Airways Inc; 4.6 m fuselage stretch.

N20ST (C/N 4561) Delivered 11-74 to Saturn; TIA, 12-76, thence TransAmerica, 1979.

N21ST (C/N 4586) Delivered 4-75 to Saturn; TIA, 12-76, thence TransAmerica, 1979.

LOCKHEED MODEL 382E-33C L-100-20 HERCULES (for Philippines) (C/N 4593) One civil aircraft, registered RP-C101, for commercial sale to the Government of the Republic of the Philippines; 2.5 m fuselage stretch.

RP-C101 (C/N 4593) Delivered to the Philippines Government, 5-75, for use by Philippine Aerospace Development Corp, PADC); leased to Philippine Aero Transport, 5-75; returned to PADC, 10-78.

LOCKHEED MODEL 382G-34C L-100-30 HERCULES (C/N 4610) One civil aircraft, registered *N108AK,* for commercial sale to Alaska International Air (AIA); 4.6 m fuselage stretch.

N108AK (C/N 4610) Completed 7-75. Purchased by AIA, then Page Airways Inc, but not delivered. Sold to Uganda Airlines and delivered direct, 8-75, as *5X-UCF.* To Uganda Air Cargo (*The Silver Lady*), 1981–82.

LOCKHEED MODEL 382G-35C L-100-30 HERCULES (for South Africa) (C/Ns 4673, 4676, 4679, 4684, 4691, 4695, 4698 and 4701) Eight civil aircraft registered *ZS-JIV, ZS-JVL, ZS-JIX, ZS-JIY, ZS-JIZ, ZS-JJA,* and *ZS-JVM,* for commercial sale to Safair Freighters, South Africa; 4.6 m fuselage stretch.

ZS-JIV (C/N 4673) Delivered to Safair, 7-76.

ZS-JVL (C/N 4676) Delivered to Safair, 7-76.

ZS-JIW (C/N 4679) Delivered to Safair, 7-76.

ZS-JIX (C/N 4684) Delivered to Safair, 8-76.

ZS-JIY (C/N 4691) Delivered to Safair, 9-76; leased to Air Botswana, 10-79, as *A2-ABZ.*

ZS-JIZ (C/N 4695) Delivered to Safair, 10-76.

ZS-JJA (C/N 4698) Delivered to Safair, 10-76.

ZS-JVM (C/N 4701) Delivered to Safair, 12-76; leased to Air Botswana, 10-79, as *A2-ACA*. Employed on Red Cross operations, 1980; relief supply flights to the Lebanon, 6-82 to 7-82.

LOCKHEED MODEL 382C-45D C-130H HERCULES (for Brazil) (C/Ns 4570, 4602 and 4630) Three standard military transports, FAB Nos *2463* to *2465;* for the *Fuerza Aerea Brasileira* (FAB, Brazilian Air Force). Delivery in 1975.

2463 (C/N 4570) Delivered 3-75. *1° Escuadrao, 1° Grupo*, FAB, Galeao, Rio de Janeiro, damaged while taxying after landing gear failure, Andrews AFB, 7-12-78.

2464 (C/N 4602) Delivered 7-75. *1° Escuadrao, 1° Grupo*, FAB, Galeao, Rio de Janeiro, 1975–80.

2465 (C/N 4630) Delivered 11-75. *2° Escuadrao, 1° Grupo*, FAB, Galeao, Rio de Janeiro, 1975–77; *2° Escuadrao, Grupo de Transporte de Tropas*, Campo dos Afoncos, 1978–79.

LOCKHEED MODEL 382C-46D C-130H HERCULES (for Saudi Arabia) (C/Ns 4605, 4607 to 4609, 4612, 4614, 4618, 4633, 4634 and 4637) Ten standard military transports, RSAF Nos *102, 463* to *465, 1601* to *1605* and *462* respectively, for the Royal Saudi Air Force. Delivered during 1975.

102 (C/N 4605) Delivered 7-75. VC-130H VIP aircraft; Royal Flight, No 1 Sqn, RSAF, Jeddah and Riyadh, 1975–80. Re-registered *111*, in 1977.

463 (C/N 4607) Delivered 7-75. No 4 Sqn, RSAF, Jeddah, 1975–80.

464 (C/N 4608) Delivered 7-75. No 4 Sqn, RSAF, Jeddah, 1975–80.

465 (C/N 4609) Delivered 8-75. No 4 Sqn, RSAF, Jeddah, 1975–80.

1601 (C/N 4612) Delivered 8-75. No 16 Sqn, RSAF, Jeddah, 1975–80.

1602 (C/N 4614) Delivered 9-75. No 16 Sqn, RSAF, Jeddah, 1975–80.

1603 (C/N 4618) Delivered 9-75. No 16 Sqn, RSAF, Jeddah, 1975–80.

1604 (C/N 4633) Delivered 11-75. No 16 Sqn, RSAF, Jeddah, 1976–80.

1605 (C/N 4634) Delivered 11-75. No 16 Sqn, RSAF, Jeddah, 1976–80.

462 (C/N 4637) Delivered 12-75. No 4 Sqn, RSAF, Jeddah, 1976–80.

LOCKHEED MODEL 382C-47D KC-130H HERCULES (for Brazil) (C/Ns 4625 and 4636) Two tanker aircraft, FAB Nos *2461* and *2462,* for the *Fuerza Aerea Brasileira* (FAB, Brazilian Air Force). Delivery in 1975.

2461 (C/N 4625) Delivered 10-75. *2° Esquadrao, 1° Grupo de Transporte*, FAB, Campo dos Afoncos, Rio de Janeiro, 1976–80.

2462 (C/N 4636) Delivered 11-75. *2° Esquadrao, 1° Grupo de Transporte*, FAB, Campo dos Afoncos, Rio de Janeiro, 1976–80.

LOCKHEED MODEL 382C-48D C-130H HERCULES (for Argentina) (C/Ns 4576 and 4578) Two standard military transports, FAA Nos *TC-67* and *TC-68,* for the *Fuerza Aerea Argentina* (FAA, Argentine Air Force). Delivery in 1975.

TC-67 (C/N 4576) Delivered 3-75. *1 Esc de Transporte, 1 Brigada Aerea*, FAA, El Palomar, 1975–81.

TC-68 (C/N 4578) Delivered 3-75. *1 Esc de Transporte, 1 Brigada Aerea*, FAA, El Palomar, 1975–81.

LOCKHEED MODEL 382C-49D C-130H HERCULES (for Nigeria) (C/Ns 4619, 4624, 4638, 4639, 4649 and 4650) Six standard military transports, FNAF Nos *910* to *915,* for the Federal Nigerian Air Force (FNAF). Delivery between 9-75 and 2-76.

910 (C/N 4619) Delivered 9-75. Re-registered in turn *AT-619* (7-77), *AT-450* (8-77), *ATG-619* (1979). Based at Lagos.

911 (C/N 4624) Delivered 10-75. Re-registered in turn *AT-634* (6-77), *AT-624* (8-77), *NAF911* (1978). Based at Lagos.

912 (C/N 4638) Delivered 12-75. Re-registered in turn *AT-744* (6-77), *AT-638* (8-77), *NAF912* (1978). Based at Lagos.

913 (C/N 4639) Delivered 1-76. Re-registered in turn *AT-639* (7-77), *NAF639* (1978), *NAF913* (10-78). Based at Lagos.

914 (C/N 4649) Delivered 2-76. Re-registered in turn *AT-649* (7-77), *NAF914* (8-78). Based at Lagos.

915 (C/N 4650) Delivered 2-76. Re-registered in turn *AT-650* (7-77), *NAF650* (8-78), *NAF915* (10-78). Based at Lagos.

LOCKHEED MODEL 382C-52D C-130H HERCULES (for Israel) (C/Ns 4653, 4662, 4668, 4680, 4686 and 4692) Six standard military transports, registered *4X-FBQ, 4X-FBS, 4X-FBT, 4X-FTU, 4X-FBW* and *4X-FBX*, for the Israel Defence Force/Air Force. Delivered in 1976.

4X-FBQ, *75-0534* (C/N 4653) Delivered 6-76. Carried IDF/AF No '420'. Damaged by wheelbrake fire, 1-79.

4X-FBS, *75-0535* (C/N 4662) Delivered 4-76. Carried IDF/AF No '427'.

4X-FBT, *75-0536* (C/N 4668) Delivered 5-76. Carried IDF/AF No '435'.

4X-FBU, *75-0537* (C/N 4680) Delivered 7-76. Carried IDF/AF No '448'.

4X-FBW, *75-0538* (C/N 4686) Delivered 8-76. Carried IDF/AF No '436'.

4X-FBX, *75-0539* (C/N 4692) Delivered 9-76. Carried IDF/AF No '428'.

LOCKHEED MODEL 382C-53D KC-130H HERCULES (for Israel) (C/Ns 4660 and 4664) Two tanker aircraft, USAF Nos *75-0540* and *75-0541* (registered *4X-FBY* and *4X-FBZ*), for the Israel Defence Force/Air Force. Delivery in 1976.

4X-FBY, *75-0540* (C/N 4660) Delivered 4-76. Carried IDF/AF No '422'.

4X-FBZ, *75-0541* (C/N 4664) Delivered 5-76. Carried IDF/AF No '455'.

LOCKHEED MODEL 382C-54D C-130H HERCULES (for Greece) (C/Ns 4622, 4632, 4665 and 4672) Four standard military transports, HAF Nos *741* to *744,* for the *Elliniki Aéroporia* (Hellenic Air Force, HAF). Delivery in 1975–76.

741 (C/N 4622) Delivered 9-75. No 355/356 *Mira*, HAF, Eleusis, 1976–82.

742 (C/N 4632) Delivered 10-75. No 335/356 *Mira*, HAF, Eleusis, 1976–82.

743 (C/N 4665) Delivered 5-76. No 355/356 *Mira*, HAF, Eleusis, 1976–82.

744 (C/N 4672) Delivered 6-76. No 355/356 *Mira*, HAF, Eleusis, 1976–82.

LOCKHEED MODEL 382C-55D KC-130H (TK-10) HERCULES (for Spain) (C/Ns 4642, 4648 and 4652) Three tanker aircraft, SpAF Nos *TK10-5* to *TK10-7,* for the

Ejército del Aire (Spanish Air Force, EdA). Delivery in 1976.
TK10-5 (C/N 4642) Delivered 1-76. *Escuadron 301, Mando Aviacion Tactica,* EdA, Valenzuela-Zaragoza ('301-05'), 1976–78; *Escuadron 312,* MAT, EdA, 1979–81.
TK10-6 (C/N 4648) Delivered 2-76. *Escuadron 301,* MAT, Eda, Valenzuela-Zaragoza ('301-06'), 1976–78; *Escuadron 312,* MAT, EdA, 1979–81.
TK10-7 (C/N 4652) Delivered 3-76. *Escuadron 301,* MAT, EdA, Valenzuela-Zaragoza ('301-07'), 1976–78; *Escuadron 312,* MAT, EdA, 1979–81.

LOCKHEED MODEL 382C-56D C-130H HERCULES (for Sweden) (C/N 4628) One standard military transport, *Flygvapnet* No *84003,* for *Flygvapnet* (Swedish Air Force). Delivered 10-75.
84003 (C/N 4628) *Flygflottilj 7, Flygvapnet,* Satenäs, 1976–82.

LOCKHEED MODEL 382C-57D C-130H HERCULES (for Malaysia) (C/Ns 4656, 4661, 4674, 4685, 4690 and 4697) Six standard military transports, RMAF Nos *FM-2401* to *FM-2406,* for the *Tentara Udara Diraja Malaysia* (Royal Malaysian Air Force, RMAF). Delivery 1976.
FM-2401 (C/N 4656) Delivered 3-76. No 14 Sqn, RMAF, Kuala Lumpur, 1976–80.
FM-2402 (C/N 4661) Delivered 4-76. No 14 Sqn, RMAF, Kuala Lumpur, 1976–80.
FM-2403 (C/N 4674) Delivered 6-76. No 14 Sqn, RMAF, Kuala Lumpur, 1976–80.
FM-2404 (C/N 4685) Delivered 7-76. No 14 Sqn, RMAF, Kuala Lumpur, 1976–80.
FM-2405 (C/N 4690) Delivered 8-76. No 14 Sqn, RMAF, Kuala Lumpur, 1977–80.
FM-2406 (C/N 4697) Delivered 10-76. No 14 Sqn, RMAF, Kuala Lumpur, 1977–80.

LOCKHEED MODEL 382C-58D KC-130R HERCULES (C/Ns 4702 and 4712) Two tanker aircraft, USAF Nos 75-0554 and 75-0555 (US Navy Nos *160020* and *160021*), for the US Marine Corps. Delivered in 1976–77.
160020, *75-0554* (C/N 4702) Delivered 11-76. VMGR-352, MCAS El Toro, California, 1977–80.
160021, *75-0555* (C/N 4712) Delivered 1-77. VMGR-352, MCAS El Toro, California, 1977–80.

LOCKHEED MODEL 382C-59D C-130H HERCULES (for Greece) (C/Ns 4716, 4720, 4723, 4724, 4727, 4729, 4732 and 4734) Eight standard transports, USAF Nos *75-0542* to *75-0549* (HAF Nos *745* to *752), for the Elliniki Aéroporia* (Hellenic Air Force, HAF). Delivery in 1977.
745, *75-0542* (C/N 4716) Delivered 1-77. No 355/356 *Mira,* HAF, Eleusis, 1977–82.
746, *75-0543* (C/N 4720) Delivered 2-77. No 355/356 *Mira,* HAF, Eleusis, 1977–82.
747, *75-0544* (C/N 4723) Delivered 3-77. No 355/356 *Mira,* HAF, Eleusis, 1977–82.
748, *75-0545* (C/N 4724) Delivered 3-77. No 355/356 *Mira,* HAF, Eleusis, 1977–82.
749, *75-0546* (C/N 4727) Delivered 4-77. No 355/356 *Mira,* HAF, Eleusis, 1977–82.
750, *75-0547* (C/N 4729) Delivered 4-77. No 355/356 *Mira,* HAF, Eleusis, 1977–82.
751, *75-0548* (C/N 4732) Delivered 5-77. No 355/356 *Mira,* HAF, Eleusis, 1977–82.
752, *75-0549* (C/N 4734) Delivered 5-77. No 355/356 *Mira,* HAF, Eleusis, 1977–82.

LOCKHEED MODEL 382C-60D C-130H HERCULES

(for Saudi Arabia) (C/Ns 4737, 4740, 4741, 4745, 4751, 4754 to 4756, and 4758) Nine standard transports, RSAF Nos *112, 466, 467, 1615, 468, 469, 1618, 1619* and *470* respectively, for the Royal Saudi Air Force (RSAF). Delivery in 1977.
112 (C/N 4737) delivered 6-77. Became VC-130H VIP transport (mod by Lockheed Aircraft Service); No 1 Sqn, RSAF, Riyadh. Damaged by fire in wheel bay, 1981, but repaired.
466 (C/N 4740) Delivered 6-77. No 4 Sqn, RSAF, Jeddah, 1977–80.
467 (C/N 4741) Delivered 6-77. No 4 Sqn, RSAF, Jeddah, 1977–80.
1615 (C/N 4745) Delivered 7-77. No 16 Sqn, RSAF, Jeddah, 1977–80.
468 (C/N 4751) Delivered 8-77. No 4 Sqn, RSAF, Jeddah, 1977–80.
469 (C/N 4754) Delivered 9-77. No 4 Sqn, RSAF, Jeddah, 1977–80.
1618 (C/N 4755) Delivered 9-77. No 16 Sqn, RSAF, Jeddah, 1977–80.
1619 (C/N 4756) Delivered 10-77. No 16 Sqn, RSAF, Jeddah, 1977–80.
470 (C/N 4758) Delivered 10-77. No 4 Sqn, RSAF, Jeddah, 1977–80.

LOCKHEED MODEL 382C-61D KC-130H HERCULES (for Saudi Arabia) (C/Ns 4746 and 4750) Two tanker aircraft, RSAF Nos *1616* and *1617,* for the Royal Saudi Air Force (RSAF). Delivery in 1977.
1616 (C/N 4746) Delivered 7-77. No 16 Sqn, RSAF, Jeddah, 1977–81.
1617 (C/N 4750) Delivered 9-77. No 16 Sqn, RSAF, Jeddah, 1977–81.

LOCKHEED MODEL 382C-63D C-130H HERCULES (for Philippines) (C/Ns 4704 and 4726) Two standard military transports, PhAF Nos '*4704*' and '*4726*', for the Philippines Air Force. Delivered in 1976–77.
'4704' (C/N 4704) Delivered 11-76. 222nd Heavy Lift Sqn, 205th Heavy Lift Wing, Mactan AB, 1977–81.
'4726' (C/N 4726) Delivered 8-77. 222nd Heavy Lift Sqn, 205th Heavy Lift Wing, Mactan AB, 1977–81.

LOCKHEED MODEL 382C-64D C-130H HERCULES (for Egypt) (C/Ns 4707, 4709, 4714, 4719, 4721 and 4728) Six standard military transports, USAF Nos *76-1598* to *76-1603* (registered *SU-BAA* to *SU-BAF*), for the Air Force of the Arab Republic of Egypt (AFARE). Delivery in 1976–77.
SU-BAA, *1270, 76-1598* (C/N 4707) Delivered 12-76. AFARE Transport Wing, Cairo West. Participated in commando raid against terrorists at Larnaca, Cyprus, 19-2-78; severely damaged by fire and written off.
SU-BAB, *1271, 76-1599* (C/N 4709) Delivered 12-76. AFARE Transport Wing, Cairo West, 1977–82.
SU-BAC, *1272, 76-1600* (C/N 4714) Delivered 1-77. AFARE Transport Wing, Cairo West, 1977–82.
SU-BAD, *1273, 76-1601* (C/N 4719) Delivered 1-77. AFARE Transport Wing, Cairo West, 1977–82.
SU-BAE, *1274, 76-1602* (C/N 4271) Delivered 3-77. AFARE Transport Wing, Cairo West, 1977–82.
SU-BAF, *1275, 76-1603* (C/N 4728) Delivered 1-77. AFARE Transport Wing, Cairo West, 1977–82.

LOCKHEED MODEL 382C-65D LC-130R HERCULES (C/Ns 4725 and 4731) Two ski-equipped transports, USAF Nos *76-0491* and *76-0492,* US Navy Nos *160740* and *160741,* purchased for the US National Science

Foundation (NSF) and operated by the US Navy. Delivered in 1977.

***160740**, 76-0491* (C/N 4725) Delivered 4-77. US Navy Squadron VXE-6, Christchurch, New Zealand ('XD-2'), 1977–82.

***160741**, 76-0492* (C/N 4731) Delivered 5-77. VXE-6. Christchurch, New Zealand, ('XD-1'), 1977–82.

LOCKHEED MODEL 382C-66D C-130H HERCULES (for Zaïre) (C/N 4736) One standard military transport, registered *9T-TCG*, for the *Force Aérienne Zaïroise* (Zaïre Air Force, ZAF). Delivered in 1977.

9T-TCG (C/N 4736) Delivered 5-77. 19 Wing, *1ere Groupement Aérien*, Kinshasa, 1977–79.

LOCKHEED MODEL 382C-67D C-130H HERCULES (for Morocco) (C/Ns 4713, 4717, 4733, 4738, 4739 and 4742) Six standard military transports, registered *CN-AOG* to *CN-AOL*, for *Al Quwwat Aljawwiya Almalakiya Marakishiya* (Royal Maroc Air Force). Delivery in 1977.

CN-AOG (C/N 4713) Delivered 1-77. Aircraft 'G', based at Kenitra, 1977–80.

CN-AOH (C/N 4717) Delivered 2-77. Aircraft 'H', based at Kenitra; shot down by SAM fired by Polisario rebels, Guelta Zemmour, West Sahara, 1981.

***CN-AOI*,** (C/N 4733) Delivered 8-77. Aircraft 'I', based at Kenitra, 1977–80.

CN-AOJ (C/N 4738) Delivered 6-77. Aircraft 'J', based at Kenitra, 1977–81.

CN-AOK (C/N 4739) Delivered 6-77. Aircraft 'K', based at Kenitra; damaged wing in taxying collision with hangar, Bierset, Belgium, 14-7-81.

CN-AOL (C/N 4742) Delivered 7-77. Aircraft 'L', based at Kenitra, 1977–80.

LOCKHEED MODEL 382C-68D KC-130R HERCULES (C/Ns 4768, 4770, 4773 and 4776) Four tanker aircraft, USAF Nos *77-0321* to *77-0324*, US Navy Nos *160625* to *160628*, for the US Marine Corps. Delivery in 1978.

***160625**, 77-0321* (C/N 4768) Marine Refuelling Squadron VMGR-252, MCAS Cherry Point, North Carolina, 1978–81.

***160626**, 77-0322* (C/N 4770) VMGR-252, MCAS Cherry Point, North Carolina, 1978–81.

***160627**, 77-0323* (C/N 4773) VMGR-252, MCAS Cherry Point, North Carolina, 1978–81.

***160628**, 77-0324* (C/N 4776) VMGR-252, MCAS Cherry Point, North Carolina, 1978–81.

LOCKHEED MODEL 382C-69D C-130H HERCULES (for Cameroon) (C/Ns 4747 and 4752) Two standard military transports, registered *TJ-XAC* and *TJ-XAD*, for *l'Armée de l'Air du Cameroun* (Air Force of the Cameroon Republic, AFCR). Delivery in 1977.

TJ-XAC (C/N 4747) Delivered 8-77. Based at Douala, 1977–82.

TJ-XAD (C/N 4752) Delivered 9-77. Based at Douala, 1977–82.

LOCKHEED MODEL 382C-70D HC-130H HERCULES (C/Ns 4757, 4760, 4762 and 4764) Four search and rescue aircraft, USAF Nos *77-0317* to *77-0320*, USCG Nos *CG1600* to *CG1603*, for the US Coast Guard. Delivery in 1977.

***77-0317**, CG1600* (C/N 4757) Delivered 10-77. Based at Kodiak, Alaska, *c*1979. Crashed 3 miles S Attu airport, Aleutian Islands, 30-7-82.

***77-0318**, CG1601* (C/N 4760) Delivered 11-77. Based at Kodiak, Alaska, *c*1978–79.

***77-0319**, CG1602* (C/N 4762) Delivered 11-77. Based at Kodiak, Alaska, *c*1978–79.

***77-0320**, CG1603* (C/N 4764) Delivered 12-77. Based at Kodiak, Alaska, *c*1978–79.

LOCKHEED MODEL 382C-71D C-130H HERCULES (for Australia) (C/Ns 4780, 4782 to 4791, and 4793) 12 standard military transports, RAAF Nos *A97-001* to *A97-012*, for the Royal Australian Air Force. Delivery in 1978, replacing C-130As.

***A97-001**, 7T-0001* (C/N 4780) Delivered 7-78; No 36 Sqn, Richmond, NSW, 1978–82.

***A97-002**, 7T-0002* (C/N 4782) Delivered 7-78; No 36 Sqn, Richmond, NSW, 1978–82.

***A97-003**, 7T-0003* (C/N 4783) Delivered 7-78; No 36 Sqn, Richmond, NSW, 1978–82.

***A97-004**, 7T-0004* (C/N 4784) Delivered 8-78; No 36 Sqn, Richmond, NSW, 1978–82.

***A97-005**, 7T-0005* (C/N 4785) Delivered 8-78; No 36 Sqn, Richmond, NSW, 1978–83.

***A97-006**, 7T-0006* (C/N 4786) Delivered 8-78; No 36 Sqn, Richmond, NSW, 1978–82.

***A97-007**, 7T-0007* (C/N 4787) Delivered 8-78; No 36 Sqn, Richmond, NSW, 1978–82.

***A97-008**, 7T-0008* (C/N 4788) Delivered 9-78; No 36 Sqn, Richmond, NSW, 1978–83.

***A97-009**, 7T-0009* (C/N 4789) Delivered 9-78; No 36 Sqn, Richmond, NSW, 1979–83.

***A97-010**, 7T-0010* (C/N 4790) Delivered 9-78; No 36 Sqn, Richmond, NSW, 1979–83.

***A97-011**, 7T-0011* (C/N 4791) Delivered 10-78; No 36 Sqn, Richmond, NSW, 1978–83.

***A97-012**, 7T-0012* (C/N 4793) Delivered 10-78; No 36 Sqn, Richmond, NSW, 1979–83.

LOCKHEED MODEL 382C-72D C-130H HERCULES (for Bolivia) (C/Ns 4744 and 4759) Two standard military transports, FABol Nos *TAM-90* and *TAM-91*, for the *Fuerza Aérea Boliviana* (FABol). Delivery in 1977.

TAM-90 (C/N 4744) Delivered 7-77 and operated by *Transportes Aéreos Militares* (TAM) as *CP-1375*; crashed during night take-off at Panama-Tacumen, 28-9-79.

TAM-91 (C/N 4759) Delivered 10-77 and operated by TAM as *CP-1376*, 1978–81.

LOCKHEED MODEL 382C-73D C-130H HERCULES (for Portugal) (C/Ns 4749 and 4753) Two standard military transports, FAP Nos *6801* and *6802*, for the *Forca Aérea Portuguesa* (Portuguese Air Force, FAP). Delivered 1977.

6801 (C/N 4749) Delivered 8-77. *Esquadra* 501, FAP, Montijo, 1978–81.

6802 (C/N 4753) Delivered 9-77. *Esquadra* 501, FAP, Montijo, 1978–81.

LOCKHEED MODEL 382C-74D C-130H HERCULES (for Ecuador) (C/Ns 4743 and 4748) Two standard military transports, FAE Nos *743* and *748*; for the *Fuerza Aerea Ecuatoriana* (Ecuador Air Force, FAE). Delivered in 1977.

743 (C/N 4743) Delivered 7-77. No 11 Sqn, FAE, 1977–81; registered *HC-SAN*, 1980. Hit mountain near Quito, 29-4-82.

748 (C/N 4748) Delivered 8-77. No 11 Sqn, FAE, 1977–78; crashed in the Pichincha Mountains, Ecuador, 12-7-78.

LOCKHEED MODEL 382C-75D EC-130Q HERCULES (C/N 4781) One communications aircraft, US Navy Nos *160608*, for the US Navy, delivered in 1978 for communication with nuclear submarines.

160608 (C/N 4781) TACAMO programme. Navy Squadron VQ-4, NAS Patuxent River, Maryland, 1978–80.

LOCKHEED MODEL 382E-36C L-100-20 HERCULES (for Gabon) (C/N 4710) One civil aircraft, registered *TR-KKB*, for Gabon; delivered in 1976.

TR-KKB (C/N 4710) Delivered 12-76. Based at Libreville, 1977–82, and employed in the construction of the Trans Gabon Railway. Leased to Pelita for transmigration.

LOCKHEED MODEL 382E-37C L-100-20 HERCULES (for Peru) (C/Ns 4706, 4708 and 4715) Three civil aircraft, FAP Nos *382*, *383* and *384*, purchased by the Peruvian Government for use by the *Fuerza Aérea del Peruviana* (Peruvian Air Force, FAP), in 1976–77. 2.5 m fuselage stretch.

382 (C/N 4706) Delivered 12-76. Based at Jorge Chavez, 1977–80.

383 (C/N 4708) Delivered 12-76. Based at Jorge Chavez, 1977–80.

384 (C/N 4715) Delivered 1-77. Based at Jorge Chavez, 1977–80.

LOCKHEED MODEL 382G-38C L-100-30 HERCULES (C/N 4763) One civil aircraft, registered *N108AK*, for commercial sale by Lockheed Aircraft Corporation in 1977. 4.6 m fuselage stretch.

N108AK (C/N 4763) Delivered 11-77 to Alaska International Air. Sold to Cargomasters, 8-82, as *VH-CYO*

LOCKHEED MODEL 382G-39C L-100-30 HERCULES (for Zaïre) (C/N 4796) One civil aircraft, registered *9Q-CBJ*, for commercial sale by Lockheed Aircraft Corporation in 1978. 4.6 m fuselage stretch.

9Q-CBJ (C/N 4796) Delivered 11-78 to SCIBE-Zaïre, 1978–82.

LOCKHEED MODEL 382G-40C L-100-30 HERCULES (C/N 4798) One civil aircraft, registered *N4301M*, for commercial sale by Lockheed Aircraft Corporation in 1978. 4.6 m fuselage stretch.

N4301M (C/N 4798) Completed 11-78. Sold to AIA, 4-79, as *N501AK*. Sold to United Trade International, thence to Pan Aviation Inc, Miami, 1-81. Sold to United African Airlines, 10-82, as *5A-DJQ*.

LOCKHEED MODEL 382G-41C L-100-30 HERCULES (for Indonesia) (C/N 4800) One civil aircraft, Indonesian AF No *A-1314*, for commercial sale to the Government of the Republic of Indonesia. Equipped as VIP transport and operated by *Tentara Nasional Indonesia-Angkatan Udara* (Indonesian Air Force, TNI-AU). Delivery in 1978. 4.6 m fuselage stretch.

A-1314 (C/N 4800) Delivered 12-78. Frequently operated by No 31 Sqn, TNI-AU, Halim, 1979–81.

LOCKHEED MODEL 382G-42C L-100-30 HERCULES (for Canada) (C/N 4799) One civil aircraft, registered *C-GHPH*, for commercial sale to Pacific Western Airlines (PWA). Delivery in 1978. 4.6 m fuselage stretch.

C-GHPH (C/N 4799) Delivered to PWA, 12-78.

LOCKHEED MODEL 382G-43C L-100-30 HERCULES (C/Ns 4824, 4826 and 4828) Three civil aircraft, registered *PK-PLU* to *PK-PLW*, for commercial sale to the Mitsui Corporation in 1979. 4.6 m fuselage stretch.

PK-PLU (C/N 4824) Delivered 7-79 to Mitsui Corp; leased to Pelita Air Service (*Bina*), 7-79.

PK-PLV (C/N 4826) Delivered 8-79 to Mitsui Corp; leased

to Pelita Air Service (*Hanonen*), 8-79.

PK-PLW (C/N 4828) delivered 9-79 to Mitsui Corp; leased to Pelita Air Service (*Sentiaki*), 9-79.

LOCKHEED MODEL 382E-44C L-100-20 HERCULES (C/Ns 4830 and 4832) Two civil aircraft, registered *N4080M* and *N4081M*, for commercial sale by Lockheed Aircraft Corporation in 1979. 2.5 m fuselage stretch.

N4080M (C/N 4830) Completed 9-79. Sold and delivered to TAAG-Angola Airlines, 10-79, as *D2-EAS*. Shot down by heat-seeking missile near Mongua, Angola, 16-5-81.

N4081M (C/N 4832) Completed 10-79. Sold and delivered to TAAG-Angola Airlines, 10-79, as *D2-THA*.

LOCKHEED MODEL 382G-45C L-100-30 HERCULES (for Bolivia) (C/N 4833) One civil aircraft, registered *N4083M*, for commercial sale by the Lockheed Aircraft Corporation in 1979. 4.6 m fuselage stretch.

N4083M (C/N 4833) Sold to Bolivian Government, 10-79, and flown by the Bolivian Air Force; leased to *Transporte Aereo Boliviano*, 10-79, as *CP1564*.

LOCKHEED MODEL 382C-76D C-130H HERCULES (for Sudan) (C/Ns 4766, 4767, 4769, 4771, 4774 and 4775) Six standard military transports, Sudan AF Nos *1100* to *1105*, for *Al-Jawwiya As-Sudaniya* (Sudan Air Force). Delivery in 1978.

***1100*, 78-0745** (C/N 4766) Delivered 1-78. Also flown by Sudan Airways as *ST-AHR*.

***1101*, 78-0746** (C/N 4767) Delivered 2-78. Sudan AF, probably based at Khartoum.

***1102*, 78-0747** (C/N 4769) Delivered 3-78. Sudan AF, 1978–81. (Was the 1,500th Hercules completed).

***1103*, 78-0748** (C/N 4771) Delivered 4-78. Sudan AF, 1978–81.

***1104*, 78-0749** (C/N 4774) Delivered 5-78. Sudan AF, 1978–81.

***1105*, 78-0750** (C/N 4775) Delivered 5-78. Sudan AF, 1978–81.

LOCKHEED MODEL 382C-77D C-130H HERCULES (for Philippines) (C/N 4761) One standard military transport, PhAF No *'4761'*, for the Philippine Air Force. Delivery in 1977.

'4761' (C/N 4761) Delivered 11-77. 222d Heavy Airlift Sqn, 205th Heavy Airlift Wing, PhAF, Mactan AB, 1978–81.

LOCKHEED MODEL 382C-78D C-130H HERCULES (for Portugal) (C/Ns 4772, 4777 and 4778) Three standard military transports, FAP Nos *6803* to *6805*, for the *Forca Aérea Portuguesa* (FAP, Portuguese Air Force). Delivery in 1978.

6803 (C/N 4772) Delivered *c*4-78. *Esquadra* 501, FAP, Montijo, 1978–81.

6804 (C/N 4777 Delivered *c*6-78. *Esquadra* 501, FAP, Montijo, 1978–81.

6805 (C/N 4778) Delivered *c*6-78. *Esquadra* 501, FAP, Montijo, 1978–81.

LOCKHEED MODEL 382C-79D C-130H HERCULES (for Gabon) (C/N 4765) One standard military transport, civil registered *TR-KKC*, for Gabon; delivery in 1977.

TR-KKC (C/N 4765) Delivered 12-77. Based at Libreville, 1978–82, and employed in the construction of the Trans Gabon Railway.

LOCKHEED MODEL 382C-80D C-130H HERCULES (1978 USAF Appropriations for the Air National Guard). (C/Ns 4815 and 4817 to 4823) Eight standard military transports, USAF Nos *78-0806* to *78-0813*, for the US Air

National Guard (ANG). Specification essentially as for the 1962 USAF Appropriations, as progressively updated. Delivery in 1979.

78-0806 (C/N 4815) Delivered 6-79. 185th TAS, 137th TAW, Oklahoma ANG, 1979–81.

78-0807 (C/N 4817) Delivered 5-79. 185th TAS, 137th TAW, Oklahoma ANG, 1979–81.

78-0808 (C/N 4818) Delivered 5-79. 185th TAS, 137th TAW, Oklahoma ANG, 1979–81.

78-0809 (C/N 4819) Delivered 6-79. 185th TAS, 137th TAW, Oklahoma ANG, 1979–81.

78-0810 (C/N 4820) Delivered 6-79. 185th TAS, 137th TAW, Oklahoma ANG, 1979–81; underwent flight tests with drag-reducing ventral fins.

78-0811 (C/N 4821) Delivered 6-79. 185th TAS, 137th TAW, Oklahoma ANG, 1979–81.

78-0812 (C/N 4822) Delivered 7-79. 185th TAS, 137th TAW, Oklahoma ANG, 1979–81.

78-0813 (C/N 4823) Delivered 7-79. 185th TAS, 137th TAW, Oklahoma ANG, 1979–81.

LOCKHEED MODEL 382C-81D C-130H HERCULES (for Egypt) (C/Ns 4792, 4794, 4795, 4797 and 4802 to 4811) 14 standard military transports for the Egyptian Air Force (USAF Nos *78-0755* to *78-0768*, EAF Nos *1276* to *1289*, registered *SU-BAH* to *SU-BAV*). Delivered between 10-78 and 3-79.

1276, *78-0755* (C/N 4792, *SU-BAH*) Delivered 10-78. Crashed with ammunition load after take-off from Cairo-West, 5-81.

1277, *78-0756* (C/N 4794, *SU-BAI*) Delivered 10-78; based Cairo-West, 1979–82.

1278, *78-0757* (C/N 4795, *SU-BAJ*) Delivered 11-78; based Cairo-West, 1979–81.

1279, *78-0758* (C/N 4797, *SU-BAK*) Delivered 11-78; based Cairo-West, 1980–81.

1280, *78-0759* (C/N 4802, *SU-BAL*) Delivered 1-79; based Cairo-West, 1980–81.

1281, *78-0760* (C/N 4803, *SU-BAM*) Delivered 1-79; based Cairo-West, 1980–81.

1282, *78-0761* (C/N 4804, *SU-BAN*) Delivered 1-79; based Cairo-West, 1980–81.

1283, *78-0762* (C/N 4805, *SU-BAP*) Delivered 1-79; based Cairo-West, 1980–81.

1284, *78-0763* (C/N 4806, *SU-BAQ*) Delivered 2-79; based Cairo-West, 1980. Evacuated Palestinian wounded, Cyprus to Egypt, 18-12-83.

1285, *78-0764* (C/N 4807, *SU-BAR*) Delivered 2-79; based Cairo-West, 1980–82.

1286, *78-0765* (C/N 4808, *SU-BAS*) Delivered 2-79; based Cairo-West, 1980–82.

1287, *78-0766* (C/N 4809, *SU-BAT*) Delivered 3-79; based Cairo-West, 1981–82.

1288, *78-0767* (C/N 4810, *SU-BAU*) Delivered 3-79; based Cairo-West, 1981–82.

1289, *78-0768* (C/N 4811, *SU-BAV*) Delivered 3-79; based Cairo-West, 1981.

LOCKHEED MODEL 382C-82D KC-130H HERCULES (for Argentina) (C/Ns 4814 and 4816) Two tanker aircraft for the *Fuerza Aerea Argentina* (FAA Nos *TC-69* and *TC-70*).

TC-69 (C/N 4814) Delivered 4-79; based El Palomar, 1979–82.

TC-70 (C/N 4816) Delivered 5-79; based El Palomar, 1979–82.

LOCKHEED MODEL 382C-83D C-130H HERCULES (for Jordan) (C/N 4779) One standard military transport for the Royal Jordanian Air Force (RJAF No *144*).

144 (C/N 4779) Delivered *c*6-78. No 3 Sqn, RJAF, Amman; re-registered *744*, and later *344*.

LOCKHEED MODEL 382C-84D C-130H HERCULES (for Venezuela) (C/N 4801) One standard military transport for the *Fuerza Aerea Venezolana* (FAV No *3134*).

3134 (C/N 4801) Delivered 12-78; Esc/1, *Grupo de Transporte*, Caracas, 1979–80.

LOCKHEED MODEL 382C-85D EC-130Q HERCULES (C/Ns 4867, 4896, 4901, 4904 and 4832) Five communications aircraft for the US Navy Nos *161223*, *161494* to *161496* and *161531*. Delivered between 12-80 and 9-82.

161223 (C/N 4867) Delivered 12-80. Employed in TACAMO operations, 1981–82.

161494 (C/N 4896) Delivered 9-81. Employed in TACAMO operations, 1981–82.

161495 (C/N 4901) Delivered 10-81. Employed in TACAMO operations, 1982

161496 (C/N 4904) Delivered 11-81. Employed in TACAMO operations, 1982

161531 (C/N 4932) Delivered 9-82. Employed in TACAMO operations, 1982–83.

LOCKHEED MODEL 382C-86D C-130H HERCULES (for Yemen) (C/Ns 4825 and 4827) Two standard military transports for the Yemen Arab Republic Air Force (YARAF Nos *1150* and *1160*).

1150 (C/N 4825) Delivered 1-80; based at Hodeida, 1980–81.

1160 (C/N 4827) Delivered 1-80; based at Hodeida, 1980–81.

LOCKHEED MODEL 382C-87D C-130H HERCULES (for Ecuador) (C/N 4812) One standard transport for the *Fuerza Aerea Ecuatoriana* (FAE No *FAE-812*).

FAE-812 (C/N 4812) Delivered 4-79. Replaced aircraft lost in 1978 (C/N 4748); based at Quito.

LOCKHEED MODEL 382C-88D C-130H HERCULES (1979 USAF Appropriations for the Air National Guard). (C/Ns 4852 and 4854 to 4860) Eight standard military transports, USAF Nos *79-0473* to *79-0480*, updated specification, but otherwise similar to 1962 USAF Appropriations. Delivery in 1980.

79-0473 (C/N 4852) Delivered 5-80. 183d TAS, 172d TAG, Mississippi ANG, 1980–82.

79-0474 (C/N 4854) Delivered 5-80. 183d TAS, 172d TAG, Mississippi ANG, 1980–82.

79-0475 (C/N 4855) Delivered 6-80. 183d TAS, 172d TAG, Mississippi ANG, 1980–82.

79-0476 (C/N 4856) Delivered 6-80. 183d TAS, 172d TAG, Mississippi ANG, 1980–82.

79-0477 (C/N 4857) Delivered 6-80. 183d TAS, 172d TAG, Mississippi ANG, 1980–82.

79-0478 (C/N 4858) Delivered 7-80. 183d TAS, 172d TAG, Mississippi ANG, 1980–82.

79-0479 (C/N 4859) Delivered 7-80. 183d TAS, 172d TAG, Mississippi ANG, 1980–82.

79-0480 (C/N 4860) Delivered 7-80. 183d TAS, 172d TAG, Mississippi ANG, 1980–82.

LOCKHEED MODEL 382C-89D C-130H HERCULES (for Jordan) (C/N 4813) One standard military transport for the Royal Jordanian Air Force (RJAF No *345*).

345 (C/N 4813) Delivered 4-79; No 3 Sqn, RJAF, Amman, 1979–81.

LOCKHEED MODEL 382C-90D C-130H HERCULES (for Niger) (C/Ns 4829 and 4831) Two standard military transports for the *Force Aérienne du Niger* (registered *5U-MBD* and *5U-MBH).*

5U-MBD (C/N 4829) Delivered 1-80; based at Niamey, 1980–81.

5U-MBH (C/N 4831) Delivered 1-80; based at Niamey, 1980–81.

LOCKHEED MODEL 382C-92D C-130H (T-10) HERCULES (for Spain) (C/Ns 4835 and 4836) Two standard military transports for the *Ejército del Aire* (EdA Nos *T10-8* and *T10-9*).

T10-8, *311-05* (C/N 4835) Delivered 11-79; *Escuadron* 311, 1980–82.

T10-9, *311-06* (C/N 4836) Delivered 11-79; *Escuadron* 311, 1980–82.

LOCKHEED MODEL 382-93D C-130H HERCULES (for Saudi Arabia) (C/N 4837) One transport for the Royal Saudi Air Force (RSAF No *MS 019*). Modified by Lockheed Aircraft Services, Ontario, to hospital aircraft (registered *N4098M*).

MS 019 (C/N 4837) Delivered 8-80; based at Jeddah, 1981.

LOCKHEED MODEL 382C-94D C-130H HERCULES (for Indonesia) (C/Ns 4838 and 4840) Two standard transport aircraft for *Tentara Nasional Indonesia -Angkatan Udara* (TNI-AU Nos *A-1315* and *A-1316*).

A-1315 (C/N 4838) Delivered 12-79; No 31 Sqn, TNI-AU, Halim, 1980–82.

A-1316 (C/N 4840) Delivered 1-80; No 31 Sqn, TNI-AU, Halim, 1980–82.

LOCKHEED MODEL 382C-95D C-130H (T-10) HERCULES (for Spain) (C/N 4841) One standard military transport for the *Ejército del Aire* (EdA No *T10-10*).

T10-10, *312-04* (C/N 4841) Delivered 1-80; *Escuadron 312*, EdA, 1981–82.

LOCKHEED MODEL 382C-96D KC-130H HERCULES (for Saudi Arabia) (C/Ns 4872 and 4873) Two tanker aircraft for the Royal Saudi Air Force (RSAF Nos *1620* and *1621*).

1620 (C/N 4872) Delivered 2-81; No 16 Sqn, RSAF, Jeddah, 1981–82.

1621 (C/N 4873) Delivered 2-81; damaged on delivery flight when liferaft came adrift; repaired by Marshall of Cambridge, England; No 16 Sqn, 1981–82.

LOCKHEED MODEL 382C-97D C-130H-MP HERCULES (for Malaysia) (C/Ns 4847, 4849 and 4866) Three maritime patrol aircraft for the Government of Malaysia (TUDM Nos *FM 2451-FM 2453*).

FM 2451 (C/N 4847) Delivered 4-80.

FM 2452 (C/N 4849) Delivered 4-80.

FM 2453 (C/N 4866) Delivered 12-80.

LOCKHEED MODEL 382C-98D KC-130H (TK-10) HERCULES (for Spain) (C/Ns 4871 and 4874) Two tanker aircraft for the *Ejército del Aire* (EdA Nos *TK10-11* and *TK10-12*).

TK10-11, *312-05* (C/N 4871) Delivered 11-80; *Escuadron 312*, EdA, 1981–82.

TK10-12, *312-06* (C/N 4874) Delivered 12-80; *Escuadron 312*, EdA, 1981–82.

LOCKHEED MODEL 382C-1E C-130H HERCULES

(for Thailand) (C/Ns 4861 to 4863) Three standard transports for the Royal Thai Air Force (RTAF Nos *60101* to *60103*).

60101 (C/N 4861) Delivered 4-80; 6th Wing, Don Muang, 1980–82.

60102 (C/N 4862) Delivered 8-80; 6th Wing, Don Muang, 1981–82.

60103 (C/N 4863) Delivered 8-80; 6th Wing, Don Muang, 1981–82.

LOCKHEED MODEL 382C-2E C-130H HERCULES (for Singapore) (C/Ns 4842 and 4844) Two standard transports for the Republic of Singapore Air Force (RSingAF Nos *730* and *731*).

730 (C/N 4842) Delivered 1-80; No 121 Sqn, RSingAF, Tengah, 1980–81.

731 (C/N 4844) Delivered 2-80; No 121 Sqn, RSingAF, Tengah, 1980–81.

LOCKHEED MODEL 382T-3E C-130H-30 HERCULES (for Indonesia) (C/Ns 4864, 4865 and 4868 to 4870) Five military transports with 4.6 m fuselage stretch, for *Tentara Nasional Indonesia - Angkatan Udara* (TNI-AU Nos *A-1317* to *A-1321*). Were the first military transports with fuselage stretch production built.

A-1317 (C/N 4864) Delivered 9-80; No 31 Sqn, TNI-AU, Halim, 1981–83.

A-1318 (C/N 4865) Delivered 9-80; No 31 Sqn, TNI-AU, Halim, 1981–83.

A-1319 (C/N 4868) Delivered 10-80; No 31 Sqn, TNI-AU, Halim, 1981–83.

A-1320 (C/N 4869) Delivered 10-80; No 31 Sqn, TNI-AU, Halim, 1981–83.

A-1321 (C/N 4870) Delivered 10-80; No 31 Sqn, TNI-AU, Halim, 1981–83.

LOCKHEED MODEL 382C-4E C-130H HERCULES (for Saudi Arabia) (C/Ns 4843 and 4845) Two special passenger-limousine aircraft for the Saudi Royal Flight (RSAF Nos *HZ-HM5* and *HZ-HM6*).

HZ-HM5 (C/N 4843) Delivered 7-80; Saudi Royal Flight (operated by Saudia, also as *HZ-114*).

HZ-HM6 (C/N 4845) Delivered 7-80; Saudi Royal Flight (operated by Saudia, also as *HZ-115*).

LOCKHEED MODEL 382C-5E C-130H HERCULES (1980 USAF Appropriations for Air National Guard) (C/Ns 4900, 4902, 4903, 4905, 4906, 4908 and 4910) Seven standard transports, USAF Nos *80-0320* to *80-0326*, updated specification as for 1979 Appropriations. Delivery in 1981.

80-0320 (C/N 4900) Delivered 9-81; 158th TAS, 165th TAG, Georgia ANG, 1982–83.

80-0321 (C/N 4902) Delivered 9-81; 158th TAS, 165th TAG, Georgia ANG, 1982–83.

80-0322 (C/N 4903) Delivered 9-81; 158th TAS, 165th TAG, Georgia ANG, 1982–83.

80-0323 (C/N 4905) Delivered 10-81; 158th TAS, 165th TAG, Georgia ANG, 1982–83.

80-0324 (C/N 4906) Delivered 10-81; 158th TAS, 165th TAG, Georgia ANG, 1982–83.

80-0325 (C/N 4908) Delivered 11-81; 158th TAS, 165th TAG, Georgia ANG, 1982–83.

80-0326 (C/N 4910) Delivered 12-81; 158th TAS, 165th TAG, Georgia ANG, 1982–83.

LOCKHEED MODEL 382C-6E C-130H HERCULES (for Singapore) (C/Ns 4846 and 4848) Two standard transports for the Republic of Singapore Air Force (RSingAF Nos

732 and *733*).

732 (C/N 4846) Delivered 4-80; No 121 Sqn, RSingAF, Tengah, 1980–82.

733 (C/N 4848) Delivered 5-80; No 121 Sqn, RSingAF, Tengah, 1980–82.

LOCKHEED MODEL 382C-8E C-130H HERCULES (for Sweden) (C/Ns 4881, 4884, 4885, 4887 and 4890) Five standard transports for the *Flygvapnet* (Nos *84004* to *84008*).

84004 (C/N 4881) Delivered 3-81; *Flygflottilj 7*, Satenäs; carried '844'; 1981–83.

84005 (C/N 4884) Delivered 5-81; *Flygflottilj 7*, Satenäs; carried '845'; 1981–83.

84006 (C/N 4885) Delivered 5-81; *Flygflottilj 7*, Satenäs; carried '846'; 1981–83.

84007 (C/N 4887) Delivered 5-81; *Flygflottilj 7*, Satenäs; carried '847'; 1981–83.

84008 (C/N 4890) Delivered 5-81; *Flygflottilj 7*, Satenäs; carried '848'; 1981–83.

LOCKHEED MODEL 382C-9E C-130H-MP HERCULES (for Indonesia) (C/N 4898) One maritime patrol aircraft for *Tentara Nasional Indonesia-Angkatan Udara* (TNI-AU No *A-1322*).

A-1322 (C/N 4898) Delivered 11-81; No 31 Sqn, TNI-AU, Halim, 1982–83.

LOCKHEED MODEL 382C-11E C-130H HERCULES (for Morocco) (C/Ns 4875 to 4877, 4888 and 4892) Five transports for the Royal Moroccan Air Force (registered *CNA-OM* to *CNA-OQ*).

CNA-OM (C/N 4875) Stored as *N4130M* (?), 1-81; delivered 8-81.

CNA-ON (C/N 4876) Stored as *N4233M*, 1-81; delivered 8-81.

CNA-OO (C/N 4877) Stored as *N4137M* (?), 1-81; delivered 8-81.

CNA-OP (C/N 4888) Stored as *N4162M*, 4-81; delivered 8-81.

CNA-OQ (C/N 4892) Delivered 8-81.

LOCKHEED MODEL 382C-12E KC-130H HERCULES (for Morocco) (C/Ns 4907 and 4909) Two tanker aircraft for the Royal Moroccan Air Force (registered *CNA-OR* and *CNA-OS*).

CNA-OR (C/N 4907) Delivered 5-82.

CNA-OS (C/N 4909) Delivered 5-82.

LOCKHEED MODEL 382C-13E C-130H HERCULES (for Oman) (C/N 4878) One military transport for the Sultan of Oman's Air Force (SOAF No *501*; USAF No *81-0001*).

501, 81-0001 (C/N 4878) Registered *N4138M*; delivered 4-81.

LOCKHEED MODEL 382C-14E C-130H HERCULES (for Abu Dhabi) (C/Ns 4879 and 4882) Two military transports for the United Emirates Air Force (UEAF Nos *1213* and *1214*).

1213 (C/N 4879) Delivered as N4140M, 6-81; based at Abu Dhabi, 1981–83.

1214 (C/N 4882) Delivered as N4147M, 6-81; based at Abu Dhabi, 1981–83.

LOCKHEED MODEL 382T-15E C-130H-30 HERCULES (for Indonesia) (C/N 4899) One military transport with 4.6 m fuselage stretch for *Tentara Nasional Indonesia-Angkatan Udara* (TNI-AU No *A-1323*).

A-1323 (C/N 4899) Delivered 8-81; No 31 Sqn, TNI-AU, Halim, 1982–83.

LOCKHEED MODEL 382T-16E C-130H-30 HERCULES (for Algeria) (C/Ns 4894 and 4897) Two transports with 4.6 m fuselage stretch for the Algerian Air Force (registered *7T-VHN* and *7T-VHO*).

7T-VHN (C/N 4894) Completed, 7-81; delivered 12-81.

7T-VHO (C/N 4897) Completed, 8-81; delivered 12-81.

LOCKHEED MODEL 382G-44C L-100-30 HERCULES (for Dubai) (C/N 4834) One commercial transport with 4.6 m fuselage stretch for the Dubai Government.

N4085M (as delivered; C/N 4834) Delivered 1-81; damaged in violent hailstorm at Dubai, 30-4-81; repaired by Marshall of Cambridge, England.

LOCKHEED MODEL 382G-46C L-100-30 HERCULES (C/N 4839) Commercial demonstration aircraft built for use by Lockheed Aircraft Company (registered *N4110M*), with 4.6 m fuselage stretch.

N4110M (C/N 4839) Completed 3-80; demonstrations until 8-80. Sold to Wirtschaftflug, Frankfurt-am-Main, as *D-ACWF*, 10-81.

LOCKHEED MODEL 382E-47C L-100-20 HERCULES (for Peru) (C/Ns 4850 and 4835) Two transports for the *Fuerza Aerea Peruana* (FAP Nos *FAP-397* and *FAP-398*) with 2.5 m fuselage stretch. Aircraft stored (second aircraft as *N4119M*) from 4-80 awaiting financing by Lockheed Financing Corporation.

FAP-397 (C/N 4850) Delivered to Peru, 3-81; *Grupo 41*, Jorge Chavez, 1981–83.

FAP-398 (C/N 4853) Delivered to Peru, 3-81; *Grupo 41*, Jorge Chavez, 1981–83.

LOCKHEED MODEL 382G-48C L-100-30 HERCULES (for Mexico) (C/N 4851) One commercial transport for *Petroléos Mexicanos* (Pemex, *XC-EXP*); 4.6 m fuselage stretch.

XC-EXP (C/N 4851) Delivered, 4-80, to Pemex.

LOCKHEED MODEL 382G-51C L-100-30 HERCULES (for Algeria) (C/Ns 4880, 4883 and 4886) Three commercial transports for *Air Algerie* (registered *7T-VHG*, *7T-VHK* and *7T-VHL*) with 4.6 m fuselage stretch.

7T-VHG (C/N 4880) Originally registered *N4148M*; delivered *Air Algerie*, 5-81.

7T-VHK (C/N 4883) Originally registered *N4152M*; delivered *Air Algerie*, 7-81.

7T-VHL (C/N 4886) Originally registered *N4160M*; delivered *Air Algerie*, 1-82.

LOCKHEED MODEL 382G-52C L-100-30 HERCULES (for Indonesia) (C/N 4889) One commercial transport with 4.6 m fuselage stretch for Pelita Air Services (*PK-PLR*)

PK-PLR (C/N 4889) Delivered to Pelita Air Services, 5-81.

LOCKHEED MODEL 382G-53C L-100-30 HERCULES (for Zaïre) (C/N 4891) One commercial transport with 4.6 m fuselage stretch for SCIBE-Zaïre.

N4170M (C/N 4891) Delivered to SCIBE-Zaïre, 16-6-81; sold to LADE, Argentina, as *LQ-FAA*, 1982.

LOCKHEED MODEL 382G-54C L-100-30 HERCULES (for Ecuador) (C/N 4893) One transport with 4.6 m fuselage stretch for the *Fuerza Aerea Ecuatoriana* (FAE).

FAE 893 (C/N 4893) Delivered as *N4175M*, 7-81, to FAE.

LOCKHEED MODEL 382G-55C L-100-30 HERCULES (for Gabon) (C/N 4395) One transport with 4.6 m fuselage stretch for the *Force Aérienne Gabonaise*.

TR-KKD (C/N 4395) Delivered 7-81 to Gabon; allocated for Presidential use, 9-81, and named *N'tem*.

LOCKHEED MODEL 382C-18E C-130H HERCULES (1981 USAF Appropriations for Air Force Reserve) (C/Ns 4939, and 4941 to 4946) Seven standard transports updated to 1980 specification, USAF Nos *81-0626* to *81-0631*, and *80-0332*, not respectively. Delivery in 1982.
81-0626 (C/N 4939) Delivered 2-10-82. 700th TAS, Dobbins AFB, Georgia. *City of Marietta.*
81-0627 (C/N 4941) Delivered 29-10-82. 700th TAS, Dobbins AFB, Georgia.
81-0628 (C/N 4942) Delivered 8-11-82. 700th TAS, Dobbins AFB, Georgia.
80-0332 (C/N 4943) Delivered 16-11-82. 700th TAS, Dobbins AFB, Georgia. (1980 number not explained.)
81-0629 (C/N 4944) Delivered 24-11-82; 700th TAS, Dobbins AFB, Georgia.
81-0630 (C/N 4945) Delivered 6-12-82. 700th TAS, Dobbins AFB, Georgia.
81-0631 (C/N 4946) Delivered 14-12-82. 700th TAS, Dobbins AFB, Georgia.
LOCKHEED MODEL 382C-19E C-130H HERCULES (for Oman) (C/N 4916) One standard military transport for the Sultan of Oman's Air Force (SOAF), completed in 1982.
502, 82-0050 (C/N 4916) Delivered to SOAF, 2-82.
LOCKHEED MODEL 382C-21E C-130H-30 HERCULES (for Indonesia) (C/Ns 4925 and 4927) Two military transports with 4.6 m fuselage stretch, for *Tentara Nasional Indonesia-Angkatan Udara* (TNI-AU Nos *A-1321* and *A-1324*).
A-1321 (C/N 4925) Delivered 21-5-82. Note: The C-130H-30 (C/N 4870), previously registered as *A-1321*, re-registered *A-1341* to avoid duplication.
A-1324 (C/N 4927) Delivered to TNI-AU, 11-6-82.
LOCKHEED MODEL 382C-22E HC-130H HERCULES (C/N 4931) One search and rescue aircraft for the US Coast Guard (USCG No *CG1790*).
CG1790 (C/N 4931) Delivered in 1982; USCG Station allocation not yet known.
LOCKHEED MODEL 382C-24E C-130H HERCULES (for Egypt) (C/Ns 4936 to 4938) Three standard military transports for the Egyptian Air Force (EAF); delivery in 1982.
SU-BEW, 1290 (C/N 4936) Delivered 13-9-82.
SU-BEX, 1291 (C/N 4937) Delivered 22-9-82.
SU-BEY, 1292 (C/N 4938) Delivered 1-10-82.
LOCKHEED MODEL 382C-25E C-130H HERCULES (for Algeria) (C/Ns 4911 to 4914, 4930, 4934 and 4935) Seven standard military transports for the Algerian Air Force (*Force Aérienne Algérienne*) for delivery in 1982.
7T-WHT (C/N 4911) Delivered to Algeria, 1-82; to Algerian AF, 4-82.
7T-WHS (C/N 4912) Delivered to Algeria, 1-82; to Algerian AF, 5-82.
7T-WHY (C/N 4913) Delivered to Algeria, 2-82; to Algerian AF, 6-82.
7T-WHZ (C/N 4914) Delivered to Algeria, 2-82; to Algerian AF, 6-82.
7T-WHI (C/N 4930) Delivered to Algeria, c18-8-82.
7T-WHF (C/N 4934) Delivered to Algeria, c17-9-82.
7T-WHE (C/N 4935) Delivered to Algeria, c28-9-82.
LOCKHEED MODEL 382C-26E C-130H HERCULES (for Saudi Arabia) (C/Ns 4915 and 4922) Two standard military transports for the Royal Saudi Air Force (RSAF),
N4185M (C/N 4915) Delivered to RSAF, 17-8-82. RSAF No

not yet known.
N4190M (C/N 4922) Delivered to RSAF, 31-8-82; Autopax version. RSAF No not yet known.
LOCKHEED MODEL 382C-27E C-130H HERCULES (for Japan) (C/Ns 4976, 4980 and two others) Four standard military transports purchased on government-to-government basis for the Japanese Air Self Defence Force (JASDF). USAF Nos *82-0051* and *82-0052* and two others.
82-0051 (C/N 4976) ff 28-9-83; delivered 12-83 to JASDF; to operate from Honshu.
82-0052 (C/N 4980) Planned delivery 12-83.
LOCKHEED MODEL 382C-28E C-130H HERCULES (for Jordan) (C/N 4920) One standard military transport for the Royal Jordanian Air Force (RJAF No *346*).
346 (C/N 4920) Delivered to RJAF, 4-5-82.
LOCKHEED MODEL 382C-29E KC-130H HERCULES (for Morocco) (C/N 4940) One tanker for Royal Maroc Air Force. Contract not completed at 8-82.
LOCKHEED MODEL 382T-30E C-130H-30 HERCULES (for Algeria) (C/Ns 4919 and 4921) Two military transports with 4.6 m fuselage stretch for Algerian Air Force (*Force Aérienne Algérienne*) for delivery in 1982.
7T-WHM (C/N 4919) Delivered to Algerian Air Force, 21-7-82.
7T-WHP (C/N 4921) Delivered to Algerian Air Force, 16-9-82.
LOCKHEED MODEL 382C-31E C-130H HERCULES (for Algeria) (C/Ns 4924, 4926 and 4928) Three standard military transports originally initiated against part of an order from Morocco, purchased for the Algerian Air Force for delivery in 1982.
7T-WHR (C/N 4924) Delivered to Algerian Air Force, 6-82.
7T-WHQ (C/N 4926) Delivered to Algerian Air Force, 6-82.
7T-WHJ (C/N 4928) Delivered to Algerian Air Force, 7-82.
LOCKHEED MODEL 382C-31E C-130H HERCULES (for Jordan) (C/N 4929) One standard military transport originally initiated against part of an order from Morocco, purchased for the Royal Jordanian Air Force in 1982. Delivered as *N4204M*.
347, N4204M (C/N 4929) Delivered to RJAF, 25-8-82, and became *347*.
LOCKHEED MODEL 382C-32E C-130H HERCULES (for Saudi Arabia) (C/N 4918) One hospital aircraft for the Royal Saudi Air Force. (RSAF No and delivery date not yet known.)
LOCKHEED MODEL 382G-57C L-100-30 HERCULES (for Indonesia) (C/Ns 4917 and 4923) Two commercial transports purchased by the Indonesian government in 1982.
PK-PLS (C/N 4917) Delivered to Indonesia, 3-82; to Pelita Air Service, 4-82.
PK-PLT (C/N 4923) Delivered to Indonesia, 17-6-82; for Pelita Air Service.
LOCKHEED MODEL 382G-59C L-100-30 HERCULES (for Kuwait) (C/Ns 4949, 4951, 4953 and 4955) Four military transports with 4.6 m fuselage stretch for the Kuwait Air Force (KAF Nos *322* to *325*) for delivery in 1983.
KAF 322 (C/N 4949) Delivered c1-83.
KAF 323 (C/N 4951) Delivered c2-83.
KAF 324 (C/N 4953) Delivered c2-83.
KAF 325 (C/N 4955) Delivered c3-83.
LOCKHEED MODEL 382C-33E C-130H HERCULES (for Oman) (C/N 4948) One military transport for the Sultan of Oman's Air Force (SOAF) (USAF No *82-0053*).

***503**, 82-0053* (C/N 4948) Delivered to SOAF, *c*1–83.

LOCKHEED MODEL 382C-34E KC-130T HERCULES (C/Ns 4972, 4974, 4978 and 4981) Four tankers for the US Marine Corps. Delivery scheduled in 1983 but USMC Nos not yet known.

LOCKHEED MODEL 382C-35E C-130H HERCULES (1982 USAF Appropriations) No contract at 1-82 and USAF Nos not yet known. At least eight aircraft (C/Ns 4968, 4970, 4971, 4973, 4975, 4977, 4979 and 4982).

LOCKHEED MODEL 382C-37E HC-130H-7 HERCULES (C/Ns 4947, 4958, 4966, 4967 and 4969) Five search and rescue aircraft with T56A-7 turboprops for the US Coast Guard. USCG Nos *CG1700* to *CG1704*. Contracted 30-9-82 for delivery in 1983 and service at Clearwater, Florida. (Note: The HC-130H-7 C/N 4959 had originated as an L-100-30 ordered by Iraq; other similar aircraft are said to be scheduled for delivery in 1984 and these may also be taken from the Iraqi order; see below).

* * *

At the time of writing, the manufacture of approximately 30 further Hercules had been initiated; some had been completed and were awaiting Contract finalisation, and others were awaiting specification notification. Of these, three aircraft were Model 382T C-130H-30s (C/Ns 4957, 4959 and 4961) scheduled for sale to the Nigerian Air Force, and five were Model 382G L-100-30s (C/Ns 4954, 4956, 4960, 4964 and 4965) scheduled for sale to Iraq; C/Ns 4933 (a Model 382T, C-130H-30, completed as *N4206M*), 4950 (a Model 382G L-100-30), 4952 (a Model 383T C-130H-30), and 4962/4963 (two Model 382G L-100-30s) were awaiting sale Contracts to unspecified purchasers.

Index

In the interests of space, Appendix 2 has been indexed only in respect of C-130 derivatives and overseas user nations and airlines.

The livery of CF-DSX initially unchanged after transfer to Echo Bay Mines Ltd; it was later painted with a read cheat line (Echo Bay Mines Ltd).